T2-FHP-889

Econometric Society Monographs in Quantitative Economics

Advances in Econometrics

Econometric Society Publication No. 2

Books in both the Econometric Society Monographs in Pure Theory and the Econometric Society Monographs in Quantitative Economics are numbered in a single sequence for the purposes of the Econometric Society. A complete listing of books in the Econometric Society Monographs in Quantitative Economics are given on the following page.

Econometric Society Monographs in Quantitative Economics

The Econometric Society is an international society for the advancement of economic theory in relation to statistics and mathematics. The Econometric Society Monograph Series in Quantitative Economics is designed to promote the publication of original research contributions of high quality in mathematical economics and in theoretical and applied econometrics.

Other titles in
Econometric Society Monographs in Quantitative Economics:
W. Hildenbrand: *Advances in Economic Theory*

Advances in Econometrics

INVITED PAPERS FOR THE FOURTH WORLD CONGRESS
OF THE ECONOMETRIC SOCIETY
AT AIX-EN-PROVENCE, SEPTEMBER 1980

Edited by

WERNER HILDENBRAND
Rheinische Friedrich-Wilhelms-Universität Bonn

with the assistance of Heike Schmidt

CAMBRIDGE UNIVERSITY PRESS

Cambridge
London New York New Rochelle
Melbourne Sydney

Published by the Press Syndicate of the University of Cambridge
The Pitt Building, Trumpington Street, Cambridge CB2 1RP
32 East 57th Street, New York, NY 10022, USA
296 Beaconsfield Parade, Middle Park, Melbourne 3206, Australia

First published 1982

Printed in the United States of America

Library of Congress Cataloging in Publication Data

Econometric Society.
Advances in econometrics.

(Econometric Society monographs in
quantitative economics; no. 2)
1. Econometrics—Congresses. I. Hildenbrand,
Werner, 1936- . II. Title. III. Series.
HB139.E27 1982 330′.028 81-18171

ISBN 0 521 24572 9 AACR2

Contents

Part IV: Small-sample distribution theory

Part V: Topics in time-series analysis

Part VI: Testing for causation and exogeneity

Contributors

T. W. Anderson
Department of Statistics
Stanford University
Stanford, California, U.S.A.

Zbigniew Czerwiński
Instytut Cybernetyki Ekonomicznej
Akademia Ekonomiczna w Poznaniu
Poznań, Poland

G. B. A. Evans
Faculty of Economics and Politics
University of Cambridge
Cambridge, England

John Geweke
Department of Economics
University of Wisconsin
Madison, Wisconsin, U.S.A.

C. W. J. Granger
Department of Economics
University of California, San Diego
La Jolla, California, U.S.A.

Jerry A. Hausman
Department of Economics
Massachusetts Institute of Technology
Cambridge, Massachusetts, U.S.A.

James J. Heckman
Department of Economics
University of Chicago
Chicago, Illinois, U.S.A.

R. E. Kalman
Swiss Federal Institute of Technology, Zürich
Zürich, Switzerland, and
University of Florida
Gainesville, Florida, U.S.A.

Daniel McFadden
Department of Economics
Massachusetts Institute of Technology
Cambridge, Massachusetts, U.S.A.

P. C. B. Phillips
Department of Economics
Cowles Foundation for Research in Economics
Yale University
New Haven, Connecticut, U.S.A.

Thomas J. Rothenberg
Department of Economics
University of California, Berkeley
Berkeley, California, U.S.A.

N. E. Savin
Trinity College
University of Cambridge
Cambridge, England

Burton Singer
Department of Mathematical Statistics
Columbia University
New York, U.S.A.

Wladyslaw Welfe
Faculty of Economics and Sociology
Institute of Econometrics and Statistics
University of Lodz
Lodz, Poland

Editorial preface

All the contributions published in this book and in its companion volume, *Advances in Economic Theory,* have been presented as "invited symposia" at the Fourth World Congress of the Econometric Society at Aix-en-Provence, in September 1980. The topics and speakers for the sixteen invited symposia were chosen by the Program Committee. The purpose of these symposia was to survey as completely as possible those areas in economic theory and econometrics where important research has come to light during the last five years since the Third World Congress. All but one of the invited symposia are included in these volumes and, according to subject, they are published either in this volume on econometrics, or in the volume on economic theory.

The Editor would like to acknowledge the cooperation of the contributors and the assistance of Heike Schmidt in the preparation of the manuscript.

Werner Hildenbrand
Chairman of the Program Committee
of the Fourth World Congress
of the Econometric Society

PART I

QUALITATIVE RESPONSE MODELS

CHAPTER 1

Qualitative response models

Daniel McFadden

1 The problem

Econometrics is concerned with understanding and predicting the behaviors of economic agents. Some behavioral responses are structurally or observationally qualitative (categorical, discrete), rather than continuous. This is a survey of models and methods that have been developed for the analysis of qualitative responses.

Table 1.1 gives examples of economic qualitative responses. Empirical studies have concentrated on a constellation of problems in labor supply, such as occupational choice and employment status, and on travel behavior. The models that have been developed are strongly influenced by the specific features of these applications.

The examples in Table 1.1 are classified by economic agent: household, firm, or an interaction of agents. There are several other aspects of qualitative responses that may affect the choice of an appropriate method for analysis. First, the categorical response may be binomial (yes/no) or multinomial, and multinomial responses may be either naturally ordered or unordered. For example, the number of children is naturally ordered, whereas the brand of automobile purchased is not.

Second, the primary purpose of examining qualitative responses may be an intrinsic interest in explaining and forecasting the observed categorical behavior, or it may be the correction of biases induced by self-selection into a target population. For example, occupational choice is of direct interest because of its impact on labor supply, but it is also a potential source of bias in a study of labor hours supplied by a self-selected population of independent professional workers.

Third, qualitative response models may be classified into the standard

Table 1.1 *Examples of economic qualitative responses*

Household
Occupation (Boskin, 1974; Hay, 1979; Poirier, 1978)
Marital status
Number of children (Heckman & Willis, 1975; Gronau, 1973)
Housing tenure (Maddala & Trost, 1978; Lee & Trost, 1978; Li, 1977)
Durable purchase/brand choice (Dubin & McFadden, 1980; Brownstone, 1978; Hausman, 1979; Cragg, 1971)
Migration (Schultz, 1975; Moses et al., 1967)
Education level (Fuller et al., 1980; Miller & Radner, 1970)
Travel model (Domencich & McFadden, 1975; Adler & Ben-Akiva, 1975)
Employment status (Hall, 1970; Heckman & Willis, 1977)

Firm
Operate/shutdown
Plant location
Product lines
Hiring/firing (Schwartz, 1976)
Freight shipment mode (Winston, 1980)

Multiagent
Merger/takeover status of firms
Excess supply/demand (Quandt, 1978, Maddala & Nelson, 1975)
Bilateral negotiations contract/strike (Farber, 1978)

econometric categories of single-equation models, multivariate reduced-form models, and simultaneous-equation models. In addition, there are descriptive models for discrete data that do not assume a causal structure.

2 Extending the standard econometric model to qualitative responses

An introduction to qualitative response models that emphasizes their connection to standard econometrics starts from the conventional single-equation or reduced-form model

(1) $$y_t = x_t\beta + \epsilon_t$$

where $t = 1, \ldots, T$ indexes sample observations, y_t is an observed vector of continuous response variables, x_t is an observed array of continuous or discrete explanatory variables, and ϵ_t is an unobserved disturbance. The disturbances usually are assumed to have a convenient cumulative distribution function $F(\epsilon \mid x)$, such as multivariate normal. Then the model is completely characterized, up to the unknown parameter vector β and parameters of the error distribution, by the conditional distribution of y_t given x_t, $F(y_t - x_t\beta \mid x_t)$. In economic applications, $x_t\beta$ may have a structure derived exactly or approximately from theory. For example, in a consumer demand study, $x_t\beta$ may be determined by Roy's identity from an indirect utility function.

The conventional model is extended to qualitative responses by introducing intermediate unobserved or latent variables. Define

$$(2) \qquad y_t^* = x_t\beta + \epsilon_t$$

where y_t^* is an $M \times 1$ vector of latent variables, with an observed qualitative variable y_t satisfying

$$(3) \qquad \begin{aligned} y_{mt} &= 1 \quad \text{if} \quad y_{mt}^* \geqslant y_{nt}^* \quad \text{for} \quad n = 1, \ldots, M \\ &\ 0 \quad \text{otherwise} \end{aligned}$$

Thus, only the qualitative information on which component of the latent vector is largest is observed.

As in the conventional model, $x_t\beta$ may have a structure derived from economic theory. For example, the latent vector may specify the levels of indirect utility associated with discrete alternatives in a consumer choice problem.

The nonlinear transformation (3) can be modified in a variety of ways to handle multivariate multinomial or ordered responses, simultaneous determination of y_t^*, state dependence on lagged values of y_t, and truncation or censoring of observations. This transformation may reflect structural discreteness in behavior, such as choice of number of children, or it may reflect classification imposed in the process of observation, such as dichotomization of continuously graded dwellings into standard and substandard categories.

Suppose, as in the conventional model, that the unobserved disturbance ϵ has a convenient cumulative distribution function $F(\epsilon \mid x)$. Let $I(y, y^*)$ be an indicator function for the set of y^* such that y and y^* satisfy (3):

$$(4) \qquad \begin{aligned} I(y, y^*) &= 1 \quad \text{if} \quad y_m = 1 \quad \text{and} \quad y_m^* \geqslant y_n^* \quad \text{for} \quad n = 1, \ldots, M \\ &= 0 \quad \text{otherwise} \end{aligned}$$

Just as in the conventional case, the qualitative response model is characterized by the conditional distribution of y_t given x_t. This distribution satisfies

$$(5) \qquad P(y_t \mid x_t) = \int I(y_t, x_t\beta + \epsilon) F(d\epsilon \mid x_t)$$

The term $P(y_t \mid x_t)$ is the response (choice) probability. The notation $P(i \mid x_t)$, where $i = 1, \ldots, M$, will also be used for this probability, with

$P(i \mid x_t)$ denoting the probability that component i of the observed vector y given by (3) equals 1. Note that $P(y_t \mid x_t)$ will depend on the unobserved parameter vector β and parameters of the error distribution F.

The formulation of qualitative responses in terms of latent-variable models is due to Goldberger (1971), Heckman (1976a), Amemiya (1976), and Lee (1981). The last two reports give generalizations of (3) that yield a variety of structural, ordered, truncated, and censored response models.

3 An example: multinomial logit analysis of ownership of a durable

3.1 *The model*

A qualitative response model that has been widely used in studies of consumer choice is the multinomial logit (MNL) model,

$$P(i \mid x_t) = \frac{\exp(x_{it}\beta)}{\exp(x_{1t}\beta) + \cdots + \exp(x_{Mt}\beta)} \qquad (i = 1, \ldots, M) \tag{6}$$

where β is a $K \times 1$ vector of unknown parameters, x_{it} is a $1 \times K$ vector of explanatory variables associated with alternative i, and

$$x_t = (x_{1t}, \ldots, x_{Mt}).$$

The MNL model can be derived from the latent variable model given in equations (2) and (3) by specifying the distribution of the disturbances $\epsilon_t = (\epsilon_{1t}, \ldots, \epsilon_{Mt})$ to be independent identical type I extreme value:

$$F(\epsilon_t \mid x_t) = \exp[-\exp(-\epsilon_{1t})] \ldots \exp[-\exp(-\epsilon_{Mt})] \tag{7}$$

This result is demonstrated by a straightforward integration in (5); see the work of McFadden (1973) and Yellot (1977).

If the response is postulated to be the result of classical economic optimization, then $x_{it}\beta$ should have the properties of an indirect utility function, reflecting preference maximization conditioned on discrete alternative i. For a firm decision problem, $x_{it}\beta$ should have the properties of a real profit function conditioned on the discrete alternative. Sources for the conventional theory of profit and indirect utility functions are the works of McFadden (1978a) and Diewert (1978); the use of these forms in a discrete choice context has been studied by Duncan (1980a), McFadden (1979a), and Dubin and McFadden (1980).

The disturbance ϵ_t in the latent variable model yielding the MNL form may have the conventional econometric interpretation of the impact of factors known to the decision-maker but not to the observer. However, it is also possible that a disturbance exists in the decision protocol of the economic agent, yielding stochastic choice behavior. These alternatives cannot ordinarily be distinguished unless the decision protocol is observable or unless individuals can be confronted experimentally with a variety of decisions.

Interpreted as a stochastic choice model, the MNL form is used in psychometrics and is termed the Luce strict utility model. In this literature, $v_{it}=x_{it}\beta$ is interpreted as a scale value associated with alternative i. The appropriate references are the works of Luce (1959, 1977) and Marschak (1960).

3.2 *Interpretation of variables*

The vector of explanatory variables x_{it} in the MNL model can be interpreted as attributes of alternative i. Note that components of x_{it} that do not vary with i cancel out of the MNL formula (6), and the corresponding component of the parameter vector β cannot be identified from observations on discrete responses.

Some components of x_{it} may be alternative-specific, resulting from the interaction of a variable with a dummy variable for alternative i. This is meaningful if the alternatives are naturally indexed. For example, in a study of ownership of a durable, the alternative of not holding the durable is naturally distinguished from all the alternatives in which the durable is held. On the other hand, if there is no link between the true attributes of an alternative and its index i, as might be the case for the set of available dwellings in a study of housing purchase behavior, alternative dummies are meaningless.

Attributes of the respondent may enter the MNL model in interactions with attributes of alternatives or with alternative-specific dummies. For example, income may enter an MNL model of the housing purchase decision in interaction with a dwelling attribute, such as price, or with a dummy variable for the nonownership alternative.

A case of the MNL model frequently encountered in sociometrics is that in which the variables in x_{it} are all interactions of respondent attributes and alternative-specific dummies. Let z_t be a $1\times s$ vector of respondent attributes and δ_{im} be a dummy variable that is 1 when $i=m$, but 0 otherwise. Define the $1\times sM$ vector of interactions

$$x_{it} = (\delta_{i1}z_t, \ldots, \delta_{iM}z_t)$$

and let $\beta'=(\beta_1', \ldots, \beta_M')$ be a commensurate vector of parameters.

Then

$$
(8)\quad \begin{aligned} P(i \mid x_t) &= \frac{\exp(x_{it}\beta)}{\exp(x_{1t}\beta) + \cdots + \exp(x_{Mt}\beta)} \\ &= \frac{\exp(z_t\beta_i)}{\exp(z_t\beta_1) + \cdots + \exp(z_t\beta_M)} \end{aligned}
$$

An identifying normalization, say $\beta_1 = 0$, is required. This model has been analyzed further by Goodman (1972b) and Nerlove and Press (1976).

3.3 *Estimation*

Consider a sample of observations (x_t, y_t) for $t = 1, \ldots, T$, with y_{it} being a count of the number of times response i is observed for case t. Without repetitions, y_t has exactly one component equal to 1, the rest being 0. With repetitions, y_t is a vector of nonnegative integers. Let $r_t = y_{1t} + \cdots + y_{Mt}$.

The maximum likelihood method is most commonly used to estimate the parameters of the MNL model. The likelihood function is

$$
(9)\quad \begin{aligned} L_t(\beta) &= \frac{1}{T} \sum_{t=1}^{T} \sum_{i=1}^{M} y_{it} \ln P(i \mid x_t) \\ &= \frac{1}{T} \sum_{t=1}^{T} \left[\sum_{i=1}^{M} y_{it} x_{it}\beta - r_t \ln \sum_{i=1}^{M} \exp(x_{it}\beta) \right] \end{aligned}
$$

This function is concave in β, and it can be maximized by a variety of computationally efficient iterative algorithms, such as those of Newton-Raphson or Berndt and associates (1974). A convenient convergence criterion is obtained by considering iterates $\beta^{(k)}$, defining

$$
\lambda^{(k)} = (1 + \beta^{(k)\prime}\beta^{(k)})^{-1/2},
$$

and iterating until changes in $(\lambda^{(k)}, \beta^{(k)}/\lambda^{(k)})$ are small. If $\lim \lambda^{(k)} > 0$, then $\beta^{(k)}$ has a limit point, and any of its limit points is a maximum likelihood estimator. If $\lim \lambda^{(k)} = 0$, then $\beta^{(k)}/\lambda^{(k)}$ has a limit point β^* such that the observed choices are nonstochastic maximands of $x_{it}\beta^*$.

Provided that an identification condition is met, the likelihood function will have a unique maximum with a probability approaching 1 as $T \to \infty$. Mild regularity conditions on the explanatory variables are sufficient to establish that the maximum likelihood estimator is consistent uniformly asymptotically normal (CUAN) and asymptotically efficient; see the work of McFadden (1973) and Manski and McFadden (1981).

An alternative to maximum likelihood estimation is to use nonlinear least-squares:

$$\min_{\beta} \frac{1}{T} \sum_{t=1}^{T} \sum_{i=1}^{N} (y_{it} - r_t P(i \mid x_t))^2 \tag{10}$$

Under the same regularity conditions as used with the maximum likelihood procedure, the nonlinear least-squares estimator is CUAN. If a generalized least-squares weighting is used, this estimator can be made asymtotically efficient. The nonlinear least-squares criterion is not concave in β, and some care must be taken to avoid subsidiary maxima.

When repetitions are observed and the counts y_{it} are large, the MNL model parameter vector can be estimated consistently (as the $r_t \rightarrow \infty$) by applying least squares to

$$\ln(y_{iy}/y_{1t}) = (x_{it} - x_{1t})\beta + \eta_{it} \tag{11}$$

This method is due to Berkson (1955b) and Theil (1969). A generalized least-squares transformation is required for efficiency.

Anemiya (1978c) has shown that with an order T^{-2} bias correction, the maximum likelihood estimator has higher second-order efficiency than the nonlinear least-squares estimator or the Berkson-Theil estimator.

3.4 *An empirical example*

As an example of application of an MNL model, consider the decision whether or not to own a clothes dryer, and, if so, whether it is to be electric or gas. The sample includes 1,408 households from a 1975 U.S. national survey of residential appliance holdings and energy use patterns conducted by the Washington Center for Metropolitan Studies. The explanatory variables used in this example are the following:

CDOPCOST: clothes dryer operating cost, constructed using 1975 prices of gas and electricity (tail block rate), standardized test-load energy requirements, and assumed frequency of use depending on household size

CDCPCOST: clothes dryer capital cost, constructed using 1975 construction cost indicator estimates of appliance and installation charges, plus an additional charge for connecting gas or 220-volt electrical service in dwelling, if not already available

GASAV: gas availability, defined as the proportion of dwellings in the area with gas service

OWN: homeowner dummy, equal to 1 for homeowners and 0 otherwise

PERSONS: number of persons, defined as the total number in the household, including children

Table 1.2 *A model of clothes dryer ownership*

Variable	Coefficient	Standard error
CDOPCOST	−.0144	.0050
CDCPCOST	−.0160	.0012
GASAV1	−1.27	.48
OWN1	−.60	.28
PERSONS1	.075	.057
C1	2.10	.47
GASAV3	−1.56	.50
OWN3	−1.59	.27
PERSONS3	−.40	.05
C3	.02	.57
Log likelihood		
For MLE	−1304	
Dummies only	−1499	
Degrees of freedom	2806	
Number of cases	1408	

Alternatives: 1, electric dryer; 2, gas dryer; 3, no dryer.

Table 1.3 *Variable means*

	Sample mean		
Variable	Alternative 1 (electric)	Alternative 2 (gas)	Alternative 3 (none)
CHOICE	.447	.235	0.318
CDOPCOST	31.17	7.56	0
CDCPCOST	233.20	258.80	0
OWN	.873		
PERSONS	3.31		
GASAV	.719		

In addition, C1 and C3 denote dummy variables for alternative 1 (electric dryer) and alternative 3 (no dryer). Interactions between respondent attributes and alternative dummies are denoted by appending the alternative number. Thus, OWN1 = OWN*C1 is the interaction that is 1 for a homeowner in alternative 1 and 0 otherwise. Similarly, GASAV3 = GASAV*C3, etc.

The estimated model is given in Table 1.2. The estimated coefficients can be interpreted as taste weights in an indirect utility function that is additively separable in (real) income and has a demand for the service of

Table 1.4 *Elasticities at variable means*

	Elasticity of proportion choosing		
Elasticity with respect to	Alternative 1 (electric)	Alternative 2 (gas)	Alternative 3 (none)
Electric operating cost	−.25	(.20)	(.20)[a]
Gas operating cost	(.03)	−.08	(.03)
Electric capital cost	−2.1	(1.7)	(1.7)
Gas capital cost	(1.0)	−3.2	(1.0)

[a] The circled elasticities indicate common values imposed by the MNL structure.

the appliance that is price-inelastic. A limitation of this specification is that it ignores the dynamics of durable purchase decisions, treating historical ownership as if it were a contemporary purchase. This is correct only under the implausible assumption that there is a perfect rental market without transactions costs, or else that costs have not shifted or were perfectly anticipated since date of purchase.

Table 1.3 gives the sample means of the explanatory variables in this MNL model, as well as the dependent variable CHOICE. Table 1.4 gives elasticities computed at sample means. The estimated coefficients and elasticities indicate substantial consumer response to both capital and operating costs. The coefficients yield a very high implicit discount rate of 111%. This may be due in part to the limitations of the variable specification and MNL model structure. If 1975 operating costs are substantially higher than anticipated at date of purchase, this will tend to bias upward the estimated discount rate. In Section 4.6 some evidence is presented indicating that the MNL model structure is incorrect, and a more suitable specification leads to a lower estimated discount rate. It should be noted that implicit discount rates in the 30% to 150% range are not uncommon in empirical studies of appliance purchase behavior.

4 Properties of the MNL model

4.1 *The property of independence from irrelevant alternatives*

Suppose in the MNL model, equation (6), that the vector x_{it} of explanatory variables associated with alternative i depends solely on the attributes of i, possibly interacted with attributes of the respondent. That is, x_{it} does not depend on the attributes of alternatives other than i.

Then the MNL model has the independence from irrelevant alternatives (IIA) property, which states that the odds of i being chosen over j are independent of the availability or attributes of alternatives other than i and j. In symbols, this property can be written

$$\text{(12)} \qquad \ln \frac{P(i \mid x_t)}{P(j \mid x_t)} = (x_{it} - x_{jt})\beta, \quad \text{independent of } x_{mt} \text{ for } \quad m \neq i,j$$

or, for $i \in A \equiv \{1, \ldots, J\} \subseteq C \equiv \{1, \ldots, M\}$,

$$\text{(13)} \qquad P(i \mid x_{1t}, \ldots, x_{mt}) \equiv P(i \mid x_{1t}, \ldots, x_{Jt}) P(A \mid x_{1t}, \ldots, x_{mt})$$

where $P(A \mid x_{1t}, \ldots, x_{mt}) \equiv \sum_{i \in A} P(i \mid x_{1t}, \ldots, x_{mt})$.

An implication of the IIA property is that the cross-elasticity of the probability of response i with respect to a component of x_{jt} is the same for all i. This can be seen in Table 1.4 for the clothes dryer model. This property is theoretically implausible in many applications. For example, one would anticipate that the cross-elasticity of the electric clothes dryer probability with respect to gas price would be higher than the corresponding elasticity for the no clothes dryer probability. Nevertheless, empirical experience is that the MNL model is relatively robust, as measured by goodness of fit or prediction accuracy, in many cases in which the IIA property is theoretically implausible.

4.2 *An approximation property*

The restrictive IIA feature of the MNL model is present only when the vector x_{it} for alternative i is independent of the attributes of alternatives other than i. When this restriction is dropped, the MNL form is sufficiently flexible to approximate any continuous positive choice probability model on a compact set of the explanatory variables. Specifically, if $P(i \mid x_t)$ is continuous, then it can be approximated globally to any desired degree of accuracy by an MNL model of the form

$$\text{(14)} \qquad \tilde{P}(i \mid x_t) = \frac{\exp(z_{it}\beta)}{\exp(z_{1t}\beta) + \cdots + \exp(z_{mt}\beta)}$$

where $z_{it} = z_{it}(x_t)$ is an arithmetic function of the attributes of all available alternatives, not just the attributes of alternative i. This approximation has been termed the universal logit model. The result follows easily from a global approximation of the vector of logs of choice probabilities by a multivariate Bernstein polynomial; details are given in the work of McFadden (1981).

The universal logit model can describe any pattern of cross-elasticities.

Thus, it is not the MNL form per se, but rather the restriction of x_{it} to depend only on attributes of i, that implies the IIA restrictions.

In practice, the global approximations yielding the universal logit model may be computationally infeasible or inefficient. In addition, the approximation makes it difficult to impose or verify consistency with economic theory. The idea underlying the universal logit model does suggest some useful specification tests (McFadden, Tye, & Train, 1976).

4.3 *The expected utility property*

Consider the latent variable model $y_{it}^* = x_{it}\beta + \epsilon_{it}$, with ϵ_{it} independently identically type I extreme value distributed. As noted earlier, this model yields the MNL form for the choice probabilities. Form the expectation of the maximum of the latent variables,

$$(15) \qquad Y_t^* = E_\epsilon \max y_{it}^*$$

A direct integration establishes that this expectation has the form

$$(16) \qquad Y_t^* = .5771 + \ln[\exp(x_{1t}\beta) + \cdots + \exp(x_{Mt}\beta)]$$

If in a consumer choice problem y_{it}^* is interpreted as the (random) indirect utility of alternative i, then Y_t^* is the expected maximum indirect utility.

The gradient of expected maximum indirect utility equals the vector of choice probabilities:

$$(17) \qquad \partial Y^*/\partial(x_{it}\beta) = P(i \mid x_t) \quad (i = 1, \ldots, M)$$

This is a variant of Roy's identity. Hence the MNL model can be interpreted as the demand function for fractional consumption of the alternatives by a single social consumer with the expected utility function. Then Y_t^* can be interpreted as an exact measure of social welfare, or consumer's surplus. This interpretation simplifies benefit–cost calculations involving discrete choice and can be used to justify the shortcut of modeling discrete choice as fractional consumption rates of the representative consumer. The expected utility property of the MNL model is discussed further by Ben-Akiva and Lerman (1979) and McFadden (1981).

4.4 *Aggregation of alternatives*

In some applications, such as choice of college or choice of dwelling, the consumer faces a large number of alternatives. It may then be necessary for practical data collection and computation to aggregate relatively homogeneous alternatives into a smaller number of primary types.

Suppose elemental alternatives are doubly indexed ij, with i denoting primary type and j denoting alternatives within a type. Let r_i denote the proportion of all alternatives that are of type i. Suppose choice among all alternatives is described by the MNL model. Then choice among primary types is described by MNL probabilities of the form

$$(18) \qquad P(i|x_t) = \frac{\exp(x_{it}\beta + \ln r_i + w_{it})}{\Sigma_k \exp(x_{kt}\beta + \ln r_k + w_{kt})}$$

where x_{it} is the mean within type i of the vectors x_{ijt} of explanatory variables for the alternative ij, and w_{it} is a correction factor for heterogeneity within type i that satisfies

$$(19) \qquad w_{it} = \ln \frac{1}{Mr_i} \sum_{j=1}^{Mr_i} \exp[(x_{ijt} - x_{it})\beta]$$

with M equal to the total number of alternatives. If the alternatives within a type are homogeneous, then $w_i = 0$.

A useful approximation to w_i can be obtained if the deviations $x_{ijt} - x_{it}$ within type i can be treated as independent random drawings from a multivariate distribution that has a cumulant generating function $W_{it}(\cdot)$. If the number of alternatives within a type Mr_i is large, then the law of large numbers implies that w_i converges almost surely to $w_i = W_{it}(\beta)$. For example, if $x_{ijt} - x_{it}$ is multivariate normal with covariance matrix Ω_{it}, then $w_i \approx W_{it}(\beta) \equiv \beta'\Omega_{it}\beta/2$.

A practical method for estimation is to assume within-type homogeneity or to use the normal approximation to w_i, with Ω_{it} either fitted from data or treated as parameters with some identifying restrictions over i and t. Then β can be estimated by maximum likelihood estimation for equation (18). The procedure can be iterated using intermediate estimates of β in the exact formula for w_i. Data collection and processing can be reduced by sampling elemental alternatives to estimate w_i. However, it is then necessary to adjust the asymptotic standard errors of coefficients to include the effects of sampling errors on the measurement of w_i. Further discussion of aggregation of alternatives in an MNL model can be found in the work of McFadden (1978b).

4.5 *Sampling alternatives*

A second method of reducing the scale of data collection and computation in the MNL model is to sample a subset of the full set of alternatives. The IIA property of the MNL model implies that the conditional probabilities of choosing from a restricted subset of the full choice set equal the choice probabilities when the choice set equals the restricted set. Then the MNL model can be estimated from data on alternatives sampled from the full choice set. In particular, the MNL model can be estimated from data on binary conditional choices. Further, subject to one weak restriction, biased sampling of alternatives can be compensated for within the MNL estimation.

Let $C=\{1,\ldots,M\}$ denote the full choice set, and $D\subseteq C$ a restricted subset. The protocol for sampling alternatives is defined by a probability $\pi(D\mid i_t,x_t)$ that D will be sampled, given observed explanatory variables x_t and choice i_t. For example, the sampling protocol of selecting the chosen alternative plus one nonchosen alternative drawn at random satisfies

$$\text{(20)} \qquad \begin{aligned} \pi(D\mid i_t,x_t) &= 1/(M-1) \quad \text{if} \quad D=\{i_t,j\}\subseteq C, \quad i_t\neq j \\ &= 0 \quad \text{otherwise} \end{aligned}$$

Let D_t denote the subset selected for case t. The weak regularity condition is as follows.

Positive conditioning property: If an alternative $j\in D_t$ were the observed choice, there would be a positive probability that the sampling protocol would select D_t; that is, if $j\in D_t$, then $\pi(D_t\mid j,x_t)>0$.

If the positive conditioning property and a standard identification condition hold, then maximization of the modified MNL log likelihood function

$$\text{(21)} \qquad \frac{1}{T}\sum_{t=1}^{T}\ln\frac{\exp[x_{i_t}\beta+\ln\pi(D_t\mid i_t,x_t)]}{\sum_{j\in D_t}\exp[x_j\beta+\ln\pi(D_t\mid j,x_t)]}$$

yields consistent estimates of β. This result is proved by showing that equation (21) converges almost surely uniformly in β to an expression that has a unique maximum at the true parameter vector; details are given in the work of McFadden (1978b). When π is the same for all $j\in D_t$, the terms involving π cancel out of the preceding expression. This is termed the uniform conditioning property; example (20) satisfies this property.

Note that the modified MNL log likelihood function (21) is simply the conditional log likelihood of the i_t, given the D_t. The inverse of the information matrix for this conditional likelihood is a consistent estimator of the covariance matrix of the estimated coefficients, as usual.

4.6 *Specification tests for the MNL model*

The MNL model in which the explanatory variables for alternative i are functions solely of the attributes of that alternative satisfies the restrictive IIA property. An implication of this property is that the model structure and parameters are unchanged when choice is analyzed conditional on a restricted subset of the full choice set. This is a special case of uniform conditioning from the preceding section on sampling alternatives.

The IIA property can be used to form a specification test for the MNL model. Let C denote the full choice set, and D a proper subset of C. Let $\hat{\beta}_C$ and $\hat{V}_C$ denote parameter estimates obtained by maximum likelihood on the full choice set, and the associated estimate of the covariance matrix of the estimators. Let $\hat{\beta}_D$ and $\hat{V}_D$ be the corresponding expressions for maximum likelihood applied to the restricted choice set D. (If some components of the full parameter vector cannot be identified from choice within D, let $\hat{\beta}_C$, $\hat{\beta}_D$, $\hat{V}_C$, and $\hat{V}_D$ denote estimates corresponding to the identifiable subvector.) Under the null hypothesis that the IIA property holds, implying the MNL specification, $\hat{\beta}_D-\hat{\beta}_C$ is a consistent estimator of zero. Under alternative model specifications where IIA fails, $\hat{\beta}_D-\hat{\beta}_C$ will almost certainly not be a consistent estimator of zero. Under the null hypothesis, $\hat{\beta}_D-\hat{\beta}_C$ has an estimated covariance matrix $\hat{V}_D-\hat{V}_C$. Hence the statistic

$$S = (\hat{\beta}_D - \hat{\beta}_C)(\hat{V}_D - \hat{V}_C)^{-1}(\hat{\beta}_D - \hat{\beta}_C) \tag{22}$$

is asymptotically chi-square, with degrees of freedom equal to the rank of $\hat{V}_D-\hat{V}_C$.

This test has been analyzed by Hausman and McFadden (1980). Note that this is an omnibus test that may fail because of misspecifications other than IIA. Empirical experience and limited numerical experiments suggest that the test is not very powerful unless deviations from the MNL structure are substantial.

When applied to the clothes dryer ownership model estimated in Section 3, with the restricted set D excluding the no dryer alternative, this test rejects the MNL structure. The test is given in Table 1.5.

A more classical specification test for the MNL form can be derived by nesting this model in a more general family and carrying out a Lagrange multiplier test. For example, the nested MNL model discussed in Section 6.1 has in this application the form

$$P_{it} = \exp(x_{it}\beta + \delta_{iD}(1 - 1/\lambda)(I_t - x_{it}\beta))/\Delta_t \tag{23}$$

where $C=A\cup D$, δ_{iD} is an indicator for $i\in D$, and

$$I_t = \lambda \ln \sum_{i\in D} \exp(x_{it}\beta/\lambda) \tag{24}$$

$$\Delta_t = \sum_{j\in A} \exp(x_{jt}\beta) + \exp(I_t)$$

Table 1.5 *A test of the MNL specification*

	Estimated coefficients			
	3-Alternative model		2-Alternative model	
Variable	Coefficient	Standard error	Coefficient	Standard error
CDOPCOST	−.0144	.0050	−.0364	.0070
CDCPCOST	−.0160	.0012	−.0168	.0014
GASAV1	−1.27	.48	−1.74	.51
OWN1	−.60	.28	−.63	.30
PERSONS1	.075	.057	.24	.08
C1	2.10	.47	2.57	.50
GASAV3	−1.56	.50	—	—
OWN3	−1.59	.27	—	—
PERSONS3	−.40	.05	—	—
C3	.02	.57	—	—
Log likelihood	−1304		−489.4	
Degrees of freedom	2806		955	
Number of observations	1408		961	

Specification test statistic: $S = 20.8$ ($\chi^2_{.99}(6) = 16.8$)

Conclusion: Reject MNL specification for 3-alternative choice at the 99% level.

When the "independence parameter" λ equals one, this model reduces to the simple MNL model. The Lagrange multiplier test statistic for this hypothesis has the general form

$$(25)\qquad LM = L_\lambda'[EL_\lambda L_\beta' - (EL_\lambda L_\lambda')(EL_\beta L_\beta')^{-1}(EL_\beta L_\lambda')]^{-1}L_\lambda / T$$

where

$$(26)\qquad L = \frac{1}{T}\sum_{t=1}^{T}\sum_{i\in C} y_{it}\ln P_{it}$$

is the normalized log likelihood function with

$$(27)\qquad y_{it} \begin{array}{ll} = 1 & \text{if } i \text{ is chosen in case } t \\ = 0 & \text{otherwise} \end{array}$$

and L_λ, L_β are gradients evaluated at $\lambda = 1$ and the maximum likelihood estimate of β from the MNL model. Under the null hypothesis, LM has a chi-squared distribution with one degree of freedom.

For this problem,

$$(28)\qquad L_\beta = \frac{1}{T}\sum_{t=1}^{T}\sum_{i\in C}(y_{it} - P_{it})x_{it}$$

$$(29)\qquad L_\lambda = \frac{1}{T}\sum_{t=1}^{T}\sum_{i\in D}(y_{it}-P_{it})(I_t - X_{it}\beta)$$

$$(30)\qquad TEL_\lambda^2 = \frac{1}{T}\sum_{t=1}^{T}\left[\sum_{i\in D} P_{it}(I_t - x_{it}\beta)^2 - \left(\sum_{i\in D} P_{it}(I_i - x_{it}\beta)\right)^2\right] \equiv V_{\lambda\lambda}$$

$$(31)\qquad TEL_\beta L_\beta' = \frac{1}{T}\sum_{t=1}^{T}\sum_{i\in C} P_{it}(x_{it}-x_{ct})'(x_{it}-x_{ct}) \equiv V_{\beta\beta}$$

$$(32)\qquad TEL_\lambda L_\beta' = \frac{1}{T}\sum_{t=1}^{T}\sum_{i\in D} P_{it}(I_t - x_{it}\beta)(\chi_{it}-\chi_{ct}) \equiv V_{\lambda\beta}$$

$$(33)\qquad x_{ct} = \sum_{i\in C} P_{it}x_{it}$$

yielding a final form for the test statistic

$$(34)\qquad LM = \left[\sum_{t=1}^{T}\sum_{i\in D}(y_{it}-P_{it})(I_t - x_{it}\beta)\right]^2 / T(V_{\lambda\lambda} - V_{\lambda\beta}V_{\beta\beta}^{-1}V_{\lambda\beta}')$$

where I_t from (24) is evaluated at $\lambda=1$.

5 General probabilistic choice systems

5.1 *History*

Econometric models of qualitative responses can be traced to four literatures: early work in econometrics on truncated and discrete responses, biometrics, psychometrics, and sociometrics. A schematic outline of these developments is given in Figure 1.1.

The concepts of stochastic choice behavior and random utility maximization, and a number of concrete choice models, are drawn from psychometrics (Thurstone, 1927; Luce, 1959, 1977; Tversky, 1972a, 1972b).

Biometrics has contributed a variety of models and statistical methods, including ordered discrete response models and maximum chi-square procedures for estimation (Berkson, 1955b; Cox, 1972; Finney, 1971).

From sociometrics have come methods for analyzing contingency table data, particularly discrete analysis of variance (Goodman, 1972b; Haberman, 1974; Bishop et al., 1975).

Early work in econometrics included the development of maximum likelihood methods for nonlinear models specific to applications, notably the contributions of Tobin (1958), Quandt (1968), Goldberger (1964), and Warner (1962).

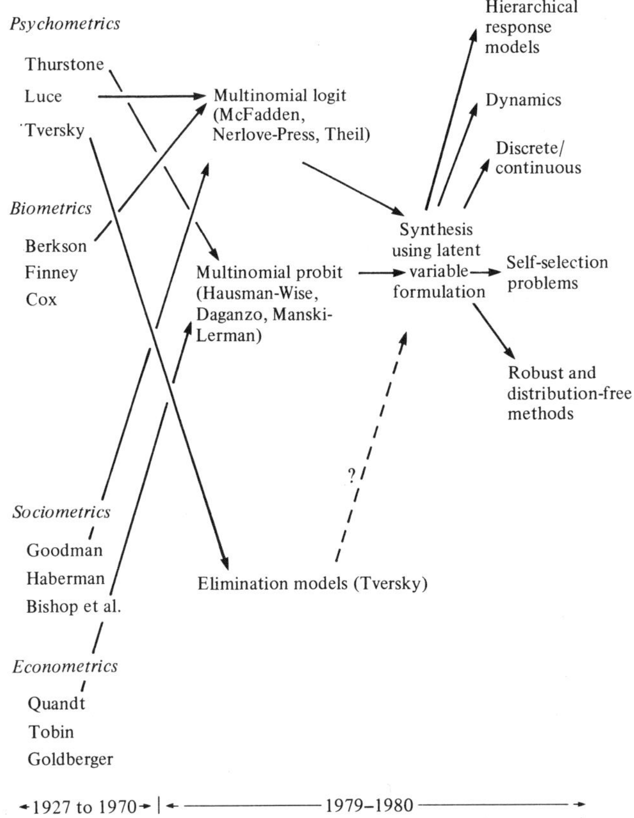

Figure 1.1. Historical development of qualitative response models.

From these origins have come three major families of models for discrete data analysis, the MNL model discussed earlier and the multinomial probit and elimination models to be discussed next. The first developments of these models were largely independent of one another and of the mainstream of econometrics. More recently, reformulation of these models in terms of latent variables has integrated them into classical econometrics and suggested a variety of extensions and solutions. Key references for this synthesis are the works of Goldberger (1971), Amemiya (1973, 1975), Heckman (1974, 1976b), Lee (1981), and Maddala (1977b).

Six areas of current research are outlined in the following sections: hierarchical response or decision-tree models; dynamics and the analysis of discrete panel data; combined continuous and discrete variable models; self-selection problems in sample surveys; robust and distribution-free methods.

5.2 *Multinomial probit*

Consider the latent variable model for discrete responses, $y_t^* = x_t\beta + \epsilon_t$ and $y_{mt} = 1$ if $y_{mt}^* \geqslant y_{nt}^*$ for $n = 1, \ldots, M$, from equations (2) and (3). If ϵ_t is assumed to be multivariate normal, the resulting discrete response model is termed the multinomial probit (MNP) model. The binary case has been used extensively in biometrics (Finney, 1971). The multivariate model has been investigated by Bock and Jones (1968), McFadden (1976b, 1981), Hausman and Wise (1978), Daganzo (1980), and Lerman and Manski (1981).

A form of the MNP model with a plausible economic interpretation is $y_t^* = x_t\alpha_t$, where α_t is multivariate normal with mean β and covariance matrix Ω and represents taste weights that vary randomly in the population. Note that this form implies $E\epsilon_t = 0$ and $\text{cov}(\epsilon_t) = x_t\Omega x_t'$ in the latent variable model formulation. If x_t includes alternative dummies, then the corresponding components of α_t are additive random contributions to the latent values of the alternatives. Generally some normalizations are required in this model for identification.

When correlation is permitted between alternatives, so that $\text{cov}(\epsilon_t)$ is not diagonal, the MNP model does not have the IIA or related restrictive properties, and it permits very general patterns of cross-elasticities. This is true in particular for the random taste weight version of the MNP model when components of α_t corresponding to attributes that vary across alternatives are random.

Evaluation of MNP probabilities for M alternatives generally requires evaluation of $(M-1)$-dimensional orthant probabilities. (The exceptions are factor models with a small number of factors, which yield very special and generally implausible covariance structures.) For $M \leqslant 3$, the MNP procedure is comparable to MNL in computation. However, for $M \geqslant 5$, the computation time required for numerical integration of the required orthant probabilities is excessive.

A quick, but crude, approximation to MNP probabilities approximates the maximum of two normal variates by a normal variate (Clark, 1961; Daganzo, 1980). This approximation is good for nonnegatively correlated variates of equal variance, but it is poor for negative correlations or unequal variances. The method tends to overestimate small probabilities. For assessments of this method, see the work of Horowitz (1979b) and McFadden (1981).

A potentially rapid method of fitting MNP probabilities is to draw realizations of α_t repeatedly and use the latent variable model to update relative frequencies, starting from some approximation such as the Clark procedure. This requires a large number of simple computer tasks and can be programmed quite efficiently. However, it is difficult to compute small probabilities accurately by this method (Lerman & Manski, 1981).

Computation is the primary impediment to widespread use of the MNP model, which otherwise has the elements of flexibility and ease of interpretation desirable in a general-purpose qualitative response model. Implementation of a fast and accurate approximation to the MNP probabilities remains an important research problem.

5.3 *Elimination models*

An elimination model views choice as a process in which alternatives are screened from the choice set, using various criteria, until a single element remains. It can be defined by the probability of transition from a set of alternatives to any subset, $Q(D|C)$. If the transition probabilities are stationary, then the choice probabilities satisfy the recursion formula

$$(35) \qquad P(i|C) = \sum_{D} Q(D|C)P(i|D)$$

where $P(i|C)$ is the probability of choosing i from set C.

Elimination models were introduced by Tversky (1972a) as a generalization of the Luce model to allow dependence between alternatives. An adaptation of Tversky's elimination by aspects (EBA) model suitable for econometric work takes transition probabilities to have an MNL form,

$$(36) \qquad Q(D|C) = \exp(x_D\beta_D) / \sum_{\substack{A \subseteq C \\ A \neq C}} \exp(x_A\beta_A)$$

where x_D is a vector of attributes common to and unique to the set of alternatives in D.

When $\exp(x_B\beta_B) = 0$ for sets B of more than one element, this model reduces to the MNL model. Otherwise, it does not have restrictive IIA-like properties.

The elimination model is not known to have a latent variable characterization. However, it can be characterized as the result of maximization of random lexicographic preferences. The model defined by equations (35) and (36) has not been applied in economics. However, if the common unique attributes x_D can be defined in an application, this should be a straightforward and flexible functional form.

An elimination model that can be derived from latent variables is the generalized extreme value (GEV) model introduced by McFadden (1978b, 1981). Define scale values

(37) $$z_{it} = x_{it}\beta \quad (i \in C = \{1, \ldots, M\})$$

and recursively for subsets $D \subseteq C$,

(38) $$z_{Dt} = \theta_D \ln \sum_{\substack{A \subseteq D \\ A \neq D}} \exp(z_{At}/\theta_D)$$

where $0 < \theta_D \leqslant 1$. The response probabilities are defined by the recursion (35) with MNL transition probabilities

(39) $$Q(D \mid C) = \exp(z_{Dt}/\theta_C) / \sum_{\substack{A \subseteq C \\ A \neq C}} \exp(z_{At}/\theta_C)$$

Note that the recursion (38) defines a function $z_{Ct} = H(z_{1t}, \ldots, z_{Mt})$ of the scale values for the alternatives. The response probabilities satisfy

(40) $$P(i \mid x_t) = \partial H(z_{1t}, \ldots, z_{Mt}) / \partial z_{it}$$

If the parameters θ satisfy $\theta_A \leqslant \theta_D$ for $A \subseteq D$, then this model is obtained from the latent variable model $y_t^* = x_t\beta + \epsilon_t$, with ϵ_t having a multivariate type I extreme value distribution of the form

(41) $$\mathrm{Prob}(\epsilon_t \leqslant \epsilon) = \exp[-\exp H(-\epsilon_1, \ldots, -\epsilon_M)]$$

Further, this model has the expected utility property that

$$H(x_{1t}\beta, \ldots, x_{Mt}\beta)$$

is the expected value of the maximum latent variable, except for an inessential constant, and can be interpreted as an exact measure of social welfare. These results are obtained by straightforward generalizations of the corresponding arguments for the MNL model.

The parameter θ_A in this elimination model can be interpreted as a measure of the degree of independence of the alternatives within A. When all the θ values are 1, this model reduces to a simple MNL model. Alternatively, when θ_A is near 0, the elimination model treats A essentially as if it contained a single alternative with a scale value equal to the maximum of the scale values of the elements in A.

Inspection of the two elimination models just described suggests that they are comparable in terms of flexibility and complexity. Other things being equal, the GEV model will tend to imply sharper discrimination among similar alternatives than the EBA model. Limited numerical experiments have suggested that the two models will be difficult to distinguish empirically.

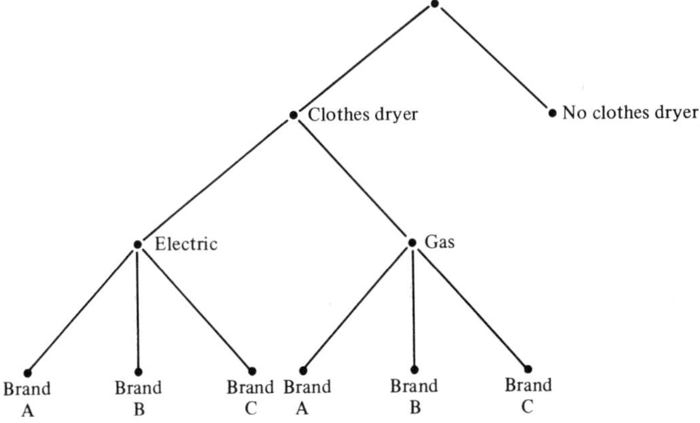

Figure 1.2. A decision hierarchy.

6 Current research

6.1 *Hierarchical response models*

When asked to describe the decision process leading to qualitative choice, individuals often depict a hierarchical or treelike structure in which alternatives are grouped into types that are "similar." The decision protocol is then to eliminate types, proceeding down the tree until a single alternative remains. An example of a decision tree is shown in Figure 1.2. Either of the elimination models described in the preceding section can be specialized to describe hierarchical responses by permitting transitions from a mode only to one of the modes immediately below it in the tree. Hierarchical decision models have been discussed further by Tversky and Sattath (1979) and McFadden (1981).

A useful feature of hierarchical models is that they can be estimated consistently by a sequential procedure. First, the parameters of the transition probabilities at the bottom of the tree are estimated using conditional choice data. Then one works up the tree, using previously estimated parameters to construct the variables entering the transition probabilities at each stage. At each stage, the transition probabilities are MNL functional forms, permitting straightforward maximum likelihood estimation. Estimated standard errors must be corrected for the use of variables constructed using previous estimates (Amemiya, 1978d; McFadden, 1981).

A hierarchical elimination model based on the generalized extreme value model described earlier generalizes the MNL model to a nested multinomial logit (NMNL) structure. Each transition in the tree is described by an MNL model, with one of the variables being an "inclusive value" that summarizes the attributes of alternatives below a node. An independence parameter at each node in the tree discounts the contribution to value of highly similar alternatives.

For the example of the clothes dryer tree in Figure 1.2, index the ownership (dryer/no dryer) decision by h, the electric or gas type decisions by g, and the brand decision by b. Then the response probability can be written as a product of transition probabilities,

$$P_{bgh} = P_{b|gh} P_{g|h} P_h \tag{42}$$

(For the no dryer alternative, the set of available b and g is of course empty, and $P_{b|gh}$ and $P_{g|h}$ are 1, by convention.) The transition probabilities have the MNL forms

$$P_{b|gh} = \exp(x_{bgh}\alpha)/\sum_c \exp(x_{cgh}\alpha) \tag{43}$$

$$P_{g|h} = \exp(y_{gh}\beta + I_{gh}\theta)/\sum_s \exp(y_{sh}\beta + I_{sh}\theta) \tag{44}$$

$$P_h = \exp(z_h\gamma + J_h\lambda)/\sum_k \exp(z_k\gamma + J_k\lambda) \tag{45}$$

where α, β, γ, θ, and λ are parameters and I_{gh} and J_h are inclusive values satisfying

$$I_{gh} = \ln \sum_c \exp(x_{cgh}\alpha) \tag{46}$$

$$J_h = \ln \sum_s \exp(y_{sh}\beta + I_{sh}\theta) \tag{47}$$

The function

$$K = \ln \sum_h \exp(z_h\gamma + J_h\lambda) \tag{48}$$

generates the response probabilities, satisfying $\partial K/\partial(x_{bgh}\alpha) = P_{bgh}$, and can be interpreted as an exact measure of social utility. The parameters θ and λ are measures of the independence of brands and types of dryers, respectively. They must satisfy $0<\theta,\ \lambda\leqslant 1$. When both equal 1, this model reduces to the simple MNL model.

The NMNL model has been used extensively in transportation demand applications (Ben-Akiva, 1973, 1974; Domencich & McFadden, 1975; McFadden, Talvitie, et al., 1977; McFadden, 1979b). Estimated sequentially, it has proved computationally tractable for large problems. The presence of the inclusive value coefficients, or independence measures, permits cross-elasticities to vary across branches of the tree. Further discussion of the statistical issues in estimation of the NMNL model can be found in the work of Amemiya (1978d) and McFadden (1981, 1980).

6.2 *Dynamic models*

The probabilistic response models discussed earlier in this chapter were developed primarily for analysis of sample survey data and usually have been given a static interpretation or have been interpreted as transition probabilities, with previous state entered as an explanatory variable. Formally, these models can be extended to the analysis of discrete panel data (a time series of observations on discrete responses of a cross section of respondents) by treating each possible response history as a discrete alternative. However, a much more fruitful approach is to extend the conventional econometric tools for the analysis of combined cross-sectional time series using a latent variable formulation of the discrete response problem. Within this framework, a variety of effects can be taken into account, including autocorrelated latent variables, components of variance error structure with individual effects (population heterogeneity), state dependence, and dynamic selection. This topic has been developed in great depth by Heckman (1974, 1978b, 1981b, 1981c), Heckman and McCurdy (1979), Heckman and Willis (1975), Heckman and Flinn (1980), and Lee (1980b).

Alternative dynamic structures often can be tested by examining time sequences of responses (Heckman, 1978b; Chamberlain, 1980).

Many familiar results for dynamic linear models carry over to the discrete response framework. However, in contrast to the linear (normal) case, conditional distributions are not characterized by their first two moments and must be analyzed explicitly. This makes a difference, for example, in the specification of initial conditions (Heckman, 1981c) and in testing causality (Chamberlain, 1980).

Most dynamic applications have used multivariate normal disturbances that permit the introduction of components of variance structure. This leads to MNP choice probabilities. As a consequence, computation limits problem size. Factor-analytic models can reduce computation, but they have restricted covariance structures that may be implausible for some applications.

An extensive survey of dynamic discrete data analysis can be found in the work of Heckman (Chapter 2 of this volume).

6.3 *Discrete/continuous systems*

In some applications, discrete response is one aspect of a larger joint decision that also involves continuous variables. For example, labor supply decisions involve discrete choice of occupation and continuous hours of work supplied. It is necessary to account correctly for the joint determination of the discrete and continuous responses in statistical analysis of such problems. Further, there may be direct interest in the interaction of these variables or in the economic theory of their joint determination.

Statistical analysis of joint discrete/continuous systems can be carried out by maximum likelihood methods or by computationally easier two-step procedures. In essence, these methods estimate reduced-form (marginal) equations and then use these estimates to obtain consistent estimators for the structural equations. Developments of these methods can be found in the work of Heckman (1978a), Amemiya (1974b), Lee (1980a), Maddala and Trost (1980), and Hay (1979). If response is the result of classical economic optimization, then cross-equation restrictions on functional forms are implied between the discrete-choice and continuous-choice equations. These conditions may be imposed to increase the efficiency of estimation, or they may be tested. For applications to the theory of the firm, see the work of Duncan (1980a) and McFadden (1979a), and for consumer theory, see the work of Dubin and McFadden (1980).

6.4 *Self-selection problems*

Qualitative response is sometimes a confounding factor in econometric analysis of a continuous phenomenon because of self-selection. For example, the analysis of housing expenditures using a sample of renters may be confounded by self-selection resulting from the purchase/rent decision. The switching regression problem, analyzed extensively for application to markets in disequilibrium, is a second example of self-selection (Quandt, 1972; Poirier & Ruud, 1980).

Models of the same mathematical structure as discrete/continuous choice models can be used to correct self-selection biases (Heckman, 1976b; Hausman & Wise, 1977; Maddala, 1977a; Lee, 1980a).

Self-selection is a special case of biased or stratified sampling. In general, stratified sampling can be turned to the advantage of the econometrician by using estimators that correct bias and extract maximum information from samples (Manski & Lerman, 1977; Manski & McFadden, 1980; Cosslett, 1980a; McFadden 1979c); the last work generalizes an efficient nonclassical maximum likelihood estimator developed by Cosslett to give an efficient procedure that is practical for many self-selection problems.

6.5 *Robust and distribution-free methods*

Parametric methods such as the MNL model are obtained from latent variable models under very special, and possibly unrealistic, variable and error specifications. The robustness of such models with respect to specification error is problematic. A battery of specification tests for diagnostic purposes is needed, as well as methods for accommodating errors in variables and calculating estimators that are robust or distribution-free.

The nonlinearity of the qualitative response models greatly complicates the search for robust methods. Common statistical approaches to robust estimation depend heavily on linear structures. Manski (1975) and Cosslett (1980b) have developed distribution-free methods for estimating some families of discrete choice models.

7 Conclusion

The development of tools for analysis of discrete response data has opened to econometric investigation a spectrum of significant economic behavior, particularly in labor economics, demographics, location theory, and consumer demand for major durables. The current literature provides a number of practical general-purpose econometric models for discrete data analysis and, in addition, suggests approaches for the development of models specific to particular applications.

Formulation of qualitative response problems in terms of latent variables has made it possible to tie this subject to the main body of econometrics. This has opened the way to extending to qualitative response problems the full range of econometric techniques, particularly structural estimation, time series analysis, and robust methods. Qualitative response problems have opened a new series of questions, arising from the nonlinearity of the models and from attention to self-selection issues, that are important to the development of this subject and illuminating for econometrics in general.

REFERENCES

Adler, T., and Ben-Akiva, M. 1975. "A Joint Frequency, Destination and Mode Choice Model for Shopping Trips." *Transportation Research Record* 569: 136–50.

Aitchison, J., and Bennett, J. 1970. "Polychotomous Quantal Response by Maximum Indicant." *Biometrika* 57: 253–62.

Aitchison, J., and Silvey, S. 1957. "The Generalization of Probit Analysis to the Case of Multiple Responses." *Biometrika* 44: 131–40.

Amemiya, T. 1973. "Regression Analysis When the Dependent Variable Is Truncated Normal." *Econometrica* 41: 997–1016.

Amemiya, T. 1974a. "Bivariate Probit Analysis: Minimum Chi-Square Methods." *Journal of the American Statistical Association* 69: 940–4.

Amemiya, T. 1974b. "Multivariate Regression and Simultaneous Equation Models When the Dependent Variables Are Truncated Normal." *Econometrica* 42: 999–1012.

Amemiya, T. 1974c. "A Note on the Fair and Jaffee Model." *Econometrica* 42: 759–62.

Amemiya, T. 1975. "Qualitative Response Models." *Annals of Economic and Social Measurement* 4: 363–72.

Amemiya, T. 1976. "The Maximum Likelihood, the Minimum Chi-Square, and the Non-linear Weighted Least Squares Estimator in the General Qualitative Response Model." *Journal of the American Statistical Association* 71: 347–51.

Amemiya, T. 1978a. "The Estimation of a Simultaneous Equation Generalized Probit Model." *Econometrica* 46: 1193–205.

Amemiya, T. 1978b. "A Note on the Estimation of a Time Dependent Markov Chain Model." Department of Economics, Stanford University.

Amemiya, T. 1978c. "The n^2-Order Mean Squared Errors of the Maximum Likelihood and the Minimum Logit Chi-Square Estimates." Technical report 267, Institute of Mathematical Studies in the Social Sciences, Stanford University.

Amemiya, T. 1978d. "On a Two-Step Estimation of a Multivariate Logit Model." *Journal of Econometrics* 8: 13–21.

Amemiya, T. 1979. "The Estimation of a Simultaneous Equation Tobit Model." *International Economic Review* 20: 169–81.

Amemiya, T., and Nold, F. 1975. "A Modified Logit Model." *Review of Economics and Statistics* 57: 255–7.

Anscombe, E. J. 1956. "On Estimating Binomial Response Relations." *Biometrika* 43: 461–4.

Antle, C., Klimko, L., and Harkness, W. 1970. "Confidence Intervals for the Parameters of the Logistic Distribution." *Biometrika* 57: 397–402.

Ashford, J. R., and Sowden, R. R. 1970. "Multivariate Probit Analysis." *Biometrics* 26: 535–46.

Ashton, W. 1972. *The Logit Transformation.* New York: Hafner.

Atkinson, A. 1972. "A Test of the Linear Logistic and Bradley-Terry Models." *Biometrika* 59: 37–42.

Barlettt, M. S. 1935. "Contingency Table Interactions." *Journal of the Royal Statistical Society* (Supplement) 2: 248–52.

Ben-Akiva, M. 1973. "Structure of Passenger Travel Demand Models." Transportation Research Board Record, No. 526, Washington, D.C.

Ben-Akiva, M. 1974. "Multi-Dimensional Choice Models: Alternative Structures of Travel Demand Models." Transportation Research Board Special Report 149, Washington, D.C.

Ben-Akiva, M., and Lerman, S. 1974. "Some Estimation Results of a Simultaneous Model of Auto Ownership and Mode Choice to Work." *Transportation* 3: 357–76.

Ben-Akiva, M., and Lerman, S. 1979. "Disaggregate Travel and Mobility Choice Modes and Measures of Accessibility." In *Behavioral Travel Modelling,* edited by D. Hensher and P. Stopher, pp. 654–79. London: Coom Helm.

Berkson, J. 1949. "Application of the Logistic Function to Bioassay." *Journal of the American Statistical Association* 39: 357–65.

Berkson, J. 1951. "Why I Prefer Logits to Probits." *Biometrika* 7: 327–39.

Berkson, J. 1953. "A Statistically Precise and Relatively Simple Method of Estimating the Bio-Assay with Quantal Response, Based on the Logistic Function." *Journal of the American Statistical Association* 48: 565–99.

Berkson, J. 1955a. "Estimate of the Integrated Normal Curve by Minimum Normit Chi-Square with Particular Reference to Bio-assay." *Journal of the American Statistical Association* 50: 529–49.

Berkson, J. 1955b. "Maximum Likelihood and Minimum Chi-Square Estimations of the Logistic Function." *Journal of the American Statistical Association* 50: 130–61.

Berndt, E., Hall, B., Hall, R., and Hausman, J. 1974. "Estimation and Inference in Non-Linear Structural Models." *Annals of Economic and Social Measurement* 3: 653–66.

Bishop, T., Fieberg, S., and Holland, P. 1975. *Discrete Multivariate Analysis.* Cambridge: MIT Press.

Block, H., and Marschak, J. 1960. "Random Orderings and Stochastic Theories of Response." In *Contributions to Probability and Statistics,* edited by I. Olkin, pp. 97–132. Stanford University Press.

Bock, R. D., and Jones, L. 1968. *The Measurement and Prediction of Judgement and Choice.* San Francisco: Holden-Day.

Boskin, M. 1974. "A Conditional Logit Model of Occupational Choice." *Journal of Political Economy* 82: 389–98.

Boskin, M. 1975. "A Markov Model of Turnover in Aid to Families with Dependent Children." *Journal of Human Resources* 10: 467–81.

Brownstone, D. 1978. "An Econometric Model of Consumer Durable Choice and Utilization Rate." Paper IP-258, Center for Research in Management Science, University of California, Berkeley.

Cardell, S. 1977. "Multinomial Logit with Correlated Stochastic Terms." Working paper, Charles River Associates.

Chamberlain, G. 1980. "On the General Non-Equivalence of Granger and Sims Causality." Working paper, Department of Economics, University of Wisconsin.

Chambers, E. A., and Cox, D. R. 1967. "Discrimination between Alternative Binary Response Models." *Biometrika* 54: 573–8.

Clark, C. 1961. "The Greatest of a Finite Set of Random Variables." *Operations Research* 9: 145–62.

Cook, P. 1975. "The Correctional Carrot: Better Jobs for Parolees." *Policy Analysis* 1: 11–54.

Cosslett, S. 1978. "Efficient Estimation of Discrete-Choice Models from Choice-Based Samples." Ph.D. dissertation, Department of Economics, University of California, Berkeley.

Cosslett, S. 1980. "Estimation of Random Utility Models with Unknown Probability Distribution." Presented to CEME conference on discrete econometrics.

Cosslett, S. 1981. "Efficient Estimators of Discrete Choice Models." In *Structural Analysis of Discrete Data,* edited by C. Manski and D. McFadden, pp. 51–111. Cambridge: MIT Press.

Cox, D. 1958. "The Regression Analysis of Binary Sequences." *Journal of the Royal Statistical Society* (Series B) 820: 215–42.

Cox, D. 1966. "Some Procedures Connected with the Logistic Response Curve." In *Research Papers in Statistics,* edited by F. David, pp. 55–71. New York: Wiley.

Cox, D. 1970. *Analysis of Binary Data.* London: Methuen.

Cox, D. R. 1972. "The Analysis of Multivariate Binary Data." *Applied Statistics* 21: 113–20.

Cox, D., and Snell, E. 1968. "A General Definition of Residuals." *Journal of the Royal Statistical Society* (Series B) 30: 248–65.

Cox, D., and Snell, E. 1971. "On Test Statistics Calculated from Residuals." *Biometrika* 58: 589–94.

Cragg, J. G. 1971. "Some Statistical Models for Limited Dependent Variables with Application to the Demand for Durable Goods." *Econometrica* 39: 829–44.

Cragg, J., and Uhler, R. 1970. "The Demand for Automobiles." *Canadian Journal of Economics* 3: 386–406.

Cripps, T. F., and Tarling, R. J. 1974. "An Analysis of the Duration of Male Unemployment in Great Britain 1932–1973." *Economic Journal* 84: 289–316.

Daganzo, C. 1980. *Multinomial Probit.* New York: Academic.

Daganzo, C., Bouthelier, F., and Sheffi, Y. 1977. "Multinomial Probit and Qualitative Choice: A Computationally Efficient Algorithm." *Transportation Science* 11: 338–58.

Dagenais, M. G. 1975. "Application of a Threshold Regression Model to Household Purchases of Automobiles." *Review of Economics and Statistics* 57: 275–85.

Daly, A., and Zachary, S. 1979. "Improved Multiple Choice Models." In *Identifying and Measuring the Determinants of Mode Choice,* edited by D. Hensher and O. Dalvi, pp. 187–201. London: Teakfield.

Debreu, G. 1960. "Review of R. D. Luce Individual Choice Behavior." *American Economic Review* 50: 186–8.

Diewert, E. 1978. "Duality Approaches to Microeconomic Theory." Technical Report 281, Institute of Mathematical Studies in the Social Sciences, Stanford University.

Domencich, T., and McFadden, D. 1975. *Urban Travel Demand: A Behavioral Analysis.* Amsterdam: North-Holland.

Dubin, J., and McFadden, D. 1980. "An Econometric Analysis of Residential Electrical Appliance Holdings and Usage." Working paper, Department of Economics, Massachusetts Institute of Technology.

Duncan, G. 1978. "Specification and a Simple Estimator for the Mixed, Continuous/Discrete Dependent Variable Model in Classical Production Theory." Working paper, Department of Economics, Washington State University.

Duncan, G. 1980a. "Formulation and Statistical Analysis of the Mixed Continuous/Discrete Variable Model in Classical Production Theory." *Econometrica* 48: 839–52.

Duncan, G. 1980b. "Mixed Continuous Discrete Choice Models in the Presence of Hedonic or Exogenous Price Functions." Working paper, Department of Economics, Washington State University.

Efron, B. 1975. "The Efficiency of Logistic Regression Compared to Normal Discriminant Analysis." *Journal of the American Statistical Association* 70: 892–8.

Fair, R. C., and Jaffee, D. M. 1972. "Methods of Estimation for Markets in Disequilibrium." *Econometrica* 40: 497–514.

Farber, H. 1978. "Bargaining Theory, Wage Outcomes, and the Occurrence of Strikes." *American Economic Review* 68: 262–71.

Farber, H., and Saks, D. 1981. "Why Workers Want Unions." *Journal of Public Economics,* to appear.

Finney, D. 1964. *Statistical Method in Bio-Assay.* London: Griffin.

Finney, D. 1971. *Probit Analysis.* Cambridge University Press.

Friedman, P. 1973. "Suggestions for the Analysis of Qualitative Dependent Variables." *Public Finance Quarterly* 1: 345–55.

Fuller, W., Manski, C., and Wise, D. 1980. "New Evidence on the Economic Determinants of Post-Secondary Schooling Choices." J.F.K. School of Government Discussion Paper 9UD. Unpublished manuscript.

Gart, J., and Zweifel, J. 1967. "On the Bias of Various Estimators of the Logit and Its Variance." *Biometrika* 54: 181–7.

Gillen, D. W. 1977. "Estimation and Specification of the Effects of Parking Costs on Urban Transport Mode Choice." *Journal of Urban Economics* 4: 186–99.

Goldberger, A. S. 1964. *Econometric Theory.* New York: Wiley.

Goldberger, A. S. 1971. "Econometrics and Psychometrics: A Survey of Communalities." *Psychometrika* 36: 83–107.

Goldberger, A. S. 1973. "Correlations Between Binary Outcomes and Probabilistic Predictions." *Journal of the American Statistical Association* 68: 84.

Goldfeld, S. M., and Quandt, R. E. 1972. *Nonlinear Methods in Econometrics.* Amsterdam: North-Holland.

Goldfeld, S., and Quandt, R. 1973. "The Estimation of Structural Shifts by Switching Regressions." *Annals of Economic and Social Measurement* 2: 475–85.

Goldfeld, S., and Quandt, R. 1976. "Techniques for Estimating Switching Regressions." In *Studies in Non-Linear Estimation,* edited by S. Goldfeld and R. Quandt, pp. 3–37. Cambridge: Ballinger.

Goodman, L. A. 1970. "The Multivariate Analysis of Qualitative Data: Interactions Among Multiple Classifications." *Journal of the American Statistical Association* 65: 226–56.

Goodman, L. A. 1971. "The Analysis of Multidimensional Contingency Tables: Stepwise Procedures and Direct Estimation Methods for Building Models for Multiple Classifications." *Technometrics* 13: 33–61.

Goodman, L. A. 1972a. "A Modified Multiple Regression Approach to the Analysis of Dichotomous Variables." *American Sociological Review* 37: 28–46.

Goodman, L. A. 1972b. "A General Model for the Analysis of Surveys." American Journal of Sociology 77: 1035–86.

Goodman, L. A. 1973. "Causal Analysis of Panel Study Data and Other Kinds of Survey Data." *American Journal of Sociology* 78: 1135–91.

Goodman, I., and Kruskal, W. 1954. "Measures of Association for Cross Classifications." *Journal of the American Statistical Association* 49: 732–64.

Goodman, L. A., and Kruskal, W. H. 1954. "Measures of Association for Cross Classification II, Further Discussion and References." *Journal of the American Statistical Association* 54: 123–63.

Griliches, Z., Hall, B. H., and Hausman, J. A. 1978. "Missing Data and Self-Selection in Large Panels." *Annals de l'Insee* 30–31: 137–76.

Grizzle, J. 1962. "Asymptotic Power of Tests of Linear Hypotheses Using the Probit and Logit Transformations." *Journal of the American Statistical Association* 57: 877–94.

Grizzle, J. 1971. "Multivariate Logit Analysis." *Biometrics* 27: 1057–62.

Gronau, R. 1973. "The Effect of Children on the Housewife's Value of Time." *Journal of Political Economy* 81: s168–99.

Gronau, R. 1974. "Wage Comparisons – A Selectivity Bias." *Journal of Political Economy* 82: 1119–43.

Gurland, J., Lee, I., and Dahm, P. 1960. "Polychotomous Quantal Response in Biological Assay." *Biometrics* 16: 382–98.

Haberman, S. 1974. *The Analysis of Frequency Data.* University of Chicago Press.

Haldane, J. 1955. "The Estimation and Significance of the Logarithm of a Ratio of Frequencies." *Annals of Human Genetics* 20: 309–11.

Hall, R. 1970. "Turnover in the Labor Force." *Brookings Papers on Economic Activity* 3: 709–56.

Harter, J., and Moore, A. 1967. "Maximum Likelihood Estimation, from Censored Samples, of the Parameters of a Logistic Distribution." *Journal of the American Statistical Association* 62: 675–83.

Hausman, J. 1978. "Specification Tests in Econometrics." *Econometrica* 46: 1251–71.

Hausman, J. 1979. "Individual Discount Rates and the Purchase and Utilization of Energy Using Durables." *Bell Journal of Economics* 10: 33–54.

Hausman, J., and McFadden, D. 1980. "A Specification Test for the Multinomial Logit Model," Working paper, Department of Economics, Massachusetts Institute of Technology.

Hausman, J. A., and Wise, D. A. 1976. "The Evaluation of Results from Truncated Samples: The New Jersey Negative Income Tax Experiment." *Annals of Economic and Social Measurement* 5: 421–45.

Hausman, J. A., and Wise, D. A. 1977. "Social Experimentation, Truncated Distributions and Efficient Estimation." *Econometrica* 45: 319–39.

Hausman, J. A., and Wise, D. A. 1978. "A Conditional Probit Model for Qualitative Choice: Discrete Decisions Recognizing Interdependence and Heterogeneous Preferences." *Econometrica* 46: 403–26.

Hausman, J. A., and Wise, D. 1981. "Stratification on Endogenous Variables and Estimation: The Gary Experiment." In *Structural Analysis of Discrete Data,* edited by C. Manski and D. McFadden, pp. 365–91. Cambridge: M.I.T. Press.

Hay, J. 1979. "An Analysis of Occupational Choice and Income." Ph.D. dissertation, Yale University.

Heckman, J. 1974. "Shadow Prices, Market Wages, and Labor Supply." *Econometrica* 42: 679–94.

Heckman, J. 1976a. "Simultaneous Equations Model with Continuous and Discrete Endogenous Variables and Structural Shifts." In *Studies in Non-Linear Estimation,* edited by S. Goldfeld and R. Quandt, pp. 235–72. Cambridge: Ballinger.

Heckman, J. 1976b. "The Common Structure of Statistical Models of Truncation, Sample Selection and Limited Dependent Variables and a Simple Estimation for Such Models." *Annals of Economic and Social Measurement* 5: 475–92.

Heckman, J. J. 1978a. "Dummy Exogenous Variables in a Simultaneous Equation System." *Econometrica* 46: 931–59.

Heckman, J. 1978b. "Simple Statistical Models for Discrete Panel Data Developed and Applied to Test the Hypothesis of True State Dependence Against the Hypothesis of Spurious State Dependence." *Annals de l'INSEE* 30–1: 227–69.

Heckman, J. 1979. "Sample Selection Bias as a Specification Error." *Econometrica* 47: 153–61.

Heckman, J. 1981a. "Heterogeneity and State Dependence in Dynamic Models of Labor Supply." In *Conference on Low Income Labor Markets,* edited by S. Rosen. University of Chicago Press.

Heckman, J. 1981b. "Statistical Models for the Analysis of Discrete Panel Data." In *Structural Analysis of Discrete Data,* edited by C. Manski and D. McFadden, pp. 114–78. Cambridge: M.I.T. Press.

Heckman, J. 1981c. "The Incidental Parameters Problem and the Problem of Initial Conditions in Estimating a Discrete Stochastic Process and Some Monte Carlo Evidence on Their Practical Importance." In *Structural Analysis of Discrete Data,* edited by C. Manski and D. McFadden, pp. 179–5. Cambridge: M.I.T. Press.

Heckman, J., and Flinn, C. 1980. "Models for the Analysis of Labor Force Dynamics." Working Paper, Department of Economics, University of Chicago.

Heckman, J., and McCurdy, T. 1980. "A Dynamic Model of Female Labor Supply." *Review of Economic Studies* 47: 47–74.

Heckman, J., and Singer, B. (eds). 1980. *Longitudinal Labor Market Studies: Theory, Methods and Empirical Results.* Social Science Research Council Monograph. New York: Academic.

Heckman, J., and Willis, R. 1975. "Estimation of a Stochastic Model of Reproduction: An Econometric Approach." In *Household Production and Consumption,* edited by N. Terleckyj, pp. 99–138. New York: National Bureau of Economic Research.

Heckman, J., and Willis, R. 1977. "A Beta Logistic Model for the Analysis of Sequential Labor Force Participation of Married Women." *Journal of Political Economy* 85: 27–58.

Horowitz, J. 1979a. "Identification and Diagnosis of Specification Errors in the Multinomial Logit Model." Mimeograph, Environmental Protection Agency.

Horowitz, J. 1979b. "A Note on the Accuracy of the Clark Approximation for the Multinomial Probit Model." Mimeograph, Department of Transportation, Massachusetts Institute of Technology.

Horowitz, J. 1980. "The Accuracy of the Multinomial Logit Model as an Approximation to the Multinomial Probit Model of Travel Demand." *Transportation Research* (Part B).

Horowitz, J. 1981. "Sampling, Specification and Data Errors in Probabilistic Discrete Choice Models." In *Applied Discrete Choice Modelling,* edited by D. Hensher and L. Johnson, pp. 417–35. London: Croom Helm.

Hulett, J. R. 1973. "On the Use of Regression Analysis with a Qualitative Dependent Variable." *Public Finance Quarterly* 1: 339–44.

Ito, T. 1980. "Methods of Estimation for Multi-Market Disequilibrium Models." *Econometrica* 48: 97–126.

Joreskog, K., and Goldberger, A. 1975. "Estimation of a Model with Multiple Indicators and Multiple Causes of a Single Latent Variable Model. *Journal of the American Statistical Association* 70: 631–9.

Kiefer, N. 1978. "Discrete Parameter Variation: Efficient Estimation of a Switching Regression Model." *Econometrica* 46: 427–34.

Kiefer, N. M. 1979. "On the Value of Sample Separation Information." *Econometrica* 47: 997–1003.

Kiefer, N., and Neumann, G. 1979. "An Empirical Job Search Model with a Test of the Constant Reservation Wage Hypothesis." *Journal of Political Economy* 87: 89–107.

King, M. 1980. "An Econometric Model of Tenure Choice and Demand for Housing as a Joint Decision." Working paper, Department of Economics, University of Birmingham.

Kohn, M., Manski, C., and Mundel, D. 1976. "An Empirical Investigation of Factors Influencing College Going Behavior." *Annals of Economic and Social Measurement* 5: 391–419.

Ladd, G. 1966. "Linear Probability Functions and Discriminant Functions." *Econometrica* 34: 873–85.

Lave, C. 1970. "The Demand for Urban Mass Transit." *Review of Economics and Statistics* 52: 320–3.

Lee, L. F. 1978. "Unionism and Wage Rates: A Simultaneous Equation Model with Qualitative and Limited Dependent Variables." *International Economic Review* 19: 415–33.

Lee, L. F. 1979. "Identification and Estimation in Binary Choice Models with Limited (Censored) Dependent Variables." *Econometrica* 47: 977–96.

Lee, L. F. 1980a. "Specification Error in Multinomial Logit Models: Analysis of the Omitted Variable Bias." Working paper, Department of Economics, University of Minnesota.

Lee, L. F. 1980b. "Statistical Analysis of Econometric Models of Discrete Panel Data." Working paper, Department of Economics, University of Minnesota.

Lee, L. F. 1981. "Simultaneous Equations Models with Discrete and Censored Variables." In *Structural Analysis of Discrete Data,* edited by C. Manski and D. McFadden, pp. 346–64. Cambridge: M.I.T. Press.

Lee, L. F., Maddala, G. S., and Trost, R. P. 1979. "Testing for Structural Change by D-Methods in Switching Simultaneous Equation Models." *Proceedings of the American Statistical Association* forthcoming.

Lee, L. F., and Trost, R. P. 1978. "Estimation of Some Limited Dependent Variable Models with Applications to Housing Demand." *Journal of Econometrics* 8: 357–82.

Lerman, S. R. 1977. "Location, Housing, Automobile Ownership and Mode to Work: A Joint Choice Model." Transportation Research Board Record No. 610, Washington, D.C.

Lerman, S., and Manski, C. 1980. "Information Diffusion in Discrete Choice Contexts." Presented to CEME conference on discrete econometrics.

Lerman, S., and Manski, C. 1981. "On the Use of Simulated Frequencies to Approximate Choice Probabiities." In *Structural Analysis of Discrete Data,* edited by C. Manski and D. McFadden, pp. 305–19. Cambridge: M.I.T. Press.

Li, M. 1977. "A Logit Model of Home Ownership." *Econometrica* 45: 1081–97.

Little, R. E. 1968. "A Note on Estimation for Quantal Response Data." *Biometrika* 55: 578–9.

Luce, R. D. 1959. *Individual Choice Behavior: A Theoretical Analysis.* New York: Wiley.

Luce, R. D. 1977. "The Choice Axiom After Twenty Years." *Journal of Mathematical Psychology* 15: 215–33.

Luce, R. D., and Suppes, P. 1965. "Preference, Utility, and Subjective Probability." In *Handbook of Mathematical Psychology III,* edited by R. Luce, R. Bush, and E. Galanter, pp. 249–410. New York: Wiley.

Maddala, G. S. 1977a. "Self-Selectivity Problem in Econometric Models." In *Applications of Statistics,* edited by P. Krishniah. Amsterdam: North-Holland.

Maddala, G. S. 1977b. "Identification and Estimation Problems in Limited Dependent Variable Models." In *Natural Resources, Uncertainty and General Equilibrium Systems: Essays in Memory of Rafael Lusky,* edited by A. S. Blinder and P. Friedman, pp. 423–50. New York: Academic.

Maddala, G. S. 1978. "Selectivity Problems in Longitudinal Data." *Annals de l'INSEE* 30-1: 423–50.

Maddala, G. S., and Lee, L. F. 1976. "Recursive Models with Qualitative Endogenous Variables." *Annals of Economic and Social Measurement* 5: 525–45.

Maddala, G., and Nelson, F. 1974. "Maximum Likelihood Methods for Markets in Disequilibrium." *Econometrica* 42: 1013–30.

Maddala, G. S., and Nelson, F. D. 1975. "Switching Regression Models with Exogenous and Endogenous Switching." *Proceedings of the American Statistical Association* (Business and Economics Section) 423–6.

Maddala, G. S., and Trost, R. 1980. "Asymptotic Covariance Matrices of Two-Stage Probit and Two-Stage Tobit Methods for Simultaneous Equations Models with Selectivity." *Econometrica* 48: 491–503.

Manski, C. 1975. "Maximum Score Estimation of the Stochastic Utility Model of Choice." *Journal of Econometrics* 3: 205–28.

Manski, C. 1977. "The Structure of Random Utility Models." *Theory and Decision* 8: 229–54.

Manski, C. 1981. "Structural Models for Discrete Data." *Sociological Methodology* pp. 58–109.

Manski, C., and Lerman, S. 1977. "The Estimation of Choice Probabilities from Choice-Based Samples." *Econometrica* 45: 1977–88.

Manski, C., and McFadden, D. 1981. "Alternative Estimates and Sample Designs for Discrete Choice Analysis." In *Structural Analysis of Discrete Data,* edited by C. Manski and D. McFadden, pp. 2–50. Cambridge: M.I.T. Press.

Marschak, J. 1960. "Binary-Choice Constraints and Random Utility Indicators." In *Mathematical Methods in the Social Sciences,* edited by K. Arrow, S. Karlin, and P. Suppes, pp. 312–29. Stanford University Press.

McFadden, D. 1973. "Conditional Logit Analysis of Qualitative Choice Behavior." In *Frontiers in Econometrics,* edited by P. Zarembka, pp. 105–42. New York: Academic.

McFadden, D. 1974. "The Measurement of Urban Travel Demand." *Journal of Public Economics* 3: 303–28.

McFadden, D. 1976a. "A Comment on Discriminant Analysis 'Versus' Logit

Analysis." *Annals of Economics and Social Measurement* 5: 511–23.

McFadden, D. 1976b. "Quantal Choice Analysis: A Survey." *Annals of Economic and Social Measurement* 5: 363–90.

McFadden, D. 1976c. "The Revealed Preferences of a Public Bureaucracy." *Bell Journal* 7: 55–72.

McFadden, D. 1978a. "Cost, Revenue, and Profit Functions." In *Production Economics,* edited by M. Fuss and D. McFadden, pp. 3–110. Amsterdam: North-Holland.

McFadden, D. 1978b. "Modelling the Choice of Residential Location." In *Spatial Interaction Theory and Residential Location,* edited by A. Karlquist et al., pp. 75–96. Amsterdam: North-Holland.

McFadden, D. 1979a. "Econometric Net Supply Systems for Firms with Continuous and Discrete Commodities." Working paper, Department of Economics, Massachusetts Institute of Technology.

McFadden, D. 1979b. "Quantitative Methods for Analysing Travel Behavior of Individuals." *Behavioral Travel Modelling,* edited by D. Hensher and P. Stopher, pp. 279–318. London: Croom Helm.

McFadden, D. 1979c. "Econometric Analysis of Discrete Data." Fisher-Schultz Lecture, Econometric Society, Athens.

McFadden, D. 1981. "Econometric Models of Probabilistic Choice." In *Structural Analysis of Discrete Data,* edited by C. Manski and D. McFadden, pp. 198–272. Cambridge: M.I.T. Press.

McFadden, D., Puig, C., and Kirschner, D. 1977. "Determinants of the Long-Run Demand for Electricity." *Proceedings of the American Statistical Association,* Business and Economics Section, Vol. 1.

McFadden, D., and Reid, F. 1975. "Aggregate Travel Demand Forecasting from Disaggregated Behavioral Models." Transportation Research Board Record 534: 24–37, Washington, D.C.

McFadden, D., Talvitie, A., et al. 1977. "Demand Model Estimation and Validation." Final Report Series, Vol. 5. Urban Travel Demand Forecasting Project, Institute of Transportation Studies, University of California, Berkeley.

McFadden, D., Tye, W., and Train, K. 1976. "An Application of Diagnostic Tests for the Independence from Irrevelent Alternatives Property of the Multinomial Logit Model." Transportation Research Board Record No. 637, pp. 39–45, Washington, D.C.

McKelvey, R., and Zovoina, W. 1975. "A Statistical Model for the Analysis of Ordinal Level Dependent Variables." *Journal of Mathematical Sociology* 4: 103–20.

Miller, L., and Radner, R. 1970. "Demand and Supply in U.S. Higher Education." *American Economic Review* 60: 326–34.

Moore, D. H. 1973. "Evaluation of Five Discrimination Procedures for Binary Variables." *Journal of the American Statistical Association* 68: 399–404.

Moses, L., Beals, R., and Levy, M. 1967. "Rationality and Migration in Ghana." *Review of Economics and Statistics* 49: 480–6.

Mosteller, F. 1968. "Association and Estimation in Contingency Tables." *Journal of the American Statistical Association* 63: 1–28.

Nelson, F. 1977. "Censored Regression Models with Unobserved Stochastic Censoring Thresholds." *Econometrica* 6: 309–27.

Nelson, F. S., and Olsen, L. 1978. "Specification and Estimation of a Simultaneous Equation Model with Limited Dependent Variables." *International Economic Review* 19: 685–710.

Nerlove, M. 1978. "Econometric Analysis of Longitudinal Data: Approaches, Problems and Prospects, The Econometrics of Panel Data." *Annals de l'INSEE* 30–1: 7–22.

Nerlove, M., and Press, J. 1973. "Univariable and Multivariable Log-Linear and Logistic Models." RAND report No. R-1306-EDA/NIH.

Nerlove, M., and Press, S. 1976. "Multivariate and Log Linear Probability Models for the Analysis of Qualitative Data." Discussion paper, Department of Economics, Northwestern University.

Oliveira, J. T., de 1958. "Extremal Distributions." *Revista de Faculdada du Ciencia, Lisboa* (Serie A) 7: 215–27.

Olsen, R. J. 1978a. "Comment on 'The Effect of Unions on Earnings and Earnings on Unions: A Mixed Logit Approach'." *International Economic Review* 19: 259–61.

Olsen, R. J. 1978b. "Tests for the Presence of Selectivity Bias and Their Relation to Specifications of Functional Form and Error Distribution." Working paper No. 812, revised, Institute for Social and Policy Studies, Yale University.

Olsen, R. J. 1980a. "A Least Squares Correction for Selectivity Bias." *Econometrica* 48: 1815–20.

Olsen, R. 1980b. "Distributional Tests for Selectivity Bias and a More Robust Likelihood Estimator." Working paper, Institute for Social and Policy Studies, Yale University.

Olsen, R. 1980c. "Estimating the Effect of Child Mortality on the Number of Births." Economic Growth Center, Yale University.

Plackett, R. L. 1974. *The Analysis of Categorical Data.* London: Charles Griffin.

Poirier, D. J. 1977. "The Determinants of Home Buying" in *The New Jersey Income-Maintenance Experiment.*" In Vol. II, *Expenditures, Health and Social Behavior, and the Quality of the Evidence,* edited by H. W. Watts and A. Rees, pp. 73–91. New York: Academic.

Poirier, D. J. 1978. "A Switching Simultaneous Equation Model of Physician Behavior in Ontario." In *Structural Analysis of Discrete Data: with Econometric Applications,* edited by D. McFadden and C. Manski, pp. 392–421. Cambridge: M.I.T. Press.

Poirier, D., and Ruud, P. 1980. "On the Appropriateness of Endogenous Switching." *J. Econometrics,* forthcoming.

Pollakowski, H. 1974. "The Effects of Local Public Service on Residential Location Decision: An Empirical Study of the San Francisco Bay Area." Ph.D. dissertation, Department of Economics, University of California, Berkeley.

Pollakowski, H. 1980. *Residential Location and Urban Housing Markets.* Lexington, Mass.: D.C. Heath.

Quandt, R. 1956. "Probabilistic Theory of Consumer Behavior." *Quarterly Journal of Economics* 70: 507–36.

Quandt, R. 1968. "Estimation of Modal Splits." *Transportation Research* 2: 41–50.

Quandt, R. 1970. *The Demand for Travel.* London: D.C. Heath.

Quandt, R. E. 1972. "A New Approach to Estimating Switching Regressions." *Journal of the American Statistical Association* 67: 306–10.

Quandt, R. 1978. "Test of the Equilibrium vs Disequilibrium Hypothesis." *International Economic Review* 19: 435–52.

Quandt, R., and Baumol, W. 1966. "The Demand for Abstract Travel Modes: Theory and Measurement." *Journal of Regional Science* 6: 13–26.

Quandt, R. E., and Ramsey, J. B. 1978. "Estimating Mixtures of Normal Distributions and Switching Regressions." *Journal of the American Statistical Association* 71: 730–52.

Quigley, J. M. 1976. "Housing Demand in the Short-Run: An Analysis of Polytomous Choice." *Explorations in Economic Research* 3: 76–102.

Radner, R., and Miller, L. 1975. *Demand and Supply in U.S. Higher Education.* New York: McGraw-Hill.

Richards, M. G., and Ben-Akiva, M. 1974. "A Simultaneous Destination and Mode Choice Model for Shopping Trips." *Transportation* 3: 343–56.

Rosen, H., and Small, K. 1979. "Applied Welfare Economics with Discrete Choice Models." Working paper 319, National Bureau of Economic Research.

Sattath, S., and Tversky, A. 1977. "Additive Similarity Trees." *Psychometrika* 42: 319–45.

Schultz, T. P. 1975. "The Determinants of Internal Migration in Venezuela: An Application of the Polytomous Logistic Model." Presented at the Third World Congress of the Econometric Society, Toronto, Canada.

Sickles, R. C., and Schmidt, P. 1978. "Simultaneous Equation Models with Truncated Dependent Variables: A Simultaneous Tobit Model." *Journal of Economics and Business* 31: 11–21.

Sjöberg, L. 1977. "Choice Frequency and Similarity." *Scandinavian Journal of Psychology* 18: 103–15.

Spilerman, S. 1972. "Extensions of the Mover-Stayer Model." *American Journal of Sociology* 78: 599–626.

Stewman, S. 1976. "Markov Models of Occupational Mobility: Theoretical Development and Empirical Support." *Journal of Mathematical Sociology* 4: 201–45.

Swartz, C. 1976. "Screening in the Labor Market: A Case Study." Ph.D. dissertation, University of Wisconsin, Madison.

Talvitie, A. 1972. "Comparison of Probabilistic Modal-Choice Models: Estimation Methods and System Inputs." Highway Research Board Record 392, pp. 111–20.

Theil, H. 1969. "A Multinomial Extension of the Linear Logit Model." *International Economic Review* 10: 251–9.

Theil, H. 1970. "On the Estimation of Relationships Involving Qualitative Variables." *American Journal of Sociology* 76: 103–54.

Thurstone, L. 1927. "A Law of Comparative Judgement." *Psychological Review* 34: 273–86.

Tobin, J. 1958. "Estimation of Relationships for Limited Dependent Variables." *Econometrica* 26: 24–36.

Train, K. 1978. "A Validation Test of a Disaggregate Mode Choice Model." *Transportation Research* 12: 167–74.

Train, K., and McFadden, D. 1978. "The Goods/Leisure Tradeoff and Disaggregate Work Trip Mode Choice Models." *Transportation Research* 12: 349–53.

Tversky, A. 1972a. "Choice by Elimination." *Journal of Mathematical Psychology* 9: 341–67.

Tversky, A. 1972b. "Elimination by Aspects: A Theory of Choice." *Psychological Review* 79: 281–99.

Tversky, A., and Sattath, S. 1979. "Preference Trees." *Psychology Review* 86: 542–73.

Venti, S., and Wise, D. 1980. "Test Scores and Self-Selection of Higher Education." Presented to CEME conference on discrete econometrics.

Walker, S., and Duncan, D. 1967. "Estimation of the Probability of an Event as a Function of Several Independent Variables." *Biometrika* 54: 167–79.

Warner, S. 1962. *Stochastic Choice of Mode in Urban Travel.* Evanston: Northwestern University Press.

Warner, S. L. 1963. "Multivariate Regression of Dummy Variates under Normality Assumptions." *Journal of the American Statistical Association* 58: 1054–63.

Westin, R. 1974. "Predictions from Binary Choice Models." *Journal of Econometrics* 2: 1–16.

Westin, R. B., and Gillen, D. W. 1978. "Parking Location and Transit Demand: A Case Study of Endogenous Attributes in Disaggregate Mode Choice Functions." *Journal of Econometrics* 8: 75–101.

Williams, H. 1977. "On the Formation of Travel Demand Models and Economic Evaluation Measures of User Benefit." *Environment Planning* A9: 285–344.

Willis, R., and Rosen, S. 1979. "Education and Self-Selection." *Journal of Political Economy* 87: 507–36.

Winston, C. 1981. "A Disaggregate Model of the Demand for Intercity Freight Transport." *Econometrica* 49: 981–1006.

Yellot, J. 1977. "The Relationship Between Luce's Choice Axiom, Thurstone's Theory of Comparative Judgement, and the Double Exponential Distribution." *Journal of Mathematical Psychology* 15: 109–44.

Zellner, A., and Lee, T. 1965. "Joint Estimation of Relationships Involving Discrete Random Variables." *Econometrica* 33: 382–94.

PART II

STRUCTURAL ANALYSIS OF LONGITUDINAL DATA

CHAPTER 2

The identification problem in econometric models for duration data

James J. Heckman and Burton Singer

Econometric models for the analysis of duration data have recently come into widespread use in economics. Recent studies of employment and nonemployment (Flinn & Heckman, 1982a; Heckman & Borjas, 1980), unemployment (Flinn & Heckman, 1982b; Kiefer & Neumann, 1981; Lancaster & Nickell, 1980; Toikka, 1976), fertility (Gomez, 1980), strike durations (Kennan, 1980; Lancaster, 1972), and infant mortality (Harris, 1980) have estimated econometric models for durations of events. All of these models have two features in common: they are nonlinear in an essential way, and the methods used to secure estimates of structural models require strong a priori assumptions about the functional forms of estimating equations. Most of these studies have also assumed that the distributions of the unobserved variables in these models are of a simple parametric form. The choice of these distributions usually is justified on the basis of familiarity, ease of manipulation, and considerations of computational cost.

Because of the novelty of the new methods, it is not yet widely appreciated that empirical estimates obtained from these models are extremely sensitive to the choice of a priori identifying assumptions. This chapter will demonstrate this point and present an analysis of identification problems in models for the analysis of duration data. We shall demon-

This research was supported by NSF grant SOC-77-27136 and SES-810 7963. We are indebted to Gary Skoog, C. Flinn, and G. Yates for numerous valuable comments. We retain responsibility for any errors in this chapter. George Yates also performed the calculations. This paper was also presented at the summer meetings of the Econometric Society, San Diego, June 1981.

strate that current practice overparameterizes econometric duration models. We shall relax the strong distributional assumptions imposed in previous work and present methods for estimating structural parameters of interest that impose fewer arbitrary a priori identifying assumptions. A nonparametric procedure for consistently estimating the distribution of unobservables and the structural parameters of duration models will be proposed and implemented.

This chapter will also develop nonparametric tests of an important hypothesis: that, controlling for unobserved variables, there is no duration dependence; that is, duration times are exponentially distributed once the intrusive effect of omitted variables is eliminated. These procedures are also useful in determining the degree of model complexity required in fitting duration models to data. Use of these procedures enables the analyst to avoid overfitting the data with elaborate econometric models that cannot be supported by the data.

This chapter is in five sections. Section 1 presents a simple continuous-time model of an unemployed worker's search for an acceptable job. This model is offered as an example of the class of interesting econometric models to which our analysis applies. Section 2 presents examples of the sensitivity of the empirical estimates of the parameters of duration models to alternative assumptions about the specification of structural equations and distributions of unobserved variables. Section 3 presents the main identification analysis of this chapter. Section 4 presents our ideas on the estimation of the distribution functions of the unobservables. Section 5 presents empirical evidence on the performance of the proposed estimators.

Most of the analysis in this chapter is for the frequently encountered case in which the analyst has only one spell of an individual history per person. Identification analysis for multiple-spell data is considered in a companion report not yet in circulation.

1 A structural duration model

In this section we shall present a simple structural model to fix ideas and to demonstrate the sort of economic model for duration data that our econometric methods can be used to estimate and assess. The economic model is a two-state model of employment and unemployment. The econometric model to be presented is new, although the essential ingredients are taken from the standard theory of search (DeGroot, 1970; Lippman & McCall, 1976; Ross, 1970).

Unemployed individuals are assumed to search for acceptable job offers. The instantaneous cost of search is c. Job offers are assumed to arrive at the jump times of a Poisson process with parameter λ. Thus the probability that a wage offer is received in a "small" time interval Δt is $\lambda\Delta t$, and the probability of receiving more than one offer is negligibly small.

Successive wage offers are independent realizations from a common known wage distribution $F(x)$. Recall of wage offers is not possible. All jobs have an associated instantaneous permanent termination rate of σ. The instantaneous rate of interest is r. To simplify the analysis, we assume that the agent does not drop out of the labor force.

$V(t)$ is defined as the value of search in period t of the consumer's life. Using standard dynamic programming arguments, the value of search can be decomposed into three components plus a remainder term. We assume initially that individuals are infinitely lived.

$$V(t) = -\frac{c\Delta t}{1+r\Delta t} + \frac{(1-\lambda\Delta t)}{1+r\Delta t} V(t+\Delta t)$$

$$+\frac{\lambda\Delta t}{1+r\Delta t} E\max\left[\frac{x}{r+\sigma} + \int_{t+\Delta t}^{\infty} \sigma \exp[-(\tau-t-\Delta t)(\sigma+r)] V(\tau)\, d\tau; V(t+\Delta t)\right] + o(\Delta t) \tag{1.1}$$

The first term on the right-hand side is the discounted value of search costs over the next small interval of time. The second term is the probability of not receiving an offer times the discounted value of search at time $t+\Delta t$. The third term is the probability that an acceptable wage offer is received times the discounted value of the expectation of the maximum of the two options that confront a worker who gets a wage at $t+\Delta t$:[1] to continue search (with value $V(t+\Delta t)$) or to take a job that has some probability of permanent layoff. The present value of the wage stream is $x/(r+\sigma)$. $\int_{t+\Delta t}^{\infty} \sigma \exp[-(\tau-t-\Delta t)(\sigma+r)] V(\tau)\, d\tau$ is the expected value of search to a worker terminated at time $t+\Delta t$. The model possesses a certain reservation-value property; that is, if $[x/(r+\sigma)] + \int_{t+\Delta t}^{\infty} \sigma \exp[-(\sigma+r)(\tau-t-\Delta t)] V(\tau)\, d\tau > V(t+\Delta t)$, the person accepts wage offer x. $V(t+\Delta t)$ is the reservation value. The remainder term is defined so that $\lim_{\Delta t\to 0} o(\Delta t)/\Delta t \to 0$. We assume that parameter values are such that $V(t) \geqslant 0$ for all t.

Collecting terms and passing to the limit, we conclude that the value of search satisfies the following integrodifferential equation:

$$\frac{dV(t)}{dt} = -c - rV(t) + \lambda \int_{B(t)}^{\infty} \left(\frac{x}{r+\sigma} + \int_t^{\infty} \sigma e^{-(\sigma+r)(\tau-t)} V(\tau)\, d\tau - V(t) \right) dF(x) \tag{1.2}$$

where $B(t) = (r+\sigma) V(t) - (r+\sigma) \int_t^{\infty} \sigma \exp[-(\sigma+r)(\tau-t)] V(\tau)\, d\tau$. This expression simplifies, if it is assumed that jobs are permanent $(\sigma=0)$. In this case, equation (1.2) becomes

$$\frac{dV(t)}{dt} = -c - rV(t) + \lambda \int_{rV(t)}^{\infty} \left(\frac{x}{r} - V(t) \right) dF(x) \tag{1.3}$$

For a stationary environment with infinitely lived individuals $dV(t)/dt = 0$, so that $V(t) = V$, and equation (1.2) may be written as

$$c + rV = \frac{\lambda}{\sigma + r} \int_{rV}^{\infty} (x - rV)\, dF(x) \tag{1.4}$$

The optimal policy is very simple for this case. For any $x > rV$, the individual accepts x. The probability that an offer is unacceptable is $F(rV)$. The probability that an unemployment duration T_u exceeds t_u is given from the following calculation. The probability of j offers in time t_u is

$$\text{Prob}(j \text{ offers} \mid t_u) = \frac{(\lambda t_u)^j}{j!} \exp(-\lambda t_u) \tag{1.5}$$

The probability that none of the j offers is acceptable is $[F(rV)]^j$. Assuming independence of the arrival times and the wage offers, the *survivor function* $P(T_u > t_u)$ is

$$\begin{aligned} P(T_u > t_u) &= \sum_{j=0}^{\infty} \frac{(\lambda t_u)^j}{j!} \exp(-\lambda t_u) [F(rV)]^j \\ &= \left(\sum_{j=0}^{\infty} \frac{[\lambda F(rV) t_u]^j}{j!} \exp(-\lambda F(rV) t_u) \right) \\ &\quad \times \exp[-\lambda(1 - F(rV)) t_u] \\ &= \exp[-\lambda(1 - F(rV)) t_u] \end{aligned} \tag{1.6}$$

The stationary search model produces a duration model with a constant hazard rate $h(t_u)$, where

$$(1.7) \qquad h(t_u) = -\frac{d \ln P(T_u > t_u)}{dt_u} = \lambda(1 - F(rV))$$

A model with a constant hazard is said to exhibit no duration dependence.

By assumption, in the more general model, with $\sigma \neq 0$, employment spells terminate at an exponential rate. Thus the probability that employment duration T_e exceeds t_e is

$$(1.8) \qquad P(T_e > t_e) = \exp(-\sigma t_e)$$

so the hazard rate for employment spells is σ.

Stationarity is a strong assumption to invoke. As noted by DeGroot (1970) and Gronau (1971), if individuals have finite lives, nonstationarity is induced. Suppose that the maximum age is A. The value function must be modified to incorporate a finite-life correction. Then $dV(t)/dt < 0$, and $V(A) = 0$, because there is no return to search at the end of life.[2]

In order to focus on essential ideas, suppose that $\sigma = 0$, so that jobs are permanent. In this model, individuals have, at most, one spell of unemployment. The reservation wage property characterizes this model, because $dV(t)/dt < 0$. The probability that an unemployment spell T_u exceeds t_u is given by the following argument.

Conditional on j arrivals of wages in time t_u, the density of interarrival times $\tau_1, \ldots, \tau_j$ is multivariate uniform

$$(1.9) \qquad g(\tau_1, \ldots, \tau_j \mid j, t_u) = j!(t_u)^{-j}$$

where $0 \leqslant \tau_1 \leqslant \tau_1 + \tau_2 \leqslant \cdots \leqslant t_u$. For the individual to remain unemployed at time t_u, each offer must be less than the reservation wage at the time the offer is received. Conditional on interarrival times $\tau_1, \ldots, \tau_j$, this probability is $\prod_{i=1}^{j} F(q(t_i))$, where $q(t) = rV(t_i)/(1 - \exp[-r(A - t_i)])$ and $t_i = \sum_{l=1}^{i} \tau_l$. Equation (1.5) gives the probability that j offers are received.

Then the probability that an unemployment spell exceeds t_u is

$$(1.10) \qquad P(T_u > t_u) = \sum_{j=0}^{\infty} \text{Prob}(j \text{ offers} \mid t_u) \times \underset{0 \leqslant t_1 \leqslant t_2 \ldots \leqslant t_j \leqslant t_u}{\int \cdots \int} g(t_1, \ldots, t_j \mid j, t_u) \prod_{i=1}^{j} F(q(t_i))\, dt_1 \ldots dt_j$$

We establish the convention that the multiple integral inside the sum is unity when $j = 0$.

Because $V(t)$ is a monotonically declining function of time, the hazard function is increasing with spell length; that is,

$$-\frac{d\ln P(T_u > t_u)}{dt_u} > 0$$

Thus the model exhibits positive duration dependence. This is so because the reservation wage $rV(t)$ is decreasing while the rate of wage arrivals and the distribution of wages remain unchanged.

Specific functional forms are useful in estimating explicitly formulated parametric econometric models. Suppose that $F(x)$ is a finite-variance Pareto distribution, so that

$$(1.11) \quad dF(x) = \phi x^{\beta} dx, \quad \infty > x \geqslant c_2 > 0, \quad \beta < -2, \quad \phi = \frac{-(\beta+1)}{(c_2)^{\beta+1}}$$

The assumption of a Pareto distribution for wage offers is not necessarily at odds with the commonly held belief that wages are distributed log normal provided that ϕ varies across individuals and is approximately log normal.

For this wage distribution, equation (1.4) for a stationary environment is

$$(1.12) \quad c + rV = \frac{\phi\lambda(rV)^{\beta+2}}{(\sigma + r)(\beta + 1)(\beta + 2)}$$

This equation can be solved for rV in terms of λ, ϕ, β, σ, and c. Estimates of the hazard function produce estimates of

$$(1.13) \quad \lambda(1 - F(rV)) = -\frac{\lambda\phi}{\beta + 1}(rV)^{\beta+1}$$

Even if we know r and estimate σ from the duration distribution of employment spells (equation (1.8)), the model is hopelessly underidentified.

Data on accepted wages give further information. The distribution of accepted wages is conditional on $x \geqslant rV$. This distribution may be written as

$$(1.14) \quad g(x \mid x \geqslant rV) = -\frac{(\beta + 1)x^{\beta}}{(rV)^{\beta+1}}, \quad x \geqslant rV$$

The mean and variance of the accepted wage offer distribution are

$$E(x \mid x \geqslant rV) = \frac{\beta + 1}{\beta + 2} rV$$

$$\text{VAR}(x \mid x \geqslant rV) = (rV)^2 \frac{(1 + \beta)}{(\beta + 3)(2 + \beta)^2}$$

For a homogeneous population, with large samples, it is possible to use sample moments of the accepted wage data to consistently estimate β and rV. From the estimated hazard, it is possible to estimate $\lambda\phi$ (see equation (1.13)). Using equation (1.12), it is possible to estimate c, because rV, β, and σ are known. It is impossible to separately estimate λ and ϕ in this model.

A test of the Pareto assumption is also possible: accepted wages are Pareto-distributed (see equation (1.14)). Using data on accepted wages and estimates of β and rV, it is possible to compute a modified Kolmogorov-Smirnov statistic to compare empirical accepted wage offer distributions with the theoretical wage offer distributions. In performing this test it is important to follow the suggestion of Durbin (1974) and correct the standard Kolmogorov-Smirnov test for estimation of β and rV.[3]

The assumption of population homogeneity is convenient but unlikely. In virtually every study in economics in which this assumption has been subject to test, it has been rejected. Individuals may differ in ϕ, β, r, c, or σ. For simplicity, suppose that in the simple Pareto search model the only source of population heterogeneity is in ϕ. Let the density of ϕ be $m(\phi)$. The survivor function conditional on ϕ may be written as

$$(1.15) \quad P(T > t \mid \phi) = e^{-b\phi t} \quad \text{where} \quad b = \frac{-\lambda}{\beta + 1}(rV)^{\beta+1}$$

Given ϕ, there is a constant hazard.

The population survivor function is given by

$$(1.16) \quad P(T > t) = \int P(T > t \mid \phi) m(\phi)\, d\phi$$

$$= \int e^{-b\phi t} m(\phi)\, d\phi$$

By direct manipulation we conclude that the population hazard function is

$$(1.17) \quad h(t) = \frac{\int_0^\infty b\phi e^{-b\phi t} m(\phi)\, d\phi}{\int_0^\infty e^{-b\phi t} m(\phi)\, d\phi}$$

Straightforward application of the Cauchy-Schwartz theorem for integrals demonstrates (see Theorem 1 in Section 3) that

$$\frac{dh(t)}{dt} \leqslant 0$$

The population hazard exhibits negative duration dependence. Intuitively, this result arises because of a dynamic selection process. High-ϕ

individuals are selected out of a sample over time, leaving low-ϕ individuals behind. Thus the observed escape rate from unemployment (or hazard) declines in a sample of heterogeneous individuals. This phenomenon has been noted by many analysts (Heckman & Willis, 1977; Salant, 1977; Silcock, 1954). Uncorrected heterogeneity results in apparent negative duration dependence in models with no duration dependence at the individual level.

To estimate the model free of such heterogeneity bias, it is necessary somehow to control for the heterogeneity. Three procedures have been advocated in recent work. Only one of these is feasible for single-spell data. That procedure is the random effect method. In most applications a particular parametric functional form is assumed for $m(\phi)$, and the parameters of this density are estimated by maximum likelihood, along with the remaining parameters of the model. This procedure can be interpreted as an empirical Bayes procedure for estimating the prior distribution of ϕ (Maritz, 1970). The sensitivity of model estimates to the assumed functional form of $m(\phi)$ will be demonstrated later.

Two other procedures for controlling for ϕ require multiple-spell data and will not be discussed at length in this chapter. The first method treats ϕ as a fixed effect. Using data on repeated spells of unemployment for each person, and assuming ϕ is the same in all such spells, it is possible to consistently estimate each person's ϕ. As the number of spells per person becomes unbounded, the estimated ϕ converges to the true ϕ, and from these estimates it is possible to use panel data to construct an empirical distribution of ϕ that converges to the true distribution. In large samples, with many unemployment spells per person, maximum likelihood estimators of ϕ and the model parameters possess desirable statistical properties. The requirement that the number of spells per person must be large makes this estimator of little use in practical work. Monte Carlo evidence is mixed on the performance of this estimator in the case of a small number of spells per person (Heckman, 1981; Wright & Douglas, 1976). A second procedure, developed in psychometrics (Andersen, 1973, 1980), and recently popularized in econometrics by Chamberlain (1982), is special to the case in which the density of duration times conditional on ϕ is a member of the exponential family of probability laws. For multiple-spell data, a conditioning argument can be developed to eliminate the fixed effect ϕ and to estimate the remaining parameters of the model free of heterogeneity bias.

To control for measured variation in explanatory variables, it is possible to parameterize λ, β, σ, and c as functions of observables. Econometric procedures for the estimation of duration models have been presented by Flinn and Heckman (1982a, b). They proposed maximum likelihood estimators of the random-effect duration model with measured and unmeasured explanatory variables. Using maximum likelihood, it is possible to impose restrictions such as equation (1.12) on the estimated hazard function.

An explicit parametric model for the nonstationary search model presented earlier is not easy to write down or estimate. This is typically the case for most theoretical models of labor force dynamics in nonstationary environments. If wage offers are Pareto-distributed, with the density given in equation (1.10), and jobs last forever $(\sigma=0)$, the time rate of change in $V(t)$ may be written as

$$\frac{dV(t)}{dt} = -c - rV(t) + \left(\frac{\lambda\phi}{(\beta+1)(\beta+2)}\right)\left(\frac{r}{1-e^{-r(A-t)}}\right)^{\beta+1} [V(t)]^{\beta+2}, \quad V(A) = 0$$

This equation can be solved for $V(t)$. These solutions can be inserted into equation (1.10) to produce expressions for the survivor function and the density of exit times, but no explicit formulas have been obtained. Uncorrected heterogeneity will contaminate parameter estimates, as in the simple stationary model. The estimated hazard will be biased toward negative duration dependence. Structural positive duration dependence (conditional on ϕ) may generate apparent negative duration dependence as a consequence of uncorrected heterogeneity.

2 The identification problem

The preceding section presented simple models of an unemployed worker's search behavior in stationary and nonstationary environments. That theory and other theories for durations of events produce a structural probability distribution $F(t \mid \theta)$, where θ is an unobserved heterogeneity component. Examples of such distributions are given by the complements of equations (1.6) and (1.10). The distribution of observed durations is $G(t)$, where

$$G(t) = \int F(t \mid \theta)\, d\mu(\theta) \tag{2.1}$$

where $\mu(\theta)$ is the distribution of the θ characteristics in the population. To simplify the argument, we initially assume that there are no observed explanatory variables in the model.

We may estimate $G(t)$ by a variety of nonparametric procedures, even in the presence of sample censoring of observations (Barlow et al.,

1972; Kalbfleish & Prentice, 1980). In this section we assume that $G(t)$ is known in order to focus on issues of identification that are logically prior to issues of estimation.

As economists, we are interested in determining $F(t \mid \theta)$ and in testing certain key hypotheses about it. For example, a test of the declining reservation wage hypothesis is a test of the hypothesis that $F(t \mid \theta)$ exhibits positive duration dependence, so that individuals who have been unemployed longer are more likely to exit the unemployment state.

From knowledge of $G(t)$ alone it is not possible to solve equation (2.1) for $F(t \mid \theta)$ and $d\mu(\theta)$. The following examples illustrate the point. We produce two dramatically different structural models that both generate $G(t)$ with no duration dependence.

First, let

$$F_1(t \mid \theta) = 1 - e^{-t\theta}, \quad t \geqslant 0$$

and let $\mu_1(\theta)$ put point mass on $\theta = \eta$ so that there is no population heterogeneity. Then

$$G_1(t) = 1 - e^{-t\eta}$$

and there is no apparent duration dependence in the data.

Next, let

$$F_2(t \mid \theta) = 1 - \int_c^\infty \frac{2}{(2\pi)^{1/2}} \exp(-l^2/2)\, dl, \quad t \geqslant 0$$

where $c = t(2\theta)^{-1/2}$ and

$$d\mu_2(\theta) = \eta^2 \exp(-\eta^2 \theta)\, d\theta, \quad \theta \geqslant 0$$

Then

$$G_2(t) = 1 - e^{-t\eta} = G_1(t)$$

There are two fundamentally different structural explanations for the same data. The first explanation is one of no duration dependence at the individual level. The second explanation is one of positive duration dependence at the individual level that, when contaminated by population heterogeneity, generates an aggregate duration distribution function that exhibits no duration dependence. Without further identifying information we cannot choose between these observationally equivalent explanations.

The standard practice in much recent work (Heckman & Willis, 1977; Kiefer & Neumann, 1981) has been to assume that $F(t \mid \theta)$ and $d\mu(\theta)$ are members of simple parametric families of distributions. The goal of the econometrician then becomes the estimation of the parameters of $F(t \mid \theta)$ and $d\mu(\theta)$, usually by maximum likelihood procedures. The choice of specific parametric families usually is dictated by considerations of computational cost or by appeal to familiarity with special functional forms. Sometimes the relevant economic theory can be used to suggest functional forms for $F(t \mid \theta)$, as demonstrated in the preceding section. The theory usually produces only qualitative implications. Economic theory produces no guidance on the functional form of $d\mu(\theta)$.

In order to make progress, we study equation (2.1) with $F(t \mid \theta)$ known, except, possibly, for some unknown parameters. This is a natural starting point in light of the fact that economic theory sometimes gives us insight into $F(t \mid \theta)$, whereas it rarely tells us anything about $d\mu(\theta)$. Economic models that predict no duration dependence provide very precise information about $F(t \mid \theta)$; that it is exponential.

If $F(t \mid \theta)$ were completely known, equation (2.1) could be solved for $d\mu(\theta)$ subject to standard existence conditions in the theory of Fredholm integral equations of the first kind (Tricomi, 1957, p. 150). It is unnecessary to assume a specific parametric functional form for $d\mu(\theta)$, and it may be dangerous to do so. Standard practice, which imposes arbitrary functional forms for $F(t \mid \theta)$ and $d\mu(\theta)$ onto the data, may produce estimates of key structural parameters that are wildly inaccurate. It is for this reason that we claim that current practice overparameterizes duration models. Given assumed functional forms for $F(t \mid \theta)$, it is, in principle, possible to estimate $d\mu(\theta)$ even when parameters of the structural duration distribution are estimated. Methods for estimating this distribution will be discussed in Section 4.

It might be argued that this issue is of purely theoretical concern. Once the analyst has selected a particular functional form for $F(t \mid \theta)$, specification of a parametric family for $d\mu(\theta)$ will not affect the estimates of structural parameters very much. The following empirical example demonstrates that this is not so.

The following models were fit to the data on unemployment durations used by Kiefer and Neumann; for a discussion of the data, see their 1979 article. The hazard function for the structural model is

$$\ln h(t) = \alpha x + \beta \ln t + c\theta \tag{2.2}$$

where x is a vector of control variables, $\ln t$ is duration, and θ is a heterogeneity component. If $\beta = 0$, there is no duration dependence; c is a scale parameter. Three distributions of θ were used to fit the structural model:

Table 2.1 *Kiefer–Neumann data*[a]

	Normal heterogeneity	Log normal heterogeneity	Gamma heterogeneity
Intercept	−3.92	−13.2	5.90
	(2.8)[b]	(4.7)	(3.4)
ln duration	−0.066	−0.708	−0.576
	(0.15)	(0.17)	(0.17)
Age	0.0036	−0.106	−0.202
	(0.048)	(0.03)	(0.06)
Education	0.0679	−0.322	−0.981
	(0.233)	(0.145)	(0.301)
Tenure on previous job	−0.0512	0.00419	−0.034
	(0.0149)	(0.023)	(0.016)
Unemployment benefits	−0.0172	0.0061	−0.003
	(0.0036)	(0.0051)	(0.004)
Married (0.1)	0.833	0.159	−0.607
	(0.362)	(0.30)	(0.496)
Unemployment rate	−26.12	25.8	−17.9
	(9.5)	(10.3)	(11.2)
Education × age	−0.00272	0.00621	0.0152
	(0.0044)	(0.034)	(0.0053)
Heterogeneity (c)	5.16	5.7	4.62
	(0.567)	(0.42)	(0.790)

[a]Sample size is 456; reduced-form estimates.
[b]Standard errors in parentheses.
Source: For a discussion of the data, see the work of Kiefer and Neumann (1979).

standard normal, log normal, and gamma distributions. The empirical results obtained from the continuous-time computer algorithm developed by Flinn and Heckman (1982b) are presented in Table 2.1.

Empirical estimates of the structural model are very sensitive to the specification of the distribution of unobservables. In Table 2.1 there are as many different behavioral models as there are distributions of heterogeneity imposed on the data. Ad hoc specifications of model unobservables vitally affect the empirical estimates achieved from structural duration models.

In light of this demonstrated sensitivity of estimates and model inference to ad hoc identifying assumptions, it is natural to proceed cautiously before drawing firm conclusions from econometric duration models. In the remainder of this chapter, we shall consider two approaches to the general problem of identification.

The first approach considers various test criteria for the important null hypothesis that $F(t \mid \theta)$ exhibits no duration dependence. These criteria are quite general and can also be used when $F(t \mid \theta)$ depends on time-invariant-measured explanatory variables. Various nonparametric statistical procedures are proposed. There are two ways to view these procedures: as identification theorems and also as practical procedures for model selection. If viewed as the latter, our procedures require much more investigation, especially with regard to the derivation of sampling distributions.

The second approach considers general procedures for the consistent estimation of $\mu(\theta)$ without imposing arbitrary parametric functional forms. In developing this approach, we draw on recent work in the theory of nonparametric maximum likelihood estimation (Kiefer & Wolfowitz, 1956; Laird, 1978). We present a computationally simple maximum likelihood procedure for the estimation of $\mu(\theta)$ based on the EM algorithm (Dempster et al., 1977). In some Monte Carlo investigations we find that the proposed estimator enables us to estimate the structural parameters of interest rather well, thus avoiding the sensitivity problem described earlier. We also find that for samples of size likely to be used in econometric analysis, the nonparametric maximum likelihood estimator of $\mu(\theta)$ does not, in fact, produce good estimates of the heterogeneity distribution. Thus the procedure presented here is useful in controlling for the contaminating effect of heterogeneity in a robust way, but it does not provide a very reliable estimate of the distribution of the unobservables.

3 Characterizations of duration distributions

3.1 *Nonparametric procedures to assess the structural duration model*

In this section we shall present criteria that can be used to test the null hypothesis of no structural duration dependence and that can be used to assess the degree of model complexity that is required to adequately model the duration data at hand. All of the criteria can be used for data for which only a single spell per observation is available. The criteria to be set forth here can be viewed in two ways: as identification theorems and as empirical procedures to use with data. Much further work on the derivation of sampling distributions remains to be done before most of the criteria to be set forth here can be viewed as rigorous statistical procedures.

We consider the following problem: $G(t)$ is estimated. We would like to infer properties of $F(t \mid \theta)$ in the presence of heterogeneity. Measured explanatory variables are included in θ, which is assumed to be a scalar. The procedures presented in this section do not require strong parametric assumptions about $F(t \mid \theta)$.[4]

In the ensuing analysis it is useful to distinguish two cases. The first case is that of an unrestricted $\mu(\theta)$. The second case is the finite mixtures case, in which θ assumes only a finite number of values θ_i, with associated probability mass P_i $(i=1,\ldots,I)$. In applications, the two cases are not as far apart as might first seem to be the case. By a theorem of Laird (1978), under very mild conditions, the nonparametric maximum likelihood estimator of unrestricted $\mu(\theta)$ is a finite mixture; that is, the estimated cumulative distribution function (cdf) of θ is a step function with a finite number of steps.

The most challenging case is the one in which $G(t)$ exhibits negative duration dependence. It is widely believed that it is impossible to distinguish structural negative duration dependence from a pure heterogeneity explanation of observed negative duration dependence when the analyst has access to only a single spell per observation. This belief is false. In this section we shall present several methods for distinguishing between the two explanations.

If $G(t)$ exhibits positive duration dependence for all values of t, $F(t \mid \theta)$ must exhibit positive duration dependence for some interval of θ for all values of t. Intuitively, this is so because the effect of scalar heterogeneity is to make the observed duration distribution exhibit more negative duration dependence than the structural duration distribution. We prove the following theorem.

Theorem 1: A necessary condition for $G(t)$ to exhibit positive duration dependence is for $F(t \mid \theta)$ to exhibit positive duration dependence, at least for some values θ.

Proof: The hazard function for the observed distribution is

$$h(t) = \frac{\int f(t \mid \theta)\, d\mu(\theta)}{\int (1 - F(t \mid \theta))\, d\mu(\theta)}$$

where $f(t \mid \theta)$ is the density of $F(t \mid \theta)$. (We assume a continuous cdf with a differentiable density. This assumption can be relaxed.) Direct manipulation reveals

(3.1)

$$\frac{dh(t)}{dt} = \frac{\int [\partial f(t\mid\theta)/\partial t]\, d\mu(\theta) \int (1 - F(t\mid\theta))\, d\mu(\theta) + [\int f(t\mid\theta)\, d\mu(\theta)]^2}{[\int (1 - F(t\mid\theta))\, d\mu(\theta)]^2}$$

We define the structural hazard $h(t\mid\theta)$ by $h(t\mid\theta)=f(t\mid\theta)/(1-F(t\mid\theta))$ and

$$\frac{\partial h(t\mid\theta)}{\partial t} = \frac{\partial f(t\mid\theta)/\partial t}{1 - F(t\mid\theta)} + \left[\frac{f(t\mid\theta)}{1 - F(t\mid\theta)}\right]^2 \tag{3.2}$$

Substituting for $\partial f(t\mid\theta)/\partial t$ from (3.2) into (3.1), we reach

(3.3)

$$\begin{aligned}\frac{dh(t)}{dt} &= \int (1-F(t\mid\theta))\, \frac{\partial h(t\mid\theta)}{\partial t}\, d\mu(\theta) \Big/ \int (1-F(t\mid\theta))\, d\mu(\theta) \\ &\quad + \frac{1}{[\int (1-F(t\mid\theta))\, d\mu(\theta)]^2} \\ &\quad \times \left\{\left[\int f(t\mid\theta)\, d\mu(\theta)\right]^2 \right. \\ &\quad \left. - \int \frac{f^2(t\mid\theta)}{1-F(t\mid\theta)}\, d\mu(\theta) \int (1-F(t\mid\theta))\, d\mu(\theta)\right\}\end{aligned}$$

The second term on the right-hand side is always nonpositive as a consequence of the Cauchy-Schwartz theorem for integrals (Buck, 1965, p. 123). If the left-hand side is always positive, the first term on the right-hand side must be nonnegative. Because $(1-F(t\mid\theta))$ is nonnegative everywhere, $\partial h(t\mid\theta)/\partial t$ must be positive for some values of θ. Q.E.D.

In order to test whether or not an empirical $G(t)$ exhibits positive duration dependence, we suggest use of the *total time on test statistic* (Barlow et al., 1972, p. 267). This statistic will be briefly described here. From a sample of I durations, order the first k durations starting with the smallest

$$t_1 \leqslant t_2 \leqslant \cdots \leqslant t_k \quad 1 \leqslant k \leqslant I$$

Let $D_{i:I}=[I-(i+1)](t_i-t_{i-1})$, where $t_0\equiv 0$. Define

$$V_k = k^{-1}\sum_{i=1}^{k-1}\left[\sum_{j=1}^{i} D_{j:I}\right] \Big/ k^{-1}\sum_{i=1}^{k} D_{i:I}$$

V_k is called the cumulative total time on test statistic. If the observations are from a distribution with an increasing hazard rate, V_k tends to be large. Intuitively, if $G(t)$ is a distribution that exhibits positive duration dependence, $D_{1:I}$ stochastically dominates $D_{2:I}$, $D_{2:I}$ stochastically dominates $D_{3:I}$, and so forth. Critical values for testing the null hypothesis of no duration dependence have been presented by Barlow and associates (1972, p. 269). This test can be modified to deal with censored data (Barlow et al., 1972, p. 302).

This test is valuable because it enables the econometrician to test for positive duration dependence without imposing any arbitrary parametric structure on the data. In the context of the nonstationary search model presented in Section 1, the total time on test statistic can be used to test the null hypothesis of a constant reservation wage against the alternative hypothesis of a declining reservation wage. In light of Theorem 1, evidence in favor of positive duration dependence is evidence in favor of the declining reservation wage hypothesis.

Negative duration dependence is more frequently observed in economic data. That this should be so is obvious from equation (3.3). Even when the structural hazard is positive $(\partial h(t\mid\theta)/\partial t>0)$, it often occurs that the second term on the right-hand side outweighs the first term. To investigate negative duration dependence, it is helpful to consider four families of distributions.

Let $\mathcal{G}_1=\{G:-\ln[1-G(t)]$ is concave$\}$. Membership in this class can be determined from the total time on test statistic. If $\mathcal{G}_1$ is log concave, the $D_{i:I}$ defined earlier are stochastically increasing in i for fixed I. Ordering the observations from the largest to the smallest and changing the subscripts appropriately, we can use V_k to test for log concavity.

Let $\mathcal{G}_2=\{G:G(t)=1-\exp[-\int_0^t h(u)\,du]$, with $h(u)$ nonincreasing$\}$. The distinction between $\mathcal{G}_1$ and $\mathcal{G}_2$ arises from the possibility that a hazard function may not exist if $\mathcal{G}_1(t)$ is discontinuous in t. Nonparametric procedures for estimating $h(u)$ are presented elsewhere (Barlow et al., 1972; Kalbfleish & Prentice, 1980). Empirically, it is very difficult to discriminate between the two families.

Next let $\mathcal{G}_3=\{G:G(t)=\int(1-e^{-\theta t})\,d\mu(\theta)$ for some probability measure μ on $[0,\infty)\}$. Data implying that $G\in\mathcal{G}_1$ are also widely interpreted in the economics literature as indicating that $G\in\mathcal{G}_3$. Furthermore, it is often suggested (erroneously) that $\mathcal{G}_2=\mathcal{G}_3$ and that what is referred to as negative duration dependence by a homogeneous population (i.e., $G\in\mathcal{G}_2$) cannot be distinguished from heterogeneity (meaning $G\in\mathcal{G}_3$) on the basis of duration data from a single spell. The facts are

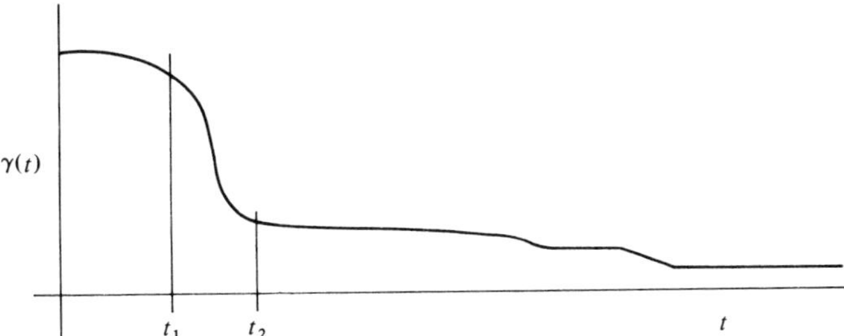

Figure 2.1. Hazard function for which equation (3.4) holds for some $t_0 \in (t_1, t_2)$.

that the inclusion $\mathcal{G}_2 \supset \mathcal{G}_3$ is proper and that a simple sufficient condition for $G \in \mathcal{G}_2$ and $G \notin \mathcal{G}_3$ is that

$$(3.4) \qquad -h''(t_0) + 3h(t_0)h'(t_0) - h^3(t_0) > 0$$

for some $t_0 > 0$. Condition (3.4) arises from the fact that $\mathcal{G}_3 = \{G : 1 - G(t)$ is completely monotone; i.e., $(-1)^n(d^n/dt^n)[1-G(t)] \geqslant 0$ for $n \geqslant 1$ and all $t \geqslant 0\}$ (Feller, 1971; Hirschman & Widder, 1955) and that $(-1)^3(d^3/dt^3)[1-G(t)]|_{t=t_0} < 0$ whenever condition (3.4) holds. This fact has been noted by other analysts (Lancaster & Nickell, 1980). To obtain further insight about condition (3.4), consider the prototype of this situation illustrated in Figure 2.1. What this implies for the qualitative character of, say, the duration of a spell of employment is the following:

1. In the early stages of a spell the individual is less likely to exit the longer that individual is employed; however, the rate of decline of the exit rate is very slow.
2. There is an intermediate period (in calendar time) during which the probability of exit per unit time declines very sharply.
3. In the later stages of the spell (i.e., $t > t_2$) the exit rate is still declining, but again at a very slow rate and approaching a constant hazard as $t \to \infty$.

Verification of condition (3.4) would require data sufficiently rich to support numerical differentiation twice. Alternatively, we could parametrically estimate $h(t)$ and ask whether or not condition (3.4) holds for some t_0 in the estimated equation.

A limiting case of $\mathcal{G}_i$ $(i = 1,2,3)$ is $\mathcal{G}_4 = \{G : G(t) = 1 - e^{-\theta t},\ t \geqslant 0$ for some $\theta > 0\}$. In the labor economics literature, an individual (or a homogeneous population) whose duration in a spell of either employment or nonemployment is governed by a member of $\mathcal{G}_4$ is said to evolve with no duration dependence during the spell. A test of the null hypothesis of no duration dependence can be based on the total time on test statistic described earlier.

For the case in which $\mu(\theta)$ is a finite discrete distribution, a test of the null hypothesis that $G \in \mathcal{G}_3$ is possible. Steutel (1967) has demonstrated that if $G \in \mathcal{G}_3$, $G(t)$ obeys an infinitely divisible law with a special known functional form for the characteristic function. The log of the characteristic function of $G(t)$ is

$$(3.5) \qquad \ln \phi(s) = isa + \int_0^\infty [e^{isx} - 1 - isx/(1+x^2)]\, w(x)\, dx$$

where a is real and

$$xw(x) = \sum_{j=1}^{n} \exp(-\theta_j x) - \sum_{k=1}^{n'} \exp(-\mu_k x)$$

where the θ_j $(j=1,\ldots,n)$ are the mass points for the heterogeneity distribution and $n'=n-1$ or $n-2$. Provided that we assume that n is known (or at least that the maximum value of n is known), it is possible to estimate a, the θ_j, and the μ_k by nonlinear regression provided we evaluate $\phi(s)$ at $s^* \geqslant n+n'-1$ values of s. Departures from the functional form indicated in equation (3.5) is evidence against the null hypothesis that $G \in \mathcal{G}_3$. One test of the mixtures of exponentials assumption is to add polynomials in s to the right-hand side of equation (3.5) and use classical testing procedures to assess departures from the mixtures of exponentials model.

Two methods of estimating the characteristic function are available. The first estimates $G(t)$ nonparametrically and then forms $\hat{\phi}(s) = \int_0^\infty e^{its}\, d\hat{G}(t)$. The second uses the estimator

$$\hat{\hat{\phi}}(s) = \frac{1}{n} \sum_{j=1}^{n} \exp(ist_j)$$

where n is sample size. Both estimators are consistent, and we conjecture that the first estimator is the more efficient of the two.

A similar testing procedure can be employed using the more familiar representation of the characteristic function of a mixture of exponentials

$$(3.6) \qquad \phi(s) = \sum_{j=1}^{n} p_j \frac{\theta_j}{\theta_j - is}$$

Departures from this functional form give evidence against the null hypothesis that $G \in \mathcal{G}_3$. Joint satisfaction of (3.5) and (3.6) constitutes powerful confirmation of the null hypothesis that $G \in \mathcal{G}_3$.[5]

There are two difficulties with this procedure. First, the choice of the set of s values to perform this test is not known to us. It can be determined, in principle, by procedures similar to those used in the theory of experimental design for nonlinear models (Chernoff, 1962). Second, the choice of n is arbitrary. In practice, as we shall demonstrate later, a small value for n produces estimates of mixing distributions that generate estimated structural distributions that closely approximate the true duration distributions.

3.2 *Nonparametric procedures to assess the mixing distribution*

In this subsection we shall consider some procedures that enable us to assess the modality of the mixing distribution. Let $\mathcal{G}_5 = \{G : G(t) = \int_0^t g(u)\, du$ and $g(t) = \int f(t \mid \theta) m(\theta)\, d\theta$ for some probability density $m(\theta)$ and $f(t \mid \theta) = k(t \mid \theta) v(t)$, where $k(t \mid \theta)$ is sign regular of order 2 $(\mathrm{SR}_2)\}$.

Sign regularity means that if $t_1 < t_2$ and $\theta_1 < \theta_2$, then

$$\epsilon_2 \det\begin{pmatrix} k(t_1 \mid \theta_1) & k(t_1 \mid \theta_2) \\ k(t_2 \mid \theta_1) & k(t_2 \mid \theta_2) \end{pmatrix} \geqslant 0$$

where ϵ_2 is either $+1$ or -1. If $\epsilon_2 = +1$, then $k(t \mid \theta)$ is called totally positive of order 2, abbreviated TP_2. From the point of view of inferring properties about the density of a mixing measure from properties of g, models with SR_2 conditional densities allow us to obtain lower bounds on the number of modes in $m(\theta)$ from knowledge of the number of modes in g/v. As an indication of the generality of models for which $k(t \mid \theta) = f(t \mid \theta)/v(t)$ satisfies SR_2, the reader should note that this includes all members of the exponential family. In fact, for the exponential family, $k(t \mid \theta)$ is TP_2. Thus an assessment of modality of an estimated density, using, for example, the procedure of Larkin (1979), is an important guide to specifying the characteristics of the density of the unobservable quantity θ.

Sign regular (particularly totally positive) kernels include many examples that are central to model specification in labor economics. In particular, if $d\nu(t)$ is any measure on $[0, +\infty)$ such that $\int_0^\infty e^{t\theta}\, d\nu(t) < +\infty$ for $\theta \in \Theta$ (an ordered set), let

$$\beta(\theta) = \frac{1}{\int_0^\infty e^{t\theta}\, d\nu(t)}$$

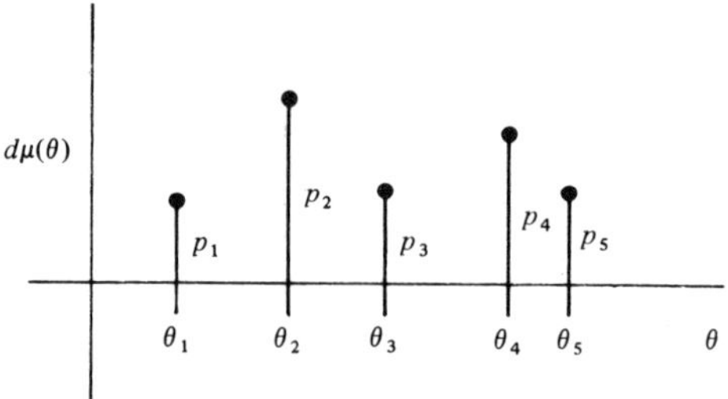

Figure 2.2.

and, in what follows, set $d\nu(t)=v(t)dt$ and $f(t\,|\,\theta)=\beta(\theta)\,e^{t\theta}v(t)$. Then the density $g(t)=\int\beta(\theta)e^{t\theta}v(t)m(\theta)\,d\theta$ governs the observable durations of spells, $f(t\,|\,\theta)$ is a member of the exponential family, and $k(t,\theta)=\beta(\theta)e^{t\theta}$ is TP_2 (Karlin, 1968). The essential point in isolating this class of duration densities is that knowledge of the number and character of the modes of g/v implies that the density, m, of the mixing measure must have at least as many modes. In particular, if g/v is unimodal, m cannot be monotonic; it must have at least one mode. More generally, if c is an arbitrary positive level and $(g(t)/v(t))-c$ changes sign k times as t increases from 0 to $+\infty$, then $m(\theta)-c$ must change sign at least k times as θ traverses the parameter set Θ from left to right (Karlin, 1968, p. 21).

The importance of this variation-diminishing character of the transformation $\int k(t,\theta)m(\theta)\,d\theta$ for modeling purposes is that if we assess the modality of g, using, for example, the method of Larkin (1979), then because v is given a priori, we know the modality of g/v, which, in turn, implies restrictions on m in fitting mixing densities to data. In terms of a strategy of fitting finite mixtures, a bimodal g/v suggests fitting a measure with support at, say, five points to the data, but subject to the constraints that $p_1<p_2$, $p_2>p_3$, $p_3<p_4$, and $p_4>p_5$, as shown in Figure 2.2.

Subsequent specification of a mixing density $m(\theta)$ to describe the same data could proceed by fitting spline polynomials with knots at $\theta_1,\ldots,\theta_5$ to the estimated discrete mixing distribution.

4 Estimating mixing distributions

4.1 *Introduction*

The preceding section presented statistical procedures that enable the econometrician to uncover essential features of structural duration distributions without having to assume arbitrary functional forms to develop estimating equations. The information obtained from these procedures is necessarily qualitative in nature.

In this section we shall present procedures that enable the econometrician to estimate the parameters of the underlying structural distribution $F(t\mid\theta)$. We consider the case in which there is some information about the functional form of this distribution, although information about certain parameter values may be lacking. We assume that there is no information about the functional form of the distribution of the unobservables $\mu(\theta)$. The goal of the analysis is to estimate the unknown parameters that determine $F(t\mid\theta)$.

As demonstrated in the simple search model presented in Section 1, economic theory sometimes provides guidance on the functional form of $F(t\mid\theta)$. Access to accepted wage offers enables the econometrician to check certain critical assumptions about this distribution. The theory provides no guidance on the issue of the correct functional form of the distribution of unobservables. As demonstrated in Section 2, alternative choices of functional forms for these distributions produce estimates of structural parameters that imply dramatically different behavioral interpretations of the same data. As discussed in Section 2, given a functional form for $F(t\mid\theta)$ and knowledge of $G(t)$ under general conditions, it is in principle possible to determine $\mu(\theta)$.

Unobserved heterogeneity is assumed to influence an individual's waiting time in a state (e.g., nonemployment or employment) in conjunction with exogenous variables X. The specification of a survivor function $S(t)$ will be of the general form

$$P(T>t\mid x(t))=S(t\mid x(t))=\int K(t\mid X(t),\theta)\,d\mu(\theta)$$

and our problem is to simultaneously estimate the mixing measure and parameters in a restrictive functional form for $K(\cdot\mid\cdot)$. An illustrative functional form that is of some generality is given by

$$\begin{aligned}1-F(t\mid X,\theta)&=K(t\mid X,\theta)\\ &=\exp\left\{-\left[\int_0^t \alpha_1 u^{\alpha_1-1}\exp(\alpha_2 X(u)+\alpha_0+\theta)\,du\right]\right\},\quad \alpha_1>0\end{aligned}\tag{4.1}$$

Some important specializations that can account for $G(t)=1-S(t)\in\mathcal{G}_1$ are the following:

(i) $\alpha_1=1$ and $X(u)$ time invariant

Then, conditional on X and θ, each individual has a constant hazard and a survivor function with distribution $G(t)=1-S(t)$ in $\mathcal{G}_3$ having a decreasing hazard due only to the mixing density $d\mu$.

(ii) $o < \alpha_1 < 1, \quad X(u) > 0, \quad \alpha_2 < 0$

Each individual has a decreasing hazard, partially as a result of the exogenous variable $X(u)$ and partially because of the intrinsic nature of the population. Because estimated values of α_1 and α_2 are very sensitive to the choice of mixing density $d\mu$, it is important to estimate this density in a nonparametric fashion before interpreting the relative importance of $X(u)$ on an individual's duration time.

(iii) $0 < \alpha_1 < 1, \quad X(u) > 0$ and increasing, $\quad \alpha_2 > 0$

If this pattern of signs for α_1 and α_2 is estimated, then $\alpha_2 X(t)$ must be sufficiently small that the population-specific parameter α_1 leads to an overall concave function

$$\int_0^t \alpha_1 u^{\alpha_1 - 1} \exp[\alpha_2 X(u) + \alpha_0]\, du$$

A sufficient condition for this is that $X(t)$ and the estimated parameters satisfy

$$\alpha_1 - 1 < -\alpha_2 \sup_{0 \leqslant t < t^*} tX'(t)$$

where t^* is the maximum duration in the sample.

4.2 *The nonparametric maximum likelihood estimator*

In this section we shall consider two specifications of $\mu(\theta)$. The first specification assumes that $\mu(\theta)$ assigns point mass P_i to a finite number of points θ_i $(i=1, \ldots, I)$. This is the standard case of finite mixtures. The upper bound on I is assumed to be known, but I, θ_i, and P_i are assumed to be unknown. In this case, classical parametric maximum likelihood procedures can be applied to estimate all the parameters of the model. A special case of this is the heterogeneity specification in the mover–stayer model (Goodman, 1961).

The first specification appears to be quite artificial. It becomes more interesting in the light of recent work by Laird (1978). In that work, $\mu(\theta)$ is an unrestricted probability distribution, which is the second and more general specification considered in this chapter. Laird demonstrated that under very weak conditions the nonparametric maximum likelihood estimator of $\mu(\theta)$, $\hat{\mu}(\theta)$, increases only at discrete points of θ; that is, the nonparametric maximum likelihood estimator of $\mu(\theta)$ is a (possibly countably infinite) discrete distribution.[6] Under somewhat stronger sufficiency conditions, the nonparametric maximum likelihood estimator is a finite mixture. The mildest set of sufficient conditions requires that the support (range) of θ be finite.

In the empirical calculations to be reported in the next section, we find that even when the underlying $\mu(\theta)$ is continuous, estimates from a finite mixtures model provide good numerical descriptions of duration data and enable us to accurately estimate structural parameters without imposing arbitrary parametric specifications of the distribution of unobservables on the data. Estimated values of P_i and θ_i are suggestive of continuous mixtures that generate the data. A surprising feature of the empirical analysis is the low value of I that is required to produce estimates of the structural duration distribution and mixing measure that produce an estimated duration distribution that is in close agreement with the data.

Because of Laird's analysis, empirical estimations of both specifications of $\mu(\theta)$ often come to the same thing. The general approach advocated in this chapter is to represent the density of $g(t)$ by

$$(4.2) \qquad g(t) = \sum_{i=1}^{I} f(t \mid \theta_i) P_i$$

and to estimate the parameters of $f(t \mid \theta)$, θ_i, and P_i by maximum likelihood.[7] Because, in practice, if only as a consequence of machine computing limits, we always assume that the range of θ is finite, we are assured by Laird's analysis that the nonparametric maximum likelihood estimator of $\mu(\theta)$ is a step function with a finite number of steps. The main difference between the two specifications is that for the more general case, in which I is unknown, classical maximum likelihood theory cannot be invoked to justify the large sample properties of the estimators. The main difficulty is that as the number of observations becomes large, I becomes large at an unknown rate. Consistency conditions for the more general case have been given by Kiefer and Wolfowitz (1956) and by our companion report (Heckman & Singer, 1981).[8]

In practice, I is unknown for either specification of $\mu(\theta)$. The only safe way to estimate P_i and θ_i without imposing false constraints is to select a large value of I, at least initially, and estimate down to a simpler model. A difficulty with this approach is that if I is selected to exceed its true value, the likelihood function is maximized on a ridge in the parameter space. In this case, standard gradient procedures are computationally unstable. For this reason, we advocate use of the EM algorithm (Dempster et al., 1977), which does not require computation of a Hessian matrix to ensure that the maximum likelihood functions converge to a (local) optimum.

To illustrate the application of this algorithm, consider the example of equation (4.1), with $X(u)$ time-invariant. The procedure to be presented here can be used for time-varying variables. We consider only the most elementary case, to avoid notational clutter.

$$K(t \mid X, \theta) = \exp[-t^{\alpha_1} \exp(\alpha_0 + \alpha_2 X + \theta)] \tag{4.3}$$

Let

$$\lambda_{il} = \exp[\alpha_0 + \alpha_2 X_l + \theta_i], \quad i = 1, \ldots, I, \quad l = 1, \ldots, L$$

L is sample size. Assume that there is no censoring or truncation, and let λ_l be an I-dimensional vector of the λ_{il}. The density of t_l is

$$f(t_l \mid \lambda_l) = \sum_{i=1}^{I} P_i(\alpha_1 t_l^{\alpha_1 - 1})\lambda_{il} \exp(-t_l^{\alpha_1}\lambda_{il})$$

The density of t_l, conditional on membership in component population i, is

$$f(t_l \mid \lambda_{il}) = \alpha_1 t_l^{\alpha_1 - 1}\lambda_{il} \exp(-t_l^{\alpha_1}\lambda_{il})$$

We seek to maximize the log likelihood

$$\mathcal{L} = \sum_{l=1}^{L} \ln f(t_l \mid \lambda_l)$$

with respect to the P_i, θ_i, and $\alpha = (\alpha_0, \alpha_1, \alpha_2)$.

Dempster and associates (1977) have demonstrated that under standard conditions the following iteration cycle maximizes the log likelihood. At the mth stage of the iteration, define $\lambda_{il}^{(m)}$, $\lambda_l^{(m)}$, $P_i^{(m)}$, and $\alpha^{(m)}$.

Define

$$P_i^{(m+1)} = \frac{1}{L} \sum_{l=1}^{L} P_i^{(m)} \left\{ \frac{f(t_l \mid \lambda_{il}^{(m)})}{\sum_{i=1}^{I} P_i^{(m)} f(t_l \mid \lambda_{il}^{(m)})} \right\}$$

The expression

$$\phi_{il}^{(m+1)} = P_i^{(m)} \left\{ \frac{f(t_l \mid \lambda_{il}^{(m)})}{\sum_{i=1}^{I} P_i^{(m)} f(t_l \mid \lambda_{il}^{(m)})} \right\}$$

can be interpreted as the posterior probability that observation l is generated by the ith component population of the mixture given values of the parameter estimates at iteration stage m. Then $P_i^{(m+1)}$ is simply the unweighted mean of these posterior probabilities.

Given $P_i^{(m+1)}$, form the following function:

$$\tilde{\mathfrak{L}}^{(m+1)} = \sum_{l=1}^{L} \sum_{i=1}^{I} [\ln f(t_l \mid \lambda_{il})] \phi_{il}^{(m+1)}$$

Given $P_i^{(m+1)}$, maximize $\tilde{\mathfrak{L}}^{(m+1)}$ with respect to θ_i $(i=1, \ldots, I)$ and α. $\tilde{\mathfrak{L}}$ is not the log likelihood $\mathfrak{L}$, even if $P_i^{(m+1)}$ is the true value of P_i. The difference between $\tilde{\mathfrak{L}}$ and $\mathfrak{L}$ is the difference between the sum of the log of an expectation ($\mathfrak{L}$) and the sum of the expectation of logs ($\tilde{\mathfrak{L}}$). For exponential models, maximizing $\tilde{\mathfrak{L}}$ by numerical methods is considerably cheaper than maximizing $\mathfrak{L}$, a fact exploited in the computational algorithm of Flinn and Heckman (1982a), who have applied the EM algorithm to estimate a general multistate duration model with a general specification for heterogeneity.

Given initial values for α, θ_i, and P_i $(i=1, \ldots, I)$, one computes the $P_i^{(1)}$, then maximizes $\tilde{\mathfrak{L}}^{(1)}$ with respect to α and the θ_i, then forms the $P_i^{(2)}$, then maximizes $\tilde{\mathfrak{L}}^{(2)}$, and so forth. This procedure is guaranteed to produce a local optimum for $\mathfrak{L}$ under standard conditions. The estimated values of P_i are constrained to lie in the unit interval.

5 Evidence on the empirical performance of the nonparametric maximum likelihood estimator

In this section we shall present some empirical evidence on the performance of the nonparametric maximum likelihood estimator of $\mu(\theta)$ discussed in Section 4. Using artificially generated samples, we implement the EM algorithm and attempt to recover the structural parameters of the model (i.e., the α) and the underlying mixing distribution ($\mu(\theta)$). Because of the limited number of sampling experiments conducted here, our analysis can be considered only as suggestive of the performance of the estimator.

Our tentative conclusions from these runs are as follows. In all runs, the structural parameters (α) are precisely estimated. A surprising finding is the apparent poor quality of the nonparametric maximum likelihood estimator as an estimator of $\mu(\theta)$ in the case of a continuous mixing distribution. Even more surprising is the fact that even though the mixing distribution is poorly estimated, the nonparametric maximum likelihood estimator produces an estimate of the cdf $G(t)$ that closely corresponds to the sample cdf, and it produces an estimate of α that is close to the true value.

We estimate various versions of the econometric model presented in equation (4.3). We write

$$(5.1) \quad F(t \mid \theta) = 1 - \exp\{-t^{\alpha_1} \exp(\alpha_0 + \alpha_2 x + \theta)\}$$

We assume that e^θ has a truncated density of the following functional form:

$$d\mu(\theta) = \frac{e^\theta(\exp - e^\theta)d\theta}{\text{Prob}(-\theta^* \leqslant \theta \leqslant \theta^*)}$$

where $\theta^* = 10^{72}$. This is a truncated gamma density for e^θ. Because of the large value of θ^*, this mixing density is essentially equivalent to an untruncated density. We impose truncation in order to be able to invoke the Laird analysis. Following the procedure outlined in Section 4, the EM algorithm is used to estimate the P_i, θ_i ($i=1, \ldots, I$) and the structural parameters (the α).

In our companion report (Heckman & Singer, 1981) we verified that for the model of equation (5.1), the nonparametric maximum likelihood estimator for $\mu(\theta)$ and the α_i ($i=1,2,3$) is consistent under certain conditions specified there. The proof is based on the Kiefer–Wolfowitz sufficiency conditions. We also verified that the nonparametric maximum likelihood estimator is a finite step function for any finite sample.

Our artificial samples are generated by the following procedure. To generate each observation, we commence by drawing a uniform random variable in the interval (0, 1). From the cdf of θ, we solve for the implied θ. Values of scalar X are taken from a standard normal random number generator. We then draw another uniform random number in the interval (0, 1). Given θ, X, and specified values of α, equation (5.1) is solved for the implied t. No censoring or truncation is imposed. Most of the results to be reported here are for samples of size 1,000 (L=1,000). This is a typical sample size encountered in microeconomic investigations. We shall report some results for different sample sizes. Because the estimation procedure does not restrict the mean of θ, α_0 is set to 0 (the mean of θ is implicit in our estimates). In each run, 10 mass points for θ are selected to commence the iterations.

We first present estimates of a model in which $\alpha_0=0$, $\alpha_1=2$, and $\alpha_2=0.5$. This is a structural model with positive duration dependence consistent with the declining reservation wage model of Section 1. The results are shown in Table 2.2. The agreement between fitted and true values of α is very high. Next we consider estimates of θ_i and P_i. These are reported under the subheading *Estimated mixing distribution*. For the starting values recorded in the first line, the EM algorithm converges to the estimates shown in the first two columns. A remarkable finding in all of our runs is a clustering phenomenon. Even though we start with 10

Table 2.2

True model	$\alpha_1 = 2$	$\alpha_2 = 0.5$
Estimated model	$\hat{\alpha}_1 = 1.947$ (0.12)[a]	$\hat{\alpha}_2 = 0.484$ (0.053)

Estimated mixing distribution

Estimated θ_i[b]	*Estimated* P_i	Estimated cdf	True cdf	Observed cdf
0.0483	0.0063	0.0063	0.0011	0.002
0.2734	0.0918	0.0981	0.0312	0.042
1.2376	0.6057	0.7038	0.3509	0.370
4.0582	0.2961	1.000	0.9152	0.917

Estimated cumulative distribution of durations vs. actual $(\hat{G}(t)$ *vs.* $G(t))$

Value of t	Estimated t cdf	Observed cdf
0.25	0.1321	0.1380
0.50	0.3775	0.3720
0.75	0.5878	0.5890
1.00	0.7339	0.7290
1.25	0.8285	0.8270
1.50	0.8876	0.8970
1.75	0.9242	0.9280
2.00	0.9471	0.9430
3.00	0.9833	0.9850
4.00	0.9933	0.9920

[a] Standard errors computed from the estimated information matrix are shown below the estimated coefficients in parentheses. $L = 1{,}000$.
[b] Starting values for θ_i are $\theta = 1, \ldots, 10$; $P_i = 0.1$, $i = 1, \ldots, 10$.

distinct values of θ_i, the algorithm eventually produces fewer than 10 distinct values, in the sense that there are several values of θ_i that are indistinguishable given the inherent numerical accuracy of the computational procedure. A complete iteration sequence documenting this clustering is reported in Appendix A. A comparison between the estimated cdf, the true cdf, and the sample cdf (based on the realized θ) is given in the final three columns. The agreement is rather poor.

Next we consider the agreement between the calculated cdf for duration times and the sample cdf. The calculated cdf is computed conditional on X values. For each observation we compute the probability that durations are less than the values of t reported in the table. In this calculation we use estimated values of θ_i, P_i, and α. Summing over all observations produces the numbers reported in the first column under

Table 2.3

True model	$\alpha_1=2$	$\alpha_2=0.5$	$\alpha_0=0$
Estimated model	—	0.496 (0.044)[a]	—

Estimated mixing distribution

Estimated θ_i[b]	*Estimated* P_i	Estimated cdf	True θ cdf	Observed cdf
0.0431	0.0062	0.0062	0.0009	0.0002
0.2569	0.0901	0.0963	0.0279	0.0390
1.1059	0.4098	0.5062	0.3031	0.3240
1.8136	0.2781	0.7842	0.5412	0.5630
5.409	0.2157	1.0000	0.9713	0.9740

Estimated cumulative distribution of durations vs. actual ($\hat{G}(t)$ *vs.* $G(t)$)

Value of t	Estimated t cdf	Observed cdf
0.2500	0.1318	0.1380
0.5000	0.3776	0.3720
0.7500	0.5867	0.5890
1.0000	0.7333	0.7290
1.2500	0.8286	0.8270
1.5000	0.8879	0.8970
1.7500	0.9244	0.9280
2.0000	0.9471	0.9430
3.0000	0.9834	0.9850
4.0000	0.9934	0.9920

[a] Standard error computed from the estimated information matrix is shown below the estimated coefficient in parentheses. $L=1{,}000$.
[b] Starting values for θ_i are $\theta=1,\ldots,10$; $P_i=0.1$, $i=1,\ldots,10$.

the subheading *Estimated cumulative distribution of durations vs. actual* ($\hat{G}(t)$ *vs.* $G(t)$). The sample histogram is recorded in the second column. The agreement between the estimated and empirical histograms is remarkably good.

Similar results are reported in Table 2.3, which displays estimates for a model in which $\alpha_0=0$, $\alpha_1=2$, and $\alpha_2=0.5$. The format of this table is the same as the format of Table 2.2. In this run, the duration dependence parameter α_1 is fixed at its true value to determine the effect of estimating one less parameter on the estimates of the mixing distribution. From the same starting values for θ_i and P_i that were used to produce the numbers reported in Table 2.2, the algorithm selects one more point of increase for the distribution of unobservables. Otherwise the story is the same as that reported in Table 2.2. These findings have been duplicated for numerous other values of α. The structural parameters are always estimated rather precisely, the cdf of θ is estimated rather imprecisely, and the estimated model fits the data rather well.

Because estimators of densities are known to converge rather slowly, we examine the behavior of the EM estimator for three sample sizes: $L=500$, $L=1{,}000$, $L=5{,}000$. We fix $\alpha_0=0$, $\alpha_1=1$, and $\alpha_2=0$ so that the model that is estimated is a pure mixture of exponentials. The same set of starting values for θ_i and P_i is employed in all runs. The results are presented in Table 2.4. More points of increase are estimated in the larger samples. But even in a sample as large as 5,000, the estimated cdf of θ is a poor indicator of the true underlying cdf. In all samples, the estimated distribution of t agrees rather closely with the empirical distribution. As expected, the fit improves with sample size.

All of the runs discussed thus far use the same set of starting values for θ_i and P_i. The final set of estimates of P_i and θ_i are, in fact, sensitive to the choice of starting values. We document this in Table 2.5. The appropriate comparison is with the first set of values in Table 2.4. An unsettling conclusion is that estimates of the mixing distribution are sensitive to the choice of starting values. The log likelihood for the $L=500$ values in Table 2.4 is -407.5977501. The log likelihood for the first set of values in Table 2.5 is -407.3143661, whereas the log likelihood value for the second set of values is -407.3142661. Using log likelihood as a measure of goodness of fit, all three sets of estimates do about equally well in fitting the empirical duration distributions.

Despite the fact that three different cdf's for θ are estimated, the predictive accuracy of the estimated cdf of t for the true cdf of t is very high and is about equally good in all models.

Much further Monte Carlo work remains to be done before any firm conclusions on the performance of the consistent nonparametric maximum likelihood estimator can be reached. Our estimates generated to date suggest the following tentative conclusions:

1 In all cases, structural parameters (the α) are precisely estimated.
2 The consistent nonparametric maximum likelihood estimator of a distribution is not a very reliable guide to the shape of the true distribution of unobservables, even in samples of size 5,000.
3 For both finite mixtures and continuous mixtures models, the estimated cdf for duration times is in close agreement with the sample cdf.

These tentative conclusions suggest one further conclusion. The consistent procedure proposed in Section 4 and implemented in Section 5

Table 2.4A *Sample size 500*

Estimates of the mixing distribution for a mixture of exponentials model

Estimated θ_i[a]	*Estimated* P_i	Estimated cdf	True cdf	Observed cdf
0.1256	0.0499	0.0498	0.0073	0.0080
1.0416	0.5817	0.6316	0.2796	0.2820
4.0510	0.3683	1.000	0.9120	0.9140

Estimated cumulative distribution of durations vs. actual ($\hat{G}(t)$ *vs.* $G(t)$)

Value of t	Estimated t cdf	Observed cdf
0.2500	0.3694	0.3720
0.5000	0.5590	0.5480
0.7500	0.6706	0.6820
1.0000	0.7443	0.7560
1.2500	0.7968	0.7860
1.5000	0.8359	0.8240
1.7500	0.8656	0.8580
2.0000	0.8886	0.8840
3.0000	0.9402	0.9520
4.0000	0.9608	0.9580

[a] Starting values for θ_i are $\theta = 1, \ldots, 10$; $P_i = 0.1$, $i = 1, \ldots, 10$; $\alpha_0 = 0$, $\alpha_1 = 1$, $\alpha_2 = 0$ fixed.

Table 2.4B *Sample size 1,000*[a]

Estimates of the mixing distribution for a mixture of exponentials model

Estimated θ_i	*Estimated* P_i	Estimated cdf	True cdf	Observed cdf
0.0429	0.00613	0.00613	0.0009	0.0020
0.2525	0.0877	0.0938	0.0270	0.0380
1.1609	0.5487	0.6426	0.3232	0.3410
3.3978	0.3127	0.9553	0.8529	0.8490
12.4452	0.0446	1.0000	0.9999	1.0001

Estimated cumulative distribution of durations vs. actual ($\hat{G}(t)$ *vs.* $G(t)$)

Value of t	Estimated t cdf	Observed cdf
0.2500	0.3653	0.3580
0.5000	0.5522	0.5450
0.7500	0.6673	0.6790
1.0000	0.7436	0.7510
1.2500	0.7971	0.7920
1.5000	0.8361	0.8240
1.7500	0.8651	0.8580
2.0000	0.8872	0.8850
3.0000	0.9366	0.9420
4.0000	0.9577	0.9580

[a] Starting values as in Table 2.4A.

Table 2.4C *Sample size 5,000*[a]

Estimates of the mixing distribution for a mixture of exponentials model

Estimated θ_i	*Estimated* P_i	Estimated cdf	True cdf	Observed cdf
0.0839	0.0141	0.0141	0.0033	0.0032
0.4323	0.1324	0.1465	0.0704	0.0686
1.0823	0.3639	0.5104	0.2944	0.2966
2.9211	0.4399	0.9503	0.7887	0.7856
4.5012	0.0497	1.0000	0.9389	0.9380

Estimated cumulative distribution of durations vs. actual ($\hat{G}(t)$ *vs.* $G(t)$)

Value of t	Estimated t cdf	Observed cdf
0.2500	0.3616	0.3582
0.5000	0.5606	0.5612
0.7500	0.6785	0.6814
1.0000	0.7535	0.7572
1.2500	0.8044	0.8036
1.5000	0.8410	0.8392
1.7500	0.8682	0.8648
2.0000	0.8892	0.8872
3.0000	0.9386	0.9412
4.0000	0.9616	0.9606

[a]Starting values as in Table 2.4A.

can be used to check the plausibility of any parametric specification of the distribution of unobserved variables. If the estimated parameters of a structural model achieved from a parametric specification of the distribution of unobservables are not too far from the estimates of the same parameters achieved from the nonparametric maximum likelihood estimator discussed in this chapter, the econometrician should have much more confidence in a particular choice of parameterization. The development of a formal test statistic to determine how far is too far is a topic for the future. Because of the consistency of the nonparametric maximum likelihood estimator, a consistent test is clearly available.

One conclusion that should *not* be drawn from the numbers reported in this section is that "it doesn't matter how one parameterizes the distribution of unobservables." The examples of Section 2 refute that contention. The fact that a variety of nonparametric maximum likelihood estimators produce estimated distribution functions for duration times that fit the data equally well does not imply that an arbitrary parametric functional form can safely be imposed on the data.

Table 2.5A *Sample size 500*; $\alpha_0 = 0$, $\alpha_1 = 1$, $\alpha_2 = 0$.

Sensitivity of estimates of θ_i and P_i to starting values

Estimated θ_i[a]	*Estimated P_i*	Estimated cdf	True cdf	Observed cdf
0.0815	0.0183	0.0183	0.0031	0.0040
0.2411	0.0514	0.0697	0.0247	0.0380
1.1165	0.5896	0.6594	0.3070	0.2940
4.2344	0.3406	1.0000	0.9241	0.9340

Estimated cumulative distribution of durations vs. actual ($\hat{G}(t)$ *vs.* $G(t)$)

Value of t	Estimated t cdf	Observed cdf
0.2500	0.3694	0.3720
0.5000	0.5584	0.5480
0.7500	0.6703	0.6820
1.0000	0.7447	0.7560
1.2500	0.7976	0.7860
1.5000	0.8369	0.8240
1.7500	0.8666	0.8580
2.0000	0.8894	0.8840
3.0000	0.9400	0.9520
4.0000	0.9604	0.9580

[a] Starting values: $\theta = (10^{-4}, 10^{-3}, 10^{-2}, 10^{-1}, 1, 10, 10^2, 10^3, 10^4, 10^5)$.
$P = (0.1, 0.1, \ldots, 0.1)$.

The fact that the structural coefficients are so well estimated, whereas the distribution of unobservables is not, suggests that specification of an erroneous but more-than-two-parameter mixing distribution may protect the analyst against the sensitivity reported in Section 2. The estimated mixing measure reported in Table 2.2 is, after all, a nine-independent-parameter distribution. A precise development of this point is a topic for the future.

6 Summary and conclusions

This chapter has explored the identification problem in econometric models for the analysis of duration data. Using both empirical and theoretical examples we have documented the sensitivity of estimates of the parameters of structural duration models to arbitrary specifications of the distribution of unobservables. These examples demonstrate that the choice of the distribution of unobservables in duration models cannot be made solely on the grounds of computational or theoretical convenience.

Table 2.5B *Sample size 500*; $\alpha_0 = 0$, $\alpha_1 = 1$, $\alpha_2 = 0$.

Sensitivity of estimates of θ_i and P_i to starting values

Estimated θ_i [a]	*Estimated P_i*	Estimated cdf	True cdf	Observed cdf
0.0815	0.0183	0.0183	0.0031	0.0040
0.2411	0.0514	0.0697	0.0249	0.0380
1.1162	0.5893	0.6590	0.3069	0.2940
4.2129	0.3383	0.9973	0.9228	0.9340
7.5887	0.0026	0.9999	0.9956	0.9900
9.1516	0.0000	1.0000	0.9989	0.9980

Estimated cumulative distribution of durations vs. actual ($\hat{G}(t)$ *vs.* $G(t)$)

Value of t	Estimated t cdf	Observed cdf
0.2500	0.3694	0.3720
0.5000	0.5583	0.5480
0.7500	0.6703	0.6820
1.0000	0.7447	0.7560
1.2500	0.7976	0.7860
1.5000	0.8369	0.8240
1.7500	0.8663	0.8580
2.0000	0.8894	0.8840
3.0000	0.9400	0.9520
4.0000	0.9604	0.9580

[a] Starting values: $\theta = (10^{-4}, 10^{-3}, 10^{-2}, 10^{-1}, 1, 10, 10^2, 10^3, 10^4, 10^5)$.
$P = (0.25, 0.20, 0.15, 0.10, 0.05, 0.05, 0.05, 0.05, 0.05, 0.05)$.

In order to avoid the arbitrariness inherent in current econometric practice, we have proposed two lines of attack on the problem of correct model specification. The first approach uses nonparametric tests of key assumptions about structural duration models. These tests can be used to assess the degree of model complexity that is required in fitting a structural duration model to a given set of data. The great advantage of these test procedures is that they do not rely on arbitrary parametric structures to extract information from the data. We have also presented some tests that enable us to assess features of the distribution of unobservables.

The second approach pursued in this chapter is consistent estimation of the distribution of the unobservables. Current practice, which specifies both the functional form of structural duration distributions and the functional form of the distribution of unobservables, overparameterizes duration models. Provided that we adopt some functional form for the structural distribution (the usual practice), it is, in principle, possible to estimate the distribution of the unobservables. Economic theory sometimes provides guidance on the nature of structural duration distributions but rarely offers guidance on the functional form of the distribution of the unobservables.

We have discussed estimation of the distribution of the unobservables of the model using a nonparametric maximum likelihood estimator and have presented a few calculations with this estimator. We have demonstrated that the nonparametric estimator of the mixing distribution enables the analyst to accurately estimate the parameters of the structural distribution. The procedure locates the unobserved mixing distribution rather well when the true distribution is discrete, as in the classical mover–stayer model. However, the nonparametric maximum likelihood estimator produces poor estimates of mixing distributions in samples of the size usually encountered in econometrics.

This chapter has analyzed a worst-case situation which is commonly encountered. Throughout this chapter we have assumed that the analyst has only one spell of an event per observation. Multiple-spell data can aid substantially in identifying the true structural duration model. Identification analysis with multiple spell data is discussed in a companion paper.

Much hard work remains to be done before all the procedures advocated in this chapter are put on firm statistical footing. Although it is possible to prove consistency of the nonparametric maximum likelihood estimator used in this chapter (Heckman & Singer, 1981), we have not yet produced a distribution theory for this estimator, although we are optimistic that it can be done. Similar remarks apply to the other test procedures discussed here.

We hope that the reader's faith in structural estimates secured from traditional methods is somewhat shaken by the examples of Section 2. The extreme sensitivity of estimates of structural models to ad hoc specifications of the distribution of the unobservables suggests that traditional procedures, while rigorously justified under strong maintained assumptions, often produce estimates that poorly describe the true behavioral models generating duration data. Because they require fewer maintained assumptions, the methods advocated in this chapter are more likely to produce reliable estimates of structural duration models.

Appendix A: Clustering of the estimated points of support in the nonparametric maximum likelihood estimator

In Section 5 of the text we reported a clustering phenomenon. Although we start each estimation run with 10 distinct points θ_i $(i=1, \ldots, 10)$, we

Table 2.6 *The clustering phenomenon: a complete iteration sequence*[a]

Iteration step	Parameters / Initial values	θ_1	θ_2	θ_3	θ_4	θ_5	θ_6	θ_7	θ_8	θ_9	θ_{10}	P_1	P_2	P_3	P_4	P_5	P_6	P_7	P_8	P_9
		10^{-4}	10^{-3}	10^{-2}	10^{-1}	1	10	10^2	10^3	10^4	10^5	0.25	0.20	0.15	0.10	0.05	0.05	0.05	0.05	0.05
1		.0616	.0617	.0625	.0712	.211	1.15	7.34	67.2	459	625	$.105\times10^{-4}$	$.84\times10^{-4}$	.0063	.0397	.145	.472	.288	.045	.0025
2		.0759	.0760	.0768	.0863	.284	1.22	6.24	51.0	270	343	$.51\times10^{-4}$	$.41\times10^{-3}$	$.31\times10^{-3}$	.0204	.113	.557	.283	.0224	$.48\times10^{-3}$
3		.0721	.0722	.0729	.0816	.316	1.24	5.67	41.7	185	221	$.41\times10^{-4}$	$.33\times10^{-3}$	$.24\times10^{-2}$	.0163	.102	.590	.274	.0151	$.19\times10^{-3}$
25		.0830	.0830	.0830	.0832	.313	1.23	4.63	12.8	17.4	17.8	$.43\times10^{-4}$	$.35\times10^{-3}$	$.26\times10^{-2}$	.0175	.0735	.618	.282	.006	$.116\times10^{-4}$
100		.0818	.0818	.0818	.0818	.250	1.14	4.29	8.3	8.84	8.87	$.4\times10^{-4}$	$.4\times10^{-3}$	$.2\times10^{-2}$	.0159	.0540	.598	.325	.0055	$.59\times10^{-4}$
200		.0814	.0814	.0814	.0814	.242	1.12	4.20	7.74	8.24	8.26	$.4\times10^{-4}$	$.3\times10^{-3}$	.0023	.0156	.0519	.590	.335	.0052	$.9\times10^{-5}$
500		.0815	.0815	.0815	.0815	.241	1.12	4.20	7.52	8.58	8.60	$.4\times10^{-4}$	$.3\times10^{-3}$	.0023	.0156	.0514	.589	.337	.0042	$.7\times10^{-5}$
900		.0815	.0815	.0815	.0815	.241	1.12	4.21	7.45	9.05	9.05	$.4\times10^{-4}$	$.3\times10^{-3}$	.0023	.0156	.0514	.589	.337	.0032	$.6\times10^{-5}$
1,200		.0815	.0815	.0815	.0815	.241	1.12	4.21	7.59	9.15	9.15	$.4\times10^{-4}$	$.3\times10^{-3}$	.0023	.0156	.0514	.589	.338	.0026	$.5\times10^{-5}$

[a] Sample size 500; $\alpha_0=0$, $\alpha_1=1$, $\alpha_2=0$ fixed.

observe that estimated values of θ_i tend to cluster. In this appendix we report the various stages of the maximum likelihood iterations for one model to document the clustering phenomenon. The clustering reported here is typical of the clustering observed in all runs. The model selected is the final model reported in Table 2.5. In Table 2.6 we report successive iteration values leading up the final optimum.

Notice how quickly the first four points of support cluster. The final two points of support move together more slowly. By iteration 25, it is apparent that the last two points are moving together.

NOTES

1 The expectation is taken with respect to the wage offer distribution, $F(x)$.
2 In place of equation (1.2) in the text, write

$$\frac{dV(t)}{dt} = -c - rV(t)$$

$$(1.2)' \qquad + \lambda \int_{B(t)}^{\infty} \left(\frac{x}{r+\sigma} (1 - \exp[-(\sigma + r)(A - t)]) \right.$$

$$\left. + \int_{t}^{A} \frac{\sigma \exp[-(\sigma+r)(\tau-t)] V(\tau)\, d\tau - V(t)}{(1-\exp[-\sigma(A-t)])} \right) dF(x)$$

where

$$B(t) = \frac{(r+\sigma)}{1 - e^{-(\sigma+r)(A-t)}} \left\{ V(t) - \int_{t}^{A} \frac{\sigma e^{-(\sigma+r)(\tau-t)}}{(1 - e^{-\sigma(A-t)})} V(\tau)\, d\tau \right\}$$

3 This sort of test has been used in the analysis of the identifying assumptions used in female labor supply (Heckman, 1976) and (incorrectly) in the empirical analysis of search unemployment (Kiefer & Neumann, 1979).
4 The assumption that θ is scalar, however, requires that measured and unmeasured explanatory variables enter additively in *F*.
5 In practice, one can avoid complex regression by estimating the moment generating function for the mixture of exponentials. In equation (3.7), replace *is* with *s*. For the moment generating function to exist, we require that $\min\{\theta_j\}_{j=1}^{n} > s$. This restriction helps, in part, to settle the problem of the optimal choice of *s*. A similar remark applies to the estimation of equation (3.6).
6 The conditions are (a) that $f(t \mid \theta)$ be analytic in θ at all points in the parameter set and (b) that if $f(t \mid \theta)$ is parameterized to depend on explanatory variables, so that if $f(t \mid \theta, \alpha X_i)$ is the density of t given θ and X_i, for any fixed set of X_i, with distinct values of X, the set

$$S=\{1, f(t\mid\theta, \alpha X_1), f(t\mid\theta, \alpha X_2), \ldots, f(t\mid\theta, \alpha X_I)\}$$

is linearly independent for all values of θ.

7 For truncated data, for which $T<\bar{T}$, replace $f(t\mid\theta)$ in equation (4.2) with $f(t\mid\theta)/F(\bar{T}\mid\theta)$. For censored data, censored at $\bar{T}$, replace $f(t\mid\theta)$ for censored observations with $1-F(\bar{T}\mid\theta)$.

8 In our companion report (Heckman & Singer, 1981) we have proved that the nonparametric maximum likelihood estimator of $\mu(\theta)$ and the structural parameters of model (4.1) are consistent under certain conditions.

REFERENCES

Andersen, E. B. 1973. *Conditional Inference and Models for Measuring.* Copenhagen: Mentalhygiejnisk Forlag.

Andersen, E. B. 1980. *Discrete Statistical Models with Social Science Applications.* Amsterdam: North-Holland.

Barlow, R. E., Bartholomew, D. J., Bremner, J. M., and Brunk, H. D. 1972. *Statistical Inference Under Order Restrictions.* London: Wiley.

Buck, R. C. 1965. *Advanced Calculus.* New York: McGraw-Hill.

Chamberlain, G. 1982. "On the Use of Panel Data." *Longitudinal Studies of the Labor Market,* edited by J. Heckman and B. Singer. New York: Academic.

Chernoff, H. 1962. *Sequential Analysis and Optimal Design.* Philadelphia: SIAM.

DeGroot, M. 1970. *Optimal Statistical Decisions.* New York: McGraw-Hill.

Dempster, A. P., Laird, N. M., and Rubin, D. B. 1977. "Maximum Likelihood from Incomplete Data Via the EM Algorithm." *Journal of the Royal Statistical Society* (Series B) 39:1–38.

Durbin, J. 1974. *Distribution Theory for Tests Based on the Sample Distribution Function.* Philadelphia: SIAM.

Feller, W. 1971. *An Introduction to Probability Theory and Its Applications, Vol. II.* New York: Wiley.

Flinn, C. and J. Heckman, 1982a. "Models for the Analysis of Labor Force Dynamics." In *Advances in Econometrics,* Vol. 1, 1982, JAI Press.

Flinn, C., and Heckman, J. 1982b. "New Methods for Analyzing Structural Models of Labor Force Dynamics." *Journal of Econometrics,* January, 1982.

Gomez, M. 1980. "Fertility in Mexico: An Empirical Analysis." Ph.D. thesis, University of Chicago.

Goodman, L. 1961. "Statistical Methods for the Mover-Stayer Model." *Journal of the American Statistical Association* 56:841–68.

Gronau, R. 1971. "Information and Frictional Unemployment." *American Economic Review* 60:290–301.

Harris, J. 1981. "Prenatal Medical Care and Infant Mortality." In *Economic Aspects of Health,* edited by V. Fuchs. Chicago: University of Chicago Press.

Heckman, J. 1976. "Sample Selection Bias as a Specification Error." Rand Corp.

Heckman, J. 1981. "The Incidental Parameters Problem and the Problem of Initial Conditions.'' In *The Structural Analysis of Discrete Data,* edited by C. Manski and D. McFadden. Cambridge: M.I.T. Press.

Heckman, J., and Borjas, G. 1980. ''Does Unemployment Cause Future Unemployment? Definitions, Questions and Answers from a Continuous Time Model of Heterogeneity and State Dependence.'' *Economica* 47:247–83.

Heckman, J., and Singer, B. 1981. ''A Method for Minimizing the Impact of Distributional Assumptions in Econometric Models for the Analysis of Duration Data.'' Unpublished manuscript, Department of Economics, University of Chicago. Forthcoming in *Econometrica.*

Heckman, J., and Willis, R. 1977. ''A Beta Logistic Model for the Analysis of Sequential Labor Force Participation of Married Women.'' *Journal of Political Economy* 85:27–58.

Hirschman, I. I., and Widder, R. V. 1955. *The Convolution Transform.* Princeton University Press.

Kalbfleish, J., and Prentice, R. 1980. *The Statistical Analysis of Failure Time Data.* New York: Wiley.

Karlin, S. 1968. *Total Positivity.* Stanford University Press.

Kennan, J. 1980. ''The Effect of Unemployment Insurance Payments on Strike Duration.'' Unpublished manuscript, Department of Economics, University of Iowa.

Kiefer, J., and Wolfowitz, J. 1956. ''Consistency of the Maximum Likelihood Estimator in the Presence of Infinitely Many Incidental Parameters.'' *Annals of Mathematical Statistics* 27:887–906.

Kiefer, N., and Neumann, G. 1979. ''An Empirical Job Search Model with a Test of the Constant Reservation Wage Hypothesis.'' *Journal of Political Economy,* pp. 69–82.

Kiefer, N., and Neumann, G. 1981. ''Individual Effects in a Nonlinear Model: Explicit Treatment of Heterogeneity in the Empirical Job Search Model.'' *Econometrica,* July, 1981.

Laird, N. 1978. ''Nonparametric Maximum Likelihood Estimation of a Mixing Distribution.'' *Journal of the American Statistical Association* 73:805–11.

Lancaster, T. 1972. ''A Stochastic Model for the Duration of a Strike.'' *Journal of the Royal Statistical Society* (Series A) 135:257–71.

Lancaster, T., and Nickell, S. 1980. ''The Analysis of Reemployment Probabilities for the Unemployed.'' *Journal of the Royal Statistical Society* (Series A) 143:141–65.

Larkin, R. 1979. ''An Algorithm for Assessing Bimodality vs. Unimodality in a Univariate Distribution.'' Unpublished manuscript, Rockefeller University.

Lippman, S., and McCall, J. 1976. ''The Economics of Job Search: A Survey.'' *Economic Inquiry* 14:113–26.

Maritz, J. 1970. *Empirical Bayes Methods.* London: Methuen.

Ross, S. M. 1970. *Applied Probability with Optimization Applications.* San Francisco: Holden-Day.

Salant, S. 1977. ''Search Theory and Duration Data: A Theory of Sorts.'' *Quarterly Journal of Economics* 1:39–58.

Silcock, H. R. 1954. ''The Phenomenon of Labor Turnover.'' *Journal of the Royal Statistical Society* (Series A) 117:429–40.

Singer, B. 1982. "Measuring Life Cycle Aspects of Employment." In *Longitudinal Studies of the Labor Market,* edited by J. Heckman and B. Singer. New York: Academic.

Steutel, F. 1967. "Note on the Infinite Divisibility of Exponential Mixtures." *Annals of Mathematical Statistics* 38:1303–5.

Toikka, R. 1976. "A Markovian Model of Labor Market Decisions by Workers." *American Economic Review* 66:821–34.

Tricomi, F. 1957. *Integral Equations.* New York: Wiley Interscience.

Wright, B. D., and Douglas, G. 1976. "Better Procedures for Simple Free Item Analysis." Research memorandum 20, Statistical Laboratory, Department of Education, University of Chicago.

PART III

EXPERIMENTATION IN ECONOMETRICS

CHAPTER 3

The effects of time in economic experiments

Jerry A. Hausman[1]

In the late 1960s and throughout the 1970s an important event has occurred for empirical economists. The United States government and other agencies have adopted the tool of experimentation to investigate important social and economic questions. To date, experiments have been conducted in income maintenance programs, electricity time-of-day prices, housing allowance subsidies, medical reimbursement, and numerous other areas.[2] These experiments have involved major expenditures of economic resources. For instance, the cost of the four negative income tax (NIT) experiments has been in excess of $100 million, and the time-of-day (TOD) price experiments have cost about $25 million. To some extent these experiments have attempted to replicate the methods developed over the past 60 years and applied with outstanding success in many biological and physical sciences. R. A. Fisher's influential work in agricultural experiments, along with the work of many other statisticians, has firmly established the usefulness of experimentation as a tool of scientific inference.

Although I do not intend to judge the overall usefulness of the many economics experiments to date, I think that a fair statement is that they have enjoyed mixed success. Much knowledge has been gained from these experiments, and many low-income individuals have benefited during the course of these experiments. On the other hand, they have not settled the questions that they were designed to answer as definitely

The research for this chapter was supported by funds from the National Science Foundation (grant 79-89120) and the Department of Health and Human Services.

as have experiments in the other sciences.[3] In this chapter I shall attempt to investigate the reasons for this lack of definite results. One problem that has arisen is that many of these experiments have tried to answer too many questions. That is, the experimental design has contained too many elements for the given size of the budget and for the precision with which econometric models can be estimated. However, the problem that I shall focus on in this chapter concerns the many important ways in which economic experiments differ from what I call classical experiments. I have attempted to organize these differences around the concept of the temporal nature of economic experiments. Most classical experimentation is essentially atemporal. Although agricultural experiments, for example, take place over time, usually only a cross-section type of analysis is considered in choosing an experimental design. Economic experiments occur over a period of time, because individuals must adjust their activities to react to the incentive structure of the experiments. The temporal nature of these experiments offers an advantage, because it allows us to learn about the permanent unobservable differences among the experimental subjects. At the same time it creates numerous analytical problems. Individuals drop out of economic experiments. If they do so in a nonrandom manner, the usual tools of experimental analysis, ANOVA and regression models, may give biased estimates. Furthermore, individuals may not demonstrate their longrun responses during the course of an experiment they know to be of limited duration. Thus, the interpretation of experimental results may pose problems. I shall attempt to investigate these advantages and problems which occur in economic experiments.

In Section 1 we shall consider optimal experimental design when the element of time is considered. Important gains in estimation efficiency occur when the temporal nature of the data is used. These gains, in turn, lead to a change in optimal experimental design. The investigation takes place within the Conlisk-Watts (1969) framework, which has been used for the NIT experiments. One of the major findings of Section 1 is that the approximately 40% rate of control observations that results from the Conlisk-Watts analysis is considerably more than is optimal when time is accounted for. In Section 2 we shall consider the problems in analysis that attrition effects and duration effects bring to economic experiments. The different economic incentives will be considered, and bias in traditional estimators will also be discussed. Lastly, in Section 3 empirical results are presented that indicate the magnitudes of the various problems. The results demonstrate conclusively that both attrition and duration have important effects on the experimental sample and on the analysis of the results. Resolution of these problems may well be necessary for the success of economics experiments to approach the success gained by the classical approach in other applications of experimental methods.

1 Efficiency issues in experimental design

We first consider the problem of how time affects optimal experimental design. The classical design literature, as characterized by the work of R. A. Fisher in his *Design of Experiments* (1971), stresses comparisons between an experimental group and a control group to measure the effect of an experimental treatment.[4] In fact, at the outset of his book, Fisher stated the most common objection to experimental evidence: "His *controls* are *totally* inadequate" (Fisher, 1971, p. 2). The outstanding contribution of the experimental design literature is to stress the concept of randomization, which attempts to remove any claim of inadequate controls. Classical experimental design theory is essentially atemporal in nature; the comparison groups, experimentals and controls, are separate entities compared at a given moment in time. However, including the element of time in experimental designs brings an important change, because experimental individuals can act partly as their own controls through the use of either preexperimental data or postexperimental data. Thus, more efficient experimental designs are possible. For a given desired level of precision, we may be able to reduce the needed sample size; alternatively, for a given sample size or experimental cost, we can attain greater statistical precision in estimating the experimental effect.[5]

To examine the effect of time in experimental design, we shall use the Conlisk-Watts (1969) framework, because it was used for all the NIT experimental designs. We begin by examining a one-way analysis-of-variance model (ANOVA). Much of the analysis of the NIT experiments has been of this form, and it seems a good place to begin. We express the model in regression form, neglecting time for now, as here y is an N vector, and each row of X has the form

$$y = X\beta + \epsilon, \qquad E\epsilon = 0, V(\epsilon) = \sigma^2 I \tag{1.1}$$

$x_j = (0, \ldots, 0, 1, 0, \ldots, 0)$, $j = 1, m$. That is, we have a 1 in the jth position, where x_1 denotes the control observations and $j = 2, m$ denote the $m-1$ experimental treatments. Typically, the NIT experiments have contained between 4 and 18 experimental treatments.[6] The Conlisk-Watts framework sets out to choose the optimal assignments of individuals to experimental treatments or control subject to a budget constraint.

Therefore, we want to choose n_j $(j=1,m)$, the number of individuals in a given row j of the design matrix.

The optimization criterion used is to minimize the variances of linear functions $P\hat{\beta}$ of the estimated coefficients. Because the covariance matrix of the estimated coefficients is orthogonal for our design, the different choices for measures of generalized variances do not raise a problem. But we will soon consider nonorthogonal designs in which questions of the trace versus the determinant and other measures arise. The Conlisk-Watts framework chooses the trace as the appropriate measure, which for $V(\hat{\beta})$ is the sum of the variances of the parameter estimates and equals $E(\hat{\beta}-\beta)'(\hat{\beta}-\beta)$.[7] To generalize slightly, we consider a weighted sum of the variance of $P\hat{\beta}$ by using a diagonal weight matrix W. Thus the objective function to be optimized is

$$\text{(1.2)} \quad \min q(n_1,\ldots,n_m) = \sigma^{-2}\operatorname{tr}[WPV(\hat{\beta})P'] = \sigma^{-2}\operatorname{tr}[P'WPV(\hat{\beta})] = \operatorname{tr}\left[D\left(\sum_{j=1}^{m} n_j x_j' x_j\right)^{-1}\right]$$

where the matrix $D=P'WP$.

The budget constraint arises from the total cost of the experiment C allocated among the different treatments, each of which costs c_j. In general, a control observation, $j=1$, is considerably less expensive than an experimental observation. The expected cost of an experimental observation varies with the generosity of the income maintenance plan offered as the experimental treatment. The cost constraint is thus $\sum_{j=1}^{m} c_j n_j \leqslant C$. The complete problem is an integer programming problem with a convex objective function subject to linear constraints.

$$\text{(1.3)} \quad \min q(n_1,\ldots,n_m) = \operatorname{tr}\left[D\left(\sum_{j=1}^{m} n_j x_j' x_j\right)^{-1}\right]$$

$$\text{s.t.} \quad \sum_{j=1}^{m} c_j n_j \leqslant C, \quad n_j \geqslant 0 \quad \text{for all } j$$

For large $N=\Sigma n_j$, a suitable approximation is to treat the n_j as continuous and to round off the results to the nearest integer. Programming problems with the concave-linear structure of equation (1.3) have been studied intensively, and well-developed computer algorithms exist to solve them.

However, for our initial ANOVA analysis we can solve equation (1.3) explicitly. Conlisk and Watts have done so for $P=I$ and have found

$$\text{(1.4)} \quad n_j = C\frac{(W_j/c_j)}{\Sigma(W_j c_j)^{1/2}}$$

We see the homogeneity properties of the n_j with respect to both C and the c_j. The optimal n_j rise with their importance in the weight function divided by their cost of observation. But the choice of $P=I$ is not very interesting in an experimental context. We are really interested in estimating the experimental effects via the contrasts, $\hat{\beta}_j - \hat{\beta}_1$. The appropriate P matrix is then an $(m-1)\times m$ matrix, with the first column of -1's and each of the remaining columns with all 0's and a single 1. Thus $P_j = [-1, 0, \ldots, 0, 1, 0, \ldots, 0]$. We set $W=I$, the identity matrix, and solve equation (1.3) to find

$$(1.5) \qquad n_1 = C\frac{((m-1)/c_1)^{1/2}}{D}, \qquad n_j = C(c_j^{-1/2}D^{-1}),$$

$$D = \left[(m-1)c_1 + \sum_{j=2}^{m} c_j\right]^{1/2}$$

Thus the result is equivalent to setting $w_1 = m-1$ in equation (1.4). Because $\hat{\beta}_1$ is used in calculating each of the $m-1$ contrasts, it becomes $m-1$ times as important as any other coefficient. We thus obtain the result that control observations can be very important when more than one experimental treatment is considered.[8] But, as we shall now see when the element of time is introduced into the experimental design considerations, individuals can act partly as their own controls, with important design consequences.

The model that we shall use to consider the question of time in experimental design is the familiar random effects model used in much of the analysis of the NIT experiments. We consider a two-period experiment and specialize equation (1.1) to

$$(1.6) \qquad \begin{aligned} &y_{it} = \mu + \beta_j\delta_{jt} + \alpha_i + \eta_{it}, \quad (t=1,2) \\ &V(\alpha_i) = \sigma_\alpha^2, \qquad V(\eta_{it}) = \sigma_\eta^2, \qquad \rho = \sigma_\alpha^2/(\sigma_\alpha^2 + \sigma_\eta^2) \end{aligned}$$

We have thus decomposed ϵ_{it} into a permanent individual component α_i and another component η_{it} assumed independent across time. The indicator variable δ_{jt} is 1 if the individual is receiving experimental treatment j in period t and 0 otherwise. The importance of the permanent individual component α_i is given by ρ, which often exceeds 0.5 in econometric studies of hours or earnings. As a very easy way to see the effect on experimental design of using individuals as their own controls, let us consider the fixed-effects estimator. For our simple case, it estimates $\hat{\beta}_j = y_{i2} - y_{i1}$, with $V(\hat{\beta}_j) = 2\sigma_\eta^2$. Within the Conlisk-Watts framework, the optimal allocation is $n_j = C/(c_j^{1/2}\Sigma c_k^{1/2})$, $n_1 = 0$. Not only has the design changed significantly, but also our estimates will be much more precise. For instance, consider the case in which $c_1 = 1$ and $c_j = 4$ for

$j = 2, \ldots, m$, with $m = 9$. For a given budget C, the new design leads to estimates of the β_j values with variances $0.704(1-\rho)$ times as large as those in the design given by equation (1.5). Thus we would do about three times as well or better letting individuals act as their own controls.[9]

But we have not necessarily done as well as possible. A more efficient estimator, the generalized least-squares (GLS) estimate, exists for the specification of equation (1.6). A caution is needed here, however. Because of the assignment procedures used in some of the NIT experiments, δ_{jt} in equation (1.6) is unlikely to be orthogonal to α_i. Whereas the fixed-effects estimator will remain unbiased (Mundlak, 1978), the GLS estimator may be biased. A specification test (Hausman, 1978) is recommended when using the NIT data within an ANOVA context. The GLS estimator takes an optimal weighted average of the fixed-effects estimator, which has variance $V(\hat{\beta}_j) = 2\sigma_\eta^2$, and the between-groups estimator, which for large N has variance $V(\tilde{\beta}_j) = 4\sigma_\alpha^2 + 2\sigma_\eta^2$. The two estimates are orthogonal, and the optimal weight can be shown to be $\Delta = (2\sigma_\eta^2)/(4\sigma_\alpha^2 + 4\sigma_\eta^2)$ (Maddala, 1971), so that $\hat{\beta}_{j,\mathrm{GLS}} = \Delta\tilde{\beta}_j + (1-\Delta)\hat{\beta}_j$. We calculate $V(\hat{\beta}_{j,\mathrm{GLS}}) = (1-\rho)^2(2\sigma_\alpha^2 + \sigma_\eta^2)(2\sigma_\eta^2 + 1)/8\sigma_\eta^2$. For $\rho = 0.5$, we find that the GLS estimator does 1.8 times as well as the fixed-effects estimator. As ρ goes to unity, the two estimators become the same, but significant improvement often occurs in practice. Now the optimal design remains the same as with the fixed-effects estimator, and we have seen that either estimator, fixed-effects or GLS, leads to substantially more precise estimates than can be obtained with ordinary least squares (OLS) or the optimal design of equation (1.5).[10]

We now want to expand our model to include time effects. But individuals cannot serve totally as their own controls, because time and the effects of the experiment will lead to y_{2t}. An acceptable experimental design will need to be able to separate time effects from experimental effects. We can continue to use equation (1.5), because $\hat{\beta}_1$, the coefficient for the control effect, will measure the effect of time. Note that the fixed-effects estimator will measure the experimental effect by $\hat{\tau}_j = (\hat{\beta}_j - \hat{\beta}_1)$, with variance $V(\hat{\tau}_j) = 4\sigma_\eta^2$. Thus, we may actually do worse than with OLS on the second-period observations. However, we can make σ_η^2 very small by observing both preexperimental and experimental data over a number of periods, so long as the number of unknown parameters does not increase too fast with the number of observations. The fixed-effects estimator now has variance $4\sigma_\eta^2/T$, whereas OLS has variance $\sigma_\alpha^2 + \sigma_\eta^2/T$, which for a T value at all large gives the advantage to the fixed-effects estimator. The question we now want to answer is whether or not the design of equation (1.5) is optimal when time is added to the specification. The answer is negative, because of the use of crossover designs (Cox, 1958, Chapter 13), as suggested by Hall (1975).[11] Let some individuals be controls in period 1 and experimentals in period 2, and vice versa. In terms of our specification, this design is equivalent to letting β_1 vary across periods as β_{1t}. Our fixed-effects estimator now becomes (for two individuals, the first assigned to β_j in period 1 and serving as a control in period 2, whereas the second person is a control in period 1 and is assigned to β_j in period 2) $\hat{\beta}_j = y_{11} - y_{21} - y_{12} + y_{22}$, with variance $V(\hat{\beta}_j) = 4\sigma_\eta^2$. But note that without any special controls for both periods, we have more observations assigned to each experimental group, and our variances will fall by 1.2 times. The random-effects estimator variance falls by a similar amount. But we may be able to do even better. Note that in each period we have eight times as many control observations as experimental observations. An optimal design will use the random-effects estimator and shift only a fraction of experimentals to control status in period 2, and vice versa. The optimal fraction depends on σ and the relative costs of sampling.

Now, this advice is too extreme for an actual experimental design, because we will still want some individuals as controls in both periods. These controls will permit estimation of the time effect without relying totally on the time orthogonization. Experimental experience might be thought to have permanent effects on behavior, so that postexperimental data would not be useful in estimation. The availability of control data from the same individuals in both periods will allow a test of this hypothesis, but even with this proviso, the example leads to two suggestions for future designs: (1) Gather more preexperimental evidence, which helps in estimation efficiency and is not too expensive to collect. (2) Have fewer pure controls, because time effects can be estimated much more accurately than experimental effects (e.g., Hausman & Wise, 1976), and the crossover design may lead to increased estimation efficiency with postexperimental data, which also are not too expensive to collect. Both of these suggestions can be incorporated into a Conlisk-Watts allocation model. When the effect of time is taken into account, the pattern of experimental and control selection may change markedly.

How well has this type of ANOVA Conlisk-Watts design worked in practice? The one NIT experiment that used it in practice was the Seattle-Denver (SIME/DIME) experiment. The number of categories was quite large in the SIME/DIME design ($m = 59$ categories). In fact, if full ANOVA had been done without deleting higher-order interactions, as the design model did, we would have had m exceeding 200. Thus, even for the comparatively large sample sizes of SIME/DIME we cannot hope to estimate precise results.[12] And when other factors such as race and city are added to the analysis, full ANOVA estimation becomes hopeless. Thus, we are left with estimating ANOVA specifications with many fewer parameters than the design uses. Perhaps a better way to use the Conlisk-Watts framework would be to consider the dual problem in equation (1.3), minimization of cost subject to constraints on estimation precision. Now we no longer use the trace, but instead have

$$(1.7) \qquad \min \sum_{j=1}^{m} c_j n_j \quad \text{s.t.} \quad \operatorname{diag}(PV(\hat{\beta})P') \leqslant W, \quad n_j \geqslant 0$$

where W is a diagonal matrix with desired variances as the nonzero elements. Here the constraint is to have the variance of each contrast that we are interested in less than or equal to a diagonal matrix with weights that signify the necessary precision. The unknown parameters necessary to use equation (1.7) are σ_ϵ^2 and ρ in the 2-period framework. Although these covariance parameters are unknown before the experiment, reasonably good estimates can be obtained from existing data sets (e.g., the SEO sample). The designer will soon see that a much greater budget is necessary or that the number of unknown β_j values will need to be decreased (i.e., the P matrix will need to be reduced in size).

The other difficulty with the Conlisk-Watts approach as used in the SIME/DIME design (as well as the Gary design) is the use of normal income or E level in the design stratification. Because c_j varies with normal income and experimental plan, the design is nonorthogonal with respect to this variable. Unfortunately, inspection of equation (1.6) indicates that normal income contains α_i, which also appears in the error term for the experimental observation. Thus, further problems are created by using all but fixed-effects-type estimators, because experimental treatment in period 2 and α_i are not uncorrelated. Various ad hoc correction methods have been used, but the correct approach is to do ANOVA with all 58 parameters present to account for all stratifying variables. I consider this problem to be the most serious failure of the NIT experimental designs. If full ANOVA cannot be done, a problem of endogenous stratification occurs (Hausman & Wise, 1980), and distributional assumptions on the stochastic terms become necessary for estimation. This removes much of the appeal of ANOVA. My suggestion here would be that one not attempt to use an income measure in the experimental design unless it is based solely on predictions from a regression on exogenous variables.[13]

We now turn from ANOVA-type designs to optimal designs for response surface problems. Equation (1.1) now contains both discrete and continuous variables. The x_{ij}'s contain both linear and nonlinear transformations of the rows of another matrix Z that contains the observable design variables. Again we assume that we have M possible rows of Z that in turn give the optimal X matrix of equation (1.1). Such a design was used in the New Jersey NIT experimental design.[14] Four points should be noted here. First, we are turning from theory-free ANOVA models to linear or nonlinear structural models that depend on correct specification. Second, Conlisk (1973) has shown that optimal designs for response surface analysis are sensitive to the correct specification, whereas ANOVA has robustness due to orthogonality of right-hand-side variables. Next, many questions can be answered only with such structural models. The sizes of income and substitution effects, deadweight loss, and participation are best determined with a structural model. Lastly, the parameterization is much more parsimonious than ANOVA. Thus, fairly precise results may be estimated for a range of programs without the necessity of including an experimental treatment for each proposed program. Of course, ANOVA designs can be estimated with a continuous parameter type of specification, but the potential efficiency losses can be large in comparison with those for an optimal response surface type of design. Given the results of previous work in labor supply, where similar elasticity results have been obtained with a large range of specifications, the response surface approach may be attractive.

The setup of the Conlisk-Watts framework remains the same as in equation (1.2): minimization of weighted generalized variance subject to a budget constraint. However, the X matrix is no longer necessarily orthogonal as it is in the ANOVA model framework. The rows of the Z matrix are chosen to cover the response space adequately. The Conlisk-Watts method then generalizes the classical result of Elfving (1952).[15] Elfving's main result is that if the set of m possible rows of Z are represented as vectors in k-dimensional space (along with their negative extensions) assumed to be the length of β, and a convex polyhedron is constructed by combining the end points, then an optimum allocation will always lie on the boundary. Thus, at most, $p(2k-p+1)/2$ design points will be chosen, where p is the rank of the P matrix. Note that this result often will put response surface designs into conflict with ANOVA type analysis, because many design points will not be chosen. Thus, tests of the functional form assumptions embedded in X will be difficult or impossible to perform. Often, constraints of the type $n_j > r$ are added to the Conlisk-Watts framework to cause all design points to be chosen. However, without r being a fairly substantial number, we cannot hope to conduct tests of very great power for our functional form.

What is the role of controls in the Conlisk-Watts framework for response surface analysis? In principle, they have no special role to play

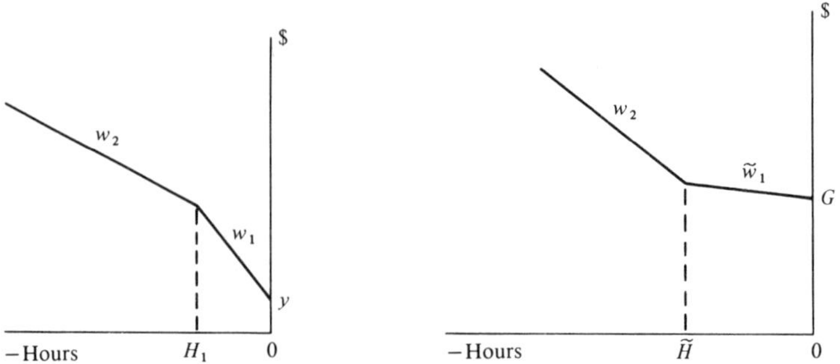

Figure 3.1. Control individual budget set. Experimental individual budget set.

as they do in the ANOVA case, where they permit calculation of the experimental effects. Because in the response surface design case we are, in principle, estimating a structural model, the unknown coefficients can be estimated solely from experimental evidence, which leads to the required variation in the right-hand-side variables. Conversely, one might argue that for a structural model no experiment may be needed at all, because the structural parameters can be estimated from nonexperimental cross-section survey data.[16] But this latter argument probably should not be taken too seriously, given the markedly different budget sets faced by NIT experimentals. Figure 3.1 indicates in a simple 2-good diagram of labor supply the difference in budget sets between controls and experimentals. In the left-hand diagram, nonlabor income is y, and the individual faces a net wage of $w_1 = w(1-t_1)$, where w is his market wage. At hours of work H_1 his earnings are such as to put him into a higher income tax bracket, so that $w_2 < w_1$. The NIT experimental individual faces the budget set on the right-hand side of Figure 3.1. He is given an income guarantee G, with $\tilde{w}_1 = w(1-t_1)$, where t_1 is around 0.5. At breakeven hours $\tilde{H}$, the income transfer has been taxed away, and he returns to the regular tax system with a greater net wage w_2. Given the convex and nonconvex budget sets faced, both controls and experimentals seem important in estimating structural models. Also, because controls were assumed to cost approximately one-fourth as much as the average experimental in designing the New Jersey NIT experiment, they were an "inexpensive" source of information. In fact, 40% of the total NIT observations were controls.

But it seems clear that preexperimental, or baseline, data give the same information that controls give. Estimation of equation (1.1) by OLS on experimental data only gives $V(\hat{\beta}) = \sigma_\epsilon^2 (X'X)^{-1}$. Now, if we decompose $\epsilon_{it} = \alpha_i + \eta_{it}$ as in equation (1.6) and consider fixed-effects estimation, we have $V(\check{\beta}) = 2\sigma_\eta^2(\check{X}'\check{X})^{-1}$, where $\check{X} = X_{i1} - X_{i2}$. In the response surface case we cannot derive analytical results as with ANOVA designs. But $(\check{X}'\check{X})$ should be at least as large as $(X'X)$, and so, in general, fixed effects with individuals acting as their own controls would seem more efficient. Now, in the response surface case the GLS estimator offers an even greater potential advantage than it did for ANOVA. To derive the optimal GLS estimator and design within the Conlisk-Watts framework, we use results from the work of Hausman (1978) and Hausman and Taylor (1980, p. 12). We define $\gamma = 1 - [\sigma_\eta^2/(\sigma_\eta^2 + 2\sigma_\alpha^2)]^{1/2}$. We then define $\tilde{X}_{it} = X_{it} - \gamma X_{i\cdot}$, where $X_{i\cdot}$ is the individual time mean. Likewise, let $\tilde{y}_{it} = y_{it} - \gamma y_{i\cdot}$, and consider the model

$$(1.8) \qquad \tilde{y}_{it} = \tilde{X}_{it}\beta + \tilde{\epsilon}_{it}, \quad t = 1, 2, \quad i = 1, \ldots, N$$

This γ transformation can be shown to lead to orthogonal $\tilde{\epsilon}_{it}$, so that OLS applied to equation (1.8) is the GLS estimator. Thus $V(\hat{\beta}_{\text{GLS}}) = [(1-\gamma)^2\sigma_\alpha^2 + (1-\gamma)\sigma_\eta^2 - \gamma^2\sigma_\eta^2/2]\cdot(\tilde{X}'\tilde{X})^{-1}$. For $\rho = 0.75$ the $\sigma_{\tilde{\epsilon}}^2$ term is 0.15 times as large as σ_η^2, whereas for $\rho = 0.5$ it is 0.41 times as large as σ_ϵ^2. Thus, substantial gains can be made so long as $(\tilde{X}'\tilde{X})$ is not too small. Now we can establish the Conlisk-Watts framework by changing equation (1.3) to read

$$(1.9) \qquad \min q(n_1, \ldots, n_m) = \operatorname{tr}\left[D\left(\sum_{j=1}^{m}\sum_{k_j=1}^{n_m} \tilde{X}_{kj}\tilde{X}'_{kj}\right)^{-1}\right]$$

$$\text{s.t.} \quad \sum_{j=1}^{m} c_j n_j \leqslant C, \quad n_j \geqslant 0 \quad \text{for all } j$$

Although closed-form analytical results cannot be determined, the general presumption in solving equation (1.9) is that the optimal design will have many fewer control observations than did the NIT experiments. Note that for controls, then, X-vector changes occur only because of time, so that for ρ at all large, γ becomes small, and the resulting $\tilde{X}$ vectors are small for controls. For experimentals, the $\tilde{X}$ vectors are much larger, because both the net wage and nonlabor income change markedly from baseline data to experimental data. For instance, nonlabor income at the origin probably changes by a factor of 6 to 10, whereas w_1 changes by a factor of about 4 for males in the sample.[17] Thus, our major conclusion is that even though control observations are estimated to be one-fourth expensive as experimental observations, we will have a greater proportion of experimentals in an optimal design when time is accounted for.

Now, a possible objection that could be raised here is that no explicit allowance is made for a time effect. In fact, we made this point earlier in our discussion of ANOVA designs. Some controls are needed if a pure time effect is to be estimated. Yet, in estimation of a structural econometric model, the time effect should be much less important than in estimation of an ANOVA specification. Consider a labor supply model from an NIT experiment. In the preexperimental period all individuals face a budget set like the left-hand side of Figure 3.1. During the experiment, individuals face the right-hand-side budget set. A structural model of labor supply specifies labor supply as a function of the after-tax wages and virtual incomes (Burtless & Hausman, 1978). It has no specific place for a time effect, because reaction to the experimental incentives comes from the wage and income response. Thus, preexperimental data are good substitutes for control data during the experiment. Again, some controls are needed to capture pure time effects, such as the collapse of a local labor market. But many fewer controls are needed in a structural model, because the relevant elasticities can be estimated from a combination of preexperimental and experimental data.

We conclude this section by briefly considering how the applications of the Conlisk-Watts design performed in practice for estimation of structural models. Two sets of structural estimates used linear structural models and attempted to account for the nonlinear budget sets while using both preexperimental and experimental observations. Hausman and Wise (1976) fit a 2-period model for New Jersey using a GLS estimator (while also accounting for sample truncation), Keeley and associates (1978) used a fixed-effects-type estimator. Both studies derived fairly precise estimates of the income and substitution effects for labor supply. However, to fully capture the complications of nonlinear budget sets such as those that appear in Figure 3.1, it seems that rather complex nonlinear structural models are required (Burtless & Hausman, 1978) for the Gary NIT experiment. Burtless and Hausman did not make use of the preexperimental evidence, but still estimated parameters quite precisely. For the types of nonlinear models used to take account of taxes, more econometric development is required before they can be used in a time series, as well as cross-sectional context. Further work on optimal design for these types of nonlinear models will also be required. Box and Lucas (1959) gave a local analysis for nonlinear models, but their analysis did not strictly apply to the taxation case, where, in a sense, the right-hand-side variables depend on the left-hand-side variable, because the net wage and virtual income are functions of the tax system and chosen hours of work.

2 Bias issues in experimental analysis

We now turn from questions of efficiency in experimental design to bias (consistency) issues in the analysis of experimental results. Because large sums of money are spent to create data of an experimental nature, we would like to consider two questions. The first question is whether or not attrition from the experiment will affect our ability to derive unbiased estimates of the experimental response within an ANOVA framework or unbiased estimates of the unknown parameters of a structural model of labor supply. The designers of the NIT experiments were aware of the possibility of attrition. In fact, Conlisk and Watts (1969, p. 154) devoted a paragraph to its possible effects on optimal experimental design. However, they were clearly thinking of random attrition, drawing an analogy to errors in laboratory experiments. But economic experiments differ in a very important manner from laboratory experiments because of the possibility of nonrandom attrition. Individuals who receive benefits from an experiment are less likely to drop out than either controls or experimentals who do not receive benefits. Thus a self-selection process is set up among experimental subjects that can bias the estimates of (population) experimental responses.

The second question we plan to look at is, apart from attrition, whether or not the estimates that are derived from a temporary experiment can be taken as unbiased estimates of the effects of nationwide adoption of a permanent NIT program.[18] At least two problems occur here. Experimental subjects know that the experiment is only temporary. Economic behavior, in most cases, is affected differently by permanent programs than by temporary programs. Perhaps even more important is the fact that in an experiment we typically see only the partial-equilibrium response of one side of the market. In a nationwide NIT program we might well expect the demand side of labor markets to respond to the different budget sets faced by low-income workers. Figure 3.1 illustrates the problem. Because the budget set under a NIT is nonconvex, an individual may well be better off by supplying hours of work equal to 0 and H^* every other period than some $H^{**} < H^*$ each period. The budget set is shifted outward by such behavior; the unknown question would be the elasticity of substitution of leisure across periods in an intertemporal utility function.[19] In a temporary experiment, such labor market behavior is unlikely because of the costs of adjusting behavior in terms of lower wages and difficulty in finding a job. But in a permanent nationwide program, employers might well find it advantageous to permit such behavior without penalty. Then experimental evidence might not provide a reliable guide to the actual effects of a permanent NIT program.

We now consider the possible effects of nonrandom attrition. As Figure 3.1 indicates, the NIT program has the effect of moving the budget set outward for an experimental individual. Thus, for an individual below breakeven hours, $\tilde{H}$, he is made better off by participating in the experiment. However, experimental individuals above breakeven hours and controls receive only a nominal payment for participating in the experiment. But a potentially important difference exists. Whereas a control is assured only of his nominal payment, an experimental individual also benefits from the insurance policy aspect of participating in the experiment. If either his market wage or actual hours of work fall unexpectedly, the individual will begin to receive experimental payments when his earnings fall below breakeven. It is well established that low-income individuals have considerable stochastic fluctuations in their earnings (Lillard & Willis, 1978). The insurance aspect of participation becomes more important the closer the individual's desired earnings are to his breakeven earnings.

To consider the possible effects of attrition on estimation, let us permit two sources of attrition: random attrition and self-selection out of the experiment. Let the self-selection depend on a choice process that compares maximized utilities inside and out of the experiment.

$$g(w,y,Z,G,t) = U_1(w_1,w_2,y,Z) + e_1 - U_2(\tilde{w}_1,w_2,G,Z) - k(Z) + e_2 \gtreqless 0 \tag{2.1}$$

Here the first utility function corresponds to not being a participant, with wages and nonlabor income corresponding to Figure 3.1. The vector Z represents socioeconomic characteristics. The second utility function corresponds to experimental participation, with $\tilde{w}_1$ the net wage and G the guarantee; $k(Z)$ is assumed a random variable that varies across the population and represents the net cost of experimental participation. The other two terms, e_1 and e_2 are assumed i.i.d. random variables. We assume that the individual drops out if equation (2.1) is positive.

Now let us consider potential bias in estimation within an ANOVA framework, assuming experimental assignment uncorrelated with α_i and η_{i1} in equation (1.6). If we do least squares using only experimental evidence, and therefore comparing controls to experimentals, we expect two effects of opposite sign. Experimental individuals who are not below breakeven hours are more likely to drop out, other things being equal. Also, individuals further away from breakeven are more probable attriters. Thus, the effect should be greater the less generous is the experimental plan (i.e., lower guarantee G or higher tax rate t_1, which lowers w_1). On the other hand, we would expect to have net cost $k(Z)$ decrease with higher income, because factors such as education and age should affect costs. But among experimentals we expect high-income individuals to be more likely to remain in the experiment. Thus, a cross-section estimate would seem likely to have an upward bias in experimental response, with the sign of the bias increasing with decreasing program generosity. Assuming joint normality in equations (1.6) and (2.1), we have the attrition specification of Hausman and Wise (1979).[20]

$$(2.2) \qquad E(y_{2i} \mid Z) = \mu + \beta_j \delta_{jt} + \sigma_{\epsilon e} \frac{\phi(g(\theta))}{\Phi(g(\theta))}$$

where $\sigma_{\epsilon e}$ is the covariance of ϵ_{it} from equation (1.6) and the stochastic term from equation (2.1) denoted e. The ratio $\phi(g(\theta))/\Phi(g(\theta))$ is a function of unknown parameters θ from equation (2.1) and is the ratio of a normal density function divided by the distribution function. Now let us consider what happens if we bring time in, through the use of preexperimental observations. The GLS estimator usually will be less biased than OLS on experimental information. We can see this effect by considering the fixed-effects estimation, which has expectation

$$(2.3) \qquad E(y_{2i} - y_{1i} \mid Z) = \beta_j \delta_{jt} + \sigma_{\epsilon e} \frac{\phi(g(\theta))}{\Phi(g(\theta))}$$

The covariance term $\sigma_{\eta e}$ should be less than $\sigma_{\epsilon e}$ because α_i has been eliminated by the differing procedure. Thus the fixed-effects estimates have less bias than the OLS estimates. Because GLS is a weighted average of fixed effects and the between estimates that has bias terms similar to equation (2.2), the final average should be less biased when preexperimental evidence is used. Thus, we evaluate potential attrition bias to be important in the case of both equations (2.2) and (2.3). However, the use of preexperimental evidence should decrease the effect of attrition on the final estimates. This analysis corroborates the findings of Hausman and Wise (1979) that inclusion of a regression specification for μ decreased markedly the effect of attrition bias on their estimates.

We now turn to possible bias effects caused by the limited duration of the experiment, a topic first analyzed by Metcalf (1973).[21] Consider a 2-period model for individuals below breakeven. For N equal periods, where the NIT experiment occurs in period 1, denote the appropriate discount rate by $R = \Sigma_{i=2}^{N} 1/(1+r)^{i-1}$. Assume perfect capital markets and assume that the market wage received does not depend on either total experience or labor market history. For a temporary experiment in period 1, the net wage is $\tilde{w}_1 = w(1-t_1)$, with t_1 around 0.5 and nonlabor income equal to the guarantee G. In period 2, the net wage is $w_2 = w(1-t_2) > w_1$, and nonlabor income is $y < G$. Indirect utility can be written as

$$V^T = V(\tilde{w}_1, Rw_2, Rp_2, G + Ry) \tag{2.4}$$

where p_1, the price of the consumption good in period 1, is numeraire, and p_2 is the price of consumption in period 2. Under a permanent NIT program, we have

$$V^P = V(\tilde{w}_1, R\tilde{w}_2, Rp_2, G(1 + R)) \tag{2.5}$$

Roy's identity gives labor supply, $h_1^T = V_{w_1}^T / V_m^T$, where subscripts denote derivatives and $m = G + Ry$, the intertemporal budget constraint. Note that, in general, we cannot say whether or not h_1^T exceeds h_1^P without more specific assumptions. The numerator is greater in the temporary case versus the permanent case, but the denominator is greater also, so long as $V_{w_1 m} < 0$. Let us consider the derivatives of labor supply with respect to G and t_1. We calculate

(2.6)

$$\frac{\partial h_1^P}{\partial G} - \frac{\partial h_1^T}{\partial G} = V_{w_1 m}^T / V_m^T - V_{w_1}^T / V_{mm}^T (-V_{w_1 m}^P / V_m^P + V_{w_1}^P / V_{mm}^P)(1+R)$$

If leisure is a normal good, then equation (2.6) is positive. But no more specific result seems possible, because the indirect utility function is being evaluated at two different points. Even the assumption of separability or additivity across periods (in either the indirect or direct utility function) leads to no more definite result. Equation (2.6) holds because we are expanding the lifetime budget set so that the individual demands more leisure in each period as G increases, with a larger derivative in the case in which his lifetime budget is greater. In a similar manner, the permanent uncompensated wage effect can be shown to be smaller for a permanent program than for a temporary program. Within an ANOVA analysis, I would expect the measured experimental effect to be a downward-biased estimate of the experimental effort under a permanent program for males that we consider in the next section. Nonexperimental cross-section results almost always find a near-zero uncompensated wage effect (Hall, 1973; Hausman, 1980). On the other hand, for the New Jersey experiment (Hausman & Wise, 1976) and for the Gary experiment (Burtless & Hausman, 1978) the income effect was found to be almost the sole explanation for experimental response. In fact, our results in the next section show a larger experimental effect for 5-year participants in SIME/DIME versus 3-year participants. Thus, equation (2.6) gives the direction of bias.[22] For females, the total direction of bias is not clear, because they also have a significant uncompensated wage effect.

We have now separately considered possible attrition effects and duration effects, but in a full model, the two effects will indeed interact. In SIME/DIME, where both 3- and 5-year experimental programs were conducted, we can attempt to measure bias. The insurance aspect of the NIT should cause less attrition among 5-year participants than among 3-year participants in SIME/DIME. But because more attrition occurs for less generous plans where the experimental effect is smaller, it would seem that even the 5-year response has a downward bias in its estimate, so that comparisons between 3-year and 5-year results are not straightforward. The empirical results in the next section support this prediction. Thus, it seems important to jointly take account of attrition and duration factors in evaluating experimental results. Again, it seems that the factor of time is extremely important in thinking about social and economic experiments.

3 Empirical results

In this section we estimate experimental effects for each of the three urban NIT experiments: New Jersey, Gary, and SIME/DIME. For each experiment we estimate an overall experiment effect and attempt to analyze the effects of attrition bias and duration bias on the results.[23] The experiments all have the same general format. Each experimental participant had an income guarantee G and a tax rate t_1. Each participant was enrolled in the experiment for 3 years, with 1 year of preexperimental or baseline data collected. Approximately one-fourth of the experimental individuals were enrolled in the experiment for either 5 years or 20 years in SIME/DIME. A group of controls was also present. They received only a nominal payment for their participation. An important fact to note is that the generosity of the experimental plans varied markedly. For instance, SIME/DIME was considerably more generous in its guarantee than the other two experiments. Thus, the experimental effects estimated across the three experiments are not directly comparable.

We limit our sample to males who were heads of households. We also consider earnings, rather than hours, to measure experimental response.

Earnings seem more appropriate, because they indicate the cost of an NIT program. The definition of attrition used is somewhat broad in scope. We include in the sample individuals who did not drop out and who did not change marital status during the experiment. The latter choice may be somewhat controversial, but because we compare preexperimental and experimental data, it does not seem correct to compare a male head of family with himself when he no longer heads a family, so that his financial obligations and experimental incentives have changed markedly. Our estimates are done on the third year of experimental data. Attrition at this point was at a maximum, so that we should be able to tell how serious a problem it is for the experimental analysis.

To describe briefly the experimental designs, we list the guarantee levels and tax rates for each of the experiments. However, as discussed in Section 1, the actual designs used were considerably more complicated; for instance, in New Jersey a quadratic response surface was used. The New Jersey experiment had four guarantee levels and three tax rates. The guarantee levels were based on the poverty level, which was adjusted for family size. In 1968, when the experiment began, the poverty level for a family of four in New Jersey was \$3,335. The four guarantee levels used in New Jersey were 0.5, 0.75, 1.0, and 1.25 times the poverty limit.[24] The three tax rates used were 0.3, 0.5, and 0.7 up to the breakeven level, where the experiment returned to the regular IRS tax schedule. For the New Jersey experiment we limit our sample to white males so that we can compare the results to previous work. In actuality, most of the sample was from Scranton, Pennsylvania. In Gary, the experiment was limited to black males. Two guarantees and two tax rates were used. The guarantee levels were 0.75 and 1.0 times the poverty limit, which was \$4,300 for a family of four in 1971 when the experiment began. The two tax rates used were 0.4 and 0.6 up to the breakeven point. Lastly, the SIME/DIME experiment, which was considerably larger than the other two experiments, had a more complex experimental treatment. Three guarantee levels were used: \$3,800, \$4,800, and \$5,600 for a family of four. The guarantees were adjusted for family size. Three tax rates were used: 0.5, 0.7, and 0.8 up to breakeven levels. However, the 0.8 tax rate decreased by 0.025 per \$1,000 earned. Two of the five 0.7 tax rate treatments had the same feature. Also, experimental treatment was stated in advance to be for wither 3 or 5 years.[25] Lastly, three different manpower counseling treatments were used with different levels of reimbursement. Thus, each experiment had numerous treatment blocks, so many that full ANOVA estimation is impractical because of small sample sizes. Instead, we estimate the mean effect of each experiment.

We now consider some evidence in an attempt to assess how serious a problem nonrandom attrition may be. Our conclusion is that the participants, both experimentals and controls, gave remarkable evidence of nonrandom attrition. In fact, nearly all the predictions of the preceding section hold in each and every case. In Table 3.1 the gross attrition data are given. Note that in each experiment greater attrition occurred among controls than among experimentals, as the model of equation (2.3) predicts. Using a normal approximation to the binomial (and assuming equal variances), in each case the hypothesis of no difference is rejected at a test level of $\alpha=0.05$. For both New Jersey and Denver the t statistic exceeds 3.0. Also note that in the Denver experiment, where two different experimental durations were used, we find that the attrition among 3-year experimental individuals exceeded the attrition among 5-year individuals.

We now take a somewhat finer look at the data to see how attrition varies with the financial generosity of each experiment. According to the results given in Section 2, we would expect low attrition for more generous financial plans with either higher guarantee levels or lower tax rates. Table 3.2 gives results for New Jersey. Note that attrition monotonically declines with the support level, except for level 0.75; for the middle quintile of preexperimental earnings the decline is strictly monotonic. On the other hand, attrition increases with an increasing tax rate monotonically in both columns. Thus, we conclude that the financial incentives of the experiment seemed to induce just the expected pattern of attrition. Lastly, note that individuals with the lowest support level, 0.50, had only a slightly lower attrition rate than did controls. Again, this is expected, because very few families would choose to live at such a low standard of living if they were below breakeven level.

For Gary, we find exactly the expected pattern of attrition. The attrition proportion for the low support level was 0.703 and for the high support level 0.607; for the low tax level it was 0.641 and for the high tax level 0.679. The pattern of results is identical for the middle quintile of the wage distribution. We now consider the results from Denver. They are the most interesting, because 3-year and 5-year experimental programs were used. Thus the effects of both attrition and duration can be investigated. The results are presented in Table 3.3. Attrition declined monotonically with support level. It was also greater in each case for the 3-year sample than for the 5-year sample. For tax rates, the results were not quite so uniform. At the highest tax rate, attrition was less than expected. Still, when we take a closer look at the data, we find that individuals with a lower tax rate, due to the 0.025 decrease, were less likely to drop out than were individuals with the corresponding higher tax rate.

Table 3.1 *Overall attrition results*

Experiment location	Overall	Experimentals	Controls
New Jersey	0.377	0.322	0.465
Gary[a]	0.693	0.662	0.740
Denver	0.302	0.286	0.344
Denver 3-year	—	0.299	—
Denver 5-year	—	0.252	—

[a] Our results show remarkably high attrition in the third year of the experiment. This problem needs further investigation.

Table 3.2 *Attrition results for New Jersey*

Support level	Overall	Middle quintile	Tax rate	Overall	Middle quintile
0.50	0.424	0.444	0.3	0.244	0.167
0.75	0.264	0.191	0.5	0.325	0.250
1.0	0.392	0.161	0.7	0.375	0.571
1.25	0.256	0.111			

Table 3.3 *Attrition results for Denver*

Support level	Overall	3-Year	5-Year	Middle quintile	Tax level	Overall	3-Year	5-Year	Middle quintile
\$3800	0.349	0.383	0.294	0.352	0.50	0.250	0.281	0.202	0.174
\$4800	0.288	0.301	0.263	0.279	0.70	0.333	0.329	0.340	0.314
\$5600	0.221	0.224	0.214	0.093	0.80	0.250	0.268	0.218	0.167

Thus, the results strongly indicate the importance of economic incentives for attrition. However, they cannot be considered conclusive, because they could represent random attrition with different attrition probabilities at different design points (a possibility pointed out to me by John Conlisk). Only within the context of a particular model specification can we test for nonrandom attrition. In our model specification, to which we now turn, we attempt to capture the possibility of nonrandom attrition with a variable that indicates whether or not the individual will be above breakeven given his preexperimental labor supply and experimental guarantee level and tax level. This specification is in keeping with our single experimental effect variable and also leads to a simpler specification of attrition.[26]

We first present empirical results for Gary and Denver using a model of attrition presented by Hausman and Wise (1979). The model has two earnings equations that correspond to equation (1.6). We specify a variance components structure with $\rho_{12}=\sigma_\alpha^2/(\sigma_\alpha^2+\sigma_\eta^2)$. We also specify a reduced-form probit equation for attrition that corresponds to equation (2.1). The crucial parameter to determine if attrition bias is important is ρ_{23}, the correlation between the experimental equation residual and the probit residual. This correlation corresponds to the bias term in equation (2.2) that occurs if attrition leads to biased estimates. We compare our results to the case of setting $\rho_{23}=0$, that is, the usual random-effects estimator that does not account for attrition.

Therefore, our model consists of the three equations

$$
\begin{aligned}
y_{i1} &= X_{i1}\beta + \epsilon_{i1} \\
y_{i2} &= X_{i2}\beta + \epsilon_{i2} \qquad (3.1)\\
A_i &= R_i\delta + \epsilon_{i3}
\end{aligned}
$$

Attrition occurs if the latent variable $A_i \leqslant 0$. The critical parameter in the determination of attrition bias is the correlation ρ_{23} between ϵ_{i2} and ϵ_{i3}. We want a method of estimation that will yield asymptotically efficient and consistent estimates of the structural parameters of equation (3.1) and will allow a convenient test of the hypothesis that $\rho_{23}=0$. We shall use a maximum likelihood procedure. We assume joint normality so that the terms ϵ_{i1}, ϵ_{i2}, and ϵ_{i3} have mean zero and covariance matrix

$$
\Sigma = \begin{bmatrix} \sigma^2 & \rho_{12}\sigma^2 & \rho_{12}\rho_{23}\sigma \\ & \sigma^2 & \rho_{23}\sigma \\ & & 1 \end{bmatrix} \qquad (3.2)
$$

where $\sigma_{11}=\sigma_{22}=\sigma^2$, and we have normalized by setting $\sigma_{33}=1$. We need to consider two possibilities: $a_i=1$ and $a_i=0$. If $a_i=1$, both y_{i1} and y_{i2} are observed, and the joint density of a_i, y_{i1}, and y_{12} is given by

$$
\begin{aligned}
f(a_i = 1, y_{i1}, y_{i2}) &= \mathrm{pr}[a_i = 1 \mid y_{i1}, y_{i2}]f(y_{i2} \mid y_{i1})f(y_{i1}) \\
&= \Phi\left[\frac{R_i\delta + (\rho_{23}/\sigma)(y_{i2}-X_{i2}\beta)}{(1-\rho_{23}^2)^{1/2}}\right]\frac{1}{(\sigma^2(1-\rho_{12}^2))^{1/2}} \qquad (3.3)\\
&\quad \cdot \phi\left(\frac{y_{12}-\rho_{12}Y_{i1}-(X_{i2}-\rho_{12}X_{i1})\beta}{(\sigma^2(1-\rho_{12}^2))^{1/2}}\right)\frac{1}{\sigma}\phi\left(\frac{y_{i1}-X_{i1}\beta}{\sigma}\right)
\end{aligned}
$$

where the first term follows from the fact that the conditional density $f(\epsilon_{13} \mid \epsilon_{12})$ is $N((\rho_{23}/\sigma)\epsilon_{i2}, 1-\rho_{23}^2)$. If $a_i=0$, y_{i2} is not observed and must be "integrated out." In this instance the fact that $f(\epsilon_{i3} \mid \epsilon_{i1})$ is $N((\rho_{12}\rho_{23}/\sigma)\epsilon_{i1},\ 1-\rho_{12}^2\rho_{23}^2)$ leads to the expression

$$f(a_1=0, y_{i1}) = \text{pr}[a_i = 0 \mid y_{i1}]f(y_{i1})$$

$$= 1-\Phi\left[\frac{R_i\delta + (\rho_{12}\rho_{23}/\sigma)(y_{i1}-X_{i1}\beta)}{(1-\rho_{12}^2\rho_{23}^2)^{1/2}}\right]\frac{1}{\sigma}\phi\left(\frac{y_{i1}-X_{i1}\beta}{\sigma}\right) \tag{3.4}$$

We form the likelihood from equations (3.3) and (3.4) and estimate the parameters via maximum likelihood. The assumption of joint normality may be problematical; for analysis of the effect of nonnormality in a more simple case, see the work of Goldberger (1980). However, the argument for log earnings to be distributed as approximately normal is fairly well accepted in the literature. Specification of nonnormal models is straightforward, as discussed earlier. However, we do not yet have computer routines to do the required numerical integration with sufficient speed to be used in an iterative program with large amounts of data.

In Table 3.4 we present the experimental results for Gary for those individuals who did not drop out of the experiment. Our specification differs from those of Hausman and Wise (1979) and Hall (1975) in that we allow for different preexperimental mean earnings and experimentals. Because of differential attrition, the mean can be different between the two groups, experimentals and controls. The first column is the random-effects estimate. Note that we find a significant experimental effect of a drop of 0.255 in earnings. We also find ρ_{12} to be quite important. Converted to a 1-year basis, it would equal 0.624, which is in line with the results of previous research. In the second column of Table 3.4 we run ANCOVA, adding as regressors age, education, and AFDC in preexperimental year. Hausman and Wise (1979) found that this specification reduced attrition bias significantly. The addition of these variables reduces the preexperimental mean difference and raises the experimental effect to 0.388, with marginal statistical significance. However, the two results on experimental differences are not significant at the usual test sizes (Hausman, 1978). In the second part of Table 3.4 we present the attrition model results. Note that the experimental effect has now fallen to 0.048, much below the previous two estimates. For the probit specification for attrition, experimental status and above break-even both have the expected signs (other variables in the probit specification are education, age, and other income). Lastly, note that the attrition parameter ρ_{23} equals -0.276, although it is not estimated very precisely. Thus, for the Gary results we find that allowing for the effects of attrition led to a large decrease in the measurement of experimental

Table 3.4 *Regression results for Gary: log earnings equations*

Variable	ANOVA specification	ANOVA specification	Attrition model	Earnings equation	Probit variables	Probit equation
Preexperiment difference	1.233	0.4818	Preexperiment difference	0.3790	Constant	0.2068
	(0.4314)	(0.3318)		(0.2572)		(0.5091)
Experimental effect	−0.2552	−0.3886	Experimental effect	−0.0481	Experimental	+0.0592
	(0.1121)	(0.2343)		(0.0270)		(0.0483)
Time (quarters)	0.0153	0.0137	Time	0.0133	Above breakeven	−0.2806
	(0.0043)	(0.0034)		(0.0053)		(0.1491)
ρ_{12}	0.243	—	ρ_{12}	0.4951	ρ_{23}	−0.276
				(0.0581)		(0.187)

Table 3.5 *Regression results for Denver: log earnings equations*

Variable	ANOVA specification	ANOVA specification	Attrition model	Earnings equation	Probit variables	Probit equation
Preexperiment difference	−0.1152 (0.1126)	−0.1411 (0.1248)	Preexperiment difference	−0.0291 0.1132	Experimental	0.2311 (0.144)
3-Year experimental effect	−0.0902 (0.0537)	−0.1245 (0.0784)	3-Year experimental effect	−0.1604 (0.1049)	5-Year experimental effect	0.2267 (0.0857)
5-Year experimental effect	−0.1036 (0.0625)	−0.1297 (0.1078)	5-Year experimental effect	−0.2248 (0.1008)	Above breakeven	−0.0141 (0.0146)
Time	0.0090 (0.0051)	0.0095 (0.0061)	Time	0.0071 (0.0058)	Manpower program	0.5752 (0.0828)
ρ_{12}	0.3440	—	ρ_{12}	0.445 (0.020)	ρ_{23}	0.271 (0.103)

Table 3.6 *Regression results for New Jersey: log earnings equations*

Variable	ANOVA specification	ANOVA specification	Attrition model	Earnings equation	Probit variables	Probit equation
Preexperiment difference	0.1942 (0.3113)	0.2321 (0.3151)	Preexperiment difference	0.1963 (0.2651)	Constant	0.2929 (0.5504)
Experimental effect	−0.1032 (0.0261)	−0.2458 (0.1301)	Experimental effect	−0.2610 (0.0909)	Experimental	0.5854 (0.3402)
Time	0.0055 (0.0069)	0.0167 (0.0208)	Time	0.0081 (0.0132)	Above breakeven	−0.7403 (0.3408)
ρ_{12}	0.456	—	ρ_{12}	0.255 (0.068)	ρ_{23}	0.709 (0.061)

effect. However, remember that attrition in our Gary sample was especially severe. This finding is what we expected from the discussion in Section 2.

We next turn to our results from Denver. The sample is much larger than that for Gary, and the amount of truncation is very much smaller. The results are presented in Table 3.5. Here the estimated results are more precise. Without attrition we measure the experimental effect to be −0.090 for 3-year people and −0.1036 for 5-year people. Thus the difference in duration does not seem to have much effect. But when we turn to the attrition specification we find that the 3-year experimental effect rises to −0.160, and the 5-year effect is measured at −0.225. Thus, when attrition is accounted for, the duration difference rises to 0.065, which leads us to suspect that the effect of limited duration experiments may well be important. By looking at the attrition specification in the probit equation, we see the reason for the change in results. Experimentals are less likely to drop out, 5-year experimentals even less so than 3-year experimentals. The preceding breakeven variable has the expected sign but is quite small in magnitude, whereas the manpower program variable is quite important. Lastly, ρ_{23} is quite significant, which implies that attrition is important for the Denver estimates.

The last set of results is for New Jersey (Table 3.6). Here we plan not only to account for attrition but also to account for single truncation in the original experimental design (Hausman & Wise, 1976). But for the current time we present results accounting only for attrition. The results again demonstrate that attrition has an important effect on the results. The experimental effect rises in magnitude from −0.103 to −0.261 when attrition is accounted for. Here the ANOVA specification comes very close to the attrition results that Hausman and Wise (1979) found in their earlier work. However, this result did not occur in the Gary and Denver results. A last unexplained result is that in Denver and New Jersey (but not Gary) the parameter ρ_{23} had the opposite sign from what we might expect.

The results of this section indicate that both attrition effects and duration effects have important bearing on the analysis of economic experiments. Because the attrition tables showed a clear reaction to the economic incentives of the experiments, we might well expect these results. But the results are not quite as straightforward as might be hoped for. We cannot simply state that failure to account for attrition biases the results upward. More investigation of the problem is required, including the interaction of attrition effects and duration effects with the experimental designs. Most important, further work on experimental design is needed to account for the attrition problem, which seems likely to be present in almost all economic experiments that take place over time.

NOTES

1 I would like to thank my collaborators over the years, David Wise, Dennis Aigner, and Gary Burtless, for adding to my knowledge in these areas. Many other people have also discussed some of the issues in this chapter with me at some time. Conversations with Herman Chernoff, Zvi Griliches, Robert Hall, Ken Kehrer, and Robert Moffitt have been especially helpful. John Conlisk provided extremely helpful comments on an initial version of the manuscript. Paul Ruud and Ken West provided research assistance.

2 Numerous demonstration programs have also been sponsored by the federal government. The programs are designed to indicate how a proposed government program would operate. However, they typically lack any consideration of experimental design. A substantial improvement might be to introduce such considerations to help in interpretation of the results.

3 I do not want to give the impression that other sciences are uniformly successful in their use of experiments. Medical experiments often lead to conflicting interpretations of the results.

4 A recent exposition of classical design theory is continued in the work of John and Quenouille (1977). An excellent introduction to the literature is provided by Aigner (1979).

5 Although these issues have been addressed in the experimental design literature, the statistical theory has been studied mainly in the design and analysis of split-plot experiments (John & Quenouille, 1977, Chapters 4–5). Also see the work of Cox (1958).

6 If stratification in design has taken place, the x vectors can be regarded as representing the interaction of experimental treatment and stratified block.

7 Other criteria have been discussed by Kiefer (1959) and Wynn (1972). Aigner (1979) gave a clear discussion of the issues.

8 However, we do not want to overemphasize the importance of controls. Instead of an estimate of an experimental effect, $\hat{\beta}_j - \hat{\beta}_1$, we might also be interested in the difference between the two experimental effects, $\hat{\beta}_j - \hat{\beta}_k$ (e.g., for a given guarantee level how experimental response changes for two different tax rates in an NIT program). Then the appropriate row of the P matrix will have 1's in the jth and kth positions. Equation (1.4) will change, in the numerator and denominator, w_j's to reflect how many 1's are in the jth column of the P matrix.

9 Hall (1975) pointed out the large gains involved in the case of all c_j's equal for one experimental treatment. He found even larger gains than I did by assuming that controls cost the same as experimentals, which probably is not true for most social experiments. Conlisk (1979) also indicated gains in estimation efficiency by making use of preexperimental data, but emphasized the importance of control observations for estimation of a time effect.

10 A natural question is how much better GLS or fixed effects do on their optimal design than on the design of equation (1.4), assuming that preexperi-

mental data exist. For fixed effects, the control observations are useless, and for GLS they help only slightly. Thus the proportion of the budget C allocated to controls divided by the ratio of c_j's gives the result. For $m=8$, $c_1=1$, $c_j=4$, $j=2$, the optimal design does 1.2 times as well.

11 The technique described by Hall has long been known in the experimental design literature as a crossover (or changeover) design (Cox, 1958). However, it has remained a controversial technique because of the possibility of bias arising from carryover effects from the treatment. For a test of carryover effects, see the work of Grizzle (1965).

12 However, P will have rank far less than 59 for most analyses, because the number of different experimental treatments equals 18. We will be interested in only these 18 treatments for population estimates.

13 This approach was used by Hausman and Tremble (1980) for an electricity usage survey. For use on income, this suggestion needs further development, because we are interested in being able to group individuals into income categories rather than predict their actual incomes.

14 A quadratic response surface in the guarantee and tax rates, with interaction terms, was used.

15 Aigner (1979) gave a clear explanation of response surface methods.

16 Although this argument is valid for the NIT case, it clearly does not hold for the time-of-day electricity experiments, where no variation in residential time-of-day prices existed before the experiments.

17 For females who head households, the changes are substantially less, because in the preexperimental period most qualify for AFDC.

18 Of course, some economic experiments, such as the time-of-day electricity experiments, are designed only to measure short-run effects. Problems of self-selection may still occur (Aigner & Hausman, 1980).

19 The length of the accounting period is crucial here. The problem will be much more severe for a monthly or quarterly accounting period than for a yearly period. Unfortunately, policy discussions seem to be tending toward shorter accounting periods for income maintenance programs.

20 Actually, the conditional expectation taken here depends only on joint normality for the specific normal density and distribution functions. The addition term remains in the more general case when appropriate conditional densities and distributions are used. However, the computational problem that arises in estimation may be considerably more difficult (Olsen, 1979). Ashenfelter (1980) also developed an interesting structural model of attrition.

21 We consider a 2-period model quite similar to that of Metcalf, although we use a duality approach that simplifies matters considerably. However, our results differ from Metcalf's in measurement of bias. His results seem correct, in general, only under the assumption that we evaluate derivatives at $G=0$, $t_1=t_2$, which is not the case when evaluating the differential response to a temporary experiment or a permanent program. Metcalf failed to notice that unless this condition holds, the labor supply derivatives differ in permanent and transitory programs, because the individual is on two different indifference curves.

22 Keeley and associates (1978) did find a significant substitution effect in SIME/DIME, but still the income effect is larger. Burtless and Greenberg (1980) found results in a statistical model in broad agreement with the theory. However, the magnitude of some of their results seems implausible. Differential

attrition may be the cause of the problem, given the results we present in the next section. Ashenfelter (1980) found no significant difference.

23 We do not attempt estimates of structural models for the three experiments. However, Hausman and Wise (1976) for New Jersey, Burtless and Hausman (1978) for Gary, and Keeley and associates (1978) for SIME/DIME fit structural labor supply models. Attrition was not accounted for in these reports.

24 In the New Jersey experiment, no one was enrolled whose preexperimental income exceeded 1.5 times the poverty limit. This sample truncation leads to important considerations for estimation (Hausman & Wise, 1976).

25 We disregard the 20-year plans, because they affect few individuals.

26 In the study of Hausman and Wise (1979), four different dummy variables were used for attrition in Gary. The estimated parameters had the expected ordering, but only two of the four estimates were precise enough to reject the hypothesis of no effect.

REFERENCES

Aigner, D. J. 1979. "A Brief Introduction to the Methodology of Optimal Experimental Design." *Journal of Econometrics* 11:7–26.

Aigner, D. J., and Hausman, J. 1980. "Correcting for Truncation Bias in the Analysis of Experiments in Time-of-Day Pricing of Electricity." *Bell Journal of Economics* 11:131–42.

Ashenfelter, O. 1980. "Discrete Choice in Labor Supply: The Determinants of Participation in the Seattle and Denver Income Maintenance Experiments." Working paper 136, Department of Economics, Princeton University.

Box, G. E. P., and Lucas, H. L. 1959. "Design of Experiments in Non-Linear Situations." *Biometrika* 46:77–90.

Burtless, G., and Greenberg, D. 1980. "Inferences Concerning Labor Supply Behavior Based on Limited-Duration Experiments." U.S. Department of Labor and SRI International.

Burtless, G., and Hausman, J. A. 1978. "The Effect of Taxation on Labor Supply: Evaluating the Gary Negative Income Tax Experiment." *Journal of Political Economy* 86:1103–30.

Chernoff, H. 1977. *Sequential Analysis and Optimal Design.* Philadelphia: Society for Industrial and Applied Mathematics.

Conlisk, J. 1973. "Choice of Response Functional Form in Designing Subsidy Experiments." *Econometrica* 41:643–56.

Conlisk, J. 1979. "Choice of Sample Size in Evaluating Manpower Programs." *Research in Labor Economics* (Supplement 1) 79–96.

Conlisk, J., and Watts, H. 1969. "A Model for Optimizing Experimental Designs for Estimating Response Surfaces." *American Statistical Association Proceedings in Social Statistics Section* 64:150–6.

Cox, D. R. 1958. *Planning of Experiments.* New York: Wiley.

Elfving, G. 1952. "Optimum Allocation in Linear Regression Theory." *Annals of Mathematical Statistics* 23:255–62.

Fisher, R. A. 1971. *The Design of Experiments,* 8th edition. New York: Hafner.

Goldberger, A. 1980. "Abnormal Selection." Mimeograph, University of Wisconsin.

Grizzle, J. E. 1965. "The Two Period Changeover Design." *Biometrics* 21:467–80.

Hall, R. E. 1973. "Wages, Income, and Hours of Work in the U.S." In *Income Maintenance and Labor Supply,* edited by G. Cain and H. Watts, pp. 102–76. Chicago: Rand McNally.

Hall, R. E. 1975. "Effects of the Experimental Negative Income Tax on Labor Supply." In *Work Incentives and Income Guarantees: The New Jersey Negative Income Tax Experiment,* edited by J. Pechman and H. Timpane, pp. 115–56. Washington, D.C.: Brookings Institution.

Hausman, J. 1978. "Specification Tests in Econometrics." *Econometrica* 46:1251–71.

Hausman, J. 1981. "The Effect of Taxes on Labor Supply." In *How Taxes Affect Economic Activity,* edited by H. Aaron and J. Pechman, pp. 27–83. Washington, D.C.: Brookings Institution.

Hausman, J., and Taylor, W. 1981. "Panel Data and Unobservable Individual Effects." *Econometrica* 49: 1377–1398.

Hausman, J., and Tremble, J. 1980. "Sample Selection for the Vermont TOD User Survey." Mimeograph, Oak Ridge National Laboratories.

Hausman, J., and Wise, D. 1976. "The Evaluation of Results from Truncated Samples: The New Jersey Income Maintenance Experiment." *Annals of Economic and Social Measurement* 5:421–45.

Hausman, J., and Wise, D. 1979. "Attrition Bias in Experimental and Panel Data: The Gary Income Maintenance Experiment." *Econometrica* 47:455–73.

Hausman, J., and Wise, D. 1981. "Endogenous Stratification and Estimation." In *Econometric Analysis of Discrete Data,* edited by C. Manski and D. McFadden. Cambridge, Mass.: MIT Press.

John, J. A., and Quenouille, M. H. 1977. *Experiments: Design and Analysis.* New York: Macmillan.

Keeley, M. C., Robins, P., Spiegelman, R., and West, R. 1978. "The Estimation of Labor Supply Models Using Experimental Data." *American Economic Review* 68:873–87.

Kiefer, J. 1959. "Optimum Experimental Designs." *Journal of the Royal Statistical Society* (B) 21:272–304.

Lillard, A., and Willis, R. J. 1978. "Dynamic Aspects of Earning Mobility." *Econometrica* 46:985–1012.

Maddala, G. S. 1971. "The Use of Variance Components Models in Pooling Cross-section and Time Series Data." *Econometrica* 39:341–58.

Metcalf, C. E. 1973. "Making Inferences from Controlled Income Maintenance Experiments." *American Economic Review* 63:478–83.

Mundlak, Y. 1978. "On the Pooling of Time Series and Cross Section Data." *Econometrica* 46:69–86.

Olsen, R. 1979. "Distributional Tests for Selectivity Bias and a More Robust Likelihood Estimator." Mimeograph, Yale University.

Wynn, H. P. 1972. "Results in the Theory and Construction of D-Optimum Experimental Designs." *Journal of the Royal Statistical Society* (B) 34:133–47.

PART IV

SMALL-SAMPLE DISTRIBUTION THEORY

CHAPTER 4

Some recent developments on the distributions of single-equation estimators

T. W. Anderson

1 Introduction

Many econometric models are based on sets of simultaneous structural equations. Although there are methods for estimating the parameters of the entire system, procedures for single equations are relevant, because often only one in a small number of equations is of interest and because such procedures are much easier to carry out than full-system methods. Recently, the properties of these single-equation methods have been investigated extensively. The purpose of this chapter is to review some of these studies. Because this chapter is limited, we shall focus our attention on the two-stage least-squares (TSLS) estimator and the limited-information maximum-likelihood (LIML) estimator, which is also known as the least-variance-ratio estimator. Much of the work reported here has involved my associates Takamitsu Sawa, Naoto Kunitomo, and Kimio Morimune. The emphasis is on comparison of the TSLS and LIML estimators based on finite-sample distributions. We shall also comment on the higher-order efficiency of the LIML estimator and some improvements.

2 The model and estimators

The (relevant) variables are $n+1$ endogenous variables and K exogenous variables observed over T time periods. The pertinent structural equation expressed in terms of T observations is

$$\mathbf{y}_1 = \mathbf{Y}_2\boldsymbol{\beta} + \mathbf{Z}_1\boldsymbol{\gamma}_1 + \mathbf{u} \tag{1}$$

where $\mathbf{y}_1$ and $\mathbf{Y}_2$ consist of T observations on 1 and n endogenous variables, respectively, $\mathbf{Z}_1$ consists of T observations on K_1 exogenous variables, $\mathbf{u}$ consists of T unobservable disturbances, $\boldsymbol{\beta}$ is a vector of n coefficients, and γ_1 is a vector of K_1 coefficients. The components of $\mathbf{u}$ are independently distributed with mean 0 and variance σ^2. The reduced form includes

$$(2) \qquad (\mathbf{y}_1 \ \mathbf{Y}_2) = (\ \mathbf{Z}_2)\begin{pmatrix} \boldsymbol{\pi}_{11} & \boldsymbol{\Pi}_{12} \\ \boldsymbol{\pi}_{21} & \boldsymbol{\Pi}_{22} \end{pmatrix} + (\mathbf{v}_1 \ \mathbf{V}_2)$$

where $\mathbf{Z}_2$ consists of T observations on K_2 exogenous variables, $\boldsymbol{\Pi}$ (partitioned into K_1 and K_2 rows and 1 and n columns, respectively) is the matrix of reduced form coefficients, and $(\mathbf{v}_1 \ \mathbf{V}_2)$ consists of disturbances. The rows of $(\mathbf{v}_1 \ \mathbf{V}_2)$ are independently distributed with means $(0, \mathbf{0}')$ and covariance matrix

$$(3) \qquad \boldsymbol{\Omega} = \begin{pmatrix} \omega_{11} & \boldsymbol{\omega}_{12} \\ \boldsymbol{\omega}_{21} & \boldsymbol{\Omega}_{22} \end{pmatrix}$$

We assume that the elements of $\mathbf{Z} = (\mathbf{Z}_1 \ \mathbf{Z}_2)$ are nonstochastic and that the rank of $\mathbf{Z}_2$ is $K_2 \geqslant n$.

The structural equation (1) is obtained from the reduced form equation (2) by multiplying on the right by $(1, -\boldsymbol{\beta}')'$. The relationships between equation (1) and the pair (2) and (3) are

$$(4) \qquad \mathbf{u} = \mathbf{v}_1 - \mathbf{V}_2\boldsymbol{\beta}$$

$$(5) \qquad \gamma_1 = \boldsymbol{\pi}_{11} - \boldsymbol{\Pi}_{12}\boldsymbol{\beta}$$

$$(6) \qquad \mathbf{0} = \boldsymbol{\pi}_{21} - \boldsymbol{\Pi}_{22}\boldsymbol{\beta}$$

$$(7) \qquad \sigma^2 = \omega_{11} - 2\boldsymbol{\omega}_{12}\boldsymbol{\beta} + \boldsymbol{\beta}'\boldsymbol{\Omega}_{22}\boldsymbol{\beta}$$

The estimator of γ_1 is obtained from estimators of $\boldsymbol{\pi}_{11}$, $\boldsymbol{\Pi}_{12}$, and $\boldsymbol{\beta}$ via equation (5). If $K_2 > n$, the sample equivalent of (6) cannot be satisfied exactly. An estimator of $\boldsymbol{\beta}$ minimizes some function of the estimated right-hand side of (6).

The matrix $\boldsymbol{\Pi}$ is estimated by least squares:

$$(8) \qquad \mathbf{P} = \begin{pmatrix} \mathbf{p}_{11} & \mathbf{P}_{12} \\ \mathbf{p}_{21} & \mathbf{P}_{22} \end{pmatrix} = (\mathbf{Z}'\mathbf{Z})^{-1}\mathbf{Z}'\mathbf{Y}$$

The estimator of $\boldsymbol{\Omega}$ is $1/T$ (or, alternatively, $1/[T-K]$) times

$$(9) \qquad \mathbf{C} = (\mathbf{Y} - \mathbf{Z}\mathbf{P})'(\mathbf{Y} - \mathbf{Z}\mathbf{P})$$

The inner products of the columns of $\mathbf{Z}_2$ orthogonal to the columns of $\mathbf{Z}_1$ compose

(10) $$\mathbf{A}_{22.1} = \mathbf{Z}_2'\mathbf{Z}_2 - \mathbf{Z}_2'\mathbf{Z}_1(\mathbf{Z}_1'\mathbf{Z}_1)^{-1}\mathbf{Z}_1'\mathbf{Z}_2$$

The effect "sum of squares" of $\mathbf{Z}_2$ (beyond the effect of $\mathbf{Z}_1$) is described by

(11) $$\mathbf{G} = \begin{pmatrix} \mathbf{p}_{21}' \\ \mathbf{P}_{22}' \end{pmatrix} \mathbf{A}_{22.1}(\mathbf{p}_{21}\ \mathbf{P}_{22})$$

The TSLS estimator is given by

(12) $$\hat{\beta}_{\mathrm{TSLS}} = \mathbf{G}_{22}^{-1}\mathbf{g}_{21}$$

which minimizes

(13) $$(1, -\hat{\beta})\mathbf{G}\begin{pmatrix} 1 \\ -\hat{\beta} \end{pmatrix} = (\mathbf{p}_{21} - \mathbf{P}_{22}\hat{\beta})'\mathbf{A}_{22.1}(\mathbf{p}_{21} - \mathbf{P}_{22}\hat{\beta})$$

The LIML estimator is given by

(14) $$\hat{\beta}_{\mathrm{LIML}} = (\mathbf{G}_{22} - \lambda_0\mathbf{C}_{22})^{-1}(\mathbf{g}_{21} - \lambda_0\mathbf{c}_{21})$$

where λ_0 is the smallest root of

(15) $$|\mathbf{G} - \lambda_0\mathbf{C}| = 0$$

It minimizes

(16) $$\frac{(1, -\hat{\beta}')\mathbf{G}\begin{pmatrix} 1 \\ -\hat{\beta} \end{pmatrix}}{(1, -\hat{\beta}')\mathbf{C}\begin{pmatrix} 1 \\ -\hat{\beta} \end{pmatrix}}$$

which is the variance ratio (the ratio of the effect sum of squares to the error sum of squares). We shall also refer to the limited-information maximum-likelihood estimator when the covariance matrix is known (LIMLK), given by

(17) $$\hat{\beta}_{\mathrm{LIMLK}} = (\mathbf{G}_{22} - \lambda_0^*\mathbf{\Omega}_{22})^{-1}(\mathbf{g}_{21} - \lambda_0^*\omega_{21})$$

where λ_0^* is the smallest root of

(18) $$|\mathbf{G} - \lambda^*\mathbf{\Omega}| = 0$$

(The distribution of the ordinary least-squares (OLS) estimator

$(\mathbf{G}_{22}+\mathbf{C}_{22})^{-1}(\mathbf{g}_{21}+\mathbf{c}_{21})$ is that of the TSLS estimator with K_2 replaced by $T-K_1$.)

The population analog of $\mathbf{G}$ is

$$\mathbf{\Theta} = \begin{pmatrix} \boldsymbol{\pi}_{21}' \\ \mathbf{\Pi}_{22}' \end{pmatrix} \mathbf{A}_{22.1} (\boldsymbol{\pi}_{21}\ \mathbf{\Pi}_{22}) \tag{19}$$

Let $\mathbf{\Theta}_{22}^{1/2}$ be a matrix such that $(\mathbf{\Theta}_{22}^{1/2})'(\mathbf{\Theta}_{22}^{1/2})=\mathbf{\Theta}_{22}=\mathbf{\Pi}_{22}'\mathbf{A}_{22.1}\mathbf{\Pi}_{22}$, the lower right-hand corner of $\mathbf{\Theta}$. Then the limiting distribution of

$$\frac{1}{\sigma}\mathbf{\Theta}_{22}^{1/2}(\hat{\boldsymbol{\beta}}-\boldsymbol{\beta}) \tag{20}$$

for TSLS, LIML, and LIMLK is the normal distribution with mean $\mathbf{0}$ and covariance matrix $\mathbf{I}$ as $\mathbf{A}_{22.1}$ grows (i.e., as $\mathbf{A}_{22.1}^{-1}\rightarrow\mathbf{0}$). In this large-sample sense, the TSLS, LIML, and LIMLK estimators are equivalent. However, in small samples their behaviors can be very different.

Some methods of comparing the behaviors of the estimators are the following:

1. Exact small-sample densities or distributions
2. Moments or other characteristics (such as the median and interquantile range) of the exact distributions
3. Approximate densities or distributions, possibly (but not necessarily) asymptotic expansions
4. Moments or other characteristics of the approximate distributions
5. Tables of the distributions for a range of parameter values
6. Tables of moments or other characteristics of distributions for a range of parameter values

3 Exact densities and distributions

The exact density of the TSLS estimator can be found from the noncentral Wishart density of the matrix $\mathbf{G}$, denoted by $W(\mathbf{\Omega}, K_2; \mathbf{\Theta})$, where $\mathbf{\Omega}$ is the covariance matrix, K_2 is the number of degrees of freedom, and $\mathbf{\Theta}$ is the sigma matrix of means. The density $\mathbf{G}$ can be transformed to the density of g_{11}, $\hat{\boldsymbol{\beta}}_{\text{TSLS}}=\mathbf{G}_{22}^{-1}\mathbf{g}_{21}$, and $\mathbf{G}_{22}$, and the marginal density of $\hat{\boldsymbol{\beta}}_{\text{TSLS}}$ can be obtained by integrating out g_{11} and $\mathbf{G}_{22}$. Richardson (1968) and Sawa (1969) found the density of the scalar $\hat{\beta}_{\text{TSLS}}$ for $n=1$ as a doubly infinite series. Basmann and associates (1971) found the density of $\hat{\boldsymbol{\beta}}_{\text{TSLS}}$ for $n=2$ and $K_2=n$, the just-identified case. Phillips (1980) found the density for arbitrary n in terms of an infinite series of zonal polynomials. However, the convergence of the series of zonal polynomials is extremely slow, and so its practical use may be limited.

Anderson and Sawa (1973), for $n=1$, transformed the distribution function $\Pr\{\hat{\beta}_{\mathrm{TSLS}} \leqslant z\}$ to $\Pr\{g_{21} \leqslant z g_{22}\} = \Pr\{g_{21} - z g_{22} \leqslant 0\}$. The quadratic form $g_{21} - z g_{22}$ in $2K_2$ variables can be transformed to diagonal form, resulting in the probability being expressed as $\Pr\{\chi_1'^2 - y\chi_2'^2 \leqslant 0\} = \Pr\{\chi_1'^2 \leqslant y\chi_2'^2\} = \Pr\{F'' \leqslant y\}$, where $\chi_1'^2$ and $\chi_2'^2$ are independent noncentral χ^2 variables with K_2 degrees of freedom, y is a function of z, and the parameters, and $F'' = \chi_1'^2/\chi_2'^2$ is a doubly noncentral F-variable with K_2 and K_2 degrees of freedom, respectively. Probabilities can be computed in terms of a doubly infinite sum of incomplete beta integrals. The probability can also be written as $\Pr\{(\chi_1'^2)^{1/3} - y^{1/3}(\chi_2'^2)^{1/3} \leqslant 0\}$. The Edgeworth expansion of the distribution of $(\chi'^2)^{1/3}$ can be used to give very accurate values for moderately large values of K_2 or the noncentrality parameter.

In obtaining these densities it is economical to transform the original distribution to a canonical form. A linear transformation of $\mathbf{G}$ (or, equivalently, of $(\mathbf{y}_1\ \mathbf{Y}_2)$) carries $\boldsymbol{\Omega}$ to $\mathbf{I}$ and $\boldsymbol{\Theta}$ to a convenient form. Then when $n=1$ the distributions depend on

$$(21)\qquad \alpha = \left(\frac{\omega_{22}}{\omega_{11.2}}\right)^{1/2}\left(\beta - \frac{\omega_{12}}{\omega_{22}}\right)$$

and

$$(22)\qquad \delta^2 = \frac{\boldsymbol{\pi}_{22}'\mathbf{A}_{22.1}\boldsymbol{\pi}_{22}}{\omega_{22}}$$

where $\omega_{11.2} = \omega_{11} - \omega_{12}^2/\omega_{22}$ is the variance of the distribution of a component of $\mathbf{v}_1$ conditioned on the corresponding component of $\mathbf{v}_2$. The standardized coefficient α depends on the difference between the structural parameter β and the regression coefficient ω_{12}/ω_{22} of a component of $\mathbf{v}_1$ on the corresponding component of $\mathbf{v}_2$. If $n \geqslant 2$, these are vector and matrix parameters; to keep the discussion in this chapter simple, we shall not treat the case of $n>1$ explicitly.

The exact density of the LIML estimator can be obtained from the noncentral Wishart density of $\mathbf{G}$ and the central Wishart density of $\mathbf{C}$, $W(\boldsymbol{\Omega}, T-K; \mathbf{0})$. Mariano and Sawa (1972) gave the density for $\hat{\beta}_{\mathrm{LIML}}$ for $n=1$ as a threefold infinite series.

The density of the LIMLK estimator is found from the noncentral Wishart density of $\mathbf{G}$. After the transformation of $\boldsymbol{\Omega}$ to $\mathbf{I}$, the density of $\arctan\hat{\beta}_{\mathrm{LIMLK}} - \arctan\beta$ depends only on δ^2. From this density, Anderson and Sawa (1982) found the density of $\hat{\beta}_{\mathrm{LIMLK}}$ as an infinite series (with confluent hypergeometric functions as coefficients) and the distribution function (for K_2 odd) as an infinite series of incomplete beta functions. For moderate and large values of δ^2, the distribution can be approximated by the noncentral F distribution.

4 Numerical computations

Anderson and Sawa (1979) gave tables of the distribution of the TSLS estimator for a range of values of α, K_2, and δ^2. A more extensive tabulation was given earlier (Anderson & Sawa, 1977). These tables agree with unpublished tables of Basmann, Eberle, and Richardson and those of Rhodes and Westbrook. The former integrated terms of the density and added them according to a convergence rule; the latter added terms of the density according to a convergence rule and numerically integrated the result. The three tabulations agree to within 1 in the third decimal place. Anderson and Sawa tabulated the distribution of the normalized estimator, that is, $\delta(\omega_{22})^{1/2}(\hat{\beta}_{\mathrm{TSLS}}-\beta)/\sigma$. This form of tabulation makes for easy interpolation, comparison between estimators, and relation to the normal distribution.

Anderson and Sawa (1977, 1978) tabulated the distribution of $\delta(\omega_{22})^{1/2}(\hat{\beta}_{\mathrm{LIMLK}}-\beta)/\sigma$. For moderate and large values of δ^2, the doubly noncentral F distribution was used; for moderate values, a finite number of terms of the infinite series was used. The tables are considered accurate to the third decimal place.

The LIML distribution presents more difficulty, because tabulation based on the threefold infinite series would be exorbitant. Instead, a simulation method was used. For each set of values of K_2, $T-K$, and δ^2 $(\alpha=0)$, 20,000 random values of $\mathbf{G}$ and $\mathbf{C}$ were constructed, and the implied values of $\hat{\beta}_{\mathrm{LIML}}$ and $\hat{\beta}_{\mathrm{LIMLK}}$ were calculated. From the difference of the empirical distribution functions, an estimate was obtained of the difference of the (true) distribution functions based on fitting a linear combination of a normal density times Hermite polynomials. In each case this estimated difference was added to the known distribution function of $\hat{\beta}_{\mathrm{LIMLK}}$ to obtain an estimate of the distribution of $\hat{\beta}_{\mathrm{LIML}}$. The distribution for $\alpha\neq 0$ can be calculated from the distribution for $\alpha=0$. Anderson, Kunitomo, and Sawa (1980) have published tables of these distributions. The errors are considered to be less than 0.004.

5 Comparison of distributions

From the tables described earlier we have prepared eight figures that display the general features of the distributions. As mentioned before, the tabulations are in terms of the normalized estimators, namely, $\hat{\beta}-\beta$ divided by the asymptotic standard error. Figures 4.1 to 4.3 present the

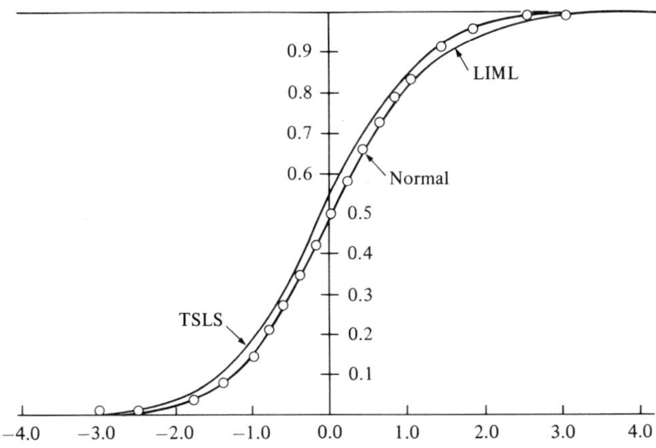

Figure 4.1. cdf's. $T-K=10$, $K_2=3$, $\alpha=1.0$, $\delta^2=100.0$. The cdf of LIMLK is indistinguishable from the cdf of LIML.

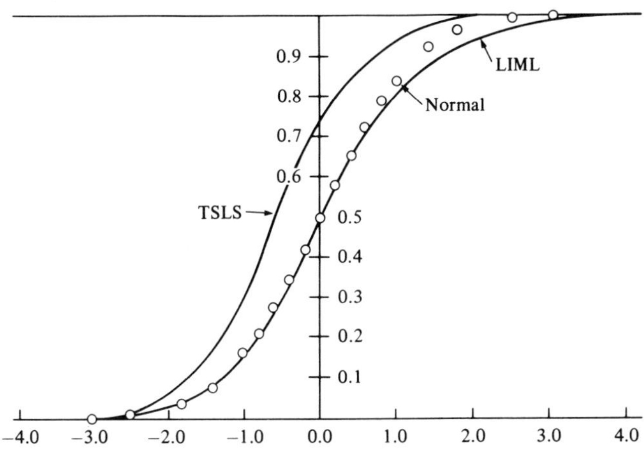

Figure 4.2. cdf's. $T-K=10$, $K_2=10$, $\alpha=1.0$, $\delta^2=100.0$. The cdf of LIMLK is indistinguishable from the cdf of LIML.

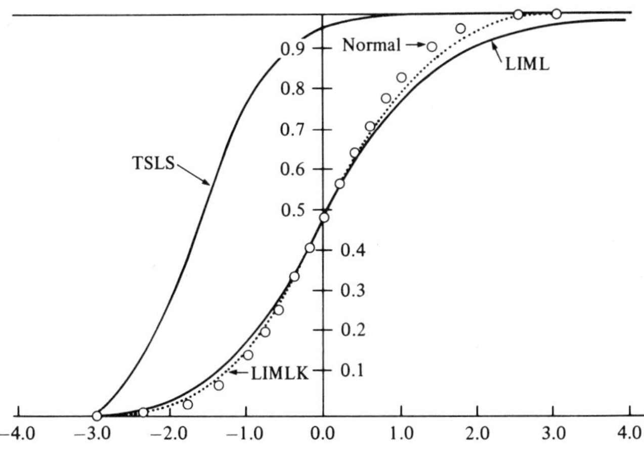

Figure 4.3. cdf's. $T-K=30$, $K_2=30$, $\alpha=1.0$, $\delta^2=100.0$.

cumulative distribution functions of the normalized TSLS, LIMLK, and LIML estimators for $\alpha=1$, $\delta^2=100$, $T-K$ relatively small, and three values of K_2. The value of δ^2 is moderate. (Anderson, Morimune, and Sawa (1978) considered it "typical" in some sense.) It will be seen that the distributions of the LIMLK and LIML estimators are fairly symmetrical about zero, with a level of about 0.5 at the value zero; that is, the distributions are approximately median-unbiased. On the other hand, the distribution of the TSLS estimator is shifted toward the left (because α is positive); the asymmetry increases with K_2. The median of each distribution is negative; for example, at $K_2=30$, the median is -1.6 (in terms of asymptotic standard deviations). There is very little difference between the distributions of the LIMLK and LIML estimators, except for large K_2, even though the number of degrees of freedom in the estimate of the covariance matrix is very small. However, the discrepancy grows as K_2 increases and is noticeable at $K_2=30$ and $T-K=30$ (a rather small value of $T-K$ compared with K_2). The distribution of the LIML estimator is a little more spread out than that of the LIMLK estimator.

It will be observed in these figures, as well as in Figures 4.4, 4.5, and 4.6, that the distributions of the normalized LIML estimator are approximately the standard normal distribution, but the tails are a little thicker. The thicker tails agree with the fact that the moments of the LIML estimator are infinite. The asymptotic theory states that these distributions approach the standard normal as $\delta^2 \to \infty$. Figure 4.4 shows the speed of approach to the standard normal distribution as δ^2 increases. At $\alpha=0$, the distribution is only slightly more spread out than the standard normal. Figure 4.5 shows how the spread tends to increase as α increases. For given α, δ^2, and K_2, the distribution of the LIML estimator approaches that of the corresponding LIMLK estimator as the number of degrees of freedom of the covariance matrix estimator increases. Figure 4.6 shows that the number of degrees of freedom $T-K$ does not matter much at moderate sizes of α and K_2.

Figure 4.7 shows the speed of approach of the distributions of the TSLS estimators to the standard normal distribution. It will be observed that the speed is much less than that of the distributions of the LIML estimators in the main body of the distributions (not in the tails). In fact, even at $\delta^2=300$ the distribution of the TSLS estimator is markedly shifted to the left of the standard normal distribution; it is primarily the shift (i.e., bias) that makes for the slowness of approach to normality. Figure 4.8 shows the effect of α. At $\alpha=0$ the distribution is symmetrical about zero; increasing α shifts the distributions to the left.

Two conclusions can be drawn from a study of the tables and graphs

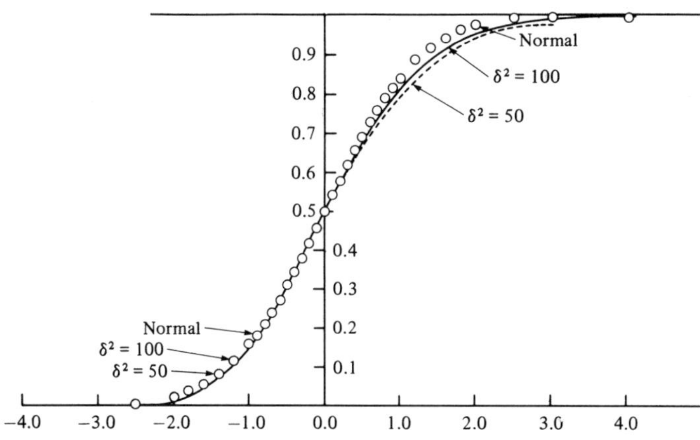

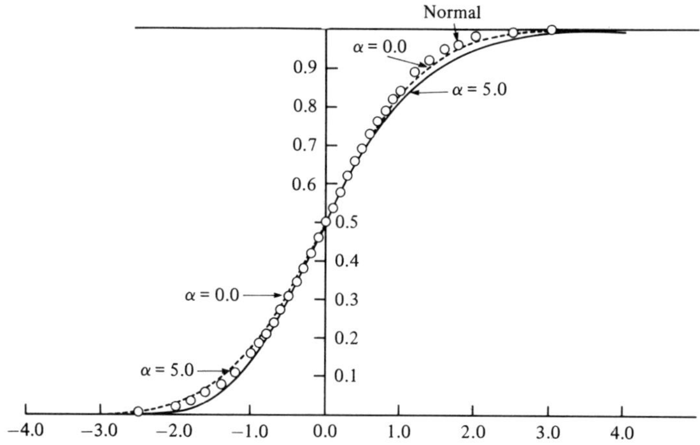

Figure 4.5. LIML. $K_2 = 10$, $T-K=30$, $\delta^2 = 100.0$. Effect of α.

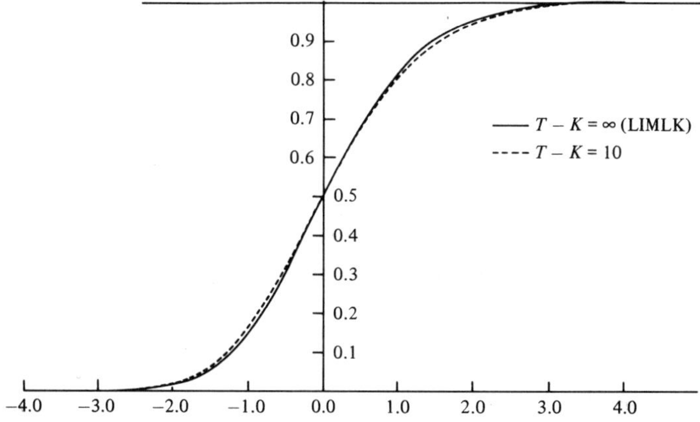

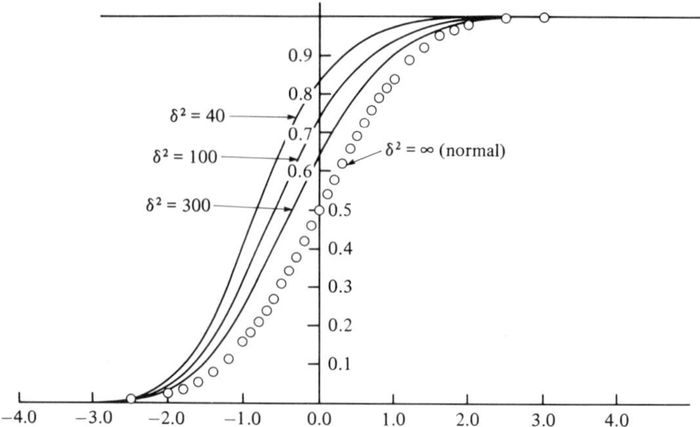

Figure 4.7. TSLS. $\alpha=1.0$, $K_2=10$. Effect of δ^2.

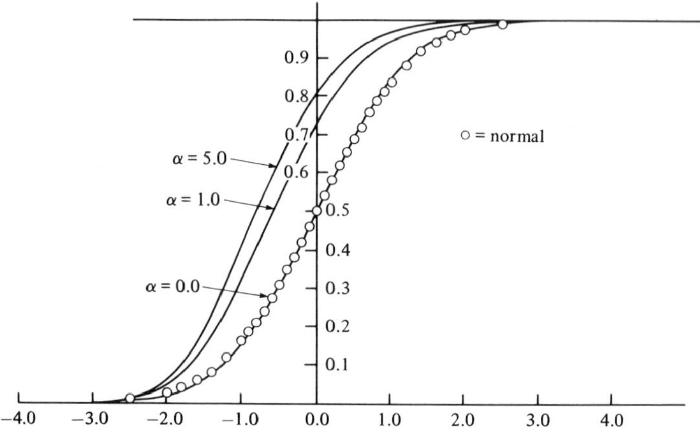

Figure 4.8. TSLS. $K_2=10$, $\delta^2=100$. Effect of α.

of the distributions. One is that the distributions of the TSLS estimators are badly distorted unless α is very small or δ^2 is very large, whereas the distributions of the LIML estimator are not distorted. The other conclusion is that the approach to the standard normal distribution is very slow for the TSLS estimator and very rapid for the LIML estimator. For many cases that occur in practice (perhaps most), the standard normal theory is inadequate for the TSLS estimator. Even though the moments of the LIML estimator are not finite, the standard normal distribution is a fairly good approximation to the actual distribution.

The features of the distributions agree with those of the asymptotic expansions (Anderson, 1974; Anderson, 1977; Anderson & Sawa, 1973); Mariano, 1973; Sargan & Mikhail, 1971). If one uses the first three terms of the asymptotic expansions of the distributions as $\delta^2 \to \infty$ (and $T \to \infty$ in the case of the LIML estimator), the mean and variance of the TSLS estimator are

$$(23) \qquad -\frac{\alpha}{\mu}(K_2 - 2), \qquad 1 - \frac{1}{\mu^2}[4(K_2 - 3)\alpha^2 + K_2 - 4]$$

respectively, and the mean and variance of the LIML estimator are

$$(24) \qquad \frac{\alpha}{\mu}, \qquad 1 + \frac{K_2 + 2 + 8\alpha^2}{\mu^2}$$

respectively, where $\mu^2 = \delta^2(1 + \alpha^2)$. Fujikoshi and associates (1979) and Kunitomo, Morimune, and Tsukuda (1980) have given asymptotic expansions for general n, but to avoid introducing more notation, we do not give details here.

6 Modified estimators

Several modifications of the estimators considered earlier have been proposed. In order to reduce bias, Sawa (1973) suggested a linear combination of the TSLS and OLS estimators, and Morimune (1978) suggested a linear combination of the TSLS and LIML estimators. Anderson suggested a different linear combination of the TSLS and LIML estimators to reduce the mean square error to order δ^{-2}. See the work of Anderson, Kunitomo, and Morimune (1980) for details.

Takeuchi (1978) has proposed the estimator

$$(25) \qquad \hat{\beta}_{\text{LIML}} - \frac{\hat{\alpha}}{\hat{\mu}}$$

where $\hat{\alpha}$ and $\hat{\mu}$ are any consistent estimators, as asymptotically unbiased to order δ^{-2}. Takeuchi and Morimune (1979) have shown that this estimator has asymptotic minimum variance to order δ^{-2}; the estimator is termed third-order-efficient.

Fuller (1977) has proposed

$$(26) \qquad (\mathbf{G}_{22} - (\lambda_0 - c/T)\mathbf{C}_{22})^{-1}(\mathbf{g}_{21} - (\lambda_0 - c/T)\mathbf{C}_{21})$$

where c is a constant, as a modification of $\hat{\beta}_{\text{LIML}}$ that has finite first and second moments. It differs from the estimator (25) by terms of order δ^{-2} for $c = 1$ and hence is also asymptotically unbiased and third-order-efficient.

Kunitomo (1982) has shown that $\hat{\beta}_{\mathrm{LIML}}$ has minimum asymptotic loss (to order δ^{-2}) among estimators that are median-unbiased to order δ^{-1} when K_2, the number of excluded exogenous variables, increases along with the sample size. This asymptotic theory is termed the large-K_2-asymptotics theory, and it may be relevant in large econometric models (Kunitomo, 1980; Morimune & Kunitomo, 1980).

It will be noted that all of these estimators with higher-order efficiency are modifications of the LIML estimator. According to our unpublished Monte Carlo experiments, the differences among modifications of the LIML estimator are negligible in many cases for practical purposes. On the other hand, as we have seen in the previous sections, the TSLS and LIML estimators are substantially different.

REFERENCES

Anderson, T. W. 1974. "An Asymptotic Expansion of the Distribution of the Limited Information Maximum Likelihood Estimate of a Coefficient in a Simultaneous Equation System." *Journal of the American Statistical Association* 69:565–72.

Anderson, T. W. 1977. "Asymptotic Expansions of the Distributions of Estimates in Simultaneous Equations for Alternative Parameter Sequences." *Econometrica* 45:509–18.

Anderson, T. W., Kunitomo, N., and Morimune, K. 1981. "Comparison of Modifications of BAN Estimators in Simultaneous Equations System." (Unpublished manuscript.)

Anderson, T. W., Kunitomo, N., and Sawa, T. 1980. "Evaluation of the Distribution Function of the Limited Information Maximum Likelihood Estimator." Technical report no. 319, Institute for Mathematical Studies in the Social Sciences, Stanford University.

Anderson, T. W., Morimune, K., and Sawa, T. 1978. "The Numerical Values of Some Key Parameters in Econometric Models." Technical report no. 270, Institute for Mathematical Studies in the Social Sciences, Stanford University.

Anderson, T. W., and Sawa, T. 1973. "Distributions of Estimates of Coefficients of a Single Equation in a Simultaneous System and Their Asymptotic Expansions." *Econometrica* 41:683–714.

Anderson, T. W., and Sawa, T. 1977. "Tables of the Distribution of the Maximum Likelihood Estimate of the Slope Coefficient and Approximations." Technical report no. 234, Institute for Mathematical Studies in the Social Sciences, Stanford University.

Anderson, T. W., and Sawa, T. 1978. "Tables of the Exact Distribution Function of the Limited Information Maximum Likelihood Estimator When the Covariance Is Known." Technical report no. 275, Institute for Mathematical Studies in the Social Sciences, Stanford University.

Anderson, T. W., and Sawa, T. 1979. "Evaluation of the Distribution Function of the Two-Stage Least Squares Estimate." *Econometrica* 47:163–83.

Anderson, T. W., and Sawa, T. 1982. "Exact and Approximate Distributions of a Maximum Likelihood Estimate of a Slope Coefficient." *Journal of the Royal Statistical Society B* (*in press*).

Basmann, R. L., Brown, F. L., Dawes, W. S., and Schoepfle, G. K. 1971. "Exact Finite Sample Density Functions of GCL Estimators of Structural Coefficients in a Leading Exactly Identifiable Case." *Journal of The American Statistical Association* 66:122–6.

Fujikoshi, Y., Morimune, K., Kunitomo, N., and Taniguchi, M. 1979. "Asymptotic Expansions of the Distributions of the Estimates of Coefficients in a Simultaneous Equation System." Technical report no. 287, Institute for Mathematical Studies in the Social Sciences, Stanford University.

Fuller, W. A. 1977. "Some Properties of a Modification of the Limited Information Estimator." *Econometrica* 45:939–53.

Kunitomo, N. 1980. "Asymptotic Expansions of the Distributions of Estimators in a Linear Functional Relationship and Simultaneous Equations." *Journal of the American Statistical Association* 75:693–700.

Kunitomo, N. 1982. "Asymptotic Efficiency and Higher Order Efficiency of the Limited Information Maximum Likelihood Estimator in Large Econometric Models." Technical report no. 365, Institute for Mathematical Studies in the Social Sciences, Stanford University.

Kunitomo, N., Morimune, K., and Tsukuda, Y. 1980. "Asymptotic Expansions of the Distributions of k-class Estimators when the Disturbances are Small." Technical report no. 307, Institute for Mathematical Studies in the Social Sciences, Stanford University.

Mariano, R. S. 1973. "Approximations to the Distribution Functions of the Ordinary Least-Squares and Two-Stage Least-Squares Estimates in the Case of Two Included Endogenous Variables." *Econometrica* 41:67–77.

Mariano, R. S. 1980. "Analytical Small Sample Distribution Theory in Econometrics: The Simultaneous Equation Case." Discussion paper 8026, Center for Operations Research and Econometrics, Universite Catholique de Louvain.

Mariano, R. S., and Sawa, T. 1972. "The Exact Finite Sample Distribution of the Limited Information Maximum Likelihood Estimate in the Case of Two Included Endogenous Variables." *Journal of the American Statistical Association* 67:159–63.

Morimune, K. 1978. "Improving the Limited Information Maximum Likelihood Estimator When the Disturbances Are Small." *Journal of the American Statistical Association* 73:867–71.

Morimune, K., and Kunitomo, N. 1980. "Improving the Maximum Likelihood Estimate in Linear Functional Relationships for Alternative Parameter Sequences." *Journal of the American Statistical Association* 75:230–7.

Phillips, P. C. B. 1980. "The Exact Distribution of Instrumental Variable Estimators in an Equation Containing $n+1$ Endogenous Variables." *Econometrica* 48:861–78.

Richardson, D. H. 1968. "The Exact Distribution of a Structural Coefficient Estimator." *Journal of the American Statistical Association* 63:1214–26.

Sargan, J. D., and Mikhail, W. M. 1971. "A General Approximation to the Distribution of Instrumental Variable Estimates." *Econometrica* 39:131–69.

Sawa, T. 1969. "The Exact Finite Sampling Distribution of OLS and 2SLS Estimators." *Journal of the American Statistical Association* 64:923–37.

Sawa, T. 1973. "Almost Unbiased Estimators in Simultaneous Equations Systems." *International Economic Review* 14:97–106.

Takeuchi, K. 1978. "Asymptotic Higher Order Efficiency of the ML Estimators of Parameters in Linear Simultaneous Equations." Presented at the Kyoto econometrics seminar meeting, Kyoto University.

Takeuchi, K., and Morimune, K. 1979. "Asymptotic Completeness of the Extended Maximum Likelihood Estimators in a Simultaneous Equation System." Unpublished manuscript.

CHAPTER 5

Best uniform and modified Padé approximants to probability densities in econometrics

P. C. B. Phillips

In this chapter, a new method of approximating the probability density functions (pdf's) of econometric estimators and test statistics is developed. It is shown that best uniform approximants to a general class of pdf's exist in the form of rational functions. A procedure for extracting the approximants is devised, based on modifying multiple-point Padé approximants to the distribution. The new approximation technique is very general and should be widely applicable in mathematical statistics and econometrics. It has the advantage, unlike the Edgeworth and saddlepoint approximations, of readily incorporating extraneous information on the distribution, even qualitative information. The new procedure is applied to a simple simultaneous-equations estimator, and it gives exceptionally accurate results even for tiny values of the concentration parameter.

1 Introduction

The idea of approximating small sample distributions, rather than extracting their exact mathematical forms, has a long history in statis-

The research reported here was supported by the NSF under Grant SES-8007571. I wish to acknowledge with many thanks the substantial contribution of Sidnie Feit in programming the computational work reported in Section 8 of this chapter. Ralph Bailey also helped with some of the original computational work on this section, and to him my thanks. It is a pleasure also to thank my secretary, Karen Marini, for her time and skill in preparing the manuscript.

tics, and a number of different techniques have been explored. Kendall and Stuart (1969) gave an introductory survey of some of these techniques in their Chapters 6, 12, and 13. Approximations are clearly of importance in those cases in which mathematical difficulties have prevented the development of an exact theory. An example is provided by regression models with lagged endogenous variables as regressors, models that are of particular relevance in econometrics. Approximations to distributions are also useful in those cases in which the exact mathematical expressions are too complicated for numerical computations. Some examples of the latter have been discussed previously (Phillips, 1980a, 1980b).

Several authors have recently obtained approximations to the distribution of econometric estimators and test statistics based on asymptotic series. The approximations used in most of these studies have been based on the first few terms of Edgeworth-type asymptotic expansions of the distribution function (df) or probability density function (pdf) of the statistic under consideration. An alternative approach that can, when it is available, provide significant improvement on the Edgeworth approximation, particularly in tail areas, is based on the method of steepest descents in contour integration. This method leads to the saddlepoint approximation. Its use was systematically explored for the first time in statistics by Daniels (1954, 1956), and it has recently been the subject of renewed interest (Daniels, 1980; Durbin, 1980a, 1980b; Holly & Phillips, 1979; Phillips, 1978a, 1978b).

Both these methods of approximation are capable of representing the exact distribution to an acceptable degree of accuracy in certain parameter environments. This has been confirmed by the numerical evaluations of Anderson and Sawa (1973, 1979), Phillips (1977a, 1978a), and Holly and Phillips (1979). Moreover, the approximate distributions that have been obtained in the literature have already given valuable information concerning the small-sample behavior of competing estimators and the adequacy of asymptotic theory in simple simultaneous equations and dynamic models. However, given the current state of our knowledge, the use of either of these methods in practical econometric work to advise on the choice of estimator and improve inferential accuracy is bound to encounter difficulites, some of them major.

First of all, there are certain parameter environments in which the performance of the approximations is poor, sometimes a good deal worse than the asymptotic distribution (particularly in the case of the Edgeworth approximation). Unfortunately, the parameter environments for which this poor performance obtains are not at all unusual. As we might expect, given that the approximations are based on asymptotic series, this problem tends to become more widespread when sample sizes are small. Some indication of the wayward nature of these approximations in certain parameter environments is already available (Phillips, 1977a, 1978a). Further documentation will be given in a companion article (Phillips, 1982).

Second, although general formulas for the Edgeworth approximation are now available (Phillips, 1977a; Sargan, 1976) and widely applicable, the saddlepoint technique is practicable only in specialized cases in which the characteristic function is available or simple integral formulas for the pdf can be used, such as in the case of ratios (Daniels, 1956), or in which there exists a set of sufficient statistics for the parameters to be estimated (Durbin, 1979b). No doubt progress will be made in tackling some of these latter difficulties, but in the meantime they remain a barrier to the general use of the procedure.

Another difficulty that can arise in the use of the saddlepoint technique is that for certain values of the argument of the pdf, singularities can occur within the strip of the imaginary axis containing the saddlepoint through which the path of integration is normally deformed. In such cases, this path of deformation is no longer permissible, and special techniques must be used to smooth the approximation past the singularity; the resulting approximants are called uniform asymptotic expansions. Uniform approximants typically are much more complicated in form than the saddlepoint approximation; an example has been given in Phillips (1978b). They are not always easy to extract, and further work will be required to splice them with the saddlepoint approximation, where it does exist, to cover the whole of the distribution.

Finally, it seems difficult to embody additional information on the distribution in question into these approximations. To take a simple example, in spite of the fact that the actual pdf is nonnegative and the df is monotonic, it is sometimes awkward to modify the Edgeworth approximations so that they share these properties. To take a more complicated example, often we know or can find the leading term in the series representation of the exact pdf (in many cases, without knowing the full expression for the pdf). Frequently this leading term has a simple algebraic form and is instrumental in determining the behavior of the exact distribution in certain domains, particularly the tails. Yet, even when this information is available, there seems to be no obvious way of building it into either the Edgeworth or the saddlepoint approximation. The resulting approximations, therefore, end up neglecting what is potentially very useful analytic information on the form of the distribution.

The purpose of this chapter is to introduce a new technique of approximating sampling distributions. The technique is quite general and should be widely applicable in mathematical statistics and econometrics. Unlike the Edgeworth and saddlepoint approximations, it has the advantage of readily incorporating extraneous information on the distribution, even qualitative information. Moreover, because the technique is not based on an asymptotic series expansion in terms of the sample size or concentration parameter, accurate approximations can be obtained even in very small samples. The technique should, therefore, be most useful in cases in which the Edgeworth and saddlepoint approximations run into difficulty. It turns out that the new approximation is close to the best uniform approximant in the class of certain rational functions. These approximants will be discussed and the class of rational functions to be used will be defined in Section 2. A general theory of best uniform approximation in the context of density approximation will be given in Sections 3 and 4. These sections will provide the theoretical basis for the new technique. Sections 5, 6, and 7 will describe the procedure and give the general formulas needed in applications. In Section 8 the method will be applied to a simple simultaneous-equations estimator, facilitating comparison between the new technique and existing techniques of approximation.

2 A general class of density functions and rational approximants

To fix ideas, we write the estimator or test statistic in which we are interested as θ_T. In what follows, we treat θ_T as a scalar, so that when dealing with estimators we are, in effect, concentrating on the marginal distribution of individual components of a complete vector of estimates. The characteristic function (cf) of θ_T is written as $\mathrm{cf}(s) = E(\exp(is\theta_T))$ and is assumed to be absolutely integrable. This implies that θ_T has a bounded continuous pdf given on inversion by

$$\text{(1)} \qquad \mathrm{pdf}(x) = \frac{1}{2\pi} \int_{-\infty}^{\infty} e^{-isx} \mathrm{cf}(s)\, ds$$

Moreover, by the Riemann–Lebesgue lemma, it follows from equation (1) that $\mathrm{pdf}(x) \to 0$ as $x \to \pm\infty$. Thus the effect of the integrability requirement on $\mathrm{cf}(s)$ is to confine our attention to the class of densities covered by the following assumption.

Assumption 1: θ_T has a continuous pdf that tends to zero at the limits of its domain of definition $(\pm\infty)$.

Note that the boundedness of the pdf now follows from its continuity and behavior at $\pm\infty$. Assumption 1 covers a wide variety of densities arising in econometric work. It can, in fact, be extended to allow for certain types of discontinuity and singularity, but this complicates the development of the approximants that follows. Therefore, in this chapter we shall keep to the class of densities defined by Assumption 1. This is sufficiently general to include all the usual simultaneous-equations estimators and test statistics, as well as their extensions to models with lagged endogenous variables as regressors and autoregressive moving-average errors.

Having defined the class of density functions, the general problem of approximation takes the following form: For a particular density function pdf(x), find an approximating function that depends on a finite number of parameters whose values are selected in such a way that the approximating function is as close, in some sense, as possible to the original density over its entire domain of definition. Once stated in this way, it is clear that there are two major components to the problem. The first is the form the approximating function should take. The second is the criterion of closeness of approximation to be used in selecting the best approximant. By a best approximant we mean the member (or members) of the given family of approximating functions whose closeness to the function pdf(x) cannot be improved by use of any other member of the same family. Thus, the second problem clearly raises the further question whether or not there exists a best approximation to pdf(x) in the given family of approximants. This question of existence will be the subject of the next section. We now define the class of approximating functions and the measure of approximation to be used in the rest of this chapter.

Definition: If $s(x)$ is a real continuous function satisfying $s(x)>0$ and $s(x)\rightarrow 0$ as $x\rightarrow\pm\infty$, then we define the class of rational approximating functions by

$$(2)\qquad R_{n,n}(x;s,\gamma) = s(x)\,\frac{P_n(x)}{Q_n(x)} = s(x)\,\frac{a_0 + a_1x + \cdots + a_nx^n}{b_0 + b_1x + \cdots + b_nx^n} \qquad (-\infty < x < \infty)$$

where (i) the numerator and denominator are reduced to their lowest degree by the cancellation of identical factors, (ii) n is an even integer, and (iii) $\gamma' = (a_0 a_1, \ldots, a_n, b_0, b_1, \ldots, b_n) \in \Gamma$, the parameter space, which is defined as the following subspace of $(2n+2)$-dimensional Euclidean space

$$\Gamma = \left\{\gamma : \sum_{i=0}^{n} b_i^2 = 1, \quad Q_n(x) > 0 \text{ for all } x \in (-\infty, \infty)\right\}$$

The condition $\sum_{i=0}^{n} b_i^2 = 1$ on the parameter space Γ is a normalization that eliminates the redundancy in the coefficients of the rational function (2). Other normalizations, such as $b_0 = 1$ or $b_n = 1$, are possible and may be more useful in applications. In fact, we shall later use the normalization $b_0 = 1$ in the application of Section 8, but the present definition of Γ is retained for the theoretical development.

The condition $Q_n(x) > 0$ ensures that the rational fractions of equation (2) have no poles on the real line and are therefore compatible with the class of density functions to be approximated. Because this is possible only when n is an even integer, we have introduced this requirement explicitly under condition (ii). On the other hand, when the density function we wish to approximate is nonzero on part, rather than all, of the real axis, it is clear that this requirement may be relaxed. Moreover, if singularities in the density function do occur on the real axis, we may remove the condition $Q_n(x) > 0$. If the position of the singularity is known, this can be incorporated directly into equation (2); otherwise, it must be approximated, and for certain values of n it may not be captured by the approximation, although whether or not this occurs will depend on the technique used to construct the approximation.

We might consider working with the somewhat wider class of rational functions for which the numerator and denominator polynomials are not necessarily of the same degree. In certain applications it may seem appropriate to make such a generalization of the class of approximants, and the theory we shall develop can be modified to take this generalization into account. However, there are various reasons why we do not choose to work with the more general class in developing our theory. The first is that the coefficient function $s(x)$ frequently will be constructed so that it captures the behavior of the exact pdf(x) as x approaches the limits of its domain. A rational fraction of equal degree is then immediately compatible with this behavior. The second is that when the numerator and denominator are of the same degree, modifications to the coefficients that are designed to avoid unwanted zeros and poles in the final approximant are easier to make. That this is of particular importance will be seen in Section 4, where the practical procedure we develop for obtaining a good approximant of the type in equation (2) is based on modifying multiple-point Padé approximants, which in crude form frequently possess zeros and poles that need to be removed in order to improve the approximation over the whole real line. Finally, numerical experience with rational function approximations in applied mathematics (Hart, 1968; Meinardus, 1967) suggests that rational fractions with numerator and denominator of equal or nearly equal degrees tend, on the whole, to give better approximations than those for which the degrees differ markedly. Taking an extreme case for comparison, polynomial approximations usually become unsatisfactory when it is necessary to approximate a function over a wide interval. Moreover, they lack the capacity to turn corners sharply and then go straight for long periods, particularly in a direction almost parallel to the horizontal axis. It is useful for a density function approximant to be capable of capturing these properties. An important feature of rational fraction approximations is that even low-degree fractions of the type in equation (2) are flexible enough to assume this behavior. This is endorsed by the large number of numerical results with rational approximants reported by Hastings (1955) and Hart (1968). It will also be confirmed in our own application of the technique reported in Section 5.

In order to develop a theory for the goodness of approximation based on members of the class (2), we introduce a norm to measure the error in the approximation. We shall use the uniform norm (also known as the Tchebycheff or L_∞ norm) defined as

$$\|f(x)\| = \sup_{x\in(-\infty,\infty)} |f(x)| \tag{3}$$

If we now let $f(x) = \text{pdf}(x) - R_{n,n}(x;s,\gamma)$ denote the approximation error, our problem is, for a given value of n and a given function $s(x)$, to find a value of γ that minimizes the maximum error. At this value of γ, $R_{n,n}(x;s,\gamma)$ is then called a best uniform (or Tchebycheff) approximation to $\text{pdf}(x)$.

Other choices of norm are certainly possible and will generally lead to different best approximations, where they exist. However, for accurately approximating $\text{pdf}(x)$ over a wide interval, the choice of the uniform norm seems very appropriate.

3 Best uniform approximation by rational functions

The theory of best uniform approximation of real continuous functions by rational fractions has a long history. One of the earliest discussions was undertaken by Tchebycheff (1859). Frobenius (1881) and Padé (1892) both systematically investigated the properties of a specialized class of rational approximants now known as Padé approximants (Section 4). In the complex domain, Runge (1885) (Rudin, 1974, Chapter 13) established the possibility of uniform approximation of analytic functions by rational fractions with preassigned poles. A general theory of approximation in the complex domain by rational functions was developed in a treatise by Walsh (1965). Extensive modern treatments of the subject covering all the classical results on the approximation of real-valued functions are given in the volumes by Rice (1964) and Meinardus (1967). Because the theory in this literature, with the exception of the work of Walsh (1965), has been concerned with the approximation of functions that are defined over compact sets, this section will be devoted to the development of a theory that is applicable over the whole real line and is therefore directly relevant to the problem of density function approximation. Our treatment of the problem will be based on the framework laid out in Section 2 and will follow the lines of Rice (1964), particularly his Section 3.8.

To establish the existence of a best uniform approximant to a given $\mathrm{pdf}(x)$ in the class of rational fractions defined by equation (2), we need to show that there exists a set of parameters γ^* for which

$$(4) \qquad \|R_{n,n}(x;s,\gamma^*) - \mathrm{pdf}(x)\| = \inf_{\gamma\in\Gamma} \|R_{n,n}(x;s,\gamma) - \mathrm{pdf}(x)\| = \rho, \quad \text{say}$$

Now, $0 \leqslant \rho < \infty$, and we can find a sequence of rational fractions $\{R_{n,n}(x;s,\gamma^{(j)})\}$ for which

$$(5) \qquad \rho_j = \|R_{n,n}(x;s,\gamma^{(j)}) - \mathrm{pdf}(x)\|$$

and

$$(6) \qquad \lim_{j\to\infty} \rho_j = \rho$$

It remains to prove that the parameter sequence $\{\gamma^{(j)}\}$ has a convergent subsequence that converges to a set of finite parameters. If we call the latter γ^*, then it will follow from equation (6) that γ^* satisfies equation (4). As discussed by Rice (1964, pp. 26–7), the crucial part of the proof of existence is to demonstrate that the parameters lie in a compact set.[1] First, we show that we may restrict our attention to bounded subsets of Γ.

Definition: Condition E of Rice (1964, p. 27). The approximating function $R_{n,n}(x;s,\gamma)$ is said to satisfy condition E for the norm $\|\ \ \|$ if, given $M<\infty$, there is an $N<\infty$ such that

$$\|R_{n,n}(x;s,\gamma)\| \leqslant M$$

implies that

$$\max_i |\gamma_i| \leqslant N$$

where $\gamma = (\gamma_i)$.

In view of equations (5) and (6), there is an integer j_0 for which

(7) $$\|R_{n,n}(x; s, \gamma^{(j)}) - \text{pdf}(x)\| \leqslant \rho + 1$$

for all $j > j_0$. Moreover, from Assumption 1 it follows that there exists $K > 0$ for which $\|\text{pdf}(x)\| \leqslant K$, and, hence, using equation (7), we have the inequality

(8) $$\|R_{n,n}(x; s, \gamma^{(j)})\| \leqslant K + \rho + 1$$

We now verify that condition E holds for the approximating function $R_{n,n}(x; s, \gamma)$.

Lemma 1: The rational fraction $R_{n,n}(x; s, \gamma)$ defined by (2) satisfies condition E for the uniform norm (3).

Proof: We consider the set

(9) $$\{\gamma : \|R_{n,n}(x; s, \gamma)\| \leqslant M, \ \ M > 0\}$$

Because $\|R_{n,n}(x; s, \gamma)\| \leqslant M$ implies that, for a given number $L > 0$,

$$\max_{x \in [-L, L]} |R_{n,n}(x; s, \gamma)| \leqslant M$$

it follows that (9) lies in the set

(10) $$\{\gamma : \max_{x \in [-L, L]} |R_{n,n}(x; s, \gamma)| \leqslant M\}$$

Now, for $x \in [-L, L]$, and taking $L > 1$, we have

(11) $$\begin{aligned} |R_{n,n}(x; s, \gamma)| &\geqslant \frac{\min_{x \in [-L, L]} |s(x)|}{\max_{x \in [-L, L]} |Q_n(x)|} |P_n(x)| \\ &\geqslant \frac{s_L (L^2 - 1)^{1/2}}{(L^{2(n+1)} - 1)^{1/2}} |P_n(x)| \end{aligned}$$

where

$$s_L = \min_{x \in [-L, L]} |s(x)| > 0$$

Thus, when γ lies in the set (10), we have

$$\frac{M(L^{2(n+1)} - 1)^{1/2}}{s_L (L^2 - 1)^{1/2}} \geqslant \max_{x \in [-L, L]} |P_n(x)| = \max_{x \in [-L, L]} \left| \sum_{i=0}^{n} a_i x^i \right|$$

and the polynomial $\Sigma_{i=0}^{n} a_i x^i$ is bounded uniformly on the interval $[-L, L]$. It follows that the coefficient parameters a_i are also bounded. Moreover, $\Sigma_{i=0}^{n} b_i^2 = 1$, by definition, so that the parameter set (10) is bounded. By implication, the same is true for the set (9), and thus $R_{n,n}(x; s, \gamma)$ satisfies condition E for the uniform norm.

This lemma shows that we can confine our attention to bounded subsets of Γ in searching for a best approximant. Hence, for all $j \geqslant j_0$, the sequence $\{\gamma^{(j)}\}$ introduced earlier lies in a bounded subset of Γ. We may, therefore, select a subsequence that converges to the vector γ^*, say. If we reindex the subsequence, we can write for the individual components of γ the following: $\lim_{j\to\infty} a_i^{(j)} = a_i^*$ and $\lim_{j\to\infty} b_i^{(j)} = b_i^*$ for $i = 0, 1, \ldots, n$.

Now it is important to note that because Γ is not closed, γ^* may or may not lie in Γ. If $\gamma^* \in \Gamma$, then $R_{n,n}(x; s, \gamma^*)$ is a rational function of the form defined in (2) and, in view of (4), is therefore a best uniform approximant of pdf(x). But, if $\gamma^* \notin \Gamma$, then $R_{n,n}(x; s, \gamma^*)$ is the limit of a sequence of functions and is not necessarily a rational function itself. In fact, it may not even be continuous (we shall give an example later in this section). However, the limit function $R_{n,n}(x; s, \gamma^*)$ will differ from a rational function, $R'_{n,n}(x; s, \gamma^*)$, say, only at a finite number of points. And, in fact, $R'_{n,n}(x; s, \gamma^*)$ is a best uniform approximant to pdf(x) in the class defined by (2).

The problem discussed in the preceding paragraph arises because although the denominator polynomial $Q_n(x) = Q_n(x; \gamma) > 0$ for $\gamma \in \Gamma$, this no longer necessarily holds when γ does not lie in Γ. Because γ^* is a subsequential limit of elements of Γ, it follows that, in the limit, $Q_n^*(x) = Q_n(x; \gamma^*)$ can have, at most, n zeros. If we let $P_n^*(x) = P_n(x; \gamma^*)$ be the limit of the numerator polynomial as $\gamma^{(j)} \to \gamma^*$, it follows that there are, at most, n points where $R'_{n,n}(x;\ s,\ \gamma^*) = s(x) P_n^*(x)/Q_n^*(x)$ is undefined. At all other points we must have $R_{n,n}(x; s, \gamma^{(j)}) = R'_{n,n}(x; s, \gamma^*)$. Moreover, because $R'_{n,n}(x; s, \gamma^*) = \text{pdf}(x) + \{R_{n,n}(x; s, \gamma^{(j)}) - \text{pdf}(x)\} + \{R'_{n,n}(x; s, \gamma^*) - R_{n,n}(x; s, \gamma^{(j)}\}$, it follows from (7) that for $j \geqslant j_0$

$$|R'_{n,n}(x; s, \gamma^*)| \leqslant K + \rho + 1 + |R'_{n,n}(x; s, \gamma^*) - R_{n,n}(x; s, \gamma^{(j)})|$$

and allowing $j \to \infty$, we deduce that

$$|R'_{n,n}(x; s, \gamma^*)| \leqslant K + \rho + 1 \tag{12}$$

Hence, for all x other than zeros of $Q_n^*(x)$, we have the inequality

$$s(x)|P_n^*(x)| \leqslant (K + \rho + 1) Q_n^*(x) \tag{13}$$

By continuity, (13) holds also when $Q_n^*(x)=0$. Thus, any real zero of $Q_n^*(x)$ is also a zero of $P_n^*(x)$, because $s(x)>0$ for all finite x. We therefore eliminate by cancellation each linear factor of $Q_n^*(x)$ corresponding to a real root of $Q_n^*(x)=0$. We call the resulting rational fraction $R'_{n,n}(x;s,\gamma^*)$ and note that for all values of x other than zeros of $Q_n^*(x)$

$$R'_{n,n}(x;s,\gamma^*) = R_{n,n}(x;s,\gamma^*)$$

whereas at the zeros $\{x_k : k=1,\ldots,m\leqslant n\}$ of $Q_n^*(x)$

$$R'_{n,n}(x_k;s,\gamma^*) = \lim_{x\to x_k} R_{n,n}(x;s,\gamma^*)$$

Finally, we note that

$$\begin{aligned}
\|R_{n,n}(x;s,\gamma^*) - \text{pdf}(x)\| &= \sup_{x\in(-\infty,\infty)} |R_{n,n}(x;s,\gamma^*) - \text{pdf}(x)| \\
&= \max\left\{ \sup_{\substack{x\in(-\infty,\infty)\\ x\neq x_k}} |R_{n,n}(x;s,\gamma^*) - \text{pdf}(x)|,\right. \\
&\qquad |R_{n,n}(x_k;s,\gamma^*) - \text{pdf}(x_k)|, \\
&\qquad\qquad \left. i=1,\ldots,m\right\} \\
&\geqslant \sup_{x\in(-\infty,\infty)} |R'_{n,n}(x;s,\gamma^*) - \text{pdf}(x)| \\
&= \|R'_{n,n}(x;s,\gamma^*) - \text{pdf}(x)\|
\end{aligned}$$

The rational function $R'_{n,n}(x;s,\gamma^*)$ is therefore a best uniform approximation of $\text{pdf}(x)$, and we have proved the following theorem.

Theorem 1: Existence of a best uniform approximant. If $\text{pdf}(x)$ satisfies Assumption 1 on $(-\infty,\infty)$, then there is a best uniform approximant to $\text{pdf}(x)$ in the class of rational functions defined by (2).

To illustrate the problem that arises in the proof of this theorem because Γ is not closed, we consider the following density function of the Pareto distribution

$$\text{pdf}(x) = \frac{ak^a}{x^{a+1}} \quad (a>0,\ x\geqslant k>0)$$

We consider the case in which $a=2$ and a class of rational approximants of the form (2) is being used with $s(x)=1/x$ $(x\geqslant k)$ and $n=4$. Now consider the sequence of approximants defined by

$$R_{4,4}(x;s,\gamma^{(j)}) = \left(\frac{2k^2}{x}\right)$$
$$\times \frac{(1/(1+k^4) - 1/2j^2)^{1/2}x^2 - (k^4/(1+k^4) - 1/2j^2)^{1/2}}{(1/(1+k^4) - 1/2j^2)^{1/2}x^4 - (k^4/(1+k^4) - 1/2j^2)^{1/2}x^2 + 1/j}$$

Thus,

$$\gamma^{(j)\prime} = \left[-\left(\frac{k^4}{1+k^4} - \frac{1}{2j^2}\right)^{1/2}, 0, \left(\frac{1}{1+k^4} - \frac{1}{2j^2}\right)^{1/2}, 0, 0; \frac{1}{j}, 0, \right.$$
$$\left. -\left(\frac{k^4}{1+k^4} - \frac{1}{2j^2}\right)^{1/2}, 0, \left(\frac{1}{1+k^4} - \frac{1}{2j^2}\right)^{1/2}\right]$$

and, as $j \to \infty$,

$$\gamma^{(j)\prime} \to \gamma^{*\prime} = \left[-\left(\frac{k^4}{1+k^4}\right)^{1/2}, 0, \left(\frac{1}{1+k^4}\right)^{1/2}, 0, 0; \right.$$
$$\left. 0, 0, -\left(\frac{k^4}{1+k^4}\right)^{1/2}, 0, \left(\frac{1}{1+k^4}\right)^{1/2}\right]$$

The limiting function is then

$$R_{4,4}(x;s,\gamma^*) = \begin{matrix} 2k^2/x^3 & \text{for} \quad x > k \\ 0 \quad \text{for} & x = k \end{matrix}$$

which is not a rational function, nor is it continuous on the interval $[k, \infty)$. However,

$$R'_{4,4}(x;s,\gamma^*) = \frac{2k^2}{x^3} \quad (x \geqslant k)$$

is rational and continuous and is clearly the best uniform approximant to $\text{pdf}(x)$ on $[k, \infty)$.

4 A convergence theorem

As the degree of the best approximating rational fraction increases, the error $E(n,s) = \| \text{pdf}(x) - R'_{n,n}(x;s,\gamma^*) \|$ must be at least as small. In fact, as Theorem 3 will show, $E(n,s) \to 0$ as $n \to \infty$, so that the best approximant $R'_{n,n}(x;s,\gamma^*)$ converges to $\text{pdf}(x)$ as $n \to \infty$. It follows that for any choice of density function satisfying Assumption 1, there is an arbitrarily close rational approximant. In this sense, the rational fractions of the class defined by equation (2) are dense in the set of density functions that satisfy Assumption 1.

Meinardus (1967) proved a related theorem on the convergence of rational fractions to a continuous function over a bounded interval.[2]

Theorem 2: The real-valued function $f(x)$ is continuous and nonnegative over the interval $[-1,1]$ and is approximated by

$$(14) \qquad R_{m,n}(x) = \frac{P_m(x)}{Q_n(x)}$$

where $P_m(x)$ and $Q_n(x)$ are polynomials with real coefficients and $Q_n(x) > 0$ for $x \in [-1,1]$.

$$E_{m,n}(f) = \inf_{R_{m,n} \in V_{m,n}} \|f - R_{m,n}\|$$

where $V_{m,n}$ is the set of all rational functions, as in (14). Then

$$\lim_{n+m \to \infty} E_{m,n}(f) = 0$$

independent of the manner in which we pass to the limit.

Proof: Meinardus (1967, pp. 158–60).

Theorem 3: If $\text{pdf}(x)$ satisfies Assumption 1 on $(-\infty, \infty)$ and

$$E(n,s) = \|\text{pdf}(x) - R'_{n,n}(x; s, \gamma^*)\|$$

where $R'_{n,n}(x; s, \gamma^*)$ is the best uniform approximant to $\text{pdf}(x)$ in the class of rational fractions defined by (2), then

$$\lim_{n \to \infty} E(n,s) = 0$$

Proof: Let $\epsilon > 0$ be arbitrarily small. Then, by Assumption 1 and the definition of $R_{n,n}(x; s, \gamma)$, there exists an $L > 0$ and large enough n for which

$$\sup_{|x| > L} |\text{pdf}(x) - R'_{n,n}(x; s, \gamma^*)| < \epsilon$$

Now,

$$\|\text{pdf}(x) - R'_{n,n}(x; s, \gamma^*)\| = \max\left\{ \max_{x \in [-L, L]} |\text{pdf}(x) - R'_{n,n}(x; s, \gamma^*)|, \right.$$

$$\left. \sup_{|x| > L} |\text{pdf}(x) - R'_{n,n}(x; s, \gamma^*)| \right\}$$

$$= \max\left\{ \max_{x\in[-L,L]} |\mathrm{pdf}(x) - R'_{n,n}(x;s,\gamma^*)|, \epsilon \right\}$$

It only remains to show that there is an n_0 for which $n > n_0$ implies that

$$\max_{x\in[-L,L]} |\mathrm{pdf}(x) - R'_{n,n}(x;s,\gamma^*)| < \epsilon \tag{15}$$

For then, because ϵ is arbitrarily small, we can approximate $\mathrm{pdf}(x)$ by $R'_{n,n}(x;s,\gamma^*)$ over the whole real line as closely as we please for sufficiently large n. Hence, $E(n,s) \to 0$ as $n \to \infty$.

In fact, equation (15) follows from Theorem 2. We need only transform $x = Ly$ with $-1 \leqslant y \leqslant 1$, and setting

$$R'_{n,n}(x;s,\gamma^*) = s(Ly)\frac{P'_n(Ly)}{Q'_n(Ly)} = \bar{s}(y)\frac{\bar{P}'_n(y)}{\bar{Q}'_n(y)}$$

$$\mathrm{pdf}(x) = \mathrm{pdf}(Ly) = \overline{\mathrm{pdf}}(y)$$

we have

$$\max_{x\in[-L,L]} |\mathrm{pdf}(x) - R'_{n,n}(x)| = \max_{y\in[-1,1]} \bar{s}(y)\left| \frac{\overline{\mathrm{pdf}}(y)}{\bar{s}(y)} - \frac{\bar{P}'_n(y)}{\bar{Q}'_n(y)} \right|$$

Because $\overline{\mathrm{pdf}}(y)/\bar{s}(y)$ is continuous and nonnegative over $[-1,1]$, it follows by Theorem 2 that equation (15) holds for n sufficiently large.

5 Local expansions for densities

The theory of the last two sections shows that for a given pdf in the class defined by Assumption 1 there exists a best rational fraction approximant of the type (2) and that, as we increase the degree of the approximant, this converges to $\mathrm{pdf}(x)$ over the entire real axis. In any practical situation, of course, we will need to prescribe the degree of the approximant to be used and attempt to find the best approximant in the given class. This normally requires numerical methods, and the algorithms discussed in the literature (Meinardus, 1967, pp. 170–1; Rice, 1964, Chapter 6) rely on knowledge of the true function values at a grid of points as well as, in certain cases, the function derivatives. This seems too much to expect in an econometric context, where, even in those cases in which the exact density function is known in analytic form, numerical computations often are impossible because of convergence problems with the multiple series representation of the density or the inadequate tabulations of the special polynomials that appear in the analytic expressions.

We are therefore left with the problem of how, in a given situation, to get close to the best approximant in the class (2) without having to rely on arbitrary evaluations of the exact distribution. The solution we present to this problem in this and succeeding sections of this chapter is based on the idea of using the local behavior of the true density in the body of the distribution and in the tails to construct a global approximation of the form (2). In principle, the procedure we develop for moving from local to global density approximations can be based on knowledge of local behavior at an arbitrary set of points. But, in practice, it will be sufficient to use information concerning the local behavior of the density in the tails and around the center of the distribution. The application we consider in Section 8 will show that this information is sufficient to secure excellent global approximations to rather complicated density functions, even with rational fractions of lower degree.

The local behavior of density functions can take the form of expansions about the value of the function at a certain point or perhaps estimates of the function values obtained from Monte Carlo simulations. We shall deal with the case in which some analytic information from local expansions is available; at the same time, it should be clear how the procedure we develop can also be used to accommodate Monte Carlo evidence.

Our present analytic knowledge of the exact distribution of a variety of econometric estimators and test statistics shows that there exists an asymptotic expansion of the density function in ascending powers of x^{-1} as the argument x approaches the limits of its domain ($\pm\infty$ or $+\infty$). In general, we can write the expansion about infinity in the form

$$\text{pdf}(x) \sim t(|x|)\{\alpha_0 + \alpha_1/x + \alpha_2/x^2 + \alpha_3/x^3 + \alpha_4/x^4 \ldots\} \tag{16}$$

as $x \to \pm\infty$. The coefficient function $t(|x|) \to 0$ as $|x| \to \infty$ and, in the case of most of the common simultaneous-equations estimators, is of the form $t(|x|) = |x|^{-k}$, where $k \geqslant 2$. Thus, in the case of the two-stage least-squares estimator, $k = l + 2$, where l is the degree of overidentification in the equation being estimated. An expansion of the type (16) was developed by Sargan and Mikhail (1971) for the instrumental variable estimator and was used by Sargan (1981) in the analysis of Monte Carlo estimates of moments that do not exist.

At points $\{d_i : i = 1, \ldots, I\}$, where pdf$(x)$ is continuously differentiable to an appropriate order, we have the Taylor expansions

$$\begin{aligned}\text{pdf}(x) = {} & \beta_{i0} + \beta_{i1}(x - d_i) + \beta_{i2}(x - d_i)^2 + \beta_{i3}(x - d_i)^3 \\ & + \beta_{i4}(x - d_i)^4 + \cdots \quad (i = 1, \ldots, I)\end{aligned} \tag{17}$$

In a number of cases we also have the analytic form of the leading term in the series representation of the density. If we denote this leading term by $w(x)$, then it will be useful to consider extensions of the expansion (17) that take the form

$$\text{(18)} \qquad \text{pdf}(x) = w(x)\{\beta_{i0} + \beta_{i1}(x - d_i) + \beta_{i2}(x - d_i)^2 + \beta_{i3}(x - d_i)^3 + \beta_{i4}(x - d_i)^4 + \cdots\}$$

There are two obvious choices of the points d_i: (i) the origin, particularly for certain test statistics like the t ratio; (ii) the true value of the relevant parameter, when pdf(x) refers to the marginal distribution of a certain estimator.

Although expansions such as (16) and (17) usually produce good approximations only in the immediate neighborhood of the point of expansion, they can be used to construct approximations that perform well outside the immediate locality of the approximation while retaining the good behavior of the original expansions within the locality. With reference to (17), the fourth-degree polynomial in x may yield a good approximation to pdf(x) in a neighborhood of the point d_i, but in most cases its performance will rapidly deteriorate outside of this neighborhood, and it will be quite inadequate as an approximation on the tails. On the other hand, the coefficients β_{i1} in the expansion (17) usually contain information that can produce greatly improved approximations outside the range in which expansion (17) itself is immediately useful. That this is so is demonstrated by the extensive practical experience with Padé approximants in the applied mathematics literature. These approximants are rational fractions for which the corresponding Taylor series matches the Taylor-series expansion of a given function to as many powers as possible. In the present context, we can refer to the following example used by Baker (1975):

$$\text{(19)} \qquad f(x) = \left(\frac{1+2x}{1+x}\right)^{1/2} = 1 + \frac{1}{2}x - \frac{5}{8}x^2 + \frac{13}{16}x^3 - \frac{141}{128}x^4 + \cdots$$

The Taylor series for $f(x)$ in (19) has radius of convergence equal to 1/2. Yet as x becomes large, $f(x)$ is a well-behaved function that tends to $\sqrt{2}$ as $x \to \infty$. Using only the first three coefficients 1, 1/2, $-5/8$ in (18), we construct the Padé approximant

$$\text{(20)} \qquad \frac{1 + (7/4)x}{1 + (5/4)x} = 1 + \frac{1}{2}x - \frac{5}{8}x^2 + \frac{25}{32}x^3 + \cdots$$

This has the same Taylor-series expansion about the origin as $f(x)$ to $O(x^2)$, and it tends to $7/5 = 1.4$ as $x \to \infty$. Thus, using only three coefficients in a local expansion about the origin, the Padé approximation (19) provides an approximation at infinity to $f(x)$ that differs at the second decimal place. Even within the radius of convergence of the Taylor expansion, expansion (20) outperforms the Taylor expansion. For instance, at $x=1/4$, $f(x)=1.0954451$, and the first three terms of the Taylor expansion give 1.0859375, whereas expansion (20) yields 1.0952381, providing accuracy to at least another decimal place.

This example suggests that Padé approximants can have the useful property of accelerating the convergence of a given power series within its circle of convergence, while at the same time considerably extending the domain over which truncated series expansions can give useful results. These features make Padé approximants attractive for constructing first-step rational fraction approximations from the information embodied in purely local density expansions such as (16), (17), or (18). Section 6 will be devoted to the algebraic details of this construction and will give the appropriate formulas.

Because the coefficients in the local expansions are needed in the construction of rational fraction approximants, we shall now give an analytic procedure for extracting local density expansions such as (16) and (17). It will be useful first to make explicit the general form of the characteristic function.

Assumption 2: (i) The characteristic function $\mathrm{cf}(s)$ has the general form

$$\mathrm{cf}(s) = \mathrm{cf}_1(s) + \mathrm{cf}_2(s) + \mathrm{cf}_3(s) \tag{21}$$

where

$$\mathrm{cf}_1(s) = e^{i\eta s} \sum_{m=0}^{M-1} p_m (is)^m$$

$$\mathrm{cf}_2(s) = e^{i\eta s} |s|^{\mu} \sum_{k=0}^{K} \sum_{l=0}^{L(k)} q_{kl} |s|^k (\ln|s|)^l,$$

$$\mu \geqslant M; \quad L(k) = 0 \quad \text{or} \quad 1 \quad \text{for all } k$$

$\mathrm{cf}_3^{(j)}(s)$ is absolutely integrable over every finite interval for $j = 0, 1, \ldots, N$, where N is the smallest integer greater than or equal to $\mu+K+1$ and $\mathrm{cf}^{(N)}(s)$ is well-behaved at infinity (Lighthill, 1958, p. 49).

(ii) The behavior of $\mathrm{cf}(s)$ as $s \to 0$ is given by the asymptotic series expansion

$$\mathrm{cf}(s) \sim e^{i\eta s}\left\{\sum_{m=0}^{M-1} p_m (is)^m + |s|^{\mu} \sum_{k=0}^{\infty} \sum_{l=0}^{L(k)} q_{ke} |s|^k (\ln|s|)^l\right\}$$

This assumption is sufficiently general to include a very wide class of distributions and should apply to most econometric estimators and test statistics in both classical and nonclassical (including dynamic-model) situations. The first component of the characteristic function $\mathrm{cf}_1(s)$ is analytic and ensures that integral moments will exist to order $M-1$ if this is an even integer and $M-2$ if $M-1$ is odd (Lukacs, 1970). In cases in which the distribution does not possess all its moments, the second component, $\mathrm{cf}_2(s)$, of (21) is important in the local behavior of $\mathrm{cf}(s)$ in the neighborhood of the origin and is, as we shall show later, instrumental in determining the form of the tails of $\mathrm{pdf}(x)$.

We start with the following two basic results that relate the tail behavior of density functions to the regularity properties of the characteristic function. They follow without difficulty from the standard discussions on this subject in the literature (Feller, 1971; Lukacs, 1970), but they also demonstrate that we need to go somewhat further to extract a tail expansion of the form (16).

Lemma 2: If the distribution with density $\mathrm{pdf}(x)$ and characteristic function $\mathrm{cf}(s)$ has finite $(M-1)$th absolute moment, then $\mathrm{cf}(s)$ is $M-1$ times continuously differentiable and the derivatives $\mathrm{cf}^{(n)}(s) \to 0$ as $s \to \pm\infty$ for each $n=0,1,\ldots,M-1$.

Proof: The first statement follows by dominated convergence from the existence of the $(M-1)$th absolute moment. The behavior of the derivatives at $\pm\infty$ follows from the representation

$$\mathrm{cf}^{(n)}(s) = \int_{-\infty}^{\infty} e^{isx}(ix)^n \mathrm{pdf}(x)\, dx$$

and, because $(ix)^n \mathrm{pdf}(x)$ is absolutely integrable on $(-\infty, \infty)$, the Riemann–Lebesgue lemma ensures that $\mathrm{cf}^{(n)}(s) \to 0$ as $s \to \pm\infty$ for each $n=0,1,\ldots,M-1$.

Lemma 3: If $\mathrm{cf}(s)$ is $M-1$ times continuously differentiable, if $\mathrm{cf}^{(n)}(s) \to 0$ as $s \to \pm\infty$, and if $\mathrm{cf}^{(n)}(s)$ is absolutely integrable for each $n=0,1,\ldots,M-1$, then

$$\mathrm{pdf}(x) = \frac{1}{2\pi}\int_{-\infty}^{\infty} e^{-isx}\mathrm{cf}(s)\, ds$$

$$= \frac{(ix)^{-M+1}}{2\pi}\int_{-\infty}^{\infty} e^{-isx}\mathrm{cf}^{(M-1)}(s)\, ds = 0(x^{-M+1})$$

as $x \to \infty$.

Proof: Erdélyi (1956, p. 47). Lemma 3 shows that $\mathrm{pdf}(x) \to 0$ as $x \to \pm\infty$ at least as fast as x^{-M+1}; but this is, in general, not a very sharp result, for if the $(M-1)$th absolute moment of the distribution exists and $\mathrm{pdf}(x)$ satisfies Assumption 1, then we would expect that $\mathrm{pdf}(x) = O(x^{-M-\delta})$ for some $\delta > 0$. For example, in the case of the Cauchy distribution, $\mathrm{cf}(s) = e^{-|s|}$, and Lemma 3 demonstrates that $\mathrm{pdf}(x) = 0(1)$, whereas, in fact, $\mathrm{pdf}(x) = O(x^{-2})$. Thus, Lemmas 2 and 3 are not very helpful in providing local expansions about infinity of the form (16).

However, a sharper result that does lead directly to the asymptotic expansion (16) can be obtained from the more explicit representation of the characteristic function (21) and the theory of Fourier transforms of generalized functions and their asymptotic expansions (Jones, 1966; Lighthill, 1958).

Theorem 4: If the distribution with density $\mathrm{pdf}(x)$ and characteristic function $\mathrm{cf}(s)$ satisfies Assumptions 1 and 2, then $\mathrm{pdf}(x)$ has the following asymptotic expansion as $|x| \to \infty$:

$$\mathrm{pdf}(x) = \frac{1}{\pi |x|^{\mu+1}} \sum_{r=0}^{K} \Bigg[\sum_{k+l=r} c_{kl} (\mathrm{sgn}(x))^k + \sum_{\substack{k+l+m=r \\ m \geqslant 1}} c_{klm} (\mathrm{sgn}(x))^k + \sum_{k+l=r} d_{kl} \ln|x| (\mathrm{sgn}(x))^k \Bigg] x^{-r} + 0(|x|^{-N})$$

where the coefficients c_{kl}, c_{klm}, and d_{kl} in this expansion are defined by equations (26) and (27), which follow, and N is the least integer $\geqslant \mu + k + 1$.

Proof: This is based on the theory of asymptotic expansions of Fourier transforms as developed by Lighthill (1958) and Jones (1966).

We shall use the notation $\mathrm{ft}_i(x)$ to denote the inverse Fourier transform of $\mathrm{cf}_i(s)$. Now, because the functions $\mathrm{cf}_i(s)$ for $i = 1, 2$ do not lie in $L(-\infty, \infty)$, the $\mathrm{ft}_i(x)$ cannot be defined in the usual way but do exist as generalized functions. In particular, the $\mathrm{cf}_i(s)$ can be defined as generalized functions, because there exists a $G > 0$ for which $(1+s^2)^{-G} \mathrm{cf}_i(s) \in L(-\infty, \infty)$ (Lighthill, 1958, p. 21). The $\mathrm{ft}_i(x)$ are then defined as the generalized functions obtained as the inverse Fourier transforms of the generalized functions $\mathrm{cf}_i(s)$ (Lighthill, 1958, p. 18).

Starting with $\mathrm{cf}_1(s)$, we write

$$\mathrm{cf}_1(s) = \lim_{t \to 0+} e^{i\eta s} \sum_{m=0}^{M-1} p_m e^{-|s|t} (is)^m$$

and then, by definition,

$$\mathrm{ft}_1(x) = \lim_{t\to 0+}\left\{\frac{1}{2\pi}\sum_{m=0}^{M-1} p_m \int_{-\infty}^{\infty} e^{-isx}e^{i\eta s}e^{-|s|t}(is)^m\,ds\right\}$$

$$= \frac{1}{2\pi}\sum_{m=0}^{M-1} p_m(-1)^m \lim_{t\to 0+}\left\{\frac{d^m}{dx^m}\int_{-\infty}^{\infty} e^{-i(x-\eta)s}e^{-|s|t}\,ds\right\}$$

(22) $$= \frac{1}{2\pi}\sum_{m=0}^{M-1} p_m(-1)^m \lim_{t\to 0+}\left\{\frac{d^m}{dx^m}\left[\int_0^{\infty} e^{[-i(x-\eta)-t]s}\,ds + \int_0^{\infty} e^{[i(x-\eta)-t]s}\,ds\right]\right\}$$

$$= \frac{1}{2\pi}\sum_{m=0}^{M-1} p_m(-1)^m\delta^{(m)}(x-\eta)$$

where $\delta(y)$ is the Dirac delta function and $\delta^{(m)}(y)$ is its mth derivative. We deduce the asymptotic behavior of $\mathrm{ft}_1(x)$ as $x\to\infty$ immediately from (22) as

(23) $\mathrm{ft}_1(x) = 0(x^{-k})$

for any value of $k>0$.

The second component is

$$\mathrm{cf}_2(s) = e^{i\eta s}\sum_{k=0}^{K}\{q_{k0}|s|^{\mu+k} + q_{k1}|s|^{\mu+k}\ln|s|\}$$

$$= e^{i\eta s}\sum_{k=0}^{K}\left[\left(q_{k0}+q_{k1}\frac{\partial}{\partial\alpha}\right)|s|^{\alpha}\right]_{\alpha=\mu+k}$$

$$= \lim_{t\to 0+} e^{i\eta s}\sum_{k=0}^{K}\left[\left(q_{k0}+q_{k1}\frac{\partial}{\partial\alpha}\right)|s|^{\alpha}e^{-|s|t}\right]_{\alpha=\mu+k}$$

On inversion, we obtain

$$\mathrm{ft}_2(x) = \lim_{t\to 0+}\left\{\frac{1}{2\pi}\sum_{k=0}^{K}\left[\left(q_{k0}+q_{k1}\frac{\partial}{\partial\alpha}\right)\int_{-\infty}^{\infty} e^{-isx}e^{i\eta s}e^{-|s|t}|s|^{\alpha}\,ds\right]_{\alpha=\mu+k}\right\}$$

$$= \lim_{t\to 0+}\left\{\frac{1}{2\pi}\sum_{k=0}^{K}\left[\left(q_{k0}+q_{k1}\frac{\partial}{\partial\alpha}\right)\right.\right.$$

$$\times\left(\int_0^\infty e^{-(iy+t)s}s^\alpha\,ds+\int_0^\infty e^{-(-iy+t)s}s^\alpha\,ds\right)\Bigg]_{\substack{\alpha=\mu+k\\ y=x-\eta}}\Bigg\}$$

$$=\frac{1}{2\pi}\sum_{k=0}^{K}\Bigg[\left(q_{k0}+q_{k1}\frac{\partial}{\partial\alpha}\right)$$

$$\times\left(\lim_{t\to 0+}\Gamma(\alpha+1)\{(t+iy)^{-\alpha-1}+(t-iy)^{-\alpha-1}\}\right)\Bigg]_{\substack{\alpha=\mu+k\\ y=x-\eta}}$$

$$=\frac{1}{2\pi}\sum_{k=0}^{K}\Bigg[\left(q_{k0}+q_{k1}\frac{\partial}{\partial\alpha}\right)\Gamma(\alpha+1)|y|^{-\alpha-1}$$

$$\times\{e^{-(i\pi/2)\,\mathrm{sgn}(y)(\alpha+1)}+e^{(i\pi/2)\,\mathrm{sgn}(y)(\alpha+1)}\}\Bigg]_{\substack{\alpha=\mu+k\\ y=x-\eta}}$$

$$=\frac{1}{2\pi}\sum_{k=0}^{K}\Bigg[\left(q_{k0}+q_{k1}\frac{\partial}{\partial\alpha}\right)$$

$$\times 2\Gamma(\alpha+1)\cos\{\tfrac{1}{2}\pi(\alpha+1)\}|y|^{-\alpha-1}\Bigg]_{\substack{\alpha=\mu+k\\ y=x-\eta}}$$

$$=\frac{1}{\pi}\sum_{k=0}^{K}\Bigg[\Gamma(\alpha+1)\cos\{\tfrac{1}{2}\pi(\alpha+1)\}$$

$$\times\{q_{k0}+(\psi'(\alpha+1)-\tfrac{1}{2}\pi\tan\{\tfrac{1}{2}\pi(\alpha+1)\}-\ln|y|)q_{k1}\}$$

$$\times|y|^{-(\alpha+1)}\Bigg]_{\substack{\alpha=\mu+k\\ y=x-\eta}}$$

where $\psi'(z)=\Gamma'(z)/\Gamma(z)$, the logarithmic derivative of the Gamma function. Thus, the asymptotic behavior of $\mathrm{ft}_2(x)$ as $x\to\infty$ is given by the series

$$\text{(24)}\qquad \mathrm{ft}_2(x)=\frac{1}{\pi}\sum_{k=0}^{K}\sum_{l=0}^{\infty}\Bigg[\Gamma(\alpha+1)\cos\{\tfrac{1}{2}\pi(\alpha+1)\}$$

$$\times\Bigg\{q_{k0}+\Bigg(\psi'(\alpha+1)-\tfrac{1}{2}\pi\tan\{\tfrac{1}{2}\pi(\alpha+1)\}$$

$$-\ln|x|+\sum_{m=1}^{\infty}\frac{1}{m}\left(\frac{\eta}{x}\right)^m\Bigg)q_{k1}\Bigg\}$$

$$\times \left. \frac{(\alpha+1)_l}{l!}\left(\frac{\eta}{x}\right)^l |x|^{-(\alpha+1)} \right]_{\alpha=\mu+k}$$

where $(\alpha+1)_l = \Gamma(\alpha+1+l)/\Gamma(\alpha+1)$.

The third component of the characteristic function is $\mathrm{cf}_3(s)$. Now, $\mathrm{ft}_3(x)$ is the inverse Fourier transform of $\mathrm{cf}_3(s)$, so that $(-ix)^N \mathrm{ft}_3(x)$ has the inverse Fourier transform $\mathrm{cf}_3^{(N)}(s)$. By Theorem 18 of Lighthill (1958, p. 49), it now follows that $(-ix)^N \mathrm{ft}_3(x) = O(1)$ as $x \to \infty$. This last result, together with equations (23) and (24), implies that as $|x| \to \infty$,

$$\mathrm{pdf}(x) = \mathrm{ft}_1(x) + \mathrm{ft}_2(x) + \mathrm{ft}_3(x)$$

$$(25) \quad = \frac{1}{\pi|x|^{\mu+1}} \sum_{k=0}^{K} |x|^{-k}\left[q'_{k0} + q'_{k1}\left\{\sum_{m=1}^{\infty}\frac{1}{m}\left(\frac{\eta}{x}\right)^m - \ln|x|\right\}\right] \times \sum_{l=0}^{\infty}\frac{(\mu+k+1)l}{l!}\left(\frac{\eta}{x}\right)^l + O(|x|^{-N})$$

$$(26) \quad = \frac{1}{\pi|x|^{\mu+1}} \sum_{r=0}^{K}\left[\sum_{k+l=r}\frac{q'_{k0}(\mu+k+1)_l\eta^l}{l!}(\mathrm{sgn}(x))^k + \sum_{\substack{k+l+m=r\\ m\geqslant 1}}\frac{q'_{k1}(\mu+k+1)_l\eta^{l+m}}{l!m}(\mathrm{sgn}(x))^k - \sum_{k+l=r}\frac{q'_{k1}(\mu+k+1)_l\eta^l}{l!}\ln|x|(\mathrm{sgn}(x))^k\right] \times x^{-r} + O(|x|^{-N})$$

where

$$q'_{k0} = \Gamma(\mu+k)\cos\{\tfrac{1}{2}\pi(\mu+k+1)\} \times \{q_{k0} + (\psi'(\mu+k+1) - \tfrac{1}{2}\pi\tan\{\tfrac{1}{2}\pi(\mu+k+1)\})q_{k1}\}$$

$$q'_{k1} = \Gamma(\mu+k)\cos\{\tfrac{1}{2}\pi(\mu+k+1)\}q_{k1}$$

and N is the least integer $\geqslant \mu+k+1$. We rewrite (26) in the form

$$(27) \quad \frac{1}{\pi|x|^{\mu+1}} \sum_{r=0}^{K}\left[\sum_{k+l=r} c_{kl}(\mathrm{sgn}(x))^k + \sum_{\substack{k+l+m=r\\ m\geqslant 1}} c_{klm}(\mathrm{sgn}(x))^k - \sum_{k+l=r} d_{kl}\ln|x|(\mathrm{sgn}(x))^k\right]x^{-r} + O(|x|^{-N})$$

and this establishes the result.

To illustrate the use of Theorem 4, we take the simple example of the Cauchy distribution with $\mathrm{cf}(s)=e^{-s}$. In this case

$$\mathrm{cf}_1(s) = 1$$

$$\mathrm{cf}_2(s) = |s| \sum_{k=0}^{K} \frac{(-1)^{k+1}}{(k+1)!} |s|^k$$

$$\mathrm{cf}_3(s) = \frac{|s|^{k+2}}{(k+2)!} e^{-\theta|s|} \quad (0<\theta<1)$$

and we deduce from (26), by setting $\mu=1$, $\eta=0$, and $q_{k1}=0$, that

$$\begin{aligned}\mathrm{pdf}(x) &= \frac{1}{\pi x^2} \sum_{r=0}^{K} \frac{(-1)^{r+1}\Gamma(r-2)\cos\{\frac{1}{2}\pi(r+2)\}}{(r+1)!} \\ &\quad \times (\mathrm{sgn}(x))^r x^{-r} + O(|x|^{-K-2}) \\ &= \frac{1}{\pi x^2} \sum_{r=0}^{K} (-1)^{r+1} \cos\{\tfrac{1}{2}\pi(r+2)\} |x|^{-r}\end{aligned}$$

Now, $\cos\{\frac{1}{2}\pi(r+2)\}$ equals $(-1)^{1/2(r+1)}$ when r is an even integer and equals zero when r is odd. Hence, setting $r=2n$ and $K=2$, we have

$$\mathrm{pdf}(x) = \frac{1}{\pi x^2} \sum_{n=0}^{N} (-1)^n (x^2)^{-n} + O((x^2)^{-(N+1)})$$

This expansion can be verified directly from the density function $\mathrm{pdf}(x)=[\pi(1+x^2)]^{-1}$ itself.

Theorem 5: If $s^N \mathrm{cf}(s)$ is absolutely integrable over $(-\infty,\infty)$, then the local expansion of $\mathrm{pdf}(x)$ about the point $x=d_i$ is given by

$$\mathrm{pdf}(x) = \sum_{j=0}^{N-1} \beta_{ij}(x-d_i)^j + O(x-d_i)^N \tag{28}$$

where

$$\beta_{ij} = \frac{1}{2\pi j!} \int_{-\infty}^{\infty} (-is)^j \exp(-isd_i)\, \mathrm{cf}(s)\, ds \quad (j=0,1,\ldots,N-1)$$

Proof: Because $s^N \mathrm{cf}(s) \in L(-\infty,\infty)$, we expand the exponential e^{-isx} in the inversion formula

$$\mathrm{pdf}(x) = \frac{1}{2\pi} \int_{-\infty}^{\infty} e^{-isx} \mathrm{cf}(s)\, ds$$

about the point $x = d_i$ and integrate term by term, giving

$$\frac{1}{2\pi j!}\sum_{j=0}^{N-1}\int_{-\infty}^{\infty}(-is)^j \exp(-isd_i)\,\mathrm{cf}(s)\,ds(x-d_i)^j$$

$$+\frac{1}{2\pi N!}\int_{-\infty}^{\infty}(-is)^N \exp(-is\tilde{d}_i)\,\mathrm{cf}(s)\,ds(x-d_i)^N$$

where $\tilde{d}_i$ lies on the line segment connecting x and d_i.

Local expansions of the type discussed in this section for the tails and the body of the distribution can also be extracted under similar conditions for the distribution function. These expansions will be useful in the development of a corresponding theory of global approximation for the distribution function rather than the density, and they will be discussed in a later paper. Expansions of this type have already been given for many of the common distributions in the statistical literature (Zelen & Severo, 1965).

6 Multiple-point Padé approximants

As discussed in the previous section, Padé approximants can be used to improve the convergence properties of local Taylor expansions, and they have the additional useful property that they frequently extend the domain over which these local expansions provide good approximations. This section will show how Padé approximants can be derived from the local density expansions (16) and (17). These approximants will provide a preliminary set of rational fractions. They can then be used directly as approximations to pdf(x) or modified so that they belong to the class of rational fractions (2) and have satisfactory global behavior. The question of modifying the preliminary rational fractions will be taken up in Section 7.

We start by writing the density function in the form

(29) $$\mathrm{pdf}(x) = s(x)\,\mathrm{pdf}_s(x) \quad (-\infty < x < \infty)$$

where $s(x)$ is a real continuous function satisfying $s(x) > 0$ over the entire real axis and $s(x) \to 0$ as $x \to \pm\infty$. This representation of pdf(x) reconciles with the class of rational fractions defined in (2) and allows us to accommodate information about the coefficient functions $t(|x|)$ and $w(x)$ that appear in the local density expansions (16) and (18). In many cases, $s(x)$ will represent the leading term in the multiple series representation of the density pdf(x), and in such cases $s(x)$ usually will be identical with $t(|x|)$ and $w(x)$. When this leading term in the density is unknown, a suitable alternative will be to set $s(x)=t(|x|)$ directly or some modified form of $t(|x|)$ that has the same asymptotic behavior but that is well behaved elsewhere on the real axis. If necessary, the expansion (18) can then be adjusted to take account of this modification so that (17) will be correct to the same number of terms.

If we write the local expansions of $\mathrm{pdf}_s(x)$ in the form

$$\text{(30)}\qquad \mathrm{pdf}_s(x) \sim \alpha_0 + \alpha_1 x^{-1} + \alpha_2 x^{-2} + \alpha_3 x^{-3} + \alpha_4 x^{-4} + \cdots \quad (x \to \pm\infty)$$

$$\text{(31)}\qquad \mathrm{pdf}_s(x) \sim \beta_{i0} + \beta_{i1}(x-d_i) + \beta_{i2}(x-d_i)^2 + \beta_{i3}(x-d_i)^3 + \beta_{i4}(x-d_i)^4 + \cdots \quad (i=1,\ldots,I), \quad x \to d_i$$

our problem is to construct a rational fraction of the form

$$\text{(32)}\qquad [n/n] = \frac{P_n(x)}{Q_n(x)} = \frac{a_0 + a_1 x + \cdots + a_n x^n}{b_0 + b_1 x + \cdots + b_n x^n} \qquad (n = \text{an even integer})$$

which has the same local behavior as (30) and (31) and to as high an order as possible. Such a rational fraction is called a multiple-point Padé approximant, and these have been discussed by Baker (1975, Chapter 8).[3]

The equations that define (32) can best be introduced by considering the approximant based on the Taylor series about a single point. We take the case of (31), with $d_i=0$, and normalize (32) by setting $b_0=1$. This normalization ensures that $Q_n(0)=1>0$, so that the $[n/n]$ approximant will not have a pole at the origin, this now being the point of expansion of the Taylor series (31). The coefficients of $[n/n]$ are now determined by the equation

$$\text{(33)}\qquad \mathrm{pdf}_s(x)Q_n(x) - P_n(x) = O(x^{2n+1})$$

Explicitly, we have the relations

$$\text{(34)}\qquad \begin{array}{llllll}
\beta_{i0} & & & & & = a_0 \\
\beta_{i1} & + \beta_{i0}b_1 & & & & = a_1 \\
\beta_{i2} & + \beta_{i1}b_1 & + \beta_{i0}b_2 & & & = a_2 \\
\beta_{i3} & + \beta_{i2}b_1 & + \beta_{i1}b_2 & + \beta_{i0}b_3 & & = a_3 \\
\cdot & \cdot & \cdot & \cdot & \cdots & \cdot \\
\beta_{in} & + \beta_{in-1}b_1 & + \beta_{in-2}b_2 & + \beta_{in-3}b_3 + & \cdots + \beta_{i0}b_n & = a_n \\
\beta_{in+1} & + \beta_{in}b_1 & + \beta_{in-1}b_2 & + \beta_{in-2}b_3 + & \cdots + \beta_{i1}b_n & = 0 \\
\cdot & \cdot & \cdot & \cdot & \cdots & \cdot \\
\beta_{i2n} & + \beta_{i2n-1} & + \beta_{i2n-2}b_2 & + \beta_{i2n-3}b_3 + & \cdots + \beta_{in}b_n & = 0
\end{array}$$

which comprise $2n+1$ equations in the $2n+1$ required coefficients of $[n/n]$, namely, $\{a_0, a_1, \ldots, a_n; b_1, \ldots, b_n\}$. Baker (1975)[4] has proved that although a solution to (34) does not necessarily exist for all positive integers n, there is an infinite subsequence $\{n_j\}$ for which the Padé approximant $[n_j/n_j]$ exists for any formal power series with $\beta_{i0} \neq 0$. Further, when the approximant $[n/n]$ exists, it is unique.[5]

We see by inspection of (34) that in order to compute the coefficients of $[n/n]$ we need the coefficients in the local expansion (31) to order $2n$. Even for low values of n this is likely to become prohibitive quite quickly when dealing with the distribution of an econometric statistic because of the increasing difficulty in extracting higher-order coefficients and the complications of the resulting formulas. Moreover, in view of the smoothness of most density functions, in practice there will be little advantage to be gained from increasing the order of contact at a particular point past $n=3$ or 4. In many cases, $n=2$ will be sufficient to provide a highly satisfactory local density approximant.[6]

Multiple-point expansions provide an excellent means of reducing the order of contact at individual points to within manageable limits while extending the domain over which the final approximant will perform well. Thus, a two-point Padé approximant $[n/n]$ might be based on the first $n+1$ equations of (34), which require local expansion coefficients up to β_{in} and a corresponding set of n equations with expansion coefficients up to order $n-1$ for a point other than the origin. These equations will then yield an approximant with contact of order n at the origin and $n-1$ at the second point.

If one of the points of local expansion is infinity, then the equations take on a slightly different form. In this case, rather than (33), we require

$$\text{pdf}_s(x)Q_n(x) - P_n(x) = O(x^{-2n-1}) \tag{35}$$

as $x \to \infty$. We then have the following explicit relations from (30), (32), and (35)

$$\begin{array}{llllll}
\alpha_0 b_n & & & & & = a_n \\
\alpha_1 b_n & + \alpha_0 b_{n-1} & & & & = a_{n-1} \\
\alpha_2 b_n & + \alpha_1 b_{n-1} & + \alpha_0 b_{n-2} & & & = a_{n-2} \\
\cdot & \cdot \quad \cdot & \cdot \quad \cdot & \cdot\cdots\cdot & \cdot\quad\cdot & \cdot \\
\alpha_n b_n & + \alpha_{n-1} b_{n-1} & + \alpha_{n-2} b_{n-2} & + \cdots & + \alpha_0 & = a_0 \\
\alpha_{n+1} b_n & + \alpha_n b_{n-1} & + \alpha_{n-1} b_{n-2} & + \cdots & + \alpha_1 & = 0 \\
\cdot & \cdot \quad \cdot & \cdot \quad \cdot & \cdot\cdots\cdot & \cdot\quad\cdot & \cdot \\
\alpha_{2n} b_n & + \alpha_{2n-1} b_{n-1} & + \alpha_{2n-2} b_{n-2} & + \cdots & \cdot \quad \cdot & = 0
\end{array} \tag{36}$$

As with (34), this is a system of $2n+1$ equations in the same number of unknown coefficients.

In the general case of expansions about arbitrary points d_i, as in (31), the equations that determine the coefficients take the form

$$\left\{\sum_{j=0}^{\infty} \beta_{ij}(x-d_i)^j\right\} Q_n(d_i + (x-d_i)) - P_n(d_i + (x-d_i)) = O((x-d_i)^{2n+1}) \quad (i=1,\ldots,I) \tag{37}$$

If we write $y=x-d_i$ and expand $Q_n(d_i+y)$ and $P_n(d_i+y)$ as

$$Q_n(d_i + y) = \sum_{k=0}^{n} b_k(d_i + y)^k = \sum_{k=0}^{n} b_k^{(i)} y^k = Q_n^{(i)}(y)$$

$$P_n(d_i + y) = \sum_{k=0}^{n} a_k(d_i + y)^k = \sum_{k=0}^{n} a_k^{(i)} y^k = P_n^{(i)}(y)$$

we have

$$b^{(i)} = K^{(i)} b, \qquad a^{(i)} = K^{(i)} a \tag{38}$$

where

$$K^{(i)} = \begin{bmatrix} 1 & d_i & d_i^2 & d_i^3 & \cdots & d_i^n \\ 0 & 1 & 2d_i & 3d_i^2 & \cdots & \binom{n}{1} d_i^{n-1} \\ 0 & 0 & 1 & 3d_i & \cdots & \binom{n}{2} d_i^{n-2} \\ \cdot & \cdot & \cdot & \cdot & \cdots & \cdot \\ 0 & 0 & 0 & 0 & \cdots & 1 \end{bmatrix}, \tag{39}$$

$$b^{(i)} = \begin{bmatrix} b_0^{(i)} \\ b_1^{(i)} \\ \cdot \\ \cdot \\ b_n^{(i)} \end{bmatrix}, \quad b = \begin{bmatrix} b_0 \\ b_1 \\ \cdot \\ \cdot \\ b_n \end{bmatrix}, \quad a^{(i)} = \begin{bmatrix} a_0^{(i)} \\ a_1^{(i)} \\ \cdot \\ \cdot \\ a_n^{(i)} \end{bmatrix}, \quad a = \begin{bmatrix} a_0 \\ a_1 \\ \cdot \\ \cdot \\ a_n \end{bmatrix}$$

and (37) becomes

$$\left(\sum_{j=0}^{\infty} \beta_{ij} y^j\right) Q_n^{(i)}(y) - P_n^{(i)}(y) = O(y^{2n+1}) \tag{40}$$

which is of the same form as (33) but in the transformed coefficients.

To work in terms of the original coefficients, we can use the transformation matrix $K^{(i)}$ in the case of the vector $a^{(i)}$, as in (38), but in view of the normalization on the vector b, we partition $K^{(i)}$ and b as follows

$$K^{(i)} = \left[\begin{array}{c|c} 1 & k^{(i)\prime} \\ \hline 0 & K_{22}^{(i)} \end{array}\right], \qquad k^{(i)\prime} = [d_i, d_i^2, d_i^3, \ldots, d_i^n]$$

$$b' = [b_0, b_*'] = [1, b_*']$$

We then have, from (38),

$$b_0^{(i)} = k^{(i)\prime} b_*, \qquad b_*^{(i)} = K_{22}^{(i)} b_*$$

We now define

$$G^{(i)} = \begin{bmatrix} 0 & 0 & 0 & \cdots & 0 \\ -\beta_{i0} & 0 & 0 & \cdots & 0 \\ -\beta_{i1} & -\beta_{i0} & 0 & \cdots & 0 \\ -\beta_{i2} & -\beta_{i1} & -\beta_{i0} & \cdots & 0 \\ \vdots & \vdots & \vdots & \vdots & \vdots \\ -\beta_{in-1} & -\beta_{in-2} & -\beta_{in-3} & \cdots & -\beta_{i0} \end{bmatrix}, \qquad g^{(i)} = \begin{bmatrix} \beta_{i0} \\ \beta_{i1} \\ \cdot \\ \cdot \\ \vdots \\ \beta_{in} \end{bmatrix}$$

The first $n+1$ equations of (34) can be written as

$$a + G^{(i)} b_* = g^{(i)}$$

or, in the general case of a local expansion about the point d_i (not necessarily the origin),

(41) $$a^{(i)} + G^{(i)} b_*^{(i)} = g^{(i)} + g^{(i)} b_0^{(i)}$$

Transforming back to the original coefficients in the rational fraction, we get

$$K^{(i)} a + G^{(i)} K_{22}^{(i)} b_* = g^{(i)} + g^{(i)} k^{(i)\prime} b_*$$

or

(42) $$K^{(i)} a + [G^{(i)} K_{22}^{(i)} - g^{(i)} k^{(i)\prime}] b_* = g^{(i)}$$

The system of equations (42) holds for each point of local expansion, that is, for $i=1, \ldots, I$ in our original notation (see equation (31)).

Note that as we have constructed (42) the system involves $n \times 1$ equations. In practice, it may be convenient to use fewer equations at each point, thus reducing the order of contact of the Padé approximant at each point and requiring less analytic information about the expansion coefficients. The procedure allows us to make up for this reduction in the number of equations at each point by increasing the number of points we use in developing the approximant. This process has the additional advantage of improving the global nature of the final approximation.

In the general case we let $K^{(i)}$ be $(m_i+1)\times(n+1)$, $G^{(i)}$ be $(m_i+1)\times m_i$, $K_{22}^{(i)}$ be $m_i \times n$, $g^{(i)}$ be $(m_i+1)\times 1$, and $k^{(i)}$ be $n+1$. The complete system of equations that determine the coefficients in the $[n/n]$ Padé approximant are then based on (36) and (42) and take the following general form:

(43)

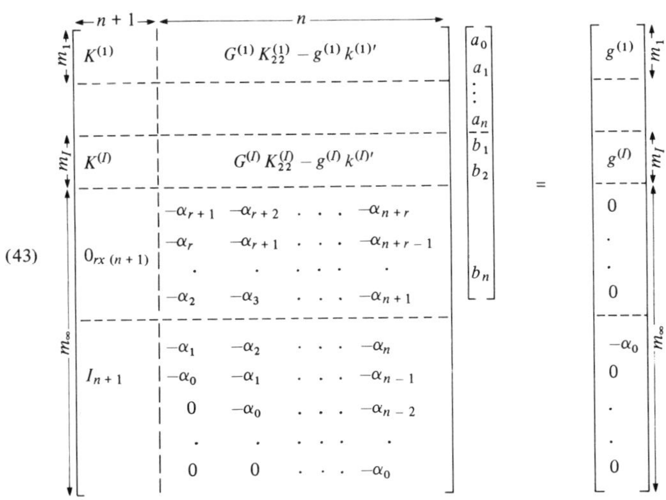

where $m_\infty = n+r+1$. In (43) we need to select I and the m_i and m_∞ in such a way that $\sum_{i=1}^{I} m_i + m_\infty \geqslant 2n+1$. In the final block of equations in (43) we shall often select $r=0$, so that $m_\infty \leqslant n+1$. As with the case of the local expansions (31) about the points d_i, this will reduce the number of final expansion coefficients that are required to solve for the $[n/n]$ Padé coefficients. In some cases (the application in Section 8 turns out to be such a case) we may have more than enough coefficients, so that $\sum m_i + m_\infty > 2n+1$, and we may neglect some equations of (43) to obtain a solution. When this happens, it would seem preferable to neglect those equations that refer to higher-order points of contact of the Padé approximant with the local expansions rather than those that refer to lower-order points of contact.

7 Modifying the Padé approximants

By solving (43) for the Padé coefficients, we obtain a preliminary rational fraction $[n/n]$ as in (32). This can be used to construct an approximation to pdf(x) of the form $s(x)[n/n] = s(x)P_n(x)/Q_n(x)$. In some cases this will turn out to be a perfectly satisfactory approximant. In others, it will need to be modified to produce a good approximation to pdf(x) over a wide interval. This is because there is nothing in the procedure outlined in Section 6 that prevents the occurrence of zeros in the polynomial $Q_n(x)$ on the real axis. These zeros induce poles in the approximant and will need to be eliminated if the approximation is to perform well, unless the zeros appear in remote and irrelevant regions of the distribution. My experience to date suggests that the latter is not usually the case. The normal occurrence is for the procedure in Section 6 to produce a preliminary approximant with either no poles at all or a pair of poles, at least one of which lies within the main body of the distribution.

In addition to unwanted poles, the $[n/n]$ Padé approximant may become zero at a finite number of points on the real axis. Because we shall, in general, have pdf$(x)>0$ for all finite x, we shall normally wish to eliminate the zeros of the approximant unless they occur well outside the region of interest in the distribution.

When poles occur, they are typically found in the bridging region between the points of local density expansion used in (43) to construct the Padé approximant. This suggests that an obvious way of helping to remove unwanted poles is to introduce an additional point of local expansion in (43), perhaps at the price of reducing the order of contact at another point. However, there is no guarantee that this method will eliminate poles, and it has the disadvantage of requiring additional information about the distribution to be operational. The procedure we shall suggest later does not suffer from these disadvantages. It will eliminate the poles, and it is sufficiently flexible to allow for additional information about the distribution to be incorporated at the time of modification, if such information is available.

Before we outline the procedure, it may be worth mentioning that the occurrence of unwanted poles in Padé approximants is a long-standing problem. The presence of poles in the approximant is one of the reasons that it is difficult to prove general theorems about the convergence of Padé approximants to a given function as the degree of the approximant increases. Many of the general results that are available (Baker, 1975, Part II) concern the convergence of subsequences as $n \to \infty$. For an example of nonconvergence, we can cite the work of Chui (1976), who proved that in the general family of entire functions there exists a function for which the sequence of $[n/n]$ Padé approximants is divergent everywhere in the whole complex plane except at the origin.

The procedure we suggest for modifying Padé approximants so that they will be well behaved over the whole real axis is based on the following simple idea. If zeros of the numerator and denominator polynomials $P_n(x)$ and $Q_n(x)$ occur on the real axis, they will occur in pairs, because n is even. We then replace the real roots of the associated quadratic equations by complex conjugate pairs in such a way that we preserve, as far as possible, the known behavior of the function at the points of local expansion. Various degrees of sophistication are possible in the practical application of this method. In fact, as we shall demonstrate in the application of Section 8, even crude adjustments that preserve only contact of order 1 at the points of local expansion seem to work remarkably well. After we have adjusted the coefficients in the Padé approximant so that $P_n(x)>0$ and $Q_n(x)>0$ throughout the real axis, we simply numerically integrate and rescale so that the area under the curve is unity.

Some of the principles involved in the method outlined in the preceding paragraph can be illustrated in the case of an approximant with $n=4$. Let the $[n/n]$ Padé approximant extracted by the procedure of Section 6 with points of local expansion at $x=0$ and $x^{-1}=0$ be given by

$$[4/4](x) = \frac{\Sigma_{i=0}^{4} a_i x^i}{\Sigma_{i=0}^{4} b_i x^i} = \frac{a_4(x-\gamma_1)(x-\gamma_2)(x-\gamma)(x-\bar{\gamma})}{b_4(x-\delta_1)(x-\delta_2)(x-\delta)(x-\bar{\delta})} \tag{44}$$

where γ_1 and γ_2 denote real zeros of the numerator and δ_1 and δ_2 denote real zeros of the denominator; $(\gamma,\bar{\gamma})$ and $(\delta,\bar{\delta})$ are complex conjugate pairs. We start by rewriting (44) in the form

$$[4/4](x) = \frac{a_4\{x^2-(\gamma_1+\gamma_2)x+\gamma_1\gamma_2\}(x-\gamma)(x-\bar{\gamma})}{b_4\{x^2-(\delta_1+\delta_2)x+\delta_1\delta_2\}(x-\delta)(x-\bar{\delta})} \tag{45}$$

We now propose to modify the coefficients of the quadratics in braces so that $[4/4](x)>0$ for all real x, while retaining the same behavior as in (45) in the neighborhood of $x=0$ and $x^{-1}=0$. We therefore define the family of functions

$$[4/4](x;\Theta) = \frac{a_4\{cx^2+dx+e\}(x-\gamma)(x-\bar{\gamma})}{b_4\{fx^2+gx+h\}(x-\delta)(x-\bar{\delta})} \tag{46}$$

where $\Theta'=(c,d,e,f,g,h)$ is a vector of real parameters to be chosen. To ensure equivalent local behavior in (45) and (46), we restrict our choice of Θ so that

(i) $c/f=1$

(ii) $e/h=\gamma_1\gamma_2/\delta_1\delta_2$

Now, (i) will ensure that $[4/4](x;\Theta)\rightarrow a_4/b_4$ as $x\rightarrow\pm\infty$, and (ii) will ensure that $[4/4](x;\Theta)\rightarrow a_4\gamma_1\gamma_2|\gamma|^2/b_4\delta_1\delta_2|\delta|^2$ as $x\rightarrow 0$.

In most cases we find that the zeros (γ_1, γ_2) and (δ_1, δ_2) occur with the same sign patterns. This is because the zeros and singularities lie in the intervals between the points (here 0 and $\pm\infty$) of local expansion. If we take the case in which both $\gamma_1\gamma_2 > 0$ and $\delta_1\delta_2 > 0$, our task is then to raise f and h from their original values in (45) so that the discriminant $g^2 - 4fh < 0$. This will require proportional changes in c and e so that (i) and (ii) remain valid. Often these automatic changes in c and e will be sufficient to ensure that there are no zeros in (46). If they are not, some small adjustment in the value of d will normally suffice. There is an added advantage to adjusting the value of d, in that simple hand calculations will show what adjustments in this parameter will improve the order of contact of (46) at the points of local expansion while preserving the desired global behavior of $[4/4](x;\Theta) > 0$ for all x. Various other scenarios for parameter changes are possible, but those we have illustrated should indicate some of the relevant considerations and the ease with which they can be performed.

The family of rational fractions (46) based on Padé approximants have introduced extra flexibility in the approximating procedure. The idea is essentially to partially reparameterize a first-stage Padé approximant so that we can achieve good global behavior by sacrificing some degree of contact at the points of local expansion. But with the new family of approximating rational fractions (46), we have the opportunity to adjust the parameters to take account of any additional information about the distribution that has not already been used in the equations (43) that define the original coefficients (perhaps less precise information based on Monte Carlo work with the same distribution).

An obvious alternative procedure for modifying the Padé approximant (45), but one I have not yet tried in application, is to use splines to bridge the intervals in which singularities and zeros occur. This method may be particularly useful in cases in which zeros and singularities occur together in close proximity.

8 An application to a simultaneous-equations estimator

We consider the single structural equation

$$y_1 = \beta y_2 + Z_1\gamma_1 + u \tag{47}$$

where y_1 and y_2 are vectors of T observations on two endogenous variables, Z_1 is a $T \times K_1$ matrix of observations on K_1 exogenous variables, and u is a vector of random disturbances. The reduced-form equations for y_1 and y_2 are

$$[y_1 \vdots y_2] = [Z_1 \vdots Z_2]\begin{bmatrix} \pi_{11} & \pi_{12} \\ \pi_{21} & \pi_{22} \end{bmatrix} + [v_1 \vdots v_2] \tag{48}$$

where Z_2 is a $T\times K_2$ matrix of observations of K_2 exogenous variables excluded from (47). We assume that the usual standardizing transformations have been carried out, so that (i) $T^{-1}Z'Z=I_K$, where $[Z=Z_1 \vdots Z_2]$, $k=k_1+k_2$, and (ii) the rows of $[v_1 \vdots v_2]$ are independent and identically distributed normal vectors with zero mean and covariance matrix equal to the identity matrix. We also assume that (47) is identified so that $K_2 \geqslant 1$.

The two-stage least-squares estimator 2SLS of β in (47) is given by the ratio $\hat{\beta}=y_2'Ry_1/y_2'Ry_2$, where $R=Z_2Z_2'$. The exact density function of $\hat{\beta}$ is known to be the doubly infinite series (Richardson, 1968)

$$\text{pdf}(x) = \frac{\exp[-(\mu^2/2)(1+\beta^2)]}{\beta(1/2,K_2/2)(1+x^2)^{(K_2+1)/2}} \sum_{j=0}^{\infty} \frac{[(K_2+1)/2]_j}{(K_2/2)_j\, j!} \times \left\{\frac{\mu^2}{2}\,\frac{(1+\beta x)^2}{1+x^2}\right\}^j {}_1F_1\left(\frac{K_2-1}{2}, j+\frac{K_2}{2}; \frac{\mu^2\beta^2}{2}\right) \tag{49}$$

which depends on the three parameters β, K_2, and $\mu^2=T\pi_{22}'\pi_{22}$.

The extensive tabulations of Anderson and Sawa (1979) show that (49) may be adequately approximated by the asymptotic normal only when μ^2 is very large; the size of μ^2 required for the asymptotic distribution to provide an adequate approximation is itself contingent on the size of β and K_2. Even for moderate values of β and K_2 the computations of Anderson and Sawa (1979) show that extremely large values of μ^2 (well over 1,000) are required to secure a satisfactory approximation.

As discussed in the introduction, other approximations to (49) that perform satisfactorily for a range of parameter values are the Edgeworth (Anderson & Sawa, 1973, 1979) and saddlepoint (Holly & Phillips, 1979) approximations. But, when μ^2 is small, both these approximations become inadequate.

In Figures 5.1, 5.2, and 5.3 we illustrate the inadequacy of these three different methods of approximation in the case in which $\beta=0.6$, $\mu^2=4.0$, and $K=4,10$. This is rather an extreme case in which μ^2 is very low (around the lower limit of μ^2 values found by Anderson and associates (1978) in their numerical computations of key parameters for actual econometric models). It has been chosen to test the adequacy of the new method of approximation discussed in the earlier sections of this chapter specifically in a case in which the existing methods break down.

Figures 5.4 to 5.8 detail the approximants obtained at each stage of the procedure outlined in the previous sections of this chapter.[7] In the

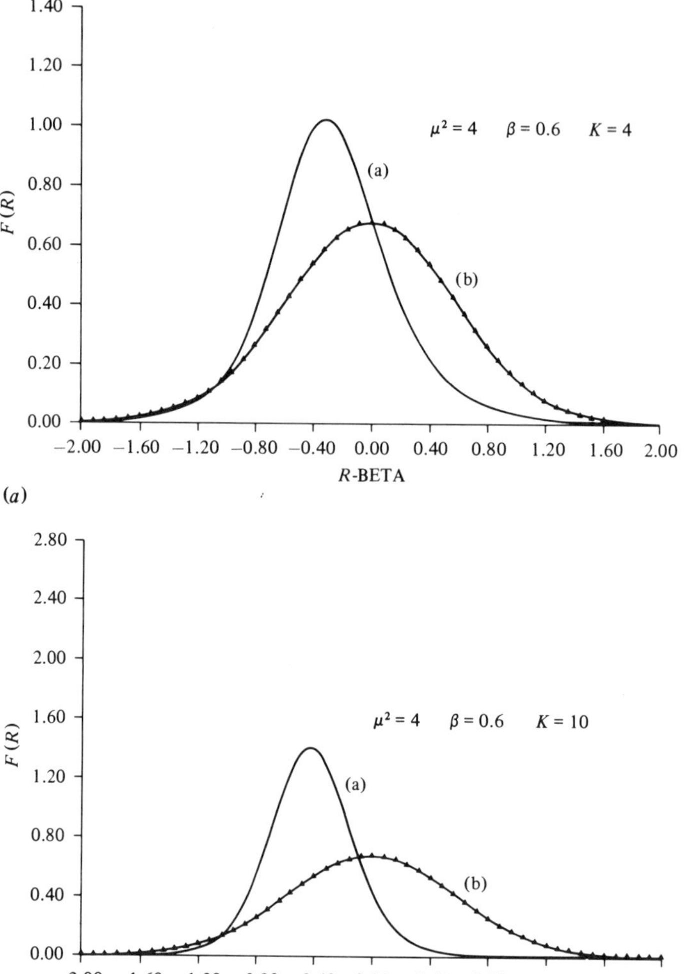

Figure 5.1. (*a*) Asymptotic normal approximation: (A) exact density; (B) asymptotic normal.
(*b*) Asymptotic normal approximation: (A) exact density; (B) asymptotic normal.

first stage of the procedure we need to select the coefficient function $s(x)$, as in equation (29). A crude choice would be $s(x) = [1 + |x|^{K_2+1}]^{-1}$, because this has the same asymptotic behavior as $|x|^{-(K_2+1)}$, which in this case is the coefficient function in the tail expansion (16), and because this function is also well behaved elsewhere on the real line. An

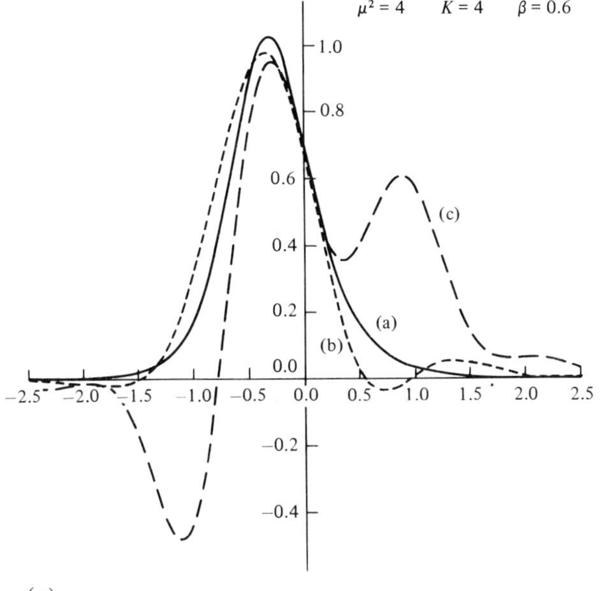

(a)

$\mu^2 = 4$ $K = 10$ $\beta = 0.6$

(b)

Figure 5.2. (*a*) Edgeworth approximation: (A) exact density; (B) $O(T^{-1/2})$; (C) $O(T^{-1})$.
(*b*) Edgeworth approximation: (A) exact density; (B) $O(T^{-1/2})$; (C) $O(T^{-1})$.

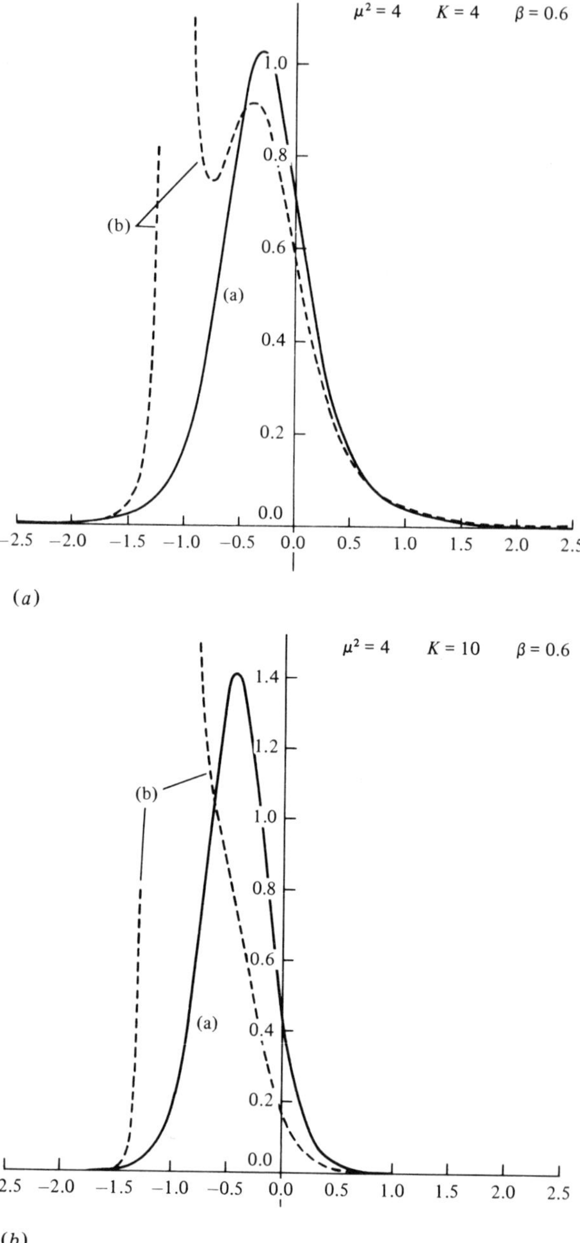

Figure 5.3. (*a*) Saddlepoint approximation: (A) exact density; (B) saddlepoint. (*b*) Saddlepoint approximation: (A) exact density; (B) saddlepoint.

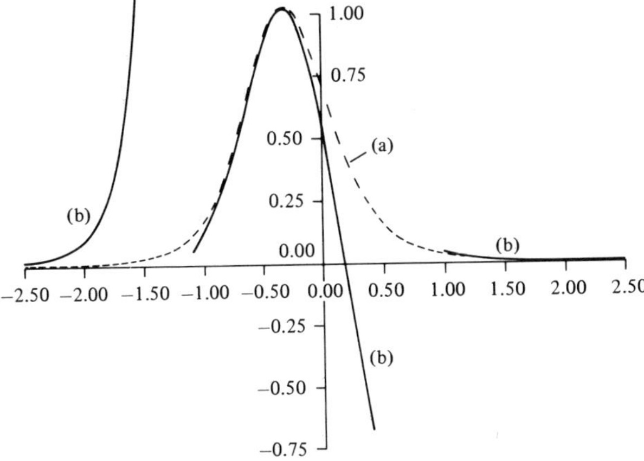

Figure 5.4. Local density approximations at the origin and in the tails to pdf(x): (A) exact density; (B) local approximations.

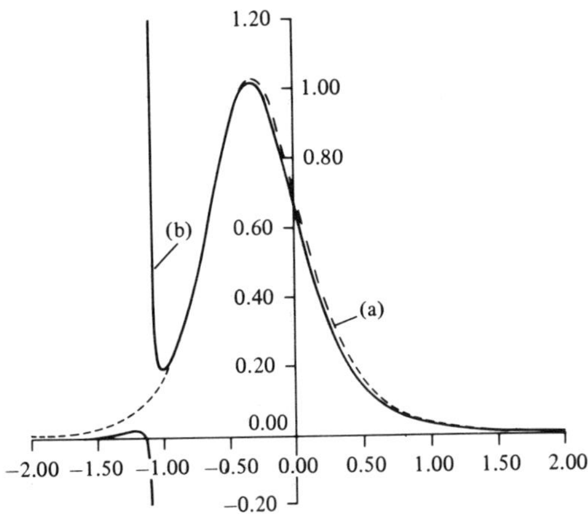

Figure 5.5. First-step [4/4] Padé approximant to pdf(x): (A) exact density; (B) Padé approximant.

alternative and better choice is the leading term in the density expansion (49), namely,

$$s(x) = \left[B\left(\frac{1}{2}, \frac{K_2}{2}\right)(1 + x^2)^{(K_2+1)/2}\right]^{-1} \tag{50}$$

This is, in fact, the pdf of $\hat{\beta}$ under the null hypothesis that $\beta=0$ and $\pi_{22}=0$ (Basmann, 1974). As mentioned in the introduction, leading

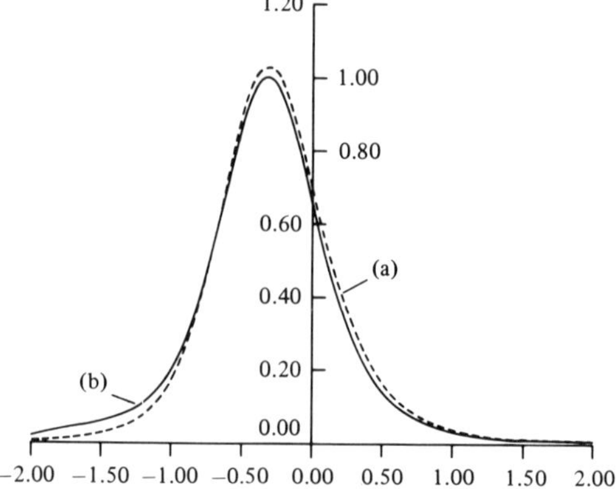

Figure 5.6. Modified Padé approximant to pdf(x); first change of coefficients: (A) exact density; (B) modified Padé approximants.

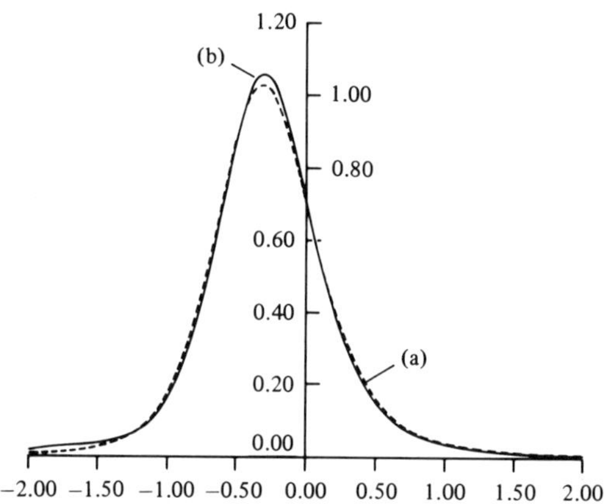

Figure 5.7. Modified Padé approximant to pdf(x); second change of coefficients: (A) exact density; (B) modified Padé approximant.

terms such as (50) in multiple series representations of density functions usually can be derived without much difficulty and often will be available even in cases in which an analytic form for the exact density has not been obtained. In the present case, a few elementary manipulations show that $\hat{\beta}$ takes the form of a standard normal variate divided by the square root of a chi square with K_2 degrees of freedom, with the numerator and denominator independent. The statistic $\hat{\beta}$ is therefore proportional to a t-variate with K_2 degrees of freedom, leading to a pdf of the form given by (50).

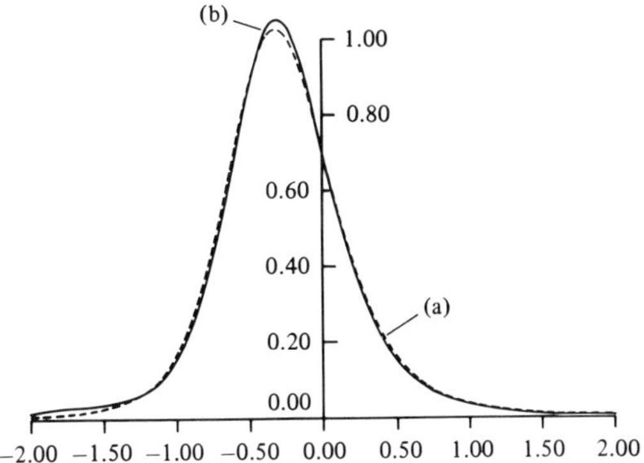

Figure 5.8. Modified Padé approximant to pdf(x) with renormalization: (A) exact density; (B) modified Padé approximant.

Writing $\mathrm{pdf}(x)=s(x)\,\mathrm{pdf}_s(x)$, as in (29), we then extract the local expansions (30) and (31) for $\mathrm{pdf}_s(x)$. The expansions we use are for the tails $(x^{-1}=0)$ and the origin $(x=0)$. The coefficients that appear in (30) and (31) are given by

$$\alpha_0 = \sum_{j=0}^{\infty} \frac{[(K+1)/2]_j}{(K/2)_j\, j!}\left(\frac{\mu^2}{2}\right)^j W(K,j)$$

$$\alpha_1 = \sum_{j=1}^{\infty} \frac{[(K+1)/2]_j 2\beta}{(K/2)_j (j-1)!}\left(\frac{\mu^2}{2}\right)^j W(K,j)$$

$$\alpha_2 = \sum_{j=1}^{\infty} \frac{[(K+1)/2]_j}{(K/2)_j (j-1)!}\left(\frac{\mu^2}{2}\right)^j [(2j-1)\beta^2-1]\, W(K,j)$$

$$\alpha_3 = \sum_{j=1}^{\infty} \frac{[(K+1)/2]_j 2\beta}{(K/2)_j (j-1)!}\left(\frac{\mu^2}{2}\right)^j \left[\frac{(2j-1)(2j-2)}{3!}\beta^2 - j\right] W(K,j)$$

$$\alpha_4 = \sum_{j=1}^{\infty} \frac{[(K+1)/2]_j}{(K/2)_j (j-1)!}\left(\frac{\mu^2}{2}\right)^j \times\left[\frac{2(2j-1)(2j-2)(2j-4)}{4!}\beta^4 - j(2j-1)\beta^2 + \frac{(j+1)}{2}\right] W(K,j)$$

and

$$\beta_0 = \sum_{j=0}^{\infty} \frac{[(K+1)/2]_j}{(K/2)_j\, j!}\left(\frac{\mu^2\beta^2}{2}\right)^j W(K,j)$$

$$\beta_1 = \sum_{j=1}^{\infty} \frac{[(K+1)/2]_j}{(K/2)_j(j-1)!} \frac{\mu^{2j}\beta^{2j-1}}{2^{j-1}} W(K,j)$$

$$\beta_2 = \sum_{j=1}^{\infty} \frac{[(K+1)/2]_j}{(K/2)_j(j-1)!} \left(\frac{\mu^{2j}\beta^{2j-2}}{2^j}\right)(1-\beta^2)W(K,j)$$

$$+ \sum_{j=2}^{\infty} \frac{[(K+1)/2]2\beta^{-2}}{(K/2)_j(j-2)!} \left(\frac{\mu^2\beta^2}{2}\right)^j W(K,j)$$

$$\beta_3 = \sum_{j=1}^{\infty} \frac{[(K+1)/2]_j(-j)}{(K/2)_j(j-1)!} \left(\frac{\mu^{2j}\beta^{2j-1}}{2^{j-1}}\right) W(K,j)$$

$$\beta_4 = \sum_{j=1}^{\infty} \frac{[(K+1)/2]_j}{(K/2)_j(j-1)!} \mu^{2j}\left[\frac{\beta^{2j}(j+1)}{2^{j+1}} - \frac{\beta^{2j-2}j}{2^j}\right] W(K,j)$$

$$+ \sum_{j=2}^{\infty} \frac{[(K+1)/2]_j}{(K/2)_j(j-2)!} \left(\frac{\mu^2}{2}\right)^j [\beta^{2j-2}j(j+1) + \tfrac{1}{2}\beta^{2j-4}]\, W(K,j)$$

where we have dropped the subscript on K_2 for convenience and where

$$W(K,j) = \exp[-\tfrac{1}{2}\mu^2(1+\beta^2)]\; {}_1F_1\left(\frac{K-1}{2}, j+\frac{K}{2}; \frac{\mu^2\beta^2}{2}\right)$$

$$= \exp(-\tfrac{1}{2}\mu^2)\; {}_1F_1\left(j+\tfrac{1}{2}, j+\frac{K}{2}; -\frac{\mu^2\beta^2}{2}\right)$$

by Kummer's transformation (Slater, 1960).

Figure 5.4 details the local density approximations to pdf(x) based on (30) and (31) with the coefficient function $s(x)$ as in (50). The approximations are good in the locality of the points of expansion, the origin, and the tails, but they start to deteriorate rapidly as we move out of the immediate vicinity. The right-hand tail expansion seems particularly good.

Figure 5.5 shows the [4/4] Padé approximant to the density (49). This has the form, in the notation of (44),

(51) $$R_{4,4}(x;s) = s(x)[4/4](x) = s(x)\frac{a_4(x-\gamma_1)(x-\gamma_2)(x-\gamma)(x-\bar{\gamma})}{b_4(x-\delta_1)(x-\delta_2)(x-\delta)(x-\bar{\delta})}$$

where

$a_4 = 4.533619$ $\qquad$ $b_4 = 1.221628$

$$\gamma_1 = -1.158240 \qquad \delta_1 = -3.567599$$

$$\gamma_2 = -0.537379 \qquad \delta_2 = -0.485485$$

$$\gamma, \bar{\gamma} = -2.133352 \pm 0.732053i \qquad \delta, \bar{\delta} = 0.310396 \pm 0.613123i$$

As a first step, approximant $R_{4,4}(x)$ is rather good, with problems occurring only in the left tail at the singularity $x=\delta_2$ (i.e., $x-\beta=\delta_2-\beta=-1.085485$ for $\beta=0.6$) and at the two zeros $x=\gamma_2, \gamma_1$ (note that the second pole occurs outside the region of immediate interest in the distribution).

The next stage in the procedure is to modify the Padé approximant (51) along the lines suggested in Section 7. We note that in the denominator the quadratic $x^2-(\delta_1+\delta_2)x+\delta_1\delta_2=x^2+4.05344x+1.7333$ has discriminant 9.497176. To remove the real zeros, we propose to replace this quadratic by

(52) $\quad 1.5x^2 + 4x + 3$

where we have raised the constant and the coefficient of x^2 and simply rounded the coefficient of x. According to the ideas outlined in Section 7, we now need to proportionately adjust the coefficient of x^2 and the constant term in one of the quadratics in the numerator. We select the quadratic $x^2-(\gamma_1+\gamma_2)x+\gamma_1\gamma_2 = x+1.695619x+0.622414$, which we need to modify in any case to remove the unwanted zeros of $R_{4,4}(x)$. Making the proportional adjustments recommended to this quadratic, we get $1.5x^2+1.695619x+1.077276$. This gives us the following modified Padé approximant after one change of coefficients:

(53)
$$R_{4,4}^{(a)}(x) = s(x) \times \frac{a_4\{1.5x^2+1.695619x+1.077276\}(x-\gamma)(x-\bar{\gamma})}{b_4\{1.5x^2+4x+3\}(x-\delta)(x-\bar{\delta})}$$

This function is graphed in Figure 5.6 against the exact density. We see that the singularity and zero problems have been eliminated, and the performance of the approximation is remarkably good. We note some reduction in the order of contact at the points of local expansion, particularly the origin (or, taking into account the change of origin on the graph, $x-\beta=-0.6$).

As suggested in Section 7, it is worthwhile to modify at least one of the remaining coefficients to improve the order of contact at the points of local expansion. Note that the success of this procedure can be measured against the original Padé approximant in the relevant localities; so we do not need a graph of the exact density to do so. Comparing the Padé and modified Padé approximants in Figures 5.5 and 5.6, it is clear that the order of contact of the modified Padé at the origin will be improved if we raise the derivative at this point ($x=0$, i.e., $x-\beta=-0.6$). This will be achieved by raising the coefficient of x in the quadratic in braces in the numerator of (53). We make a change in this coefficient from 1.69 to 2.0, giving the new modified Padé approximant

$$R_{4,4}^{(b)}(x) = s(x) \times \frac{a_4\{1.5x^2+2.0x+1.077\}(x-\gamma)(x-\bar{\gamma})}{b_4\{1.5x^2+4x+3\}(x-\delta)(x-\bar{\delta})} \tag{54}$$

This function is graphed in Figure 5.7. Even with the rather crude adjustments we have made, (54) is really an exceptionally close approximation to the true density and is well behaved over the whole real axis. A final adjustment can be made by renormalizing so that the area under (54) is unity. The adjusted curve is shown in Figure 5.8.

9 Conclusion

This chapter has introduced a new technique of approximating probability density functions. The approximating functions belong to a family of rational fractions and are sufficiently flexible to produce good approximants to a very wide class of density functions. The theory developed in Sections 3 and 4 indicates that this family of rational fractions contains approximants that are best in a well-defined sense and that will perform well in reproducing the form of the exact density functions over the entire real axis. The practical procedure for finding good approximants in this family is based on the use of multiple-point Padé approximants to construct global approximations from purely local information about the density. These multiple-point Padé approximants are then modified to ensure that they have good global behavior and to incorporate any additional information that may be available concerning the density. The application in Section 8 to an already well-established test area for density approximations illustrates that the procedure can produce exceptionally good approximations even in cases in which existing methods break down. Further refinement of the ideas laid out in Section 7 on modifying the initial Padé approximant should lead to fine approximations that are very close to the best uniform approximants discussed in Sections 2 and 3.

NOTES

1 The compact set must obtain at least in this region of the overall parameter space Γ. We can, for example, exclude as irrelevant in terms of equation (4) those regions of Γ for which the parameters yield unbounded rational fractions.
2 The Weierstrass theorem (Meinardus, 1967, p. 7) established the same result for polynomial approximants.
3 This work and others (Baker & Gammel, 1970; Saff & Varga, 1977) have provided systematic coverage of the extensive literature on the theory of Padé approximants and their applications, particularly in mathematical physics.
4 Theorem 2.4 of Baker (1975).
5 Theorem 1.1 of Baker (1975).
6 These issues will be taken up at greater length in a later paper.
7 We deal specifically with the case $\mu^2=4$, $k=4$, $\beta=0.6$. Another paper will detail more fully some numerical experience with modified Padé approximants.

REFERENCES

Anderson, T. W., Morimune, K., and Sawa, T. 1978. "The Numerical Values of Some Key Parameters in Econometric Models." Technical report no. 270, Institute for Mathematical Studies in the Social Sciences, Stanford University.

Anderson, T. W. and Sawa, T. 1973. "Distribution of Estimates of Coefficients of a Single Equation in a Simultaneous System and Their Asymptotic Expansions." *Econometrica* 41:683–714.

Anderson, T. W., and Sawa, T. 1979. "Evaluation of the Distribution Function of the Two-Stage Least Squares Estimate." *Econometrica* 47:163–83.

Baker, G. A. 1975. *The Essentials of Padé Approximants.* New York: Academic.

Baker, G. A., and Gammel, J. L. 1970. *The Padé Approximant in Theoretical Physics.* New York: Academic.

Barndorff-Nielson, O., and Cox, D. R. 1979. "Edgeworth and Saddlepoint Approximations with Statistical Applications." *Journal of the Royal Statistical Society* 41:279–312.

Basmann, R. L. 1974. "Exact Finite Sample Distributions and Test Statistics: A Survey and Appraisal." In *Frontiers of Quantitative Economics, Vol. II,* edited by M. D. Intriligator and D. A. Kendrick, pp. 209–71. Amsterdam: North-Holland.

Chui, C. K. 1976. "Recent Results on Padé Approximants and Related Problems." In *Approximation Theory II,* edited by G. G. Lorenz et al., pp. 79–115. New York: Academic.

Daniels, H. E. 1954. "Saddlepoint Approximations in Statistics." *Annals of Mathematical Statistics* 25: 631–50.

Daniels, H. E. 1956. "The Approximate Distribution of Serial Correlation Coefficients." *Biometrika* 43:169–85.

Daniels, H. E. 1980. "Exact Saddlepoint Approximations." *Biometrika* 67:59–64.

Durbin, J. 1980a. "The Approximate Distribution of Partial Serial Correlation

Coefficients Calculated from Residuals from Regression on Fourier Series." *Biometrika* 67:335–49.

Durbin, J. 1980b. "Approximations for Densities of Sufficient Statistics." *Biometrika* 67:311–33.

Erdélyi, A. 1956. *Asymptotic Expansion.* New York: Dover.

Feller, W. 1971. *An Introduction to Probability Theory and Its Applications, Vol. II.* New York: Wiley.

Frobenius, G. 1881. "Ueber Relationen zwischen den Näherungsbrüchen von Potenzreihen." *Journal für die reine und angewandte Mathematik* 90:1–17.

Hart, J. F. 1968. *Computer Approximations.* New York: Wiley.

Hastings, C. 1955. *Approximations for Digital Computers.* Princeton University Press.

Holly, A., and Phillips, P. C. B. 1979. "A Saddlepoint Approximation to the Distribution of the k-Class Estimator in a Coefficient in a Simultaneous System." *Econometrica* 47:1527–48.

Jones, D. S. 1966. *Generalized Functions.* New York: McGraw-Hill.

Kendall, M. G., and Stuart, A. 1969. *The Advanced Theory of Statistics, Vol. I.* London: Griffin.

Lighthill, M. J. 1958. *An Introduction to Fourier Analysis and Generalized Functions.* Cambridge University Press.

Lukacs, E. 1970. *Characteristic Functions.* London: Griffin.

Meinardus, G. 1967. *Approximation of Functions: Theory and Numerical Methods, Vol. 13.* New York: Springer-Verlag.

Oberhettinger, F. 1973. *Fourier Transforms of Distributions and Their Inverses.* New York: Academic.

Padé, H. 1892. "Sur la représentation approchée d'une fonction par des fractions rationelles." *Annales Scientifiques de l'Ecole Normale Supérieure* (Supplement) 9:1–93.

Phillips, P. C. B. 1977a. "Approximations to Some Finite Sample Distributions Associated with a First Order Stochastic Difference Equation." *Econometrica* 45:463–86.

Phillips, P. C. B. 1977b. "A General Theorem in the Theory of Asymptotic Expansions as Approximations to the Finite Sample Distributions of Econometric Estimators." *Econometrica* 45:1517–34.

Phillips, P. C. B. 1978a. "Edgeworth and Saddlepoint Approximations in the First-Order Non-Circular Autoregression." *Biometrika* 65:91–8.

Phillips, P. C. B. 1978b. "A Note on the Saddlepoint Approximation in a First Order Non-Circular Autoregression." Cowles Foundation discussion paper no. 487, Yale University.

Phillips, P. C. B. 1980a. "Finite Sample Theory and the Distributions of Alternative Estimators of the Marginal Propensity to Consume." *Review of Economic Studies* 47:183–224.

Phillips, P. C. B. 1980b. "The Exact Finite Sample Density of Instrumental Variable Estimators in an Equation with $n+1$ Endogenous Variables." *Econometrica* 48:861–78.

Phillips, P C. B. 1982. "Approximating the Density Functions of Simultaneous Equations Estimators." (*in press*).

Rice, J. R. 1964–7. *The Approximation of Functions, Vols. I and II.* Reading, Mass.: Addison-Wesley.

Richardson, D. H. 1968. "The Exact Distribution of a Structural Coefficient Estimator." *Journal of the American Statistical Association* 63:1214–26.
Rudin, W. 1974. *Real and Complex Analysis.* New York: McGraw-Hill.
Runge, C. 1885. "Zur Theorie der eindeutigen analytischen Funktionen." *Acta Mathematica* 6:229–44.
Saff, E. G., and Varga, R. S. 1977. *Padé and Rational Approximation.* New York: Academic.
Sargan, J. D. 1976. "Econometric Estimators and the Edgeworth Approximation." *Econometrica* 44:421–8; "Erratum." *Econometrica* 45:272.
Sargan, J. D. 1981. "On Monte Carlo Estimates of Moments Which Are Infinite." *Advances in Econometrics* (*in press*).
Sargan, J. D., and Mikhail, W. M. 1971. "A General Approximation to the Distribution of Instrumental Variable Estimators." *Econometrica* 39:131–69.
Slater, L. J. 1960. *Confluent Hypergeometric Functions.* Cambridge University Press.
Tchebycheff, P. L. 1859. "Sur les questions de minima qui se rattachent à la représentation approximative des fonctions." In *Oeuvres I,* pp. 273–378. New York: Chelsea (reprinted 1962).
Walsh, J. L. 1965. *Interpolation and Approximation by Rational Functions in the Complex Domain.* Providence, R.I.: American Mathematical Society (originally published 1935).
Zelen, M., and Severo, N. C. 1965. "Probability Functions." In *Handbook of Mathematical Functions,* edited by M. Abramowitz and I. A. Stegun, pp. 927–95. New York: Dover.

PART V

TOPICS IN TIME-SERIES ANALYSIS

CHAPTER 6

Identifiability and problems of model selection in econometrics

R. E. Kalman

1 Background and perspective

Econometrics was born in the 1920s, conceived as the embodiment of a noble dream. Today, with the hindsights of more than half a century, this dream gives way to a scenario:

"Economics deals with complex interactive phenomena. It is impossible to study quantitative relationships between important variables (say, taxation vs. savings) without reference to the context. Nor is it possible to perform experiments or make direct observations that would isolate such relationships or at least diminish the noise level under which their effects can be observed. We possess, however, innumerable time series engendered by the very economic forces we wish to uncover. By constructing models for time series we may hope to gain indirect access to the desired quantitative economic relationships because these are intrinsic in the models and therefore should be recoverable from the

The research reported here was supported in part under U.S. Air Force grant AFOSR 76-3034(D) and U.S. Army research grant DAA 29-80-C-0050 through the Center for Mathematical System Theory, University of Florida, Gainesville, FL 32611 USA.

This paper is a highly edited version of my oral presentation made at the Congress on August 30, 1980. Because of unexpected and unusual circumstances surrounding the manuscript, and also because the material has implications on statistical methodology which go far beyond the context of econometrics, a slightly revised and definitive version of this work will appear in *Developments in Statistics*, edited by Paruchuri R. Krishnaiah. New York: Academic Press, 1982.

structure and parameters of the models. Economic truths are immutable, at least in the short run, and thus there is no reason, in principle, why accurate models cannot be deduced from the available data, in spite of disturbances, errors, irrationalities, expectations, and other random influences which contaminate economic time series.''

This scenario forces the conclusion that the study of economics is a *system-theoretic* endeavor. Economics as a science must be built on methods that are effective in the exploration and explanation of interactive phenomena. The dream of econometrics has evolved into a technical problem in system theory.

But, unfortunately, the actual evolution of econometrics took a rather different route. System theory was not even in sight in the 1920s and 1930s, and econometrics soon came to be dominated by statistics. The aspiration of Haavelmo (1944) to give a solid foundation to econometrics by dogmatic application of probability theory has not been fulfilled (in the writer's opinion), no doubt because probability theory has nothing to say about the underlying system-theoretic problems.

This is 1980, and by now system theory has reached a certain level of maturity. It can provide a scientific framework within which basic ideas of economics and econometrics can be reexamined, assessed, and subjected to objective analysis and critique.

I have pointed out in several publications (Kalman, 1979a, 1979b, 1980, 1982b) that economic research cannot be done meaningfully if the modeling required for it is conceptually soft and mathematically sloppy. Procedures of economic modeling cannot be and should not be justified solely by economic reasoning.[1] Modeling has its own logic, independent of what is being modeled. And the constraints imposed by modeling logic may be far more important than mundane problems such as reliability of data, use of prior economic theory, statistical methodology, and the like. A model must explain real data; it must not be an artifact expressing the modeler's prejudices.

My publications cited earlier have been concerned with general, even philosophical, aspects of modeling. This chapter has a much narrower aim: to reexamine the notion of *identifiability*.

In econometrics, the ''thing'' to be identified is always some type of system. Under the influence of the standard statistical paradigm, econometricians have been assuming, unquestioningly and for a long time, that a system is the same as a bunch of parameters. They therefore view system identification as equivalent to parameter estimation. The system theorist disagrees.

Mathematical common sense requires that we view a system first of all as an abstract object. ''Parameters'' in the naive sense (a set of numbers without any prior restrictions) usually are not the correct description of an abstract mathematical object. The problems of parameterization enter the analysis of the system at a later stage, after the basic system description has been agreed upon.

We use here "parameterization" as a synonym for "coordinatization." This means that each member of a family of abstract objects is uniquely described by a set of numbers with explicitly given restrictions. Because parametrizations are obtained by abstract mathematical procedures, the resulting "parameters" do not necessarily possess intuitive significance; they are determined by their mathematical properties, and they are almost never unique. We can never identify "a parameter." The real meaning of "identification" is that we assign numerical values to the set of all parameters of some specified parametrization.

The many different and fuzzy uses of the word "parameter" in the scientific literature are the symptoms of conceptual confusion. To lessen this evil, we introduce in this chapter a sharp distinction between *descriptive* and *intrinsic* parameters. The former, roughly speaking, involve the notion of a parameter as normally employed in econometrics (and other applied fields); the latter refer to the parametrization of mathematical objects mentioned earlier.

Descriptive parameters are no more than a means for numerical specification of mathematical objects. The descriptive parameters do not reflect the intrinsic properties of these objects. Ultimately the system identification problem must be expressed in terms of some set of intrinsic parameters. A conceptual setup for accomplishing this already exists in system theory; it is outlined in Section 3.

Identification should be viewed as a problem in realization theory. Using the tools provided by this theory, behavioral data may be translated into a "model," that is, a collection of all systems compatible with given data. Once the model has been parameterized as an abstract object, there will be a one-to-one correspondence between behavioral parameters and model parameters. In principle, this solves the identification problem.

If the realization problem has a nonunique solution, the model will consist of a family of inequivalent systems. Then each system belonging to the model is described by two sets of (intrinsic) parameters. One set, the behavioral parameters, specifies which model the system is a part of. The other set of parameters describes the position of a given system within the family of systems that constitutes the model.

Classical statistics concentrates attention on questions such as the "estimation" of the means or variances of hypothetically postulated distributions. In much of econometrics, this point of view has been adopted uncritically for the task of "parameter identification." This is a grievous error, because usually the statistical parameters are taken in the descriptive sense and the system parameters are sought in the intrinsic sense. Hence the point of view of "parameter identification" must be gradually replaced by "system identification," followed by "system parametrization."

Econometrics has overemphasized the classical statistical paradigm while ignoring the system problem. In our view, the balance should be reversed. It is better to overemphasize the system-theoretic aspects, because there is no other way to be sure that what we have identified is a real object and not merely an artifact created by our prejudiced methodology.

To a real-world econometrician it might seem hairsplitting to claim that a model is always identifiable and yet admit that it may contain many inequivalent systems, each equally valid as a representation of behavioral data. How is he to choose between different systems all of which are part of the same model? Why can't he just say that some parameters are "unidentified"?

The appropriate reply to this complaint is that our new theoretical framework is superior to the prior ones because we can provide quantitative (and hence deeper) insights into the fundamental questions of identification. We shall see that this is possible only because in the past the concept of "identifiability" was not researched as thoroughly as it should have been.

The theoretical framework relating realization theory, identification, and parametrization is explained in Sections 2 and 3. It is illustrated in Sections 4, 5, and 6, on various levels of generality, by examples taken from econometrics. Section 7 outlines some more advanced applications of system theory.

The contribution of this chapter, it must be emphasized, does not reside in proposing a new methodology for econometrics. Rather, the contribution consists in calling attention to subtle and serious difficulties inherent in the classical approaches to econometrics.

System theory is the right theoretical framework. It *does* provide powerful new tools. These should be used. There *will be* new results and hence progress.

Many friends and colleagues have contributed to clarifying the issues discussed here. I would like to thank especially Professor M. Deistler, Technische Universität Wien; Professor M. Intriligator, University of California at Los Angeles; Professor H. Wold, Universities of Uppsala and Genève; and Drs. P. Tinsley and P. A. V. B. Swamy, Federal

Reserve Board, Washington. This chapter is dedicated to M. v. N., without whose inspiration it probably would never have been conceived.

2 Realization

The identification of econometric models from time series requires system theory at the very first step: the definition of the *model*. This may seem trivial, but in fact turns out to be crucial.

Although it is not yet worldwide practice to do so, we shall organize the identification problem as consisting of three classes of objects and two connecting operations, *given by the following scheme:*

(2.1)

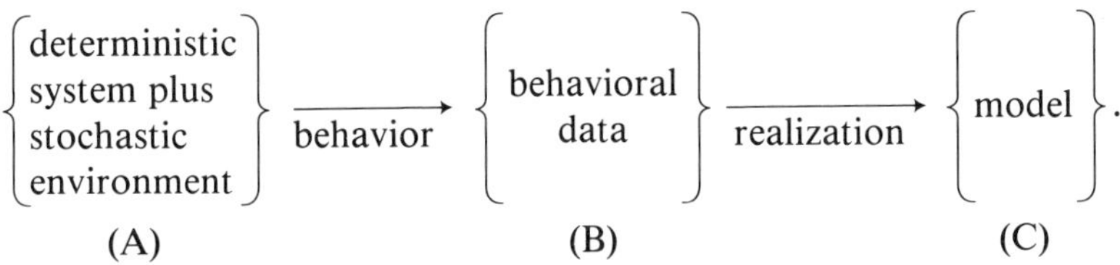

In more detail, the task is as follows:

A. Specify a class of (deterministic) *systems* and their (stochastic) *environments*. (For simplicity, we take "system" to be always deterministic and "environment" to be always stochastic. Other variants are, of course, conceivable.) The basic requirement is that the unknown real system Σ_* (which we wish to identify and which we believe to have generated the observed data) is a member of class A.

B. Specify a class of observations (measurements) that we are allowed to make on the systems and environments in class A. The totality of all such postulated observations is the *behavioral data*. In an idealized sense, it is usually the specification of a probability distribution; in the practical sense, it is usually the sample means and covariances computed from actually measured values of the observables.

A→B. Show how to compute the behavior S_Σ of each system Σ of class A. From this machinery, derive explicit conditions that allow testing any data S in class B (without knowledge of Σ) to determine whether or not S could have been generated by some Σ in class A. We call these conditions the *behavioral relations*.

C. Reversing the operation A→B, specify the class C of systems and environments that satisfy the behavioral relations for some given data S in class B. Evidently class C always includes class A, but it may be larger than class A if the original formulation of the problem did not consider all possible systems giving rise to the observed data. So class C is a kind of "closure" of class A.

B→C. Show how to compute for any given (fixed) piece of behavioral data S all systems Σ_s (in class C) compatible with it. For given S the collection Σ_s of all such systems is the *model* of S.

The arrow A→B expresses a priori information about the *behavior* of the systems in question. The arrow B→C may be regarded as the inversion of behavior (in mathematical terms, the adjoint functor of behavior). This important operation is called *realization* in system theory. Evidently the "inversion of behavior" is the principal problem studied in the theory of identification.

The essential objective in any identification problem is the quantitative determination of the model (in the special sense defined earlier). Note that the model may consist of more than one system, and the data may be explainable in more than one way. This nonuniqueness of modeling is an unavoidable feature of the identification problem. It should not be eliminated by artificial assumptions, as is sometimes done in parameter estimation methods in statistics.

Identification is not a conceptual but a mathematical problem. It can be carried out only after precise mathematical definitions have been given to the three classes of objects involved and to the operations of "behavior" and "realization." This we now proceed to do, for the basic case of deterministic linear systems.

Aa. *System.* The classical time-series literature is concerned only with linear models and the corresponding domains of probability theory. Therefore we shall also restrict our analysis (here) to linear systems and gaussian environments. The precise concept of a *linear system* has been axiomatized (Kalman, Falb, and Arbib, 1969, Chapters 1, 2, and 10). This provides a reference point to which all further definitions and results can be compared.

In the definition of a system, precise technical meaning must be given to the attributes *linear, finite* (-dimensional and finitely parametrized), *multi-input/multi-output, constant* (=time-independent in its defining properties), and *dynamical*. These words are all incorporated in the standard definition,[2] which comes in two versions. For continuous time, that is, with the time set $T=\mathbf{R}=$real numbers, a system Σ (having the foregoing attributes) is defined by

$$\text{(2.2a)} \qquad \frac{dx}{dt} = Fx + Gu(t), \qquad y(t) = Hx(t), \quad t \in \mathbf{R}.$$

For discrete time, that is, with the time set $T=\mathbf{Z}=$integers, a system Σ is given by

(2.2b) $x(t+1) = Fx(t) + Gu(t), \qquad y(t) = Hx(t), \quad t \in \mathbf{Z}.$

In (2.2a–b), the real (or complex) vectors x, u, and y are called *state, input,* and *output,* respectively; F, G, H are matrices with constant real (or complex) coefficients.

It is rather obvious from its definition that a "system" [which will be our shorthand for the precise terminology concomitant with (2.2)] is really defined by the "parameters" (entries) in (F, G, H). So we shall write simply $\Sigma := (F, G, H)$. The notations have been intentionally selected in such a way that there is no built-in distinction between the continuous-time and discrete-time cases. Most of the system-theoretic questions are purely algebraic in nature, based on properties of (F, G, H), and therefore such a distinction is not necessary; the results hold simultaneously for continuous time and discrete time.

[The idea of a "system" goes back to Newtonian mechanics, with the very important modern addition of "inputs" and "outputs." A very good mental model, especially in discrete time, is a computer. The formulation of the basic definitions is conceptually valid in complete generality, without the assumption of linearity (Kalman, Falb, and Arbib, 1969, Chapter 1). But linearity becomes essential if universal (i.e., system-theoretic) mathematical results are wanted, not just definitions. The power of mathematics, as currently applied to system theory, stems largely from the word "linear."]

Equations (2.2a–b) are sometimes known as the *internal* definition of a system. This alludes to the fact that the definition is stated in terms of the internal or *state* variables, the components of the vector x.

Ab. *Stochastic environment.* Recall that the notion of a system in the present context is always deterministic. Stochastic effects are regarded as arising from outside the system and are modeled accordingly.

Thus we need to describe all stochastic influences (disturbance inputs) acting on the system as well as the noise entering into the observations. This is done, under the general gaussian assumption, by specifying a class of means and covariances for the stochastic variables involved. Such data may refer to either a population or a sample. See the examples in Sections 4, 5, and 6.

B. *Behavior.* In the deterministic case, "observation" means, by definition, knowledge of all inputs and all outputs at given times; the state variables are always regarded as nonobservable.

In the stochastic case, exact knowledge of the inputs and outputs is replaced by specifying the probability distributions of the corresponding observables. For example, the inputs and outputs of the system may be observable only in the presence of additive noise. The nature of such noise is part of the specification of the stochastic environment. The specification of behavioral data amounts to giving the joint probability distributions of (input + noise) with (output + noise). Further discussion is deferred until the examples.

The output of a deterministic linear system must be linearly (and causally) related to its input. Taking causality for granted and then using nothing more than the mathematical definition of linearity, it follows that for a discrete-time system the relationship between input and output must take the following form:

$$(2.3) \qquad y(t) = \sum_{\tau=0}^{t-1} A_{t-\tau} u(\tau), \qquad x(0) = 0.$$

We may view (2.3) as the *behavioral* (*external*) definition of a system. Thus "behavior" for a linear discrete-time system is abstractly the same mathematical object as the infinite sequence of matrices

$$(2.4) \qquad S := (A_1, A_2, \ldots),$$

occurring in (2.3).

For continuous-time systems, S is again defined as in (2.4). [However, for such systems (2.3) must be replaced by the convolution integral; the derivation of (2.4), which we omit here, involves nontrivial mathematical considerations.]

As an illustration of the operation A→B, we determine the behavior of a system given by (2.2). This is easy. Using (2.2a) recursively gives the following definition of the elements of S_Σ:

$$(2.5) \qquad A_t := HF^{t-1}G, \quad t = 1, 2, \ldots.$$

It is clear that (2.5) are the explicit *behavioral relations* of the system $\Sigma = (F, G, H)$ with respect to the data S.

Formulas (2.5) define a mapping $\Sigma \mapsto S_\Sigma$. This mapping is necessarily surjective provided we consider only behaviors S_Σ which may have been generated by a system Σ in a prescribed class. On the other hand, the mapping is almost never injective; that is, usually there may be several systems $\Sigma_0, \Sigma_1, \ldots$ giving rise to the same behavior so that $S_{\Sigma_0} = S_{\Sigma_1} = \ldots$.

A change of coordinates in the state space X may be defined as $T: x \mapsto \hat{x}$, $\det T \neq 0$. This change of coordinates implies the relations

$$(2.6) \qquad \begin{aligned} \hat{F}T &= TF, \\ \hat{G} &= TG, \\ \hat{H}T &= H, \end{aligned}$$

between the systems $\Sigma=(F, G, H)$ and $\hat{\Sigma}=(\hat{F}, \hat{G}, \hat{H})$. Moreover, T induces a transformation $\Sigma \mapsto \hat{\Sigma}$ of the system Σ into another system $\hat{\Sigma}$ with the same behavior. [To prove this, simply substitute (2.6) into (2.5).] In other words, two systems differing only by a change of coordinates belong to the same equivalence class with respect to their behavior. We write this equivalence class as $[\Sigma]$. Thus if $\Sigma \mapsto \hat{\Sigma}$ as defined by (2.6) then $[\Sigma]=[\hat{\Sigma}]$ and $S_{\Sigma}=S_{\hat{\Sigma}}$.

It is an important system-theoretic fact that for deterministic systems the converse is also true in a certain precisely defined sense, to be discussed later.

C. *Model.* Considering again formulas (2.5), let us try to invert the arrow of calculating behavior. The problem is this: Given the left-hand side of (2.5), that is, *given some fixed behavior* S_0, *does there exist a system* Σ (or perhaps several such systems) *whose defining matrices* F, G, H *satisfy* (2.5) *for all values of* t?

This is the problem of realization. Any Σ that satisfies (2.5) for a given S_0 is called a *realization* of S_0. It is written as Σ_{S_0}. With the left-hand side given and the right-hand side unknown, formulas (2.5) are called the *realization conditions.*

If Σ is a realization, so is every system $\hat{\Sigma}$ in the equivalence class $[\Sigma]$ defined by a coordinate change. We do not regard such Σ and $\hat{\Sigma}$ as different realizations. But it may happen that the class of all realizations $\{\Sigma_{S_0}\}$ of a fixed S_0 also contains essentially different elements, that is, some Σ and $\hat{\Sigma}$ that are not equivalent under any coordinate change. In that case, the solution of the realization problem is nonunique.

It is a fundamental result of linear system theory (Kalman, 1962, 1976; Tannenbaum, 1981, Chapter VI) that for *deterministic systems the realization problem has a unique solution* provided that the realization Σ_{S_0} is "reduced" to its simplest possible ("canonical") part by discarding unnecessary state variables in (2.2a–b) and provided that uniqueness is interpreted as "modulo a change in coordinates in the state space." [Although this result is often stated in the narrow sense for finite-dimensional, constant, linear systems only, the more general wording used here is justified by analogous theorems obtained (i) in the finite-dimensional constant nonlinear (polynomial) case by Sontag and Rouchaleau (1976), (ii) in the infinite-dimensional constant linear case by Yamamoto (1981), and (iii) in the finite-dimensional nonconstant linear case by Kalman, Falb, and Arbib (1969, Appendix 10.C).]

For stochastic systems the realization problem usually has a nonunique solution, and it may even fail to have a solution at all in certain cases.

If we wish to maintain an objective point of view toward the question of identification, we must admit the possibility of only partial success in that several different systems may have to be accepted as constituting the model in the sense defined here. In other words, the mathematical facts of life concerning stochastic realization are not at all counterintuitive.

Our terminology is new in regard to the concept of model, but it could hardly be controversial. For example, Koopmans and Reiersøl (1950, p. 169) insisted that "[such a thing is acceptable] provided the temptation to specify models in such a way as to produce [unique] identifiability of relevant characteristics is resisted." The specification of the identification problem, namely the class A of systems on the left-hand side of (2.1), is essentially the choice of the modeler. He must therefore accept the consequences; his model, derived from his own assumptions by rigid logic as the realization of the stochastic behavioral data, may turn out to be nonexistent, unique, or nonunique.

3 Parametrization

Before any concrete implementation of the theoretical framework of the scheme (2.1), we must consider questions of parametrization.

This is mainly a question of numbers. Data are almost always numerical, and therefore the system or model must also be specified the same way. Trivial as it may seem, the subject is surrounded by serious misunderstandings in the econometric literature, and not only there.

As mentioned in the introduction, confusion is best avoided by making a sharp distinction here between *descriptive parameters* and *intrinsic parameters.*

The descriptive parameters are usually regarded as "free," that is, they are taken as arbitrary numbers. Thus, if a mathematical object is described by n real numbers, abstractly that object is the same as a point in $\mathbf{R}^n$. However, a class of such objects is very seldom all of $\mathbf{R}^n$. This means that restrictions must be imposed on the descriptive parameters to correctly specify the class. For example, the class of $n \times n$ matrices $\{A\}$ is the same as $\mathbf{R}^{n^2}$, but the class of nonsingular $n \times n$ matrices is specified by subjecting the descriptive parameters $a_{11}, \ldots, a_{nn}$ to the implicit condition $\det A \neq 0$.

The descriptive parameters of a linear system Σ are, of course, the entries of the matrices F, G, H.

A linear behavior S is described by specifying (in principle) all the (infinitely many) entries of the sequence of matrices $A_1, A_2, \ldots$, which are therefore collectively called *descriptive behavioral parameters.* The descriptive parameters of the stochastic environment of a system are usually the entries in covariance matrices.

Example. An elementary and classical case illustrating the difference between descriptive and intrinsic parameters is provided by rotations Γ in 2-space. A rotation may be described by a 2×2 real matrix

$$M=\begin{bmatrix} a & c \\ -c & b \end{bmatrix}, \quad a,b,c=\text{real numbers},$$

subject to the orthogonality and positivity conditions

$$MM'=I, \quad \det M>0.$$

The descriptive parameters are a, b, and c. The class $\mathfrak{M}$ of matrices corresponding to arbitrary values of a, b, and c is much larger than the class Γ of 2-rotations. Γ as a subclass of $\mathfrak{M}$ is singled out by the orthogonality conditions. These conditions subject the descriptive parameters to three algebraic identities, only two of which are independent. Therefore we conclude, but at this stage only intuitively, that a 2-rotation matrix M is described by one (independent) parameter. More mathematics will prove that every such M may be written as

$$M=\begin{bmatrix} \cos\theta & \sin\theta \\ -\sin\theta & \cos\theta \end{bmatrix}.$$

This shows that θ may be taken as the (single) intrinsic parameter. But θ is still not free; it is subject to an equivalence relation, because $M(\theta)=M(\hat{\theta})$ when $\theta\equiv\theta \bmod 2\pi$. There is then a one-to-one correspondence between M=2-rotation and the equivalence classes $[\theta]$. In other words, as an abstract mathematical object, Γ corresponds to the closed interval $[0,2\pi]$, the end-points of the interval being identified.

The descriptive parameters are subject to the implicit constraint $MM'=I$, whereas the constraint on θ is explicit. The price we pay for this is that M is now a complicated function of $[\theta]$. Moreover, the relationship between $[\theta]$ and (a,b,c) is also complicated, as $\theta:=\arccos a=\arcsin c$.

Guided by this example, we see that the *intrinsic parameters* of a class of systems should be characterized by two properties: (i) There is one and only one parameter set corresponding to any system in the class. (ii) The constraints on the parameters are explicit. These properties are, of course, crucial for any identification problem.

Parametrization of systems. Let us now illustrate the idea of intrinsic parametrizations with reference to the scheme (2.1).

The class of systems must be defined by fixing some invariant properties; for example, we may define the class as all linear n-dimensional,

m-input, p-output systems. Then the descriptive parameters, as already mentioned, are the $n(n+m+p)$ entries in the matrices $\Sigma=(F, G, H)$.

Intrinsic parametrization is concerned with the equivalence classes $[\Sigma]$, not the individual Σ's. Because equivalence, as defined by (2.6), involves the action of the general linear group on Σ, it is natural to suppose that the problem of intrinsic parametrization may be solved by defining suitable *canonical forms*[3] F_*, G_*, H_*. This is indeed true, but the problem is highly nontrivial; its first rigorous treatment goes back only to (Kalman, 1974). For details, consult Antoulas, 1981.

The main result is that the set of objects in the foregoing class form a quasi-projective algebraic variety. It follows that the entries in the canonical forms F_*, G_*, H_* may be interpreted as the local coordinates of this variety. It is a mathematical fact that no (continuous) global coordinates exist. Consequently, the *intrinsic parameters must be viewed as only locally defined.* (The local coordinate systems overlap. Together they cover the whole variety, but no single coordinate system covers all of it.) The precise description of these canonical forms (i.e., of the intrinsic parametrization) is a rather complex topic (Tannenbaum, 1981; Kalman, 1984).

Turning to the intrinsic parametrization of the behavioral data, the first requirement is to specify constraints on the data that express the basic assumption that the class of data is generated by the class of systems defined in the scheme (2.1). Because systems must be described (for practical reasons) using only finitely many parameters, the same requirement must be imposed indirectly on the behavioral data, even though initially it may be convenient to describe the latter [see (2.4)] using infinitely many (descriptive) parameters.

The mathematical techniques for accomplishing this are a part of realization theory. The well-known result, for linear systems (Kalman, Falb, and Arbib, 1969, Chapter 10), is the "rank condition"

$$(3.1) \qquad \operatorname{rank} B(S_\Sigma) \leqslant \dim \Sigma = n,$$

where $B(S_\Sigma)$ is the *behavior matrix* associated to the behavioral data S generated by the system Σ; the definition of this matrix is

$$(3.2) \qquad B(S_\Sigma) = \begin{pmatrix} A_1 & A_2 & \cdots \\ A_2 & A_3 & \cdots \\ \cdots & \cdots & \ddots \end{pmatrix}.$$

Thus the intrinsic parametrization of S requires introducing parameters in $A_1, A_2, \ldots$ in such a way that (3.1) is satisfied for various (prescribed) values of n and for all values of the intrinsic parameters of the family (F, G, H).

This difficult problem is solved with the aid of linear realization theory. In other words, we must study the second arrow in (2.1). The principal classical results (Kalman, 1962, 1976; Kalman, Falb, and Arbib, 1969, Chapter 10; Tannenbaum, 1981, Chapter VI) may be described as follows:

(a) *If S admits any finite-dimensional realization* Σ_S, *it admits a canonical realization* Σ_S^{can} (*canonical* = *reachable and observable*).

(3.3) (b) *All canonical realizations* Σ_S^{can} *belong to a single equivalence class* $[\Sigma_S^{\mathrm{can}}]$ *defined by* (2.6).

(c) $\dim \Sigma_S^{\mathrm{can}} = \operatorname{rank} B(S)$ *for all canonical realizations.*

Phrased differently, this theorem makes the following crucially important statement about the second arrow in (2.1):

(3.4) *The behavioral data for deterministic linear dynamical systems uniquely determines the model* (*which may be taken as a canonical system*).

Indeed, if a realization exists at all (in the finite-dimensional sense), it may be taken as canonical [by (3.3a)]; the model is unique because $\{\Sigma_S\}$ consists of a single equivalence class $[\Sigma_S^{\mathrm{can}}]$ so that there are no essentially different realizations [by (3.3b)]; the "size" of the realization, that is, the number of state variables, may be determined directly from the behavioral data, without having to construct the realization itself [by (3.3c)].

Another way of stating these results is to say that

(3.5) *There is a bijection between S and* $[\Sigma_S^{\mathrm{can}}]$.

Indeed, the data S uniquely determine the model $[\Sigma_S^{\mathrm{can}}]$ [because all canonical realizations belong to the same equivalence class by (3.3b)]; on the other hand, any realization (hence any canonical realization Σ_S^{can}) determines S, just by the definition of a realization.

Thus in the deterministic, linear, finite-dimensional case, the identification problem stated by (2.1) has a solution, and this solution is as nice as it could possibly be. The procedure of solution depends crucially on the idea of canonical systems, surely the major system-theoretic discovery of the 1960s. By theorem (3.3), $[\Sigma_{S_{\Sigma_*}}^{\mathrm{can}}]$ is the best conceivable substitute for the unknown real system Σ_* that generated the data S_{Σ_*} and therefore $[\Sigma_{S_\Sigma}^{\text{can}}]$ fully deserves the name "model."

We hasten to repeat that whereas the assumption "deterministic" is crucial for (3.5) to be true, "linear" and "finite-dimensional" are certainly not. See the references cited at the end of Section 2.

The bijective correspondence (3.5) between model and data implies that any intrinsic parametrization of the data determines an intrinsic parametrization for the model and vice versa.

The actual construction of a realization, which cannot be avoided in computing intrinsic parameters, may be carried out sequentially. This is the so-called partial realization theory, which is briefly discussed in Section 7.

In the historical evolution of time-series analysis, as well as in the corresponding econometric lore, there is a persistent tendency to put the cart before the horse. The usual "approach" is to try to determine the numbers (descriptive parameters) for *a* model Σ_{S_0} from the numbers (descriptive parameters) of *a* given piece of data S_0 before the relationship between S_0 and *the* model $\{\Sigma_{S_0}\}$ (in our sense) is understood.

The danger with such a procedure, used, for example, by Hannan (1979), is that the results of the study of the identification problem may be artifacts depending on the parametrization used rather than on intrinsic properties of the system that are to be identified from real data. We examine this question in connection with the classical approach to the so-called simultaneous-equation estimation problem. See also the discussion of ARMAX models in Section 6.

Parametrization is a higher-level issue; when it is done, it must be done intrinsically, not merely descriptively. It is a deep mathematical problem, too deep to be amenable to solution by "economic intuition."

Relying on the system-theoretic language already familiar to the reader, we may summarize the steps for solving the identification problem in the following way:

(I) Specify a class of systems and the environments in which the system is observed. This class must, of course, contain the model one hopes to identify from the behavioral data.

(II) Specify the class of behavioral data (=available observations). The data S_{Σ_0}, which could have been generated by a system Σ_0 specified under (I), must, of course, belong to this class.

(III) Solve the realization problem: Given any fixed behavioral data S_0 specified under (II), find all systems Σ_{S_0} in the class specified under (I) that could have generated S_0. This gives the model $\{\Sigma_{S_0}\}$ for the data S_0.

(IV) Compute the intrinsic parametrization of both the behavioral data and the family of models.

The problem of identification is now solved in principle, and in the best possible way, namely, deduced from the given data and the given (postulated) class of systems and environments.

Because of (3.5), the numerical determination of a model is automatic once the data has been parametrized. Thus there is really no problem of "parameter identification" once we regard parameters as intrinsic and not merely descriptive. There remains only the question of "parameter determination," namely, translating the parameters of the data into parameters of the model by means of the bijection given by (3.5). Sections 4 and 5 will illustrate the details of this process, by means of examples taken from econometrics.

So, at least in a somewhat oversimplified theoretical way, we have arrived at the conclusion that

(3.6) *identification* = *realization* + *parametrization.*

Evidently there is nothing in the recipe (3.6) that would preclude its applicability to stochastic identification problems. This problem has a rich literature under the label of stochastic realization theory (Kalman, 1965; Rissanen and Kailath, 1972; Faurre, 1973; Akaike, 1974; Picci, 1976, 1977; Faurre et al., 1979; Van Putten and Van Schuppen, 1979).

The reader is warned, however, that this literature deals mainly with the exact stochastic realization problem. An example of such a problem is the construction of a Markovian model from a given autocovariance function, which is a standard theoretical step in reducing the "Kalman" filtering problem to the "Wiener" filtering problem (Kalman, 1965, 1978). The mathematical treatment of these exact problems follows the pattern of deterministic realization theory, in that exact deterministic data (such as the sequence S) is simply replaced by exact stochastic data (such as an exactly given covariance function).

In the real world, alas, we are almost always confronted with the noisy stochastic realization problem, where the basic data is given in an inexact, "noisy" way. This is the situation in many of the classical problems of econometrics. "Noise" means anything about which exact information is lacking and cannot be assumed. This includes measurement errors, disturbances, departure from linearity or stationarity, etc.

The conceptual scheme of Section 2 is clearly applicable to the formulation of the noisy identification problem. But at present there is no developed theory for this problem. So, when we look at examples of identification in Sections 4 and 5, our discussion will remain necessarily sketchy and incomplete.

Yet noisy identification problems are of the greatest interest because they provide the aims of future research. These are concrete, open, system problems whose study is likely to be fairly easy and, if successful, certainly important for the advancement of econometrics.

4 Stochastic identification: example[4]

To illustrate the application of the scheme (2.1) to noisy stochastic realization, we shall now analyze a classical example. The problem is the identification of a static linear relationship, and in that sense it is trivial from the point of view of (dynamical) system theory. The identifiability aspect of this problem has been discussed in a classical paper of Koopmans[5] and Reiersøl (1950).

Consider an affine relationship between a scalar *input* u and a scalar *output* y described by two unknown parameters α and β:

$$(4.1) \quad y = \alpha + \beta u.$$

The data obtained about this relationship come from two sets of (noisy) *observations*, which we shall write, in accordance with the classical notations of Kalman filtering theory (Kalman, 1960), as

$$(4.2) \quad \begin{aligned} z_1 &= u + v_1, \\ z_2 &= y + v_2. \end{aligned}$$

Let us now formally relate this problem to the conceptual scheme (2.1).

The *deterministic system* for this problem is given by (4.1) and by the preceding specification of input, output, and observations. (In general, and also here, for stochastic systems the output is not necessarily the same as the observables.)

The *stochastic environment* of the system is specified by assumptions concerning the joint probability distributions of the variables in (4.1) and (4.2). With Koopmans and Reiersøl (1950), we assume that the scalar u is gaussian random variable, independent of the noise vector v. We specify v by assuming that it, too, is gaussian, with

$$(4.3) \quad \begin{aligned} &\text{(a)} \; Ev_1 = Ev_2 = 0, \\ &\text{(b)} \; \operatorname{cov} v_1 v_2 = 0. \end{aligned}$$

The *behavioral data* for our problem is specified by the conventional hypothesis that the probability distribution function for the observable vector z is known. Because z is gaussian, this means that we assume knowledge of the population parameters

$$\text{(4.4)} \qquad \text{behavioral data} := \{Ez, \operatorname{cov} zz'\}, \quad \text{where} \quad \operatorname{cov} zz' > 0.$$

We may also view (4.4) as specified in terms of the sample mean and the sample covariance. The questions concerning "population" versus "sample" are irrelevant for the discussion that follows.

The system and environment specified by (4.1) to (4.3) will generate a set of behavioral data. Such data cannot fail to be a subset of (4.4), for some Ez and some $\operatorname{cov} zz'$, because (4.4) is the most general data set involving two gaussian variables. In other words, our problem is to identify an affine relationship that may exist between two gaussian random variables z_1 and z_2 when this relationship is obscured by an unknown amount of noise given by the noise mechanism postulated in (4.2–4.3).

Remark. If we allowed the noise to have unknown but nonzero mean, then these unknown values Ev_1 and Ev_2 would affect the determination of the constant α in (4.1). In this case, the problem of identifying α would not be well defined, because

$$\begin{aligned} Ez_2 &= Ey + Ev_2, \\ &= \alpha + \beta Eu + Ev_2, \qquad \text{(4.5)} \\ &= \alpha + \beta Ez_1 - \beta Ev_1 + Ev_2, \end{aligned}$$

Then

$$\alpha := Ez_2 - \beta Ez_1 - (Ev_2 - \beta Ev_1).$$

This means that α could not be determined from the behavioral data but would depend also on the unknown mean of the noise. Thus α would be unidentifiable by its failure to be well defined. For the theorist, this is absurd. If we allow the noise (whose mean cannot be measured in any way, by assumption) to explain some of the affine relationship between z_1 and z_2, then we will not be identifying (4.1) at all. In other words, the mean of the noise must be regarded as part of the postulated deterministic relationship in (4.1). Thus assumption (4.3a) is forced.

[The situation encountered here is logically analogous to the physical problem of "identifying" the resistance of a resistor R_1 when the only permissible measurement is at the terminals of the parallel connection of R_1 with another resistor R_2 of unknown resistance. As far as any such measurement is concerned, it is meaningless to imagine that the actually measured $R = R_1 \| R_2$ is split in some unknown way into two externally indistinguishable parts. The fact that we may see R_1 while R_2 is hidden (say, below the circuitsboard) is irrelevant as far as identification is concerned.]

Assumption (4.3b) is also forced. For if $\operatorname{cov} v_1 v_2 \neq 0$, we can replace v_2 by $\hat{v}_2$ according to the rule

$$v_2 = \hat{\beta} v_1 + \hat{v}_2,$$

with

$$\hat{\beta} := (\operatorname{var} v_1)^{-1} \operatorname{cov} v_1 v_2 \quad \text{and} \quad \operatorname{cov} v_1 \hat{v}_2 = 0.$$

So, if $\hat{\beta} \neq 0$, the parameter β in (4.1) will not be well defined, because the linearity coefficient in the affine relationship between z_2 and z_1 depends on $\hat{\beta}$ as well as on β.

To complete the formal definition of the problem, we now introduce the descriptive parameters of the deterministic system (4.1) and its environment (4.2) and (4.3).

The system is described by

$$\begin{aligned} \delta_1 &:= \alpha, \\ \delta_2 &:= \beta. \end{aligned}$$

There are no constraints; these parameters may be regarded also as intrinsic parameters.

The environment is described by

$$\begin{aligned} \delta_3 &:= Eu, \\ \delta_4 &:= \operatorname{var} u > 0, \\ \delta_5 &:= \operatorname{var} v_1 > 0, \\ \delta_6 &:= \operatorname{var} v_2 > 0. \end{aligned}$$

The assumption that the variances are strictly positive is made to simplify the analysis that follows; this should be regarded as part of the problem specification. Remembering the positivity constraints, δ_3 through δ_6 may again be regarded as intrinsic parameters.

The data parameters are given by

$$Ez_1, \quad Ez_2; \qquad \operatorname{var} z_1, \quad \operatorname{cov} z_1 z_2, \quad \operatorname{var} z_2.$$

The last three of these are subject to the constraint $\operatorname{cov} zz' > 0$ already stated in (4.4).

We have now enough notation to write down the behavioral relations. They are obtained by computing the data covariances in terms of the parameters of the system and the environment. This is exceedingly elementary in this case; the result is

$$\begin{aligned}
&Ez_1 = \delta_3, \\
&Ez_2 = Ey = \alpha + \beta\delta_3, \\
(4.6) \quad &\operatorname{var} z_1 = \delta_4 + \delta_5, \\
&\operatorname{var} z_2 = \beta^2\delta_4 + \delta_6, \\
&\operatorname{cov} z_1 z_2 = \beta\delta_4.
\end{aligned}$$

Let us double check whether or not the behavioral data are well defined for this problem. We must show that the left-hand side of (4.6) is compatible with the specification (4.4) when $\alpha, \beta, \delta_3, \ldots, \delta_6$ have arbitrarily allowable values. For the means Ez_1 and Ez_2 this is trivial, because they need not satisfy any condition. For the covariances, the positivity of $\operatorname{cov} zz'$ follows from the assumed positivity of δ_4, δ_5, and δ_6 (*vide infra*).

Koopmans and Reiersøl (1950) assumed (4.3a) but not (4.3b). Their conclusion was that *the pair* (α, β) *is not identifiable on the basis of the data Ez and* $\operatorname{cov} zz'$.

This conclusion is not at all acceptable from the system-theoretic point of view, and not merely because β is not well defined in the absence of (4.3b).

Koopmans and Reiersøl reasoned as follows. Assuming $\operatorname{cov} zz'$ is strictly positive definite [part of the specification of the data in (4.4)], for any given value of the parameter β the obvious constraint

$$\begin{bmatrix} 1 & \beta \\ \beta & \beta^2 \end{bmatrix} \delta_4 < \operatorname{cov} zz'$$

may be satisfied by a suitably small positive choice of $\delta_4 = \operatorname{var} u$. Then the relation

$$\operatorname{cov} zz' = \begin{bmatrix} 1 & \beta \\ \beta & \beta^2 \end{bmatrix} \operatorname{var} u + \operatorname{cov} vv'$$

may always be satisfied by a suitable choice of positive values for δ_5 and δ_6. For each chosen β, the relation

$$Ez_2 = Ey = \alpha + \beta Eu = \alpha + \beta Ez_1$$

chooses a unique value of α, because Ez_1 and Ez_2 are known as part of the data specification. (Because Koopmans and Reiersøl did not specify $\operatorname{cov} v_1 v_2$, we can simply take it to be $\operatorname{cov} z_1 z_2 - \beta\delta_4$ in this argument.)

The Koopmans–Reiersøl argument reproduced here shows that the mapping "behavior" in (2.1) may send two inequivalent objects (=system+environment) into the same behavioral data. Thus one would expect the realization problem (in our sense) to have a nonunique solution. However, as to the "nonidentifiability of parameters" claimed by Koopmans and Reiersøl, the analysis must go beyond their arguments and requires detailed consideration of the parametrizations involved.

The rigorous system-theoretic analysis of the problem is the following: We determine all solution sets $(\alpha, \beta, \delta_3, \ldots, \delta_6)$ of the realization conditions (4.6) and data (4.4). The first equation is trivial. The second equation can be solved trivially for α given any value of β. Hence, only the last three equations are of interest.

A pair (β, δ_4) solving the last three equations of (4.6), if it exists at all, must satisfy the conditions

$$\text{(4.7)}\qquad \begin{aligned} &\text{(a)}\ \ \beta\delta_4 = \operatorname{cov} z_1 z_2, \\ &\text{(b)}\ \ \operatorname{var} z_1 > \delta_4 > 0, \\ &\text{(c)}\ \ \frac{\operatorname{var} z_2}{|\operatorname{cov} z_1 z_2|} > |\beta|. \end{aligned}$$

To find all solution sets (β, δ_4) of (4.7) is an elementary problem in algebraic geometry. It turns out that a solution always exists because of the assumption $\operatorname{cov} zz' > 0$. In fact, the family of all solutions is given by that segment of the hyperbola (4.7a) which is delimited by the two inequalities (4.7b–c). *Thus the solution of the realization problem is not unique.* (This is, of course, a much stronger statement than the claim of unidentifiability of Koopmans and Reiersøl.)

We may exhibit the solutions of (4.7) more directly as the single condition

$$\text{(4.8)}\qquad \rho^2_{z_1z_2} < \frac{\operatorname{var} u}{\operatorname{var} z_1} < 1,$$

where $\rho_{z_1z_2}$ is the correlation coefficient between the random variables z_1 and z_2. Inequality (4.8) shows quantitatively the influence of noise on the nonuniqueness of the identification of $\operatorname{var} u$; for low noise, $\rho_{z_1z_2} \sim 1$ and $\operatorname{var} v_1 \sim 0$, and then the identification is nearly exact.

If we fix the value of $\delta_4 = \operatorname{var} u$ so as to satisfy the requirement (4.8), every other parameter of the system plus environment is uniquely determined; for example, $\beta = (\operatorname{cov} z_1 z_2)/(\operatorname{var} u)$.

Thus, recalling *our* definition of a model as the family of all realizations of a given fixed set of behavioral data, we can say that *the model for the problem corresponds abstractly to the open interval* $(\rho^2_{z_1z_2}, 1)$; *any system plus environment in the model can be described uniquely by picking a point in this interval and specifying by it the value of* $(\text{var}\, u)(\text{var}\, z_1)^{-1}$. Thus *the model is a one-parameter family* of systems and environments.

From the theoretical point of view, this is certainly the best possible result, because it describes the model solely in terms of the intrinsic parameters of the behavioral data.

However, the transparency of the preceding statement depends very much on the type of parametrization adopted. It may be more appealing, for example, to replace (4.8) by an inequality involving the (intrinsic) parameter β. The existence of such an inequality follows from our preceding results. A simple calculation gives it to us explicitly as

$$\frac{|\text{cov}\, z_1 z_2|}{\text{var}\, z_1} < |\beta| < \frac{\text{var}\, z_2}{|\text{cov}\, z_1 z_2|}, \qquad \text{sgn}\, \beta = \text{sgn}\, \text{cov}\, z_1 z_2 \tag{4.9}$$

This is a very interesting relation, because it gives the solution of the realization problem in terms of the classical regression coefficients. They enter here in the description of the solution of the stochastic realization problem, but without having to appeal to either the assumptions or the techniques of classical statistics.

The surprising form of (4.9) suggests that stochastic realization theory (yet to be developed in detail for the noisy case treated in this section) provides in certain respects an alternative to classical statistics, as far as the use of least squares, regression analysis, and maximum likelihood is concerned. The resulting implications are explored elsewhere (Kalman, 1983) for the general case of identifying m linear relations among n noisy variables.

In econometrics, the structure (4.1) to (4.3) is usually known as the "errors-in-variables" model (Griliches, 1974). I suggest replacing this archaic and ambivalent terminology by "identification of linear relations from noisy data" (Kalman, 1982c). The essence of the problem is the extraction of the linear part of the relationship between z_1 and z_2; the statistical remainder after removing (4.1) from the data may be due to measurement errors, but it may also be due to unexplained effects, other variables, lack of linearity, etc. As I insisted earlier, all of these possibilities are subsumed under the current scientific usage of the word "noise."

The errors-in-variables model (to use the terminology that is still entrenched) has acquired a bad reputation in econometrics. This is due to the unidentifiability aspect. I do not agree with this assessment.

The setup analyzed here is identical with the one adopted by Frisch (1934) in his pioneering book. [Incidentally, he assumed both parts of (4.3)!] Especially if it is a question of identifying more than one linear relation, Frisch's problem has never received adequate mathematical study. It is impossible to avoid the conclusion (Kalman, 1982b) that the lack of progress on and the present unpopularity of Frisch's ideas are due to mathematical rather than conceptual difficulties.

To conclude, we summarize the system-theoretical critique of the Koopmans–Reiersøl claim that "(α, β) are not identifiable."

(I) Identifiability of *a* parameter is not a well-defined notion. A given parameter has no invariant meaning, because there are many different equivalent parametrizations. For example, var u and β may be used equivalently in describing the nonuniqueness of the realization.

(II) What is well defined is the abstract parametrization of the model (= all realizations). For the problem of this section, this turns out to be an open interval. How this interval is displayed in the solution of the problem depends on which particular parametrization has been adopted.

(III) It is wrong to claim that the pair (α, β) is unidentifiable; if β is given some value compatible with (4.8), then α is fixed by the second relation in (4.6). It is a certain segment of a curve in $\{(\alpha, \beta)\} = \mathbf{R}^2$ that is identified. It is meaningless to speak of the "identifiability" of an arbitrary point (α, β) on this segment or in $\mathbf{R}^2$.

Econometricians have been mesmerized for many years by the naive aspiration (as in the field statistical parameter estimation culminating in the maximum likelihood method) that every "parameter" should be given a single value as an "estimate." There is no intuitive reason for having to do so; if there is uncertainty about observing a system, as there is here, it is reasonable to look for an interval of values. And it is unreasonable to try to obtain a single value, because this necessarily involves imposing some prejudice on the data. Realization theory shows that noisy data implies an uncertain model.

The results of the analysis of identifiability carried out here are strongly linked with the initial assumptions concerning the system to be identified and its stochastic environment.

For example, Mehra (1976) has shown that the nonuniqueness of the stochastic realization in our problem (with cov $v_1 v_2 = 0$ being explicitly assumed also by him) may be removed by the following reformulation. View both u and v_1 as random sequences, and assume that the first is serially correlated and that the second is white. Then it is possible to determine uniquely var u, and hence everything else. Unfortunately, this assumption imposes certain new prejudices (see the latter part of Section 5) on the problem which should be tested against the time series $\{z_t, t = 1, 2, \ldots\}$ used to estimate (4.4). If we accept Mehra's prejudice, the problem is seen to belong to exact stochastic realization theory.

Table 6.1 *Equivalent terms*

Koopmans (1949)	This chapter
Endogenous variables	Output
Exogenous (or predetermined) variables	Input
Model (= family of structures)	Class of systems and environments
Structure	System plus stochastic environment with given parameter values
Structural parameters	Descriptive parameters
Observationally equivalent structures	Systems and environments with the same behavior
Identified (identifiable) equations	Canonical forms
Just-identified structural parameters	Coefficients in a canonical form; intrinsic parameters; local coordinates
—	Model
—	Behavior

5 Estimation of simultaneous equations

We shall now outline the application of stochastic realization theory to the standard econometric problem of estimating simultaneous (static) relationships. The discussion will be restricted here to the classical framework due to Haavelmo (1944), Koopmans (1949), and Koopmans, Rubin, and Leipnik (1950). The guiding principle is again the scheme (2.1).

To help the reader, we give in Table 6.1 a concordance between the classical terminology and that used here. [It is unfortunate that the term "structure" is technically defined by Koopmans (1949) and used in later textbooks, e.g., Theil (1971, Chapters 9 and 10) and Malinvaud (1978, Chapter 18), in a way almost opposite to its accepted meaning outside of econometrics. Structure usually connotes the general assumptions or overall framework for the analysis of a problem, never the specific parameter values; structure is bones, not flesh.]

The object of study in this section is a set of linear simultaneous equations subject to many observations of the variables,[6]

$$(5.1) \qquad By_t = Cu_t + v_t, \quad t = 1, 2, \ldots, T.$$

Here $y_t \in \mathbf{R}^p$ is the *output* vector, $u_t \in \mathbf{R}^m$ is the *input* vector, and $v_t \in \mathbf{R}^p$ is the so-called equation error or disturbance vector, which represents all the stochastic influences outside the explanatory domain of the deterministic *system* given by the pair $\Sigma = (B, C)$.

Because the object of modeling is to study the dependence of output on input, obviously the output must be uniquely determined by the input. Hence, we must (and do) assume that

$$(5.2) \qquad \det B \neq 0$$

holds for all systems (5.1) in our class.

This completes the specification of the system in (2.1). [In the present elementary treatment, we disregard the possibility of serial correlation (time correlation) for the variables in (5.1). Thus the problem treated is purely static; dynamic modeling is excluded by fiat.]

The *stochastic environment* in (2.1) is given by the second set of classical specifications for this problem. This is the following. All random variables are gaussian and

$$(5.3) \qquad \begin{aligned} &Ev = 0, \\ &\operatorname{cov} uv' = 0 \quad (' = \text{transpose}), \\ &\operatorname{cov} vv' > 0 \quad (\text{fixed but unknown}), \\ &Eu = 0, \qquad \operatorname{cov} uu' > 0. \end{aligned}$$

[Instead of population means and covariances, we may define the data (5.3) to be the sample means and sample covariances. This will amount to avoiding the standard statistical paradigm (which defines parameters via probability distributions) and working instead directly with the data, the finite time series $\{(y_t, u_t), t = 1, \ldots, T\}$. As far as the present discussion is concerned, the distinction between these two points of view is irrelevant.]

The *behavior* of the system is conventionally specified by giving the joint probability distribution of the random vectors y and u. Under the gaussian assumptions, this is equivalent to specifying

$$(5.4) \qquad E\begin{pmatrix} y \\ u \end{pmatrix} = 0, \qquad \operatorname{cov}\begin{pmatrix} yy' & yu' \\ uy' & uu' \end{pmatrix} > 0.$$

Again, it is irrelevant whether "cov" is taken in the population sense or the sample sense.

The analysis required to understand the system$\rightarrow$behavior arrow in (2.1) is very simple in this case. The first question is: What are equivalent systems?

The mathematical content of the relation $By = Cu$ is unaffected by premultiplying both sides of the equation by a nonsingular matrix.

Using (5.2), it follows that the system $(I, B^{-1}C)$ is equivalent to the system (B, C). In general, the required definition of system equivalence is then

$$(5.5) \qquad (B_1, C_1) \sim (B_2, C_2) \quad \text{if and only if} \quad B_1^{-1}C_1 = B_2^{-1}C_2.$$

The equivalence class of (B, C) evidently contains the element (I, B^{-1}, C). There is no reason not to accept the classical terminology, which calls (B, C) the *structural form* and

$$(5.6) \qquad y = Au + w, \qquad A := B^{-1}C, \qquad w := B^{-1}v$$

the *reduced form* of (5.1). Clearly, equivalent systems will yield identical behavioral data (5.4).

The next question is whether or not the specification (5.4) includes all data that may have been generated by a system and an environment according to (5.1)–(5.2). Here the resolution of this question is quite trivial. Using the machinery of conditional expectations (or regression), we get immediately

$$(5.7) \qquad A := (\operatorname{cov} yu')(\operatorname{cov} uu')^{-1}, \qquad w := y - Au, \qquad \operatorname{cov} uw' = 0.$$

We see, therefore, that *any behavioral data* (5.4) *with positive definite covariance matrix corresponds to a system and environment satisfying* (5.1)–(5.4). Moreover, the natural way of carrying out the solution of the realization problem is to determine a specific element, namely the reduced form (5.7), of the equivalence class of all systems giving rise to the data (5.4).

To complete the solution of the realization problem, it remains to determine the disturbance covariance matrix. This is easy, because it is immediate from the definition of w:

$$(5.8) \qquad \begin{aligned} \operatorname{cov} ww' &= \operatorname{cov}(y - Au)(y - Au)' \\ &= (I \quad -A) \operatorname{cov}\begin{pmatrix} yy' & yu' \\ uy' & uu' \end{pmatrix}\begin{pmatrix} I \\ -A' \end{pmatrix}. \end{aligned}$$

Thus the behavioral data and knowledge of A together uniquely determine $\operatorname{cov} ww'$.

So we have the theorem, well known in econometrics, that

(5.9) *The realization problem for (5.1), under the classical specification (5.1)–(5.4), has a unique solution modulo the equivalence relation (5.5).*

This is an example of an exact stochastic realization problem that shares the fundamental uniqueness property of exact (deterministic) realization problems.

[If the system (5.1)–(5.3) is specified in the population sense and the data (5.4) is given in the sample sense, then of course there is uncertainty in A and cov ww' because of the inaccuracy of the sampling estimates of the population covariances in (5.4). We repeat: this is *not* relevant to the questions analyzed in this chapter.]

It is a misconception to describe this result, as is often done in econometrics, by claiming that "the reduced form is uniquely identified" from the behavioral data. The reduced form (5.6) is merely one element of the equivalence class $[(B, C,)]$ and it is the equivalence class that is uniquely identified, not a particular element of it.

It is currently accepted in econometrics that the goal is the identification of parameters of the structural form (B, C), $\det B \neq 0$. Because the map $(B, C) \rightarrow B^{-1}C$ is not injective, identification in this naive sense evidently cannot be unique. To make it forcibly so, Koopmans's idea was to specify a pair (B_*, C_*) by fixing certain of its elements to be zero while retaining the other elements as free parameters. This is motivated as introducing into the identification problem further "economic" knowledge that has not been taken into account in the already given specification of the behavioral data in (5.4). Suppose (B_*, C_*) can be chosen in such a way that its free parameters are bijective with (the parameters of) A, and hence with the behavioral data. Then the parameters of (B_*, C_*) and the equations in which they appear are said to be, following Koopmans, "just identified" or "identifiable." [For mathematical reasons, there is actually no $(B_*, C_*) \neq (I, A)$ that is bijective with all A; a small set of matrices A must always be excluded (Malinvaud, 1978, p. 718).]

Considering an arbitrary pair of matrices (B, C) in (5.1) amounts to looking at descriptive parameters. Specifying zeros in (B_*, C_*) in such a way that the remaining (free) parameters are almost bijective with A amounts to looking at intrinsic parameters. [We shall not dwell here on the so-called overidentified case that implies further restrictions on A.]

The use of the word "identify" and its derivatives in the sense just explained is entrenched in econometrics. This is most unfortunate. In scientific model building the standard meaning of the word is "inferring the characteristics of a system from observations." This is quite different from the technical connotation given by Koopmans to the word "identification."

To see the issue clearly, we repeat that the behavioral data "identifies," in the honest sense of the word, only the equivalence class $[(I, A)]$. The family $\{[(I, A)]\}$ of equivalence classes is bijective with the family $\{A\}$; in other words, each equivalence class corresponds to exactly one numerical matrix A. Identification in Koopmans's sense requires picking a unique representative of the type (B_*, C_*) in (almost) every equivalence class. When this condition is satisfied, (B_*, C_*) is said to be an (almost) *canonical form* for A. [Not only is this the system-theoretic terminology, but also it agrees with old usage in pure mathematics, where a canonical form connotes a unique choice of a representative (by some abstract or concrete rule) from each member of a family of equivalence classes.]

Koopmans, Rubin, and Leipnik (1950) have resolved the problem of how to specify a valid (B_*, C_*), in other words, a canonical form for A. This is the content of the so-called "rank and order conditions for identifiability."

It is misleading to say that the free coefficients of a valid (B_*, C_*) are identified. Like the elements of A, these coefficients are merely "coordinates" for the equivalence class $[(I, A)] = [(B_*, C_*)]$. Both sets of parameters are valid coordinates. The choice between them is outside the specification of the identification problem in the sense of (2.1); it is made by the prejudice (=data-independent assumption) that assigns economic significance to the elements of (B_*, C_*) but not to those of A.

The format (I, A) is convenient for converting the numbers from the behavioral data (5.4) into the parameters of a system belonging to the equivalence class determined by the data. Once this is done, it may be useful to translate these numbers into yet another format, (B_*, C_*), which is chosen for the purpose of providing a convenient economic interpretation of the data.

The economic assumptions put into (B_*, C_*) have played no role whatever in the identification process. Translation of the data into the (B_*, C_*) format does not, in any way, test the economic hypotheses incorporated in the specifications (5.1)–(5.4). [But the (B_*, C_*) format may make such a test easier.]

There are many economically reasonable choices of canonical forms. Each should be checked against real data. If the modeler likes the numbers the realization process places into his pet (B_*, C_*), he might gain further confidence in the special economic assumptions he has built into the choice of his canonical form. But he certainly cannot claim to have "identified" those assumptions from the data; another canonical form $(B_\#, C_\#)$ may yield even nicer numbers.

Thus, accepting the environmental specification (5.3) of the classical Koopmans identification problem, there still remains the question, not treated by him, of choosing the "right" canonical form in the equivalence class (5.5).

Suppose we have found the parameters of two simultaneous equations, say,

(D_*) quantity $=\alpha$(price) $+\ \beta$(consumer income),

(S_*) quantity $=\gamma$(price) $+\ \delta$(cost of production),

corresponding to the matrix structure

$$(5.10)\quad (B_*, C_*) := \begin{pmatrix} 1 & -\alpha & \vdots & \beta & 0 \\ 1 & -\gamma & \vdots & 0 & \delta \end{pmatrix}.$$

From just the format of (5.10) it is certainly not correct to infer (as is often implied in econometrics texts) that (D_*) is "identified" as the demand equation (arguing that, in it, quantity depends on consumer income but not on cost of production) and that (S_*) is "identified" as the supply equation (because, in it, quantity depends on cost of production but not on consumer income). Any demand-supply situation must be thought of as embedded in the complicated interacting fabric of the economy; therefore it is equally reasonable (and makes perhaps better economic sense) to define another canonical form as

$$(5.11)\quad (B_\#, C_\#) := \begin{pmatrix} 1 & -a & \vdots & b & 0.01b \\ 1 & -c & \vdots & 0.1d & d \end{pmatrix}.$$

Using (5.11) will yield another set of "identified" values (a, b, d, d) for the parameters that may be rather different from the "identified" values $(\alpha, \beta, \gamma, \delta)$ obtained by using (5.10) as the canonical form.

We cannot avoid the conclusion that *it is impossible to identify demand-supply relations in the classical simultaneous-equations context without bringing in new assumptions that are unrelated to the data specified in* (5.4).

In other words, the crucial ingredient in the determination of the price elasticities of demand and supply [the parameters (α, β) or, alternatively, (a, b)] is an assumption, the choice of a specific canonical form, a choice that is made without examination of the data.

Such an assumption I propose to call *prejudice.* The preceding analysis should have convinced the reader that "prejudice" is now a well-defined technical term, meaning assumptions unrelated to data, independent of data, assumptions that cannot be verified or contradicted from data. See Kalman (1982c).

The intended intuitive meaning of "prejudice" is close to the current popular connotation of the word, which is pejorative. It must be remembered, however, that, in the modeling context, prejudice may sometimes be good and in fact most valuable, such as a brilliant assumption about the nature of the data. (Einstein's explanation of the photoelectric effect could serve as the example.)

Of course, the very specification of the system and environment could also be called a higher-level prejudice. Hence, some further comments are needed. "Linear" should not be belittled as a prejudice, because it is known that this assumption is verified in a large number of cases within the realm of investigation considered. Similarly, the standard statistical assumption of an unknown but gaussian distribution is often justified by prior experience. Nevertheless, on a higher level of modeling, it would certainly be desirable to free the current theory (and practice) of the prejudices "linear" and "gaussian."

The classical specification of the simultaneous-equation estimation model by Haavelmo, Koopmans, and the later literature contains some important lower-level prejudices. We mention three: (i) the ad-hoc separation of the variables into "exogenous" and "endogenous" groups (or, equivalently, into "input" and "output"); (ii) the requirement $\operatorname{cov} uv'=0$ in (5.3), which allows the equation errors v in (5.1) to be cross-correlated between different equations but entirely uncorrelated with the explanatory variables; (iii) the assumption that the explanatory variables have been measured exactly.

The first kind of prejudice is nicely illustrated by a well-known paper of Haavelmo (1947) concerned with the estimation of γ, the propensity to consume. Haavelmo claimed that determining γ by regression of consumption c on income y is biased (in the statistical sense) because income is not autonomous but (according to Keynesian-style economics) investment $z:=y-c$ is. Haavelmo analyzed the data in the light of this Keynesian prejudice. Regressing c on y on the assumption that income causes consumption is the application of a different prejudice. (Because it is difficult to consume without income, the latter prejudice, from classical economics, would seem reasonable to most, especially noneconomists.) The point is that both procedures are prejudiced, in the technical sense introduced in this chapter. Haavelmo did not interrogate the data with respect to the validity of his Keynesian prejudice; he simply forced the data to yield a number for γ. If Haavelmo's prejudice were applied to data where national income had been replaced by the birthdates of Babylonians and consumption by a list of telephone numbers, we would still get an unambiguous value of γ. This is computing, not identifying.

The moral of our story is clear: *The classical simultaneous-equation estimation problem is a trivial case of exact stochastic realization theory.* The theory developed by Koopmans and his followers does not deal with the identification problem per se, because that problem is preempted by the prejudicial modeling assumptions imposed at the outset on both the system and its environment. Koopmans's main result was the analysis of the restricted question of valid parametrization; he disposed of that problem completely.

The choice between two valid canonical forms (B_*, C_*) and $(B_\#, C_\#)$, which would seem to be the essence of the identification problem, is not considered in the classical simultaneous-equation estimation context. Such a choice cannot be made without going outside the classical assumptions.

The modern critique of the three prejudices of the classical simultaneous-equation literature is an urgent research topic. For a summary from a certain point of view, the reader is referred to the work of Wold (1981, Chapter 1). Some of the mathematical issues have been explored by Kalman (1982b), with a detailed analysis being given in Kalman (1982c).

6 The ARMAX model

The widespread use in econometrics of ARMAX models (Box and Jenkins, 1976) raises some system-theoretic problems that require discussion.

The general model of this type is often described in econometrics by the following relations (Hannan, 1979):

$$\sum_{r=0}^{n_1} Q_r y_{t-r} = \sum_{s=0}^{n_2} N_s u_{t-1} + v_t. \tag{6.1}$$

The vector variables u_t and y_t are the *input* and *output* of the deterministic system to be identified. The vectors v_t are additional "error" terms; they constitute the stochastic environment for the identification problem.

We shall consider here only the deterministic aspects of (6.1). The basic question to be looked at is this: In what sense does (6.1) determine a linear system? Our answer is in the form of eight remarks:

1. Equations (6.1) describe a system in the external sense; there are no state variables. The existence of state variables [and thus that of a system (2.2b) equivalent to (6.1)] is implied by realization theory. It is immaterial whether or not the modeler likes to think in terms of state variables; state variables are always part of the picture, once the concept of a linear system has been properly defined.

2. For the output sequence y_t to be uniquely determined by the input sequence u_t, we must have

$$\det Q(z) \neq 0 \tag{6.2}$$

(as a polynomial), where $Q(z)$ is the matrix polynomial

(6.3) $$Q(z) := \sum_{r=0}^{n_1} Q_r z^{n_1 - r}.$$

3. Now we can define the object $Q^{-1}(z)N(z)$, with $N(z)$ the matrix polynomial

(6.4) $$N(z) := \sum_{s=0}^{n_2} N_s z^{n_2 - s}.$$

$Q^{-1}(z)N(z)$ is a rational matrix, and therefore it has a formal Laurent series about $z = \infty$. To be able to relate this series to the transfer function of the underlying system Σ, it is necessary to assume, for reasons of causality, that

(6.5) $$Q^{-1}(z)N(z) = \text{(strictly) proper rational matrix.}$$

4. The last assumption means that

(6.6) $$Q^{-1}(z)N(z) = \sum_{t>0} A_t z^{-t},$$

where equality holds in the sense of formal power series. We are now in the situation of having given a standard external description $S = (A_1, A_2, \ldots)$ of the system in the form (2.4). Of course, S is "identifiable," by definition, because S is the data to which the identification problem is ultimately referenced.

5. Conditions for the identifiability of (6.5) are sometimes given in the literature. They usually concern some assumption about u_t (e.g., $u_t \neq 0$). We prefer not to use such terminology in talking about a system; identifiability should be an intrinsic property of S, not something that depends on the environment. It might be interesting to discuss the question of "identifying S with respect to it being imbedded in a certain signal environment," but such problems are outside the scope of the present work.

6. Evidently, the intrinsic identifiability of $(Q(z), N(z))$ used as in formula (6.6) concerns the relations between the descriptive parameters of S, given by the matrices $A_1, A_2, \ldots,$ on the one hand, and the descriptive parameters of the pair $(Q(z), N(z))$, given by the coefficient matrices $Q_0, Q_1, \ldots$ and $N_0, N_1, \ldots$ in (6.3)–(6.4), on the other hand.

Such issues can be considered only after the notion of a system is well defined. This obviously requires introducing the equivalence relation

(6.7) $$(Q(z), N(z)) \sim (\hat{Q}(z), \hat{N}(z))$$

defined by

(6.8) $$Q^{-1}(z)N(z) = \hat{Q}^{-1}(z)\hat{N}(z).$$

This relation may be viewed as a constraint imposed on the descriptive parameters given by (6.3)–(6.4). The equivalence relation (6.7) is needed to prevent the system from being ill defined because of the possibility of cancelable factors between $Q(z)$ and $N(z)$, as well as because of different conventions on normalization. [Note: The normalization used in (6.3)–(6.4) follows standard system-theoretic practice and, unfortunately, differs from that used by Hannan (1979) and by Hannan, Dunsmuir, and Deistler (1980). See the work of Antoulas (1981) for the standard notations and terminology.]

7. Conditions (6.2), (6.5), and the equivalence relation (6.7) are obviously necessary and sufficient for the abstract map

$$(6.9)\qquad (Q(z), N(z)) \mapsto S$$

given by (6.6) to be injective.

To show that (6.1) is a proper (external) definition of a system, we must establish that this map is bijective. Thus it remains to show that there exists an injective map

$$(6.10)\qquad S \mapsto (Q(z), N(z))$$

satisfying (6.6). This question requires a mathematical study.

Assuming that S has a finite-dimensional realization Σ_S, realization theory shows that there is a proper irreducible rational matrix $Z(z)$ whose formal power series agrees with the right-hand side of (5.6). It can be shown, further, that every proper rational matrix admits a factorization as $Z(z) = Q^{-1}(z)N(z)$. Alternatively, by setting up suitably defined canonical forms $(Q_*(z), N_*(z))$, it is easy to give a map $\Sigma_S \mapsto (Q_*(z), N_*(z))$ satisfying (6.6). The relevant literature and techniques have been reviewed by Antoulas (1981).

This proves the existence of an injective map (6.10). Then it follows that the correspondence between S and $(Q(z), N(z))$ can be made bijective with the aid of the conditions mentioned earlier.

The essential point to remember is that the proper definition of a linear system by (6.1) requires studying the process $(Q(z), N(z)) \mapsto Z \mapsto S \mapsto \Sigma$. Conversely, the conversion of the standard external data S into the ARMAX description is essentially a realization problem and is most easily visualized through the process $S \mapsto \Sigma \mapsto (Q(z), N(z))$. Thus, realization theory is an unavoidable part of the ARMAX problem, even before the question of parametrization arises.

The (intrinsic) parametrization of the ARMAX model is made difficult by the need for the equivalence condition (6.5). This is not at all a trivial problem. It is best studied by relating all basic definitions ultimately to the Σ definition of a system that is to be used as a reference point in comparing results. This is often missing in published papers.

8. In the work of Hannan (1979, first sentence), as well as in the work of Hannan, Dunsmuir, and Deistler (1980, p. 277, equation (4) and following), we find the astonishing statement that *the definition of a linear system is subject to conditions of stochastic nature.* Thus, within a single sentence, we are faced with the obfuscation of the two most basic principles of mathematical analysis upon which this chapter (and all of system theory) rests.

The concept of "linear" is such a basic algebraic definition that it must not be confused with anything else. Otherwise, technical use of mathematics becomes futile.

The notion of a "system," as we have argued in Section 2, should be sharply distinguished from its stochastic "environment". Failure to do so is responsible for much fuzziness in the present literature. Doing so deliberately is one of the ingredients that account for the success of the so-called Kalman filtering theory.

Subject to these technical details, however, the question of how to define a deterministic linear dynamical system (external sense) with the aid of a pair $(Q(z), N(z))$ is completely settled at the present time. The remaining problems concern a better understanding of the intrinsic parametrization.

It should be mentioned that the mathematical analysis required here is relatively recent even in system theory and was developed mainly during the last 10 years under the impetus of the book by Rosenbrock (1970).

We may again conclude that "parameter identifiability" is a non-problem for the situation formalized in terms of (6.1), unless this terminology is used merely as a code for "parametrization."

The ARMAX scheme defines a generic linear system. This is undoubtedly a major reason for the success of methods based on it. Dropping either the AR or the MA (i.e., considering only moving-average or autoregressive models), genericity is lost, and further serious conceptual and technical difficulties arise. This will be examined in the next section.

7 Applications of realization theory

"Parameter identifiability" is, intuitively, a rather appealing idea. Why did it fail to work for linear systems? The reason is simply that the development of system theory (a particular field of science) has reached a point where results from realization theory (a subfield) are now available to subject such an intuitive notion as that of "parameter identifiability" to rigorous scientific analysis. After parameter identifiability has been tested on the precise and concrete case of a linear system, it collapses as a workable concept, and yet it must work for linear systems if it is to have theoretical merit.

A similar application of system theory can be made to assess the merits of the *moving average* (MA) and *autoregressive* (AR) models. These were proposed and used by time-series analysts long before system theory existed, certainly by the late 1920s. Their study provided some of the stimuli for the early development of system theory.

Are these models good or bad? The gut response of any good system theorist is certainly: "Bad." To prove this emotional guess in a rigorous way, however, is far from easy; in fact, this became possible only after the development of the so-called partial-realization theory (Kalman, 1971, 1979c).

The partial-realization problem arises when S in (2.4) is given only partially, that is, by a finite sequence of matrices $A_1, \ldots, A_t$. Then realizations $\Sigma_t^{\min}$ of minimal dimension n_t may not be unique, but of course n_t is unique because of the requirement of minimality. The analysis of n_t as a function of t provides very important mathematical information concerning the classical realization problem (Kalman, 1984). Because n_t is a monotone, nondecreasing, integer-valued function defined on the integers, its value can change only in "jumps." The structure of these jumps turns out to satisfy strong regularity conditions (*vide infra*).

The AR and the MA schemes constitute a constructive existence proof that *for every t the partial-realization problem has a (finite) solution.* Mathematically, this is a very trivial fact. It follows, unfortunately, that this is the only system-theoretic idea inherent in AR and MA.

The (scalar) AR scheme applies if and only if n_t is a function with a single jump. This is a highly nongeneric situation. It usually does not occur in nature. Because the jumps are the basic phenomenon in the realization problem, it must be possible to find a statistical test for the occurrence of various patterns of jumps.

Such a test has not yet been developed, as far as I know. Consequently, the application of AR models to real data is system-theoretic nonsense. When an AR scheme is applied, it is usually out of pure prejudice, without statistical evidence that the very unlikely case is in fact at hand. It cannot be argued that AR fits the data, because ARMA will fit the data even better, being generic (see Section 6).

It is amusing to note that for $n=1$ it is trivially true that AR= ARMA. Consequently, there is nothing wrong in applying first order autoregression. When we attempt to go to the $n>1$ case, however, the AR idea collapses. We have here a generalization leading to a system-theoretic problem that is far more difficult than it seems. Of course, similar comments also aply to the MA scheme.

Another application of partial-realization theory concerns the parametrization of the data $S=(A_1,A_2,\ldots)$. Let us consider only the scalar case $S=(a_1,a_2,\ldots)$, where the a_i are real numbers, because the theory given in Kalman (1979c) is restricted to this case. Such a scalar sequence may be viewed, for example, as a discrete-time autocovariance function.

With this restriction, however, the theory in Kalman (1979c) applies to any such sequence (there are no conditions!). Consequently, any "data" $a_1,a_2,\ldots$ has a certain intrinsic pattern of jumps associated with it. If a jump of size $q_i:=n_{t_i}-n_{t_{i-1}}$ occurs at the time point t_i, the following statements can be made:

(i) $a_{t_i}\neq a^*_{t_i}:=$ [value of a_{t_i} computed from the (unique) partial realization based on $a_1,\ldots,a_{t_{i-1}}$, using formulas (2.5)]. This statement is meaningful because the main theorem of partial-realization theory guarantees that a jump may occur at t_i only if $a_1,\ldots,a_{t_{i-1}}$ has a unique minimal realization. So a_{t_i} is not a free parameter, because letting $a_{t_i}=a^*_{t_i}$ would contradict the intrinsic jump pattern.

(ii) After a jump of size q_i, exactly the next q_i elements $a_{t_i+1},\ldots,a_{t_i+q_i}$ of the sequence are free; that is, any values of these elements may occur without contradicting the jump pattern.

(iii) Before a jump of size q_i, exactly q_i-1 elements of the sequence are fixed, that is, they are uniquely determined via (2.5) by the minimal partial realization of the first $2n_{t_{i-1}}$ elements of the sequence.

This shows that it is naive to speak of $S=(a_1,a_2,\ldots)$ as a sequence of (intrinsic) parameters, if we take "parameter" in the usual sense of being any real number. Only the q_i elements of the sequence following the ith root jump point [type (ii)] qualify as parameters in this sense. The type (i) elements must satisfy the $\neq$ condition. The type (iii) elements (which do not occur in the generic case) are completely fixed. Moreover, and this is the crucial point, the locations of the various types of elements are fixed by the jump pattern. This is an intrinsic property of the data that has not been discovered in the time-series literature prior to Kalman (1971, 1979c).

The parametrization of S is especially important when the dimension n of the system is not fixed a priori, which is the normal situation in identification. In this case, partial realization provides a nested sequence of parametrizations for (F,G,H). This comes from the fact that n_t is monotonically increasing with t, as was pointed out 10 years ago by Rissanen (1971).

8 Conclusions

System theory is a new paradigm. It applies to economics in at least two ways: through the study of systemic properties of any economic model and through the critique of the econometric recipes of modeling. Here we have studied the second aspect.

The development of science, certainly in regard to economics, has today reached the stage where physics is no longer a good role model. The physicist's approach (first isolate a phenomenon and then try to analyze it in its simplest manifestations without regard to the context) is precisely what is inapplicable to the problems of economics, because economic phenomena are intrinsically system (context)-related.

The aspiration of econometrics, to develop hidden quantitative relationships from interrelated data, is a central problem of system theory. To be successful, econometrics and econometricians must pay close attention to more advanced problems arising from modeling; for example, the question of intrinsic parameters and their relation to real data. It is not enough to think in terms of parameters in the naive sense. We insist that the intuitive notion of "identifiability of a parameter" cannot be developed into a meaningful scientific concept. A viable alternative is provided by the apparatus of realization theory.

Let us close by recalling the position taken 25 years ago by John von Neumann (1955) is one of his last public statements. In response to a discussion topic concerning potential scientific development of economics, he denied that progress would be stopped because of the "impossibility of experiments" (classical astronomy, a science successful without experiments, being his counterexample) or blocked by "lack of data" (many scientific advances, such as Einstein's photoelectric law and even more his general relativity, were conceived when there was very little data available). The most important missing element in economics, von Neumann insisted, was the "definition of categories."

What he must have meant by this is articulated in contemporary terminology by the words "invariants," "intrinsic properties," "decomposition," etc. If modeling of economic time series is to have relevance for economic theory (and in that hope we are all united), then system theory must be able to discover von Neumann's missing categories in real data, by penetrating more deeply into the theory of models.

There are many results and much research in system theory today concerned with exactly this problem. Econometrics must also collaborate on its solution, or wither as a second-hand exercise in statistics.

The task of going from real data to economic (or any other) theory may be attacked in many ways. The scientific approach is not compulsory. Astrology has been tried. We hear the phrase "economic witch doctors" with disturbingly increasing frequency.

An optimist does not want to quarrel with declarations such as "the exposure to the 'real world' of economic policy... affirmed rather than eroded [my] belief in the usefulness and relevance of economic theory" (Whitman, 1979, p. x). Indeed, mountains are sometimes moved by innocent faith. But don't hold your breath. It is better to sit down and begin getting rid of prejudices.

NOTES

1 Economists have wasted much emotion in debunking the so-called Forrester–Meadows world model, on the grounds of obsolete data, inadequate attention to economic theory or realities, etc. Actually, this model collapses under its own weight for internal logical reasons that have nothing to do with economics (Kalman, 1980a, Section 7.1).
2 The notations in (2.2a–b), which I introduced around 1960 to honor my great teacher, F. G. H. Linear, have been universally adopted in system theory.
3 Not to be confused with canonical systems (*vide infra*).
4 This section was not part of the oral presentation.
5 I am indebted to Professor Koopmans for having pointed out to me this and other related papers of his nearly 15 years ago already.
6 I follow the conventional terminology here only as an aid to the reader who may have been educated in that way. Actually, the expression "simultaneous equation estimation" should be exorcized as quickly as possible because none of the three words occurring in it is used in the correct and accepted sense. See Kalman (1982c).

REFERENCES

Akaike, H. 1974. "Stochastic Theory of Minimal Realization." *IEEE Transactions on Automatic Control* AC-19:667–74.

Antoulas, A. 1981. "On Canonical Forms for Linear Constant Systems." *International Journal of Control* 33:95–122.

Box, G. E. P., and Jenkins, G. M. 1976. *Time Series Analysis: Forecasting and Control.* San Francisco: Holden-Day.

Faurre, P. 1973. "Réalisations markoviennes de processus stationnaires." Research Report No. 13, IRIA, Rocquencourt, France.

Faurre, P., Clerget, M., and Germain, F. 1979. *Opérateurs Rationnels Positifs: Application à l'Hyperstabilité et aux Processus Aléatoires.* Paris: Dunod.

Firsch, R. 1934. *Statistical Confluence Analysis by Means of Complete Regression Systems.* Publication No. 5, University of Oslo Economic Institute.

Griliches, Z. 1974. "Errors in Variables and Other Unobservables." *Econometrica* 42:971–98.

Haavelmo, T. 1944. "The Probability Approach in Econometrics." *Econometrica 12*, Supplement, 118 pages.

Haavelmo, T. 1947. "Methods of Measuring the Marginal Propensity to Consume." *Journal of the American Statistical Association* 42:105–22.

Hannan, E. J. 1979. "The Statistical Theory of Linear Systems." In *Developments in Statistics, Vol. 2,* edited by P. R. Krishnaiah, pp. 83–121. New York: Academic.

Hannan, E. J., Dunsmuir, W. T. M., and Deistler, M. 1980. "Estimation of Vector ARMAX Models." *Journal of Multivariate Analysis* 10:275–95.

Kalman, R. E. 1960. "A New Approach to Linear Filtering and Prediction Problems." *Journal of Basic Engineering* (*Trans. ASME*) 82D:35–45.

Kalman, R. E. 1962. "Canonical Structure of Linear Dynamical Systems." *Proceedings of the National Academy of Sciences* (*USA*) 48:596–600.

Kalman, R. E. 1965. "Linear Stochastic Filtering Theory—Reappraisal and Outlook." In *Proceedings of a Symposium on System Theory,* edited by J. Fox, pp. 197–205. New York: Polytechnic Institute of Brooklyn.

Kalman, R. E. 1971. "On Minimal Partial Realizations of a Linear Input/Output Map." In *Aspects of Network and System Theory,* edited by R. E. Kalman and N. DeClaris, pp. 385–408. New York: Holt, Rinehart & Winston.

Kalman, R. E. 1972. "Kronecker Invariants and Feedback." In *Proceedings of the 1971 NRL–MRC Conference on Ordinary Differential Equations,* edited by L. Weiss, pp. 459–71. New York: Academic.

Kalman, R. E. 1974. "Algebraic-Geometric Description of the Class of Linear Systems of Constant Dimension." In *Proceedings of the 8th Annual Princeton Conference on Information Sciences,* pp. 189–91.

Kalman, R. E. 1976. "Realization Theory of Linear Dynamical Systems." In *Control Theory and Functional Analysis, Vol. II,* pp. 235–56. Vienna: International Atomic Energy Agency.

Kalman, R. E. 1978. "A Retrospective after Twenty Years: From the Pure to the Applied." In *Applications of Kalman Filter to Hydrology, Hydraulics, and Water Resources,* edited by Chao-Lin Chiu, pp. 31–54. Pittsburgh: Department of Civil Engineering, University of Pittsburgh.

Kalman, R. E. 1979a. "A System-Theoretic Critique of Dynamic Economic Models." In *Global and Large-Scale System Models,* edited by B. Lazarevic, pp. 1–24. New York: Springer-Verlag.

Kalman, R. E. 1979b. "Theory of Modeling." In *Proceedings of the IBM System Science Symposium, Oiso, Japan,* edited by Y. Nishikawa, pp. 53–69.

Kalman, R. E. 1979c. "On Partial Realizations, Transfer Functions, and Canonical Forms." *Acta Polytechnica Scandinavica, Mathematics and Computer Science Series* 31:9–32.

Kalman, R. E. 1980. "System-Theoretic Critique of Dynamic Economic Models." *International Journal of Policy Analysis and Information Systems* 4:3–22.

Kalman, R. E. 1982a. "Dynamic Econometric Models: A System-Theoretic Critique." In *New Quantitative Techniques for Economic Analysis,* edited by G. P. Szegö, New York: Academic, pp. 19–28.

Kalman, R. E. 1982b. "System Identification from Noisy Data," *Proc. International Symposium on Dynamical Systems,* in Gainesville, FL in February 1981, edited by A. Bednarek and L. Cesari. New York: Academic Press (in press).

Kalman, R. E. 1982c. "Identification of Linear Relations from Noisy Data." to appear.

Kalman, R. E. 1984. *Realization Theory. I. Deterministic Systems* (book), to appear.

Kalman, R. E., Falb, P. L., and Arbib, M. A. 1969. *Topics in Mathematical System Theory.* New York: McGraw-Hill.

Koopmans, T. C. 1949. "Identification Problems in Economic Model Construction." *Econometrica* 17:125–44.

Koopmans, T. C., and Reiersøl, O. 1950. "The Identification of Structural Characteristics." *Annals of Mathematical Statistics* 21:165–81.

Koopmans, T. C., Rubin, H., and Leipnik, R. B. 1950. "Measuring the Equation Systems of Dynamic Economics." In *Statistical Inference in Dynamic Economic Models,* edited by T. C. Koopmans, pp. 54–231. New York: Wiley.

Malinvaud, E. 1978. *Méthodes Statistiques de l'Econométrie,* ed. 3. Paris: Dunod.

Mehra, R. K. 1976. "Identification and Estimation of the Error-in-Variables Model (EVM) in Structural Form." In *Mathematical Programming Study, Vol. 5,* pp. 191–210. Amsterdam: North-Holland.

Picci, G. 1976. "Stochastic Realization of Gaussian Processes." *Proceedings of the IEEE* 64:112–22.

Picci, G. 1977. "Some Connections between the Theory of Sufficient Statistics and the Identifiability Problem." *SIAM Journal of Applied Mathematics* 33:383–98.

Rissanen, J. 1971. "Recursive Identification of Linear Systems." *SIAM Journal on Control* 9:420–30.

Rissanen, J. and Kailath, T. 1972. "Partial Realization of Random Systems." *Automatica* 8:389–96.

Rosenbrock, H. H. 1970. *State-space and Multivariable Theory.* New York: Wiley.

Sontag, E. D., and Rouchaleau, Y. 1976. "On Discrete-Time Polynomial Systems." *Journal of Nonlinear Analysis* 1:55–64.

Tannenbaum, A. 1981. *Invariance and System Theory: Algebraic and Geometric Aspects.* Springer Lecture Notes in Mathematics No. 845. New York: Springer-Verlag.

Theil, H. 1971. *Principles of Econometrics.* New York: Wiley.

Van Putten, C., and Van Schuppen, J. H. 1979. "On Stochastic Dynamical Systems." In *Proceedings of the 4th International Symposium on the Mathematical Theory of Networks and Systems,* Delft, Netherlands (*in press*).

von Neumann, J. 1955. "The Impact of Recent Developments in Science on the Economy and on Economics" (summary of speech before the National Planning Association). *Looking Ahead* 4:11; reprinted in the author's *Collected Works, Vol. VI,* pp. 100–1.

Whitman, M. v. N., 1979. *Reflections of Interdependence: Issues for Economic Theory and U.S. Policy.* University of Pittsburgh Press.

Wold, H., editor. 1981. *The Fix-Point Approach to Interdependent Systems.* Amsterdam: North-Holland.

Yamamoto, Y. 1981. "Realization Theory of Infinite-Dimensional Linear Systems." (*in press*).

PART VI

TESTING FOR CAUSATION AND EXOGENEITY

CHAPTER 7

Causality, exogeneity, and inference

John Geweke

1 Introduction

Building on earlier work by Wiener (1956), C. W. J. Granger (1963, 1969) introduced a formalization of the concept of "causality" that applied to time series and subsequently has proved useful in empirical work. We shall refer to this formalization as Wiener–Granger causality. Let $X=\{\mathbf{x}_t, t \text{ integer}\}$ and $Y=\{\mathbf{y}_t, t \text{ integer}\}$ be two time series, and let X_t and Y_t denote their entire histories up to and including time t: $X_t=\{\mathbf{x}_t, \mathbf{x}_{t-1}, \ldots\}$, $Y_t=\{\mathbf{y}_t, \mathbf{y}_{t-1}, \ldots\}$. Let U_t denote all information accumulated as of time t, and suppose that $X_s \subseteq U_t$ if and only if $s \leqslant t$, and $Y_s \subseteq U_t$ if and only if $s \leqslant t$. If we are better able to predict $\mathbf{x}_t$ using U_{t-1} than we are using $U_{t-1} - Y_{t-1}$, then Y causes X. If we are better able to "predict" $\mathbf{x}_t$ using $U_{t-1} \cup \mathbf{y}_t$ than we are using U_{t-1}, then Y causes X instantaneously.[1]

The concept of Wiener–Granger causality has proved useful in econometric work because it is closely related to notions of causation that have been developed by philosophers of science and to the condition of exogeneity set forth three decades ago by econometricians. These relations are unfortunately not so "clear" as they are "close." In this chapter we shall survey alternative formalizations of these ideas in an attempt to clarify the relations among them. In applied work, tests for the

I am grateful to the National Science Foundation for support through grant SES-8005606 and to Susan Hudak for help with the computations. Sections 2 and 3 are based on the author's "Inference and Causality in Economic Time Series Models," forthcoming as a chapter in *Handbook of Econometrics*, edited by Z. Griliches and M. Intriligator and published by North-Holland.

absence of Wiener–Granger causality have frequently been applied as a device for describing relations among time series. We shall compare these tests and evaluate their appropriateness as a descriptive device. We begin with a succinct, but simplified, summary of this chapter's main points.

Wiener–Granger causality is not synonymous with any of the definitions of causation in the literature of the philosophy of science and would be a poor substitute for those that appear. The difficulty is that Wiener–Granger causality is a statement about predictability in the population (which makes unidirectional Wiener–Granger causality empirically refutable) but contains no reference to the notion of *systematic forcing* (Bunge, 1959, Chapter 12) that is common to classical definitions. In a universe governed by causal laws, unidirectional Wiener–Granger causal orderings may emerge, however, because systematic forcing can produce such orderings. Situations in which unidirectional causal ordering has been refuted may be of interest, insofar as they eliminate from further consideration proposed laws that imply the unidirectional ordering in question. The finding of a unidirectional causal ordering has not the significance of the discovery of a causal law, although it may suggest further research that leads to such a discovery. These ideas will be developed in detail in Section 2.

The concept of exogeneity is used in at least two ways by econometricians. In the first use, exogeneity is a property of a functioning system or a proposed model that refers to the order in which the realizations of certain variables are determined. In the special case of the complete dynamic simultaneous-equations model, the notion is equivalent to the dynamic ordering implicit in the usual dichotomy of variables into endogenous and exogenous variables. In this system there is a unidirectional Wiener–Granger causal ordering from the exogenous to the endogenous variables; refutation of such an ordering is therefore again of interest. In the second use of the word, exogeneity is that property of a group of variables that permits them to be treated as fixed for purposes of inference about certain parameters in a proposed model. Given maintained hypotheses of sufficient strength, exogeneity of this type may be refuted. We shall argue in Section 3 that situations in which maintained hypotheses of sufficient certainty are available are rare and that the relationship between Wiener–Granger causality and this type of exogeneity is tenuous.

In Section 4 we shall elaborate on the notion of feedback considered in the earlier work of Granger (1963) and suggest that measures of feedback provide a more reasonable description of the relationships between time series than do the outcomes of tests for unidirectional causal orderings. Unidirectional causal orderings frequently are events with low (or zero) prior probability, and test outcome is in any event a function of the sample. Measures of feedback are characteristics of the population, and confidence regions for these measures provide a convenient summary of the extent to which available data restrict these characteristics.

Several tests for the absence of Wiener–Granger causal orderings have been employed in the literature. Some investigators have estimated the projection of Y on X directly, correcting for serial correlation of the disturbance and using the results of Sims (1972) on the relationship between the projection and the existence of a unidirectional causal ordering. Others have exploited the relationship between the correlation of disturbances in univariate ARIMA models and the existence of such an ordering. Analytical results indicate that tests in the autoregressive models suggested immediately by Granger's definition (1969) are superior to the latter method and as good as the former; Monte Carlo evidence strongly favors this method over either of the others. Some of these considerations will be discussed in Section 5. An empirical example illustrating some of these points will be discussed in Section 6. Conclusions are summarized in the final section.

2 Wiener–Granger causality, causation, and the structure of econometric models

A variety of formal definitions of causation has been offered by philosophers of science. There are important differences in these definitions, discussion of which is well beyond the scope of this chapter. The difference between Wiener–Granger causality and formal causation is of a still greater order of magnitude. In most definitions, "cause" is similar in meaning to "force" or "produce" (e.g., Blalock, 1961, pp. 9–10), which clearly are not synonymous with "predict." The definition closest to Wiener–Granger causality is perhaps that of Feigl (1953, p. 408), in which "causation is defined in terms of predictability according to a law." As Zellner (1979) has pointed out, Wiener–Granger causality concentrates on predictability, to the exclusion of any consideration of laws. For these reasons, Wiener–Granger causality is not an acceptable substitute for other definitions of causation. However, there is no logical conflict between causation and Wiener–Granger causality once the distinction between the two is made. Indeed, the existence of causation implies predictability, at least in principle, and so the concept of Wiener–Granger causality is potentially useful in inference about laws. To assess this possibility in econometrics, it is necessary first to review and formalize some operational concepts implicit in econometric modeling.[2]

A definition of *causal ordering* in any econometric model (as opposed to the real world) was proposed by Simon (1952). Suppose S is a space of possible outcomes and that the model imposes two sets of restrictions, A and B, on these outcomes. The entire model imposes the restriction $A \cap B$ on S. Suppose that S is mapped into two spaces, X and Y, by G_X and G_Y, respectively. Then the ordered pair of restrictions (A, B) implies a causal ordering from X to Y if A restricts X (if at all) but not Y, and B restricts Y (if at all) without further restricting X. Formally, we have the following definition.

Definition: The ordered pair (A, B) of restrictions on S determines a causal ordering from X to Y if and only if $G_Y(A) = Y$ and $G_X(A \cap B) = G_X(A)$.

Perhaps the simplest example of a causal ordering that can be constructed is the following. Let $S = \{(x, y) \in \mathbf{R}^2\}$, and consider the restrictions

(A) $\qquad x = a$

(B) $\qquad y + bx = c$

on S. Let G_X map S into the x coordinate, and let G_Y map S into the y coordinate. Then (A, B) determines a causal ordering from X to Y because A determines x without affecting y, whereas B together with A determines y without further restricting x. The causal ordering is a property of the model, not a property of the restrictions on S to which the model happens to give rise. Clearly, there are many pairs of restrictions (C, D) such that $G_X(C \cap D) = G_X(A \cap B) = a$ and $G_Y(C \cap D) = G_Y(A \cap B) = c - ba$. In fact, one of these establishes a causal ordering from Y to X.

Causal orderings, or recursive models, are intended to be more than just descriptive devices. Inherent in such models is the notion that if restriction (A) is changed, the outcome will still be $A \cap B$, with B unchanged. Once the possibility of changing the first restriction in the ordered pair is granted, it makes a great deal of difference which causal ordering is inherent in the model. Different models describe different sets of restrictions on S arising from manipulation of the first restriction. Hence, attention is focused on B. We formalize the notion that B is unchanged when A is manipulated as follows.

Definition: The set $B \subseteq S$ accepts X as input if for any $A \subseteq S$ that constrains only X (i.e., $G_X^{-1}(G_X(A)) = A$), (A, B) determines a causal ordering from X to Y.

In econometric modeling, the notion that B should accept X as input is so entrenched and natural that it is common to think of B as the model itself, with little or no attention given to the set A that restricts the admissible inputs for the model, although these restrictions may be very important. Conventional manipulation of an econometric model for policy or predictive purposes assumes that the manipulated variables are accepted as input by the model.

In many applications X and Y are time series, as they were in the notation of Section 1. Consider the simple case in which X and Y are univariate, normally distributed, jointly stationary time series and S is the family of bivariate, normally distributed, jointly stationary time series. Suppose that the restriction (A) is

$$A(L)x_t = v_t$$

where $A(L)$ is one-sided (i.e., involves only nonnegative powers of the lag operator L) and has all roots outside the unit circle, and $V=\{v_t, t \text{ integer}\}$ is a serially uncorrelated, normally distributed, stationary time series. Let the restriction (B) be

$$B(L)y_t + C(L)x_t = w_t$$

where $B(L)$ has no roots on the unit circle, both $B(L)$ and $C(L)$ may be two-sided (i.e., involve negative powers of the lag operator L), and $W=\{w_t, t \text{ integer}\}$ is a serially uncorrelated, normally distributed, stationary time series independent of V. Because (A) implies $x_t=A(L)^{-1}v_t$, it establishes the first time series without restricting the second, whereas (B) implies

$$y_t = -B(L)^{-1}C(L)x_t + B(L)^{-1}v_t \tag{2.1}$$

which establishes the second without changing the first. Hence the model establishes a causal ordering from X to Y, and if for any normally distributed, jointly stationary X the outcome of the model satisfies (2.1), then (ii) accepts X as input. However, such a model might or might not be interesting for purposes of manipulation. In general, y_t will be a function of past, current, and future X, which is undesirable if (ii) is supposed to describe the relationship between actual inputs and outputs; the restriction that $B(L)$ and $C(L)$ be one-sided and that $B(L)$ have no roots inside the unit circle would obviate this difficulty.

The notion that future inputs should not be involved in the determination of present outputs is known in the engineering literature as realizability (Zemanian, 1972), and we can formalize it in our notation as follows.

Definition: The set $B \subseteq S$ is realizable with time series X as input if B accepts X as input, and $G_{X_t}(A_1) = G_{X_t}(A_2)$ implies $G_{Y_r}(A_1 \cap B) = G_{Y_r}(A_2 \cap B)$ for all $A_1 \subseteq S$ and $A_2 \subseteq S$ that constrain only X, and all $t \geq r$.

If B accepts X as input but is not realizable, then a specification of inputs up to time t will not restrict outputs, but once outputs up to time t are restricted by B, then further restrictions on inputs (those occurring after time t) are implied. This is clearly an undesirable characteristic of any model that purports to treat time in a realistic fashion.

The concepts of causal ordering, inputs, and realizability pertain to models. One can determine whether or not models possess these properties without reference to the phenomena that the models are supposed to describe. Of course, our interest in these models stems from the possibility that they do indeed describe actual phenomena. Hurwicz (1962) attributed the characteristic of *structure* to models that meet this criterion.

Definition: The set $B \subseteq S$ is structural for inputs X if B accepts X as input, and when any set $C \subseteq X$ is implemented, then $G_Y(G_X^{-1}(C) \cap B)$ is true.

Notice that the use of the word "structural" here is not the same as its use in the parlance of simultaneous-equations models. The sets of "structural," "reduced-form," and "final-form" equations are either all structural or not structural in the sense of the foregoing definition, depending on whether or not the model depicts actual phenomena.

This definition incorporates two terms that shall remain primitive: "implemented" and "true." Whether or not $G_Y(G_X^{-1}(C) \cap (B))$ is true for a given C is a question to which statistical inference can be addressed; at most, we can hope to attach a posterior probability to the truth of this statement. We can never know if $G_Y(G_X^{-1}(C) \cap (B))$ is true for any C. One can never prove that a model is structural, although by implementing one or more sets C, serious doubt could be cast on the assertion. Because the definition allows any set $C \subseteq X$ to be implemented, those implementing inputs in real time are permitted to change their plans. It seems implausible that the current outputs of an actual system should depend on future inputs as yet undetermined. We formalize this idea as follows.[3]

Axiom of causality: $B \subseteq S$ is structural for inputs X only if B is realizable with X as input.

The axiom of causality is a formalization of the idea that the future cannot cause the past, an idea that appears to be uniformly accepted in the philosophy of science, despite differences about the relationships between antecedence and causality. For example, Blalock (1961, p. 10) found this condition indispensable: "Since the forcing or producing idea is not contained in the notion of temporal sequences, as just noted, our conception of causality should not depend on temporal sequences, except for the impossibility of an effect preceding its cause." Bunge (1959, p. 67) argued that the condition is universally satisfied:

> Even relativity admits the reversal of time series of physically disconnected events but excludes the reversal of causal connections, that is, it denies that effects can arise before they have been produced... events whose order of succession is reversible cannot be causally connected with one another; at most they may have a common origin.... To conclude, a condition for causality to hold is that C [the cause] be previous to or at most simultaneous with E [the event] (relative to a given reference system).

It is important to note that the converse of the axiom of causality is the *post hoc ergo propter hoc* fallacy. The converse is fallacious because there are many $B_j \subseteq S$ that are realizable with X as input, but for which $G_Y(G_X^{-1}(C) \cap B_j) \neq G_Y(G_X^{-1}(C) \cap B_k)$, with $j \neq k$ for some choices of C. For C that have actually been implemented, B_j and B_k may, of course, produce identical outputs in spite of their logical inconsistency. One cannot establish that a restriction is structural through statistical inference, even to a specified level of a posteriori probability.[4]

3 Causality and exogeneity

The condition that Y not cause X, in the sense defined in Section 1, is very closely related to the condition that X be strictly exogenous in a stochastic model. The two are so closely related that tests of the hypothesis that Y does not cause X are often termed "exogeneity tests" in the literature (Sims, 1977a; Geweke, 1978). The strict exogeneity of X is in turn invoked in inference in a wide variety of situations, for example, the use of instrumental variables in the presence of serially correlated disturbances. The advantage of the strict exogeneity assumption is that there often is no loss in limiting one's attention to distributions conditional on strictly exogenous X, and this limitation usually results in considerable simplification of problems of statistical inference. As we shall soon see, however, the condition that Y not cause X is not *equivalent* to the strict exogeneity of X. What can be said is that if X is strictly exogenous in the complete dynamic simultaneous-equations model, then Y does not cause X, where Y is endogenous in that model. This means that tests for the absence of a Wiener–Granger causal ordering can be used to refute the strict exogeneity specification in a certain class of stochastic models, but never to establish it. In addition, there are many circumstances in which nothing is lost by undertaking statistical inference conditional on a subset of variables that are not strictly exogenous, the best known being that in which there are predetermined variables in the complete dynamic simultaneous-equations model. Unidirectional causality is therefore neither a necessary condition nor a sufficient condition for inference to proceed conditional on a subset of variables.

To establish these ideas, specific terminology is required. We begin by adopting a definition due to Koopmans and Hood (1953, pp. 117–20), as set forth by Christ (1966, p. 156).[5]

Definition: A strictly exogenous variable in a stochastic model is a variable whose value in each period is statistically independent of the values of all the random disturbances in the model in all periods.

Examples of strictly exogenous variables are provided in complete, dynamic simultaneous-equations models in which all variables are normally distributed:[6]

$$
\begin{aligned}
B(L)\mathbf{y}_t + \Gamma(L)\mathbf{x}_t &= \mathbf{u}_t \\
A(L)\mathbf{u}_t &= \epsilon_t \\
\operatorname{cov}(\epsilon_t, \mathbf{y}_{t-s}) &= 0 \quad (s > 0) \\
\operatorname{cov}(\epsilon_t, \mathbf{x}_{t-s}) &= 0 \quad (\text{all } s)
\end{aligned}
\tag{3.1}
$$

$$\text{roots of } |B(L)|,\ |A(L)| \text{ have modulus greater than 1}$$

This model is similar to that of Koopmans (1950) and to the models discussed in most econometrics texts, except that serially correlated disturbances and possibly infinite lag lengths are allowed. The system of equations $A(L)B(L)\mathbf{y}_t + A(L)\Gamma(L)\mathbf{x}_t = \epsilon_t$ is an example of the complete dynamic simultaneous-equations model discussed earlier (Geweke, 1978), in which it is shown that Y does not cause X. In view of our discussion in Section 2 and the fact that the complete dynamic simultaneous-equations model is usually perceived as a structure that accepts X as input, this implication is not surprising.

If Y does not cause X, then there exists a complete dynamic simultaneous-equations model with Y endogenous and X strictly exogenous, in the sense that there exist systems of equations formally similar to (3.1). However, none of these systems need satisfy the overidentifying restrictions in the model of interest, and in this case X is not strictly exogenous. For example, consider the case of (3.1) in which there are no exogenous variables:

$$(3.2)\qquad B(L)\mathbf{y}_t = \begin{bmatrix} \underset{l_1\times l_1}{B_{11}(L)} & \underset{l_1\times l_2}{B_{12}(L)} \\ \\ \underset{l_2\times l_1}{B_{21}(L)} & \underset{l_2\times l_2}{B_{22}(L)} \end{bmatrix} \begin{pmatrix} \underset{l_1\times 1}{\mathbf{y}_{1t}} \\ \\ \underset{l_2\times 1}{\mathbf{y}_{2t}} \end{pmatrix} = \begin{pmatrix} \underset{l_1\times 1}{\epsilon_{1t}} \\ \\ \underset{l_2\times 1}{\epsilon_{2t}} \end{pmatrix}$$

The autoregressive representation of Y is $B(0)^{-1}B(L)\mathbf{y}_t = B(0)^{-1}\epsilon_t$. If the elements in the first l_1 rows and last l_2 columns of $B(0)^{-1}B(L)$ turn out to be zeros, then Y_2 does not cause Y_1. For instance, this will always be the case if only contemporaneous values Y_2 enter the system (3.2); that is, $B_{12}(L) = B_{12}(0)$ and $B_{22}(L) = B_{22}(0)$.

If a simultaneous-equations model of the form (3.1) is hypothesized, then a finding that Y causes X is grounds for rejection of the model. A finding that Y does not cause X supports the model, in the sense that a refutable implication of the model fails to be rejected, but in the same sense the finding supports all models with the same lists of exogenous and endogenous variables.

The outcome of a test of the hypothesis that Y does not cause X is in general not equivalent to answering the question whether or not X or a subset of X can be regarded as fixed for purposes of inference. There are many examples in which this assumption is justified by a priori information, and yet y causes X. One of the most familiar is the special case of (3.2) in which $B_{12}(0) = 0$ and $\mathrm{cov}(\epsilon_{1t}, \epsilon_{2t}) = 0$. The system is block-recursive, and if all restrictions consist of exclusions of variables, then full-information maximum-likelihood estimates of the parameters in $B_{21}(L)$ and $B_{22}(L)$ coincide with maximum-likelihood estimates in the last l_2 equations computed under the assumption that $Y_{1t-1} = \{\mathbf{y}_{1t-s},\ s>0\}$ is fixed. Unless $B_{12}(L) = 0$, Y causes X. Evidently, the variables in Y_{1t-1} are predetermined, according to the generally accepted definitions of Koopmans and Hood (1953, pp. 117–21) and Christ (1966, p. 227).

Definition: A variable $\mathbf{z}_t$ is predetermined at time t if all its current and past values $Z_t = \{\mathbf{z}_{t-s},\ s \geqslant 0\}$ are independent of the vector of current disturbances in the model, $\mathbf{u}_t$, and these disturbances are serially independent.

In the foregoing examples the predetermined and strictly exogenous variables could be treated as fixed for purposes of inference, because they satisfied the condition of weak exogeneity (Engle, Hendry, & Richard, 1979).

Definition: Let $\bar{\mathbf{X}} = (\mathbf{x}_1, \ldots, \mathbf{x}_n)'$ and $\bar{\mathbf{Y}} = (\mathbf{y}_1, \ldots, \mathbf{y}_n)'$ be $n \times r$ and $n \times s$ matrices of observations on X and Y. Suppose the likelihood function $L(\boldsymbol{\theta}; \bar{\mathbf{X}}, \bar{\mathbf{Y}})$ can be reparameterized by $\boldsymbol{\lambda} = F(\boldsymbol{\theta})$, where F is a one-to-one transformation; $\boldsymbol{\lambda}' = (\boldsymbol{\lambda}_1', \boldsymbol{\lambda}_2')$, $(\boldsymbol{\lambda}_1, \boldsymbol{\lambda}_2) \in \boldsymbol{\Lambda}_1 \times \boldsymbol{\Lambda}_2$; and the investigator's loss function depends on the parameters of interest $\boldsymbol{\lambda}_1$, but not on the nuisance parameters $\boldsymbol{\lambda}_2$. Then $\bar{\mathbf{X}}$ is weakly exogenous if

$$(3.3) \qquad L(\boldsymbol{\lambda}_1, \boldsymbol{\lambda}_2; \bar{\mathbf{X}}, \bar{\mathbf{Y}}) = L_1(\boldsymbol{\lambda}_1; \bar{\mathbf{Y}} \mid \bar{\mathbf{X}}) \cdot L_2(\boldsymbol{\lambda}_2; \bar{\mathbf{X}})$$

Weak exogeneity is a sufficient condition for treating $\bar{\mathbf{X}}$ as fixed for purposes of statistical inference without loss. The joint likelihood function can always be factored as the product of a likelihood in $\bar{\mathbf{X}}$ and a likelihood in $\bar{\mathbf{Y}}$ conditional on $\bar{\mathbf{X}}$, but the parameters of interest need not be confined to the latter function, as (3.3) stipulates. Whether or not $\bar{\mathbf{X}}$ is weakly exogenous depends on the investigator's loss function.

Consider the case in which $\bar{\mathbf{X}}$ is strictly exogenous in a complete model. We denote the joint distribution of the disturbances $\bar{\mathbf{U}} = (\mathbf{u}_1, \ldots, \mathbf{u}_n)'$ in the model by $f_U^n(\bar{\mathbf{U}}; \boldsymbol{\lambda}_1)$ and the joint distribution of the exogenous variables $\bar{\mathbf{X}} = (\mathbf{x}_1, \ldots, \mathbf{x}_n)'$ in the model by $f_X^n(\bar{\mathbf{X}}; \boldsymbol{\lambda}_2)$. The model itself is $M_n(\bar{\mathbf{Y}}, \bar{\mathbf{X}}; \boldsymbol{\lambda}_1) = \bar{\mathbf{U}}$, and the condition of completeness is that the Jacobian of transformation $J(\boldsymbol{\lambda}_1)$ from $\bar{\mathbf{U}}$ to $\bar{\mathbf{Y}}$ be nonzero for all $\boldsymbol{\lambda}_1 \in \Lambda_1$. Because $\bar{\mathbf{X}}$ is strictly exogenous, the joint distribution of $\bar{\mathbf{U}}$ and $\bar{\mathbf{X}}$ is $f_U^n(\bar{\mathbf{U}}; \boldsymbol{\lambda}_1) f_X^n(\bar{\mathbf{X}}; \boldsymbol{\lambda}_2)$, and the joint distribution of $\bar{\mathbf{Y}}$ and $\bar{\mathbf{X}}$ is $f_U^n(M_n(\bar{\mathbf{Y}}, \bar{\mathbf{X}}; \boldsymbol{\lambda}_1); \boldsymbol{\lambda}_1) J(\boldsymbol{\lambda}_1) f_X^n(\bar{\mathbf{X}}; \boldsymbol{\lambda}_1)$. Consequently, the distribution of $\bar{\mathbf{Y}}$ conditional on $\bar{\mathbf{X}}$ is $f_U^n(M(Y, X; \boldsymbol{\lambda}_1)) J(\boldsymbol{\lambda}_1)$. The condition (3.3) for weak exogeneity will be met if the investigator's loss function depends only on $\boldsymbol{\lambda}_1$ and there are no cross-restrictions on $\boldsymbol{\lambda}_1$ and $\boldsymbol{\lambda}_2$. The former condition will be met if the investigator cares only about the model, and the latter may or may not be met. In many simultaneous-equations models the distribution of $\bar{\mathbf{X}}$ is of no consequence. An important class of exceptions is provided by rational-expectations models, in which behavioral parameters are generally linked to the distribution of exogenous variables; efficient estimation then requires that we work with $L(\boldsymbol{\theta}; \bar{\mathbf{X}}, \bar{\mathbf{Y}})$.

In many applications, predetermined variables will also be weakly exogenous, but this, again, need not be the case. Let $f_u^t(\mathbf{u}_t; \boldsymbol{\lambda}_1)$ be the distribution of the tth disturbance; by virtue of serial independence, $f_U^n(\bar{\mathbf{U}}; \boldsymbol{\lambda}_1) = \prod_{t=1}^n f_u^t(\mathbf{u}_t; \boldsymbol{\lambda}_1)$. Let the distribution of the vector of predetermined variables in period t, conditional on their past history, be denoted $f_x^t(\mathbf{x}_t \mid X_{t-1}; \boldsymbol{\lambda}_2)$. (Some of the predetermined variables may, in fact, be exogenous, of course.) Because the disturbances are serially independent, it is convenient to write the model for period t,

$M_t(\mathbf{y}_t, \mathbf{x}_t; \lambda_1) = \mathbf{u}_t$. The Jacobian of transformation from $\mathbf{u}_t$ to $\mathbf{y}_t$, $J_t(\lambda_1)$, is assumed to be nonzero. Let $Z = X_0, \ldots, X_{n-1}$. Then

$$L(\lambda_1, \lambda_2; \bar{\mathbf{X}}, \bar{\mathbf{Y}} \mid Z) = \prod_{t=1}^{n} f_u^t(M_t(\mathbf{y}_t, \mathbf{x}_t; \lambda_1); \lambda_1) J_t(\lambda_1) f_x^t(\mathbf{x}_t \mid X_{t-1}; \lambda_2),$$

and

$$L(\lambda_1, \lambda_2; \bar{\mathbf{Y}} \mid \bar{\mathbf{X}}, Z) = \prod_{t=1}^{n} f_u^t(M_t(\mathbf{y}_t, \mathbf{x}_t; \lambda_1); \lambda_1) J_t(\lambda_1).$$

The question whether or not there are cross-restrictions on λ_1 and λ_2 again arises in the case of predetermined variables. For example, in the block-recursive version of (3.2) in which $B_{12}(0) = 0$ and $\text{cov}(\epsilon_{1t}, \epsilon_{2t}) = 0$, λ_2 consists of the parameters in $B_{11}(0)$ and $\text{var}(\epsilon_{1t})$. So long as there is no functional dependence between these and the parameters in $B_{21}(0)$, $B_{22}(0)$, and $\text{var}(\epsilon_{2t})$, $\mathbf{y}_{1t}$ will be weakly exogenous for purposes of estimating the latter parameters.

The assertion that $\bar{\mathbf{X}}$ is weakly exogenous always relies to some degree on a priori assumptions. For example, Y_{1t} is weakly exogenous in (3.2) if $B_{12}(0) = 0$ and $\text{cov}(\epsilon_{1t}, \epsilon_{2t}) = 0$, but this assumption is by itself not refutable, as Basmann (1965) pointed out years ago. As another example, weak exogeneity of $\bar{\mathbf{X}}$ follows from strict exogeneity of X in (3.1) if all the parameters in the distribution of X are nuisance parameters. Strict exogeneity is refutable, because it implies that Y does not cause X, but it is not equivalent to a verifiable restriction on the joint distribution of Y and X. In each example, weak exogeneity can be tested only together with other restrictions on the model. Indeed, this will always be the case, because (3.3) is a condition on parameters, not a restriction on joint distributions. One can always construct a "model" for which (3.3) will be true. The fact that the constructed model may not be of substantive interest corresponds precisely to the notion that any consistent test of weak exogeneity must be a joint test of weak exogeneity and other hypotheses.

The specification of weak exogeneity is attractive because it simplifies statistical inference. To the extent that this specification is grounded in economic theory it is more attractive, and if that theory implies refutable restrictions it is more attractive still. The strict exogeneity assumption in the complete dynamic simultaneous-equations model is an example of such a specification. It often arises naturally from the assumption that the model in question has, historically, taken X as input [e.g., Koopmans's discussion (1953, pp. 31–2) of "weather" in econometric models]. It implies the refutable restriction that the endogenous variables do not cause the exogenous variables. Specifications of weak exogeneity that do not rely on strict exogeneity require assumptions about the serial correlation of disturbances that usually are more difficult to ground in economic theory. For example, if a variable is predetermined but not strictly exogenous, then there always exists a pattern of serial correlation for which the assumption that the variable is weakly exogenous will lead to inconsistent estimates. Assumptions about serial correlation in the latter case should therefore be tested, just as unidirectional causality should be tested when the weak exogeneity specification rests on strict exogeneity. In both cases, weak exogeneity will still rely on a priori assumptions; no set of econometric tests will substitute for careful formulation of the economic model.

4 Causality and feedback[7]

The empirical literature abounds with tests of independence and unidirectional causality for various pairs of time series; see the survey by Pierce and Haugh (1977). The hypotheses of independence and unidirectional causality are almost never literally entertained; rather, they are but two of many possible simplifying assumptions that are essential in econometric modeling and estimation. In fact, we expect dependence and feedback among economic time series, these terms having been given exact definition in the literature (e.g., Granger, 1963). If dependence and feedback can be measured, then their extent can be inferred, and the appropriateness of assumptions of unidirectional causality or independence can be assessed. In this section we shall show how such measures can be constructed, and in the next how one can assess the suitability of assumptions of unidirectional causality or independence in an econometric model that is to be used for prediction.

Suppose that $Z=\{z_t,\ t \text{ integer}\}$ is a wide-sense stationary, purely nondeterministic, multiple time series with a moving-average representation whose coefficients are square-summable.[8] Suppose that the spectral-density matrix of Z, $S_z(\lambda)$, satisfies the inequality $c^{-1}I_n \leqslant S_z(\lambda) \leqslant cI_n$ for some $c>1$ and almost all $\lambda \in [0, \pi]$.[9] These assumptions are somewhat less restrictive than the assumption that Z is a moving-average autoregressive process of finite order with invertible moving-average and autoregressive parts, which is sometimes taken as the point of departure in studies of the relationships of time series and econometric models (e.g., Zellner & Palm, 1974).

Suppose that $\mathbf{z}_t : m \times 1$ has been partitioned into $k \times 1$ and $l \times 1$ subvectors $\mathbf{x}_t$ and $\mathbf{y}_t$, $\mathbf{z}_t' = (\mathbf{x}_t', \mathbf{y}_t')$, reflecting an interest in causal relationships between X and Y. It can be shown (Geweke, 1982) that our assumptions are sufficient to guarantee the existence of the canonical

Table 7.1 *A canonical form for the wide-sense stationary time series* $\mathbf{z}_t' = (\mathbf{x}_t', y_t')$

(4.1) $\mathbf{x}_t = \sum_{s=1}^{\infty} E_{1s}\mathbf{x}_{t-s} + \mathbf{u}_{1t}$		
(4.2) $\mathbf{y}_t = \sum_{s=1}^{\infty} G_{1s}\mathbf{y}_{t-s} + \mathbf{v}_{1t}$		
(4.3) $\mathbf{x}_t = \sum_{s=1}^{\infty} E_{2s}\mathbf{x}_{t-s} + \sum_{s=1}^{\infty} F_{2s}\mathbf{y}_{t-s} + \mathbf{u}_{2t}$	$\mathrm{var}[\mathbf{u}_{jt}] = \Sigma_j$	$\mathrm{cov}(\mathbf{u}_{2t}, \mathbf{v}_{2t}) = C$
(4.4) $\mathbf{y}_t = \sum_{s=1}^{\infty} G_{2s}\mathbf{y}_{t-s} + \sum_{s=1}^{\infty} H_{2s}\mathbf{x}_{t-s} + \mathbf{v}_{2t}$		
(4.5) $\mathbf{x}_t = \sum_{s=1}^{\infty} E_{3s}\mathbf{x}_{t-s} + \sum_{s=0}^{\infty} F_{3s}\mathbf{y}_{t-s} + \mathbf{u}_{3t}$	$\mathrm{var}[\mathbf{v}_{jt}] = T_j$	$\Upsilon = \begin{bmatrix} \Sigma_2 & C \\ C' & T_2 \end{bmatrix}$
(4.6) $\mathbf{y}_t = \sum_{s=1}^{\infty} G_{3s}\mathbf{y}_{t-s} + \sum_{s=0}^{\infty} H_{3s}\mathbf{x}_{t-s} + \mathbf{v}_{3t}$		
(4.7) $\mathbf{x}_t = \sum_{s=1}^{\infty} E_{4s}\mathbf{x}_{t-s} + \sum_{s=-\infty}^{\infty} F_{4s}\mathbf{y}_{t-s} + \mathbf{u}_{4t}$		
(4.8) $\mathbf{y}_t = \sum_{s=1}^{\infty} G_{4s}\mathbf{y}_{t-s} + \sum_{s=-\infty}^{\infty} H_{4s}\mathbf{x}_{t-s} + \mathbf{v}_{4t}$		

form in Table 7.1. In these equations the disturbances are uncorrelated with all right-hand-side variables, and all coefficients are square-summable, as defined in note 8.

Consider $F_{Y\to X}=\ln(|\Sigma_1|/|\Sigma_2|)$ as a measure of linear feedback from Y to X. This definition has several motivations. First, because $|\Sigma_1| \geqslant |\Sigma_2|$, it is nonnegative, as any measure must be. Second, the statements that $F_{Y\to X}=0$, $\Sigma_1=\Sigma_2$, $F_{2s}\equiv 0$, and that Y does not cause X if the universe of information at t is Z_t are equivalent. Third, $F_{Y\to X}$ is a monotonic transformation of the "strength of causality $Y \Rightarrow X$," $1-|\Sigma_2|/|\Sigma_1|$, which was proposed by Granger (1963) for the case in which there is no instantaneous causality; Pierce's definition of R_+^2, which requires $k=1$, is the same as Granger's "strength." Fourth, $\exp(-F_{Y\to X})$ is the reduction in the total predictive variance of X (Granger, 1963) that can be achieved using past Y in addition to past X in prediction. Fifth, to anticipate an obvious result of the next section, the maximum-likelihood estimate of $F_{Y\to X}$ is simple to construct, and the asymptotic distribution of $F_{Y\to X}$ is the well-known chi-square under the null hypothesis $F_{Y\to X}=0$ and can be approximated under the alternative. Finally, $F_{Y\to X}$ is one term in the additive decomposition of the measure of dependence, to be introduced presently, and may itself be decomposed additively by frequency.

Symmetrically, define the measure of linear feedback from X to Y, $F_{X\to Y}=\ln(|T_1|/|T_2|)$. The measure of instantaneous linear feedback $F_{X\cdot Y}=\ln(|\Sigma_2|/|\Sigma_3|)$ has motivation similar to that of the first two measures. In particular, note that if the universe of information at t is Z_t, then $F_{X\cdot Y}\neq 0$, "X causes Y instantaneously," and "Y causes X instantaneously" are equivalent statements. A concept closely related to the notion of linear feedback is that of linear dependence. The fact that X and Y are linearly independent if and only if $|\Sigma_1|=|\Sigma_4|$ suggests the measure of linear dependence, $F_{X,Y}=\ln(|\Sigma_1|/|\Sigma_4|)$. Because instantaneous linear feedback and linear dependence are notions in which the roles of X and Y are symmetric (unlike the situation with linear feedback), $F_{X\cdot Y}$ and $F_{X,Y}$ could have been expressed in terms of the T_j rather than the Σ_j. The following result shows, among other things, that the alternative definitions would be equivalent.

Theorem: In the canonical form in Table 7.1,

(i) $$F_{X,Y} = \ln(|\Sigma_1|/|\Sigma_4|) = \ln(|T_1|/|T_4|) = \ln(|\Sigma_1|\cdot|T_1|/|\Upsilon|)$$

(ii) $$F_{Y\to X} = \ln(|\Sigma_1|/|\Sigma_2|) = \ln(|T_3|/|T_4|)$$

(iii) $$F_{X\to Y} = \ln(|\Sigma_3|/|\Sigma_4|) = \ln(|T_1|/|T_2|)$$

(iv) $$F_{X\cdot Y} = \ln(|\Sigma_2|/|\Sigma_3|) = \ln(|T_2|/|T_3|) = \ln(|T_2|\cdot|\Sigma_2|/|\Upsilon|)$$

Proof: Geweke (1982).

From this result it is immediate that $F_{X,Y}=F_{Y\to X}+F_{X\to Y}+F_{X\cdot Y}$; the measure of linear dependence is the sum of the measures of the three types of linear feedback. This result can also be used to obtain Sims's result (1972) that Y does not cause X if and only if in the linear projection of Y on future, current, and past X

$$\mathbf{y}_t = \sum_{s=-\infty}^{\infty} D_s \mathbf{x}_{t-s} + \mathbf{w}_t \tag{4.9}$$

$D_s=0$ for all $s<0$.

Further decomposition of the measures of feedback $F_{X\to Y}$ and $F_{Y\to X}$ by frequency is possible. Consider the system

$$\begin{bmatrix} E_2(L) & F_2(L) \\ H_3(L) & G_3(L) \end{bmatrix}\begin{pmatrix} \mathbf{x}_t \\ \mathbf{y}_t \end{pmatrix} = \begin{pmatrix} \mathbf{u}_{2t} \\ \mathbf{v}_{3t} \end{pmatrix} \tag{4.10}$$

constructed from equations (4.3) and (4.6) in Table 7.1. One may think of this system as one in which all instantaneous feedback has been combined with feedback from Y to X, so that the equations in Y have been purged of instantaneous feedback. This system can be inverted:

$$\begin{pmatrix} \mathbf{x}_t \\ \mathbf{y}_t \end{pmatrix} = \begin{bmatrix} E^2(L) & F^2(L) \\ H^3(L) & G^3(L) \end{bmatrix}\begin{pmatrix} \mathbf{u}_{2t} \\ \mathbf{v}_{3t} \end{pmatrix} \tag{4.11}$$

The first k equations of the new system provide a decomposition of $\mathbf{x}_t$ into distributed lags on the orthogonal, serially uncorrelated processes $\mathbf{u}_{2t}$ and $\mathbf{v}_{3t}$,

$$\mathbf{x}_t = E^2(L)\mathbf{u}_{2t} + F^2(L)\mathbf{v}_{3t} \tag{4.12}$$

and a corresponding decomposition of the spectral density $S_x(\lambda)$ into the sum of two positive semidefinite matrices,

$$S_x(\lambda) = \tilde{E}^2(\lambda)\Sigma_2\tilde{E}^2(\lambda)' + \tilde{F}^2(\lambda)T_3\tilde{F}^2(\lambda)' \tag{4.13}$$

where $\tilde{E}^2(\lambda)$ and $\tilde{F}^2(\lambda)$ are the Fourier transforms of $E^2(L)$ and $F^2(L)$, respectively. When X is univariate, $\tilde{F}^2(\lambda)T_3\tilde{F}^2(\lambda)'/S_x(\lambda)$ is the fraction of $S_x(\lambda)$ due to $\mathbf{v}_{3t}$.

This suggests the definition of the measure of linear feedback from Y to X at frequency λ,

$$f_{Y\to X}(\lambda) = \ln(|S_x(\lambda)|/|\tilde{E}^2(\lambda)\Sigma_2\tilde{E}^2(\lambda)'|) \tag{4.14}$$

The definition of feedback from X to Y at frequency λ, $F_{X\to Y}(\lambda)$, is symmetric. It can be shown (Geweke, 1982) that $1/2\pi\int_{-\pi}^{\pi} f_{Y\to X}(\lambda)\,d\lambda \leqslant F_{Y\to X}$ and $1/2\pi\int_{-\pi}^{\pi} f_{X\to Y}(\lambda)\,d\lambda \leqslant F_{X\to Y}$ and that given side conditions usually satisfied by point estimates, $1/2\pi\int_{-\pi}^{\pi} f_{Y\to X}(\lambda)\,d\lambda = F_{Y\to X}$ and $1/2\pi\int_{-\pi}^{\pi} f_{X\to Y}(\lambda)\,d\lambda = F_{X\to Y}$. Hence, the measures of feedback $F_{Y\to X}$ and $F_{X\to Y}$ can be decomposed by frequency.

5 Inference and testing

Because the concept of Wiener–Granger causality refers to predictability, the condition that Y does not cause X ought to be refutable by statistical methods. Yet the statistical theory available for this purpose is inadequate, and anything approaching a rigorous theory seems to be far off. We summarize here what has been learned about testing the proposition that Y does not cause X and about inference for the measures of feedback considered in the previous section. We do so maintaining the assumptions of Section 4; even then, difficulties arise.

The fundamental problem in inference and testing is that the second moments of multiple time series cannot reasonably be described by the unknown values of a finite number of known parameters. The problem is best known in the estimation of spectra, but it is a problem inherent in the nature of time series rather than the particular representation of time series employed. Consider, for example, inference about the parameters of (4.1). Because these are square-summable, consistent estimation of each E_{1s} is possible; one can estimate autoregressions of finite order and expand the order of the autoregression with sample size. If the rate of expansion is sufficiently slow, then consistent estimates will be obtained, although determining what rate is sufficient for this purpose is difficult (Fine & Hwang, 1979; Robinson, 1978). Inference about the E_{1s} using the usual estimated variances and covariances may not be reliable in this situation; the number of parameters estimated must grow sufficiently rapidly with sample size that mean square error is dominated by variance, not by squared bias. The lower bounds required for this purpose have yet to be established for any set of parameterizations useful in testing propositions about unidirectional causality. About all that has been done is to explore the effect of underparameterization on the distribution of test statistics by Monte Carlo methods (Guilkey & Salemi, 1981). One can ignore the parameterization problem, of course, either by assuming that there is a known finite parameterization or by assuming that there is a known rate of expansion of the parameterization such that consistent estimates whose mean square error consists entirely of variance in the limit are obtained. Either will lead to a useful asymptotic distribution theory, and for purposes of exposition we shall choose the first, because it leads to some simplifications.

Even with a known parameterization, not all procedures that have been proposed lead to test statistics with a known asymptotic distribution under the null hypothesis; see the discussion by Pierce and Haugh (1977) and the comments of Sims (1977b). There are three remaining procedures. One involves testing (4.1) as a restriction on (4.3) after truncation of lags; the first published application seems to be that of Sargent (1976). By virtue of the theorem cited in Section 4, a second similar test may be constructed by regarding (4.6) as a restriction on (4.8); the sampling properties of the resulting test statistic were studied by Geweke, Meese, and Dent (1982) and Guilkey and Salemi (1981) using Monte Carlo methods. The third test, by far the most widely applied, is based on the restriction $D_s = 0$ for $s < 0$ in (4.9), implied by the condition that Y not cause X. The first two tests require only ordinary least-squares estimation, but a correction for serial correlation is necessary in the third, because the $\mathbf{u}_{jt}$ and $\mathbf{v}_{jt}$ are white noises by construction, but $\mathbf{w}_t$ is not.

Of the three tests, the first two can be shown by analytical methods to have similar properties under the alternative as well as the null hypothesis, but the third will tend to reject the null more frequently under the alternative.[10] Monte Carlo studies indicate conclusively that the third test also rejects the null more frequently under the null hypothesis, so much so that it is reasonable to conjecture that type I errors are less than half their nominal levels in many (if not most) applications using macroeconomic data. This fact, combined with the greater computational burden imposed by the correction for serial correlation, suggests that the first two tests are preferred to the third. The first test has a slight advantage over the second, because it does not involve the use of any future values that diminish the size of the usable sample.

Once a finite parameterization for the canonical form in Table 7.1 is assumed, inference about the measures defined in the previous section is straightforward. Suppose all distributed lags have been truncated at length p, the equations are estimated by maximum likelihood conditional on presample values (i.e., by ordinary least squares), and conditional maximum-likelihood estimates $\hat{F}$ of the various measures F are then constructed in the obvious way. Under the null hypothesis of no feedback from Y to X (i.e., unidirectional causality from X to Y), $n\hat{F}_{Y\to X} \overset{a}{\sim} \chi^2(klp)$. More generally, the results of Wald (1943) imply that $n\hat{F}_{Y\to X} \overset{\dot{a}}{\sim} \chi^2(klp, nF_{Y\to X})$, the approximation being better the closer is $F_{Y\to X}$ to zero. The noncentral chi-square approximation proposed by Sankaran (1963) can be used to form approximate confidence intervals for $F_{Y\to X}$ (Geweke, 1982). Inference about other measures of feedback can be undertaken in similar fashion. Simultaneous inference about all four measures is simplified by the fact that $\hat{F}_{X\to Y}$, $\hat{F}_{Y\to X}$, and $\hat{F}_{X\cdot Y}$ are asymptotically independent. Inference about $f_{X\to Y}(\lambda)$ and $f_{Y\to X}(\lambda)$ is somewhat more difficult, because nonlinear combinations of parameters are involved. Because the null hypothesis $f_{X\to Y}(\lambda)=0$ is equivalent to linear restrictions on the coefficients H_{2s}, it is simpler to test. In interpreting these tests, it is worthwhile to note that the test statistics for the hypotheses $f_{X\to Y}(2\pi j/p)=0$, $j=0,\dots,p/2$, are asymptotically independent when p is even (Geweke, 1982). The limiting distributions of the test statistics under the null hypothesis are $\chi^2(kl)$ at frequencies 0 and π and $\chi^2(2kl)$ elsewhere.

A formal test of the hypothesis $F_{Y\to X}=0$ does not address the question whether or not it is wise to assume that Y does not cause X for purposes of prediction. Parzen (1977) considered the problem of choosing the finite-order vector autoregression whose estimates would produce minimum-mean-square-error postsample forecasts. Direct application of his solution to the present question suggests that the constraint $F_{Y\to X}=0$ should be imposed for purposes of prediction if and only if $\mathrm{tr}(\hat{\Sigma}_2^{-1}-\hat{\Sigma}_1^{-1})<(mp/n)\,\mathrm{tr}(\hat{\Sigma}_2^{-1})$, where $\hat{\Sigma}_1$ and $\hat{\Sigma}_2$ are maximum-likelihood estimates of Σ_1 and Σ_2, respectively. This approach can also be used to address the question whether or not the assumption of unidirectional causality from X to Y should have been imposed by a forecaster of X at various points in the sample period, under the assumption that model structure remained constant over the sample period.

6 Money, income, and feedback

Some of these points can be illustrated by an empirical example based on the data set used by Sims (1972). The data employed here are not quite the same as those used by Sims, because of subsequent revisions in the narrowly defined money supply (M1) and gross national product (GNP). Our GNP series is that used prior to the accounts revision; so comparison of the results reported here with those of Sims is not complicated by the substantial differences in the old and revised GNP series noted by Nelson (1979). Our sample period ends in 1969:II, whereas Sims's period ended in 1968:II.

Inference about feedback between these two series was based on ordinary least-squares estimates of equations (4.1) through (4.4), with lag lengths truncated at six quarters. In addition to the relationship between the logarithm of M1 and that of GNP investigated by Sims, we consider also the relationships between the logarithm of M1 and the logarithms of real GNP and the GNP deflator. All estimated equations include intercept and linear trend. In the investigation of all of these relationships, the effects of seasonal variation and seasonal adjustment procedures in the investigation of similar relationships have been documented by Wallis (1974) and Sims (1974). In the present case, the problem is complicated further by the fact that the real GNP and the GNP deflator are available only in seasonally adjusted form. On the assumption that seasonal variation in the logarithm of nominal GNP is due almost entirely to seasonal variation in real GNP, the ratio of unadjusted GNP to the seasonally adjusted deflator was treated as unadjusted real GNP. When equations (4.1) through (4.4) were estimated using constructed real GNP not seasonally adjusted and seasonal dummies, the results were quite similar to those obtained with seasonally adjusted real GNP and M1. The same similarity was observed in comparison of the estimated nominal GNP and M1 relationship using seasonally adjusted data and that using unadjusted data and seasonal dummies.

Estimated measures of feedback and associated statistics are presented in Table 7.2, with decompositions by frequency presented graphically in Figures 7.1 through 7.5. The relationship for which estimated measures of feedback are reported in column two of Table 7.2 and in Figure 7.2 is closest to that considered by Sims. We find that the hypothesis of no feedback from GNP to M1 is accepted at the 10% level, whereas that of no feedback from M1 to GNP is rejected at the 1% level, which is commensurate with Sims's finding. The F statistic associated with the latter hypothesis is 3.74, which is not quite as high as that reported by Sims, but the difference can be explained by the parameterization and correction for serial correlation chosen in that report (Geweke, Meese, & Dent, 1982).

Whether or not seasonal dummies are included in the estimated equations (or, alternatively, whether or not seasonally adjusted data are

Table 7.2 *Estimated measures of feedback, GNP, and M1 (1949:III–1969:II)*[a]

"GNP":	Nominal NSA	Nominal NSA	Deflator SA	Nominal NSA / Deflator SA	Nominal NSA / Deflator SA
M1:	NSA	NSA	SA	NSA	NSA
Seasonal dummies:	No	Yes	No	No	Yes
$\hat{F}_{M1\to GNP}$	0.359*** (0.077, 0.587)	0.293*** (0.037, 0.494)	0.067 (−0.054, 0.134)	0.362*** (0.079, 0.591)	0.301*** (0.042, 0.506)
$\hat{F}_{GNP\to M1}$	0.176* (−0.024, 0.322)	0.067 (−0.054, 0.135)	0.100 (−0.050, 0.196)	0.229** (0.002, 0.402)	0.142 (−0.038, 0.267)
$\hat{F}_{M1\cdot GNP}$	0.238*** (0.060, 0.487)	0.186*** (0.033, 0.411)	0.008 (0.004, 0.083)	0.205*** (0.042, 0.439)	0.145*** (0.014, 0.348)
$\hat{F}_{M1,GNP}$	0.773*** (0.286, 1.031)	0.546*** (0.094, 0.740)	0.175 (−0.094, 0.215)	0.796*** (0.337, 1.116)	0.588*** (0.184, 0.853)
$\hat{f}_{M1\to GNP}(0)$	3.285	1.253	6.045	0.006	0.068
$\hat{f}_{M1\to GNP}(\pi/8)$	0.798***	0.924***	0.073	0.769***	0.903***
$\hat{f}_{M1\to GNP}(\pi/4)$	0.564***	0.457***	0.138	0.494***	0.384***
$\hat{f}_{M1\to GNP}(\pi/2)$	0.387*	0.093	0.006	0.483**	0.118
$\hat{f}_{M1\to GNP}(3\pi/4)$	0.043	0.076	0.016	0.642*	0.116**
$\hat{f}_{M1\to GNP}(\pi)$	0.020	0.023	0.019	0.002	0.136
$\hat{f}_{GNP\to M1}(0)$	0.002	0.001	0.530	0.229	0.365
$\hat{f}_{GNP\to M1}(\pi/8)$	0.004	0.034	0.075	0.873	0.142
$\hat{f}_{GNP\to M1}(\pi/4)$	0.043	0.030	0.118	0.066	0.084
$\hat{f}_{GNP\to M1}(\pi/2)$	0.295*	0.077	0.107	0.319*	0.190
$\hat{f}_{GNP\to M1}(3\pi/4)$	0.017**	0.049	0.006	0.312**	0.052
$\hat{f}_{GNP\to M1}(\pi)$	2.20***	0.295	0.024	1.518**	0.139
H_0: $F_{M1\to GNP} = F_{GNP\to M1}$	2.196**	2.291**	0.048	1.789*	2.000**

[a] Single, double, and triple asterisks denote significance at 10%, 5%, and 1% levels, respectively; 95% confidence intervals, based on an approximate discussed elsewhere (Geweke, 1982), are shown parenthetically.

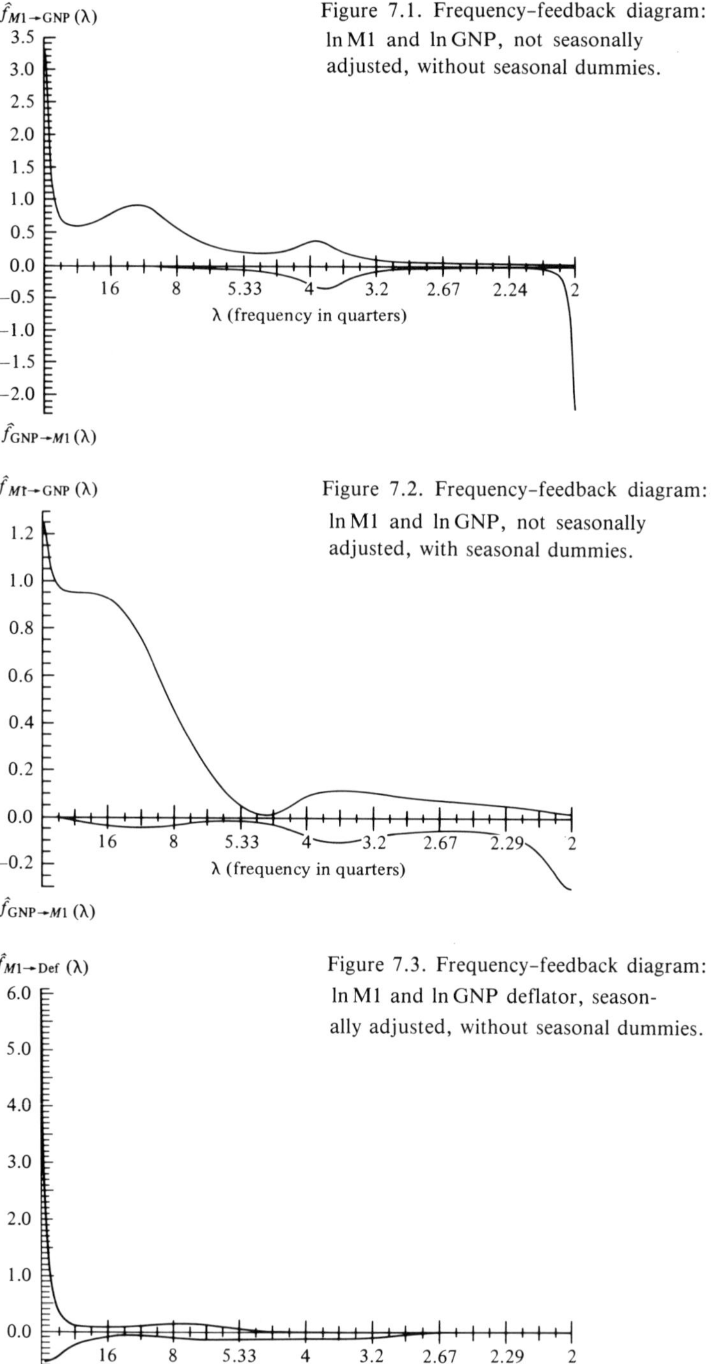

Figure 7.1. Frequency-feedback diagram: ln M1 and ln GNP, not seasonally adjusted, without seasonal dummies.

Figure 7.2. Frequency-feedback diagram: ln M1 and ln GNP, not seasonally adjusted, with seasonal dummies.

Figure 7.3. Frequency-feedback diagram: ln M1 and ln GNP deflator, seasonally adjusted, without seasonal dummies.

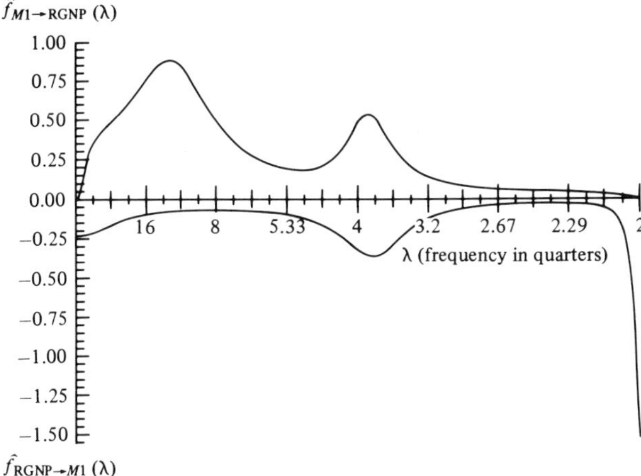

Figure 7.4. Frequency-feedback diagram: ln M1(NSA) and ln(GNP(NSA)/deflator(SA)), without seasonal dummies.

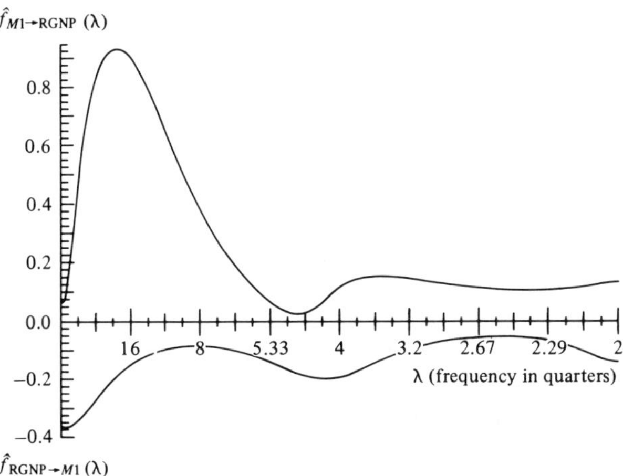

Figure 7.5. Frequency-feedback diagram: ln M1(NSA) and ln(GNP(NSA)/deflator(SA)), with seasonal dummies.

used) substantially affects the estimated feedback from nominal GNP and M1. When they are not included, estimated feedback between nominal GNP to M1 rises to 0.176 and becomes statistically significant at the 10% level. Figure 7.1 shows that most feedback from GNP to M1 occurs at the seasonal frequencies and that feedback attributed mostly to deterministic influences when dummies are included is assigned almost entirely to feedback from GNP to M1 when they are not. This seems consistent with models in which feedback from GNP to M1 arises primarily from a transactions demand for money. (It is not to say that the M1 equation in the bivariate autoregression is a money-demand equation; that is *post hoc ergo propter hoc.*)

When nominal GNP is decomposed into real and deflator components, the association between money and nominal GNP seems to arise mostly from the relationship between money and real GNP. The hypothesis that M1 and GNP deflator are uncorrelated at all leads and lags cannot be rejected at the 10% level when seasonally adjusted data are used. The hypothesis cannot be tested with seasonally unadjusted data, but questions of dependence are not obscured by seasonal adjustment methods as are those of feedback (Wallis, 1974; Geweke, 1981). In the absence of an assumed deterministic seasonal, there is strong feedback of all types between M1 and real GNP; in particular, the hypothesis that real GNP does not Wiener–Granger cause M1 is rejected at the 5% significance level. Reference to Figures 7.4 and 7.5 shows that, as was the case with nominal GNP, feedback from real GNP to M1 occurs mainly at seasonal frequencies and is reduced but not entirely eliminated by the inclusion of seasonal dummies. This also seems consistent with feedback due to transactions demand.

Further properties of money and income dynamics are suggested by the decomposition of feedback by frequency. Feedback from M1 to GNP is concentrated in those frequencies associated with the long run and the business cycle. When seasonal dummies are included, no more than 25% of the spectral density of GNP in the decomposition (4.13) is attributed to the innovation for M1 in (4.12) at periods less than six quarters, and this fraction does not rise above 50% when dummies are not included. Feedback from M1 to both nominal and real GNP at business cycle frequencies (corresponding, say, to periods of 8 to 20 quarters) is always substantial and is statistically significant at the 1% level. For frequencies less than about 0.1π (corresponding to periods longer than 5 years) the situation is markedly different. Estimated feedback from M1 to real GNP nearly vanishes in the neighborhood of the zero frequency, whereas that from M1 to the deflator increases. In the limit, less than 7% of the long-run variance of real GNP (as measured by the spectral density at $\lambda=0$) is assigned to innovations in M1; if seasonal dummies are included, the figure is 0.6%. By contrast, 99.8% of the long-run variance in prices is attributed to innovations in M1, leaving only 0.2% to be explained by innovations in prices themselves. Estimated feedback from M1 to the deflator (Def) is concentrated virtually entirely at long-run frequencies, as shown in Figure 7.3. However, very little can be inferred about the nature of feedback in the long run from these estimates, because feedback at the zero frequency is without exception insignificant even when it is large. In part, this may be due to the inclusion of a trend term in the estimated equations. More fundamentally, the failure of feedback in the long run to be significant may reflect the fact that there has been only one long-run "experiment" in the data on which to base inference.

On the whole, these findings seem consistent with monetarist models of the relationship between money and income. Business cyclical movements in real GNP are associated with innovations in the money supply; about half the variance in real GNP at periods of 2 to 4 years is attributed to these innovations. Over periods less than 1 year, feedback from M1 to real GNP is very small. Money innovations had almost no short-run influence on prices, either, over the sample period. At most, feedback from money to prices is found in moving averages of the two series of at least 10 years' duration. These findings should not convince a skeptic, even aside from the post hoc issue. The results cast some doubt on the interpretation of the postwar economy as a black box that accepted M1 as input and determined GNP as output. There is evidence of feedback from nominal and real GNP to M1 at those frequencies at which transactions demand would lead us to expect it. Although point estimates show that in the long run, money influences prices and little else happens, there is little enough information on the long run that formal inference would support many alternatives. Finally, the simple bivariate model can obscure more fundamental relationships involving other variables, a consideration that more recent work by Sims (1980) suggests may be important in the case of money and income.

7 Conclusions

We conclude with a brief summary of the main implications of the foregoing discussion.

1. Wiener–Granger causality is not equivalent to causation as defined in the literature of the philosophy of science. However, conventional structural econometric models exhibit unidirectional Wiener–Granger causality from inputs to outputs. A refutation of Wiener–Granger causality may therefore be interpreted as a refutation of a class of econometric models with specified inputs and outputs. The converse is not true; the assertion that a Wiener–Granger causal ordering implies a particular structural model amounts to the *post hoc ergo propter hoc* fallacy.

2. In structural econometric models, variables other than inputs may be regarded as predetermined, or weakly exogenous, for purposes of

estimation. A finding of unidirectional causality from a set of variables X to a set Y is therefore neither necessary nor sufficient for X to be regarded as weakly exogenous. In general, the assertion of weak exogeneity is testable only in the presence of maintained overidentifying restrictions. When prior confidence in these restrictions is about the same as that in the weak exogeneity assumption, weak exogeneity cannot be tested. This is the case in most circumstances. As a practical matter, weak exogeneity rests on a priori assumptions; certainly no set of econometric tests is an effective substitute for careful prior formulation of the model.

3. Tests of unidirectional Wiener–Granger causality that involve the estimation of linear equations containing lagged dependent variables but with serially uncorrelated disturbances are more reliable (in the sense that the actual probability of type I error is closer to the nominal probability established with reference to the asymptotic distribution theory) that those that involve the estimation of linear projections of one group of variables on another with serially correlated disturbances. Because the former are computationally simpler as well, they are to be preferred to the latter in empirical work. No test of unidirectional causality has been derived rigorously without assuming a known finite parameterization for the joint distribution of X and Y.

4. The hypothesis that the relationship between X and Y is due predominantly to feedback from X to Y in many instances corresponds more closely to prior expectations than does the hypothesis that there is unidirectional Wiener–Granger causality from X to Y. Inference about feedback from X to Y (and vice versa) is straightforward, as is the decision whether or not the assumption of unidirectional causality will improve prediction.

NOTES

1 Granger's definitions (1963, 1969) assume that the time series are stationary, that predictors are linear least-squares projections, and that mean square error is the criterion for comparison of forecasts. Although these assumptions are convenient to make when conducting empirical tests of the proposition that causality of a certain type is absent, they are not sui generis and therefore have not been imposed here.

2 Much (but not all) of what follows in this section may be found in the work of Sims (1977).

3 It may seem curious to provide the name "axiom of causality" to a statement that nowhere mentions the word "cause." The name is chosen because of Sims's result (1972) that (in our language, and with appropriate restrictions on classes of time series and predictors) B is realizable with X as input if and only if in B Wiener–Granger causality is unidirectional from X to Y.

4 Sims (1977a) has provided an extended discussion of specific pitfalls encountered in using a finding that a restriction B that is realizable with X as input is in agreement with the data to buttress a claim that B is structural.

5 We use the term "strictly exogenous" where Christ used "exogenous" in order to distinguish this concept from weak exogeneity, to be introduced shortly.

6 The strong assumption of normality is made because of the strong condition of independence in our definition of strict exogeneity. As a practical matter, quasi-maximum-likelihood methods usually are used, and the independence condition can then be modified to specify absence of correlation.

7 Material in this section is drawn from earlier work (Geweke, 1982).

8 By this we mean $\mathbf{z}_t = \sum_{s=0}^{\infty} A_s \epsilon_{t-s}$, and $\sum_{s=0}^{\infty} \|A_s\|^2 < \infty$, where $\|A_s\|$ is the square root of the largest eigenvalue of $A_s' A_s$.

9 $A \circledleq B$ indicates that $B - A$ is positive semidefinite.

10 It is not asserted that the third test is "more powerful." The reader is referred to another article (Geweke, Meese, & Dent, 1982) for a precise discussion.

REFERENCES

Basmann, R. L. 1965. "A Note on the Statistical Testability of 'Explicit Causal Chains' against the Class of 'Interdependent Models.'" *Journal of the American Statistical Association* 60:1080–93.

Blalock, H. M., Jr. 1961. *Causal Inferences in Nonexperimental Research.* Chapel Hill: University of North Carolina Press.

Bunge, M. 1959. *Causality: The Place of the Causal Principle in Modern Science.* Cambridge: Harvard University Press.

Christ, C. F. 1966. *Econometric Models and Methods.* New York: Wiley.

Engle, R., Hendry, D., and Richard, J.-F. 1979. "Exogeneity." Unpublished manuscript.

Feigl, H. 1953. "Notes on Causality." In *Readings in the Philosophy of Science,* edited by H. Feigl and M. Brodbeck, pp. 408–18. New York: Appleton-Century-Croft.

Fine, T. L., and Hwang, W. G. 1979. "Consistent Estimation of a System Order." *IEEE Transactions on Automatic Control* AC-24:387–402.

Geweke, J. 1978. "Testing the Exogeneity Specification in the Complete Dynamic Simultaneous Equation Model." *Journal of Econometrics* 7:163–85.

Geweke, J. 1981. "A Comparison of Tests of the Independence of Two Covariance-Stationary Time Series." *Journal of the American Statistical Association* 76:363–73.

Geweke, J. 1982. "The Measurement of Linear Dependence and Feedback Between Multiple Time Series." *Journal of the American Statistical Association (in press).*

Geweke, J., Meese, R., and Dent, W. 1982. "Comparing Alternative Tests of Causality in Temporal Systems: Analytic Results and Experimental Evidence." *Journal of Econometrics (in press).*

Granger, C. W. J. 1963. "Economic Processes Involving Feedback." *Information and Control* 6:28–48; also Chapter 7 of Granger, C. W. J., and Hatanaka, M. *Spectral Analysis of Economic Time Series.* Princeton University Press.

Granger, C. W. J. 1969. "Investigating Causal Relations by Econometric Models and Cross-Spectral Methods." *Econometrica* 37:424–38.

Guilkey, D. K., and Salemi, M. K. 1981. "Small Sample Properties of Three Tests for Granger-Causal Ordering in a Bivariate Stochastic System." *Review of Economics and Statistics (in press)*.

Hurwicz, L. 1962. "On the Structural Form of Interdependent Systems." In *Logic, Methodology and the Philosophy of Science,* edited by E. Nagel et al., pp. 232–9. Stanford University Press.

Koopmans, T. C. 1950. "When Is an Equation System Complete for Statistical Purposes?" In *Statistical Inference in Dynamic Economic Models,* edited by T. C. Koopmans, pp. 393–409. New York: Wiley.

Koopmans, T. C., and Hood, W. C. 1953. "The Estimation of Simultaneous Economic Relationships." In *Studies in Econometric Method,* edited by W. C. Hood and T. C. Koopmans, pp. 112–99. New Haven: Yale University Press.

Nelson, C. R. 1979. "Recursive Structure in U.S. Income, Prices and Output." *Journal of Political Economy* 87:1307–27.

Parzen, E. 1977. "Multiple Time Series: Determining the Order of Approximating Autoregressive Schemes." In *Multivariate Analysis IV,* edited by P. Krishnaiah, pp. 181–97. Amsterdam: North-Holland.

Pierce, D. A., and Haugh, L. D. 1977. "Causality in Temporal Systems: Characterizations and a Survey." *Journal of Econometrics* 5:265–93.

Robinson, P. 1978. "Distributed Lag Approximations to Linear Time-Invariant Systems." *Annals of Statistics* 6:507–15.

Sankaran, M. 1963. "Approximations to the Non-Central Chi-Square Distribution." *Biometrika* 50:199–204.

Sargent, T. J. 1976. "A Classic Macroeconometric Model of the U.S." *Journal of Political Economy* 87:207–37.

Simon, H. A. 1952. "On the Definition of the Causal Relation." *Journal of Philosophy* 49: 517–27; reprinted in Simon, H. A., ed. 1957. *Models of Man.* New York: Wiley.

Sims, C. A. 1972. "Money, Income and Causality." *American Economic Review* 62:540–52.

Sims, C. A. 1974. "Seasonality in Regression." *Journal of the American Statistical Association* 69:618–26.

Sims, C. A. 1977a. "Exogeneity and Causal Ordering in Macroeconomic Models." In *New Methods in Business Cycle Research: Proceedings from a Conference,* edited by C. A. Sims, pp. 23–44. Federal Reserve Bank of Minneapolis.

Sims, C. A. 1977b. "Comment." *Journal of the American Statistical Association* 72:23–4.

Sims, C. A. 1980. "Macroeconomics and Reality." *Econometrica* 48:1–48.

Wald, A. 1943. "Tests of Statistical Hypotheses Concerning Several Parameters when the Number of Observations is Large." *Transactions of the American Mathematical Society* 54:426–85.

Wallis, K. 1974. "Seasonal Adjustment and Relations Between Variables." *Journal of the American Statistical Association* 69:18–31.

Wiener, N. 1956. "The Theory of Prediction." In *Modern Mathematics for Engineers,* edited by E. F. Beckenback, pp. 165–90. New York: McGraw-Hill.

Zellner, A. 1979. "Causality and Econometrics." In *Three Aspects of Policy and Policymaking,* edited by K. Brunner and A. H. Meltzer, pp. 9–54. Amsterdam: North-Holland.

Zellner, A., and Palm, F. 1974. "Time Series Analysis and Simultaneous Equation Econometric Models." *Journal of Econometrics* 2:17–54.

Zemanian, A. H. 1972. *Realizability Theory for Continuous Linear Systems.* New York: Academic.

CHAPTER 8

Generating mechanisms, models, and causality

C. W. J. Granger

1 Causation

In the years 1977 to 1979, the *Social Science Citation Index* listed over 2,000 articles that used words such as *cause, causation,* and *causality* in their titles, and over 1,000 more such articles were listed in the *Science Citation Index.* The number of reports using such words in the text, but not the title, is presumably very much greater. Thus, there does seem to be clear demand for a definition of *causation.* In such circumstances, economists would expect a supply to arise, and I have attempted to supply a definition. The proposed definition tries to have both some depth and generality to it, while at the same time having a practical and usable orientation.

The definition is easily explained in terms of information sets and conditional distributions. Suppose that $\mathbf{M}_t$ is a vector of variables of interest and, at time n, consider the following information sets:

(a) Ω_n, all information available in the universe at time n.
(b) $\Omega_n - Y_n$, the universal information set apart from the past and present values $\mathbf{Y}_{n-k}$ $(k=0,1,2,\ldots)$ of a vector $\mathbf{Y}_t$.
(c) $J_n(W)$, consisting of all past and present values of the vector $\mathbf{W}_t$ [i.e., $\mathbf{W}_{n-k}$ $(k=0,1,2,\ldots)$]. $\mathbf{W}_t$ is assumed to include $\mathbf{M}_t$, thus making $J_n(W)$ a proper information set, but not $\mathbf{Y}_t$.
(d) $J_n(W, Y)$, being $J_n(W)$ plus $\mathbf{Y}_{n-k}$ $(k = 0,1,2,\ldots)$. Denote the conditional distribution of $\mathbf{M}_{n+1}$ given $J_n(W)$ by $F_c(\mathbf{x},M| W)_{n+1}$ = $\text{Prob}(\mathbf{M}_{n+1}\leqslant \mathbf{x} \,|\, J_n(W))$.

The causality definitions to be proposed use the following central axiom.

Central axiom: The cause occurs at an earlier time than the effect. Thus the future cannot cause the past or present, although expectations of the future could cause the present, provided these expectations are based on information occurring in the past.

Definitions

(a) $\mathbf{Y}_n$ does not cause $\mathbf{M}_{n+1}$ with respect to $J_n(W, Y)$ if $F_c(\mathbf{x}, M \mid W)_{n+1} = F_c(\mathbf{x}, M \mid W, Y)_{n+1}$ for all x. Thus the extra information in $\mathbf{Y}_{n-k}$ $(k \geqslant 0)$ has not affected the conditional distribution. A necessary condition in terms of statistical expectations is that

$$E[\mathbf{M}_{n+1} \mid J_n(W)] = E[\mathbf{M}_{n+1} \mid J_n(W, Y)]$$

(b) If

$$F_c(\mathbf{x}, M \mid \Omega)_{n+1} \neq F_c(\mathbf{x}, M \mid \Omega - Y)_{n+1}$$

for some x, then $\mathbf{Y}_n$ causes $\mathbf{M}_{n+1}$. Thus, $\mathbf{Y}_{n-k}$ contains information useful in characterizing $\mathbf{M}_{n+1}$ not available anywhere else. If

$$E[\mathbf{M}_{n+1} \mid \Omega_n] \neq E[\mathbf{M}_{n+1} \mid \Omega_n - Y_n]$$

then $\mathbf{Y}_n$ is said to cause $\mathbf{M}_{n+1}$, in mean.

(c) If $F_c(\mathbf{x}, M \mid W) \neq F_c(\mathbf{x}, M \mid W, Y)$ for some x, then $\mathbf{Y}_n$ is a prima facie cause of $\mathbf{M}_{n+1}$ with respect to $J_n(W, Y)$.

(d) If $E[\mathbf{M}_{n+1} \mid J_n(W)] \neq E[\mathbf{M}_{n+1} \mid J_n(W, Y)]$ then $\mathbf{Y}_n$ is a prima facie cause in mean of $\mathbf{M}_{n+1}$ with respect to $J_n(W, Y)$.

The general definition (b) involving the universal information set is a strong statement. If social scientists ever reach complete agreement on a definition of causality, this general definition may not constitute an agreed definition, but I believe that it will be an important component of it. Moving to the more constrained definitions (c) and (d) is necessary for the purely pragmatic reasons of limited data availability and sufficiently sophisticated statistical techniques. Using the constrained definitions does allow them to be operational, and I consider this gain to completely outweigh the admitted losses in moving from the general, but nonoperational, definitions. Naturally, when using the less general definitions, more care in interpretation is required. By "prima facie" is meant a possible cause that cannot be removed from consideration when using a stated information set, but it may be removed when a different information set is used. A discussion and defense of these definitions, pointing out both advantages and some difficulties, can be found in an earlier report (Granger, 1980).

A variety of tests of causation, invariably based on definition (d), causality in mean, have been proposed and have frequently been applied, although usually with very limited bivariate information sets. There does seem to be an acceptance that these definitions have some value, although this acceptance is by no means universal, as might be expected.

In this chapter I shall assume that the definitions have been accepted and consider the implications of causality ideas for theoretical modeling of interrelated variables and, in particular, of the central axiom. For convenience it is assumed that all variables are discrete statistical processes and that there exists a positive minimum causal lag that coincides with the sampling interval of the processes. A minimum causal lag means that although $\mathbf{Y}_n$ may cause $\mathbf{M}_{n+1}$, all terms $\mathbf{Y}_{n+f}$ with $0<f<1$ are not causal of $\mathbf{M}_{n+1}$, given the information set $J_n(W, Y)$. Thus, it is assumed that it takes a finite time for the individual decision-making units in the economy to realize the most recent value taken by $\mathbf{Y}$, to consider the implications of this value, and to plan and implement their reactions. Later, the case in which the sampling interval and the minimum causal interval are different will be considered, as will the possibility of instantaneous causality.

Returning now to the definition of prima facie cause in mean, given in (d), we denote the conditional zero mean component of $\mathbf{M}_t$ at time t by

$$\epsilon_t(M \mid W) = \mathbf{M}_t - E[\mathbf{M}_t \mid J_{t-1}(W)]$$

It is clear that if $J(W)$ is a proper information set, then the series $\epsilon_t(M \mid W)$ will be a vector white-noise series; that is

$$E[\epsilon_t(M \mid W)] = 0$$

and

$$E[\epsilon_t(M \mid W) \cdot \epsilon_s(M \mid W)] = 0 \quad (t \neq s)$$

The series need not be pure white noise, in that these series are uncorrelated but not necessarily independent. Now consider the expanded information set $J_{t-1}(W, Y)$ and denote

$$\begin{aligned}\delta_{t-1}(M \mid W, Y) &= E[\epsilon_t(M \mid W) \mid J_{t-1}(W, Y)] \\ &= E[M_t \mid J_{t-1}(W, Y)] - E[M_t \mid J_{t-1}(W)]\end{aligned}$$

so that

$$\epsilon_t(M \mid W) = \epsilon_t(M \mid W, Y) + \delta_{t-1}(M \mid W, Y) \tag{1}$$

This equation has a number of interesting features. Because $\delta_{t-1}(M \mid W, Y)$ is a function of quantities known at time $t-1$, it can be considered to be fully known at that time. δ_{t-1} will not be zero for all t if Y_{t-1} is causing $\mathbf{M}_t$ in mean with respect to J_{t-1}. However, the average or expected value for δ will be zero, as is seen from taking expectations in equation (1). Further, because δ_{t-1} is known at time $t-1$, it is necessarily uncorrelated with $\epsilon_t M(W, Y))$; that is

$$E[\delta_{t-1}(M|W, Y)\epsilon_t(M|W, Y)] = 0$$

because, otherwise, part of $\epsilon_t(M|W, Y)$ can be forecast (in mean) from part of J_{t-1}, which contradicts the definition of $\epsilon_t(M|W, Y)$. It then follows that expanding the information set by adding a causal variable results in the original "residual" $\epsilon_t(M|W)$ being decomposed into two terms, one of which, δ, is knowable at an earlier time. It is common to interpret residuals in models as being due to the effect of "unexpected shocks" on the system, but it is seen that this interpretation is not correct if the information set used excludes a causal variable.

It further follows, from these results, that if $\Sigma(\epsilon_t(M|W))$ is the covariance matrix of $\epsilon_t(M|W)$, and similarly for other variables, then

$$\Sigma(\epsilon_t(M|W)) = \Sigma(\epsilon_t(M|W, Y)) + \Sigma(\delta_{t-1}(M|W, Y)) \tag{2}$$

so that $\mathbf{M}_{n+1}$ is better forecast if $J_n(W, Y)$ is used rather than $J_n(W)$, in that the variance of any linear combination of the components of $\epsilon_t(M|W)$ will be larger than the variance of the same linear combination of the components of $\epsilon_t(M|W, Y)$, because $\Sigma(\delta_{t-1}(M|W, Y))$ will be a positive definite matrix if $\mathbf{Y}_n$ causes $\mathbf{M}_{n+1}$ in mean. It thus follows that causality in mean can be associated with an improved ability to forecast when a least-squares criterion is used. If other criteria are used, it may be necessary to move to the more general definition introduced in (c). A further aspect of equation (2), which will be seen later to be of some importance, is that if $\mathbf{Y}_n$ causes several components of $\mathbf{M}_{n+1}$, then $\Sigma(\delta_{t-1}(M|W, Y)$ is likely to be nondiagonal, and so even if $\Sigma(\epsilon_t(M|W, Y))$ is diagonal, $\Sigma(\epsilon_t(M|W))$ will not be. Thus, interdependence of components of $\epsilon_t(M|W)$ can be due to a missing causal variable from the information set being used.

2 Generating mechanisms

Each time period, which will be called a month, all of the variables in an economy can be considered to take observable values. For convenience, practical problems such as the precise definitions of variables, measurement errors, and delays in reporting will be ignored. As we observe that these numbers are being generated, it seems reasonable to postulate the existence of an underlying generating mechanism. Such a mechanism must produce each month a value for each component of the vector of variables of interest $\mathbf{M}_t$, and the values so produced must have all of the observed properties of $\mathbf{M}_t$ plus all relationships between components of $\mathbf{M}_t$, with each other and also with other variables. Thus, for example, if the number of employed workers is known to be a positive variable with a log normal distribution, integrated of order d, and with a specific transfer-function relationship with production, then the generating mechanism must generate a variable with these properties. Some implications of the restrictions on the mechanism have been discussed earlier (Granger, 1981). It can be argued that the major purpose of econometrics should be determination of the generating mechanism for any vector of variables, or at least to produce models that adequately approximate this mechanism. To be a potential generating mechanism, a model must have a number of properties. In particular, it must be capable of producing a value each month, so that a variable cannot depend on future values of other variables, and it must be properly normalized. Thus, a model of the form

$$a_t M_t = b_t Z_{t-1} + c W_{t+2} + e_t$$

is not acceptable as a generating function if $c \neq 0$, or if a_t can take the value zero. Also, it will not be acceptable if M_t is positive, a_t is positive, but e_t is a gaussian variable independent of the "explanatory variables," because the right-hand side of the equation could then produce negative values, or if M_t is nonseasonal, a_t and b_t are constants, but Z_t is strongly seasonal.

One obvious way to specify a generating mechanism is to use a conditional distribution, such as

$$F_c(\mathbf{x}, M \mid W)_{n+1} = \text{Prob}(\mathbf{M}_{n+1} \leqslant \mathbf{x} \mid J_n(W))$$

Thus $\mathbf{M}_{n+1}$ is conditioned on an information set $J_n(W)$ available at time n, and then values drawn from this distribution may have all of the required properties for a generating mechanism. However, this will be true only if $\mathbf{W}_n$ is selected properly. The question how to do this will be discussed in this section. It will be assumed throughout that all distribution functions are completely known, both in form and also any parameter values.

Starting with the variables of interest $\mathbf{M}_t$, suppose that it is possible to identify a set of variables $\mathbf{Z}_t$, with $\mathbf{M}_t \in \mathbf{Z}_t$ and a corresponding information set $J_t(Z) : \mathbf{Z}_{t-k}$ $(k \geqslant 0)$ such that there exist no measurable variables not in $\mathbf{Z}_t$ that cause $\mathbf{M}_{t+1}$. $J_t(Z)$ may then be called a complete and proper information set for $\mathbf{M}_{t+1}$.

Two special cases deserve separate names. If $\mathbf{Z}_t$ consists of just $\mathbf{M}_t$, then $\mathbf{M}_t$ can be called self-causal. If $\mathbf{Z}_t$ is the empty set, $\mathbf{M}_t$ can be said to be zero-causal, and it will then be just a pure white-noise vector. Clearly, any stochastic nondeterministic variable (i.e., one that cannot be completely explained by causal variables) must contain a zero-causal component. This will be true whichever of the definitions of causation introduced earlier is used.

For the moment, a further simplifying assumption will be made to facilitate discussion. If the vector $\epsilon_t(M|Z)$ consists of independent components, then the case being considered will be called *pure causal.* This case is a useful simplification, because there is no possibility of simultaneous relationships or of "instantaneous causality." It will not be argued that this is a particularly important case in practice, and ways in which the assumption of independent components can break down will be discussed in the next section.

If $J_t(Z)$ is a complete information set, the conditional distribution

$$F_c(\mathbf{x}, M|Z)_{t+1} = \text{Prob}(M_{t+1} \leqslant \mathbf{x} \,|\, J_t(Z))$$

will provide a true generating mechanism, because drawing a term from this sequence of conditional distributions at each moment of time will provide the best possible sequence for $\mathbf{M}_{t+1}$ and will completely produce all of the observable properties of the $\mathbf{M}_t$ series. Further, the "residuals" or "innovations" $\epsilon_t(M|Z)$ can now be interpreted as shocks or innovations to the system, because they cannot be partly due to missing causal variables.

If one is interested in one-step least-squares forecasting or control, the true generating mechanism, particularly $E[\mathbf{M}_{n+1} \,|\, J_n(Z)]$, provides the best possible forecasts, either conditional or unconditional. However, if one is interested in longer-term forecasting, a different situation can arise. Suppose that h-step least-squares forecasts are required, that is, $E[\mathbf{M}_{n+h} \,|\, J_n(Z)]$; then these may not be the best forecasts possible, as the following example shows. If the generating mechanism for M_t is

$$M_t = \alpha M_{t-1} + \beta Z_{t-1} + \gamma W_{t-2} + \epsilon_t$$

where ϵ_t is pure white noise, then the best one-step forecast of M_{n+1} is $\alpha M_n + \beta Z_n + \gamma W_{n-1}$, but the best two-step forecast, of M_{n+2}, will require a forecast of Z_{n+1}. Similarly, to forecast more than two steps will require forecasts of Z and W. Thus, to form optimum forecasts, it is necessary to have generating mechanisms not only for the variables of interest, $\mathbf{M}_t$, but also for some of the causal variables of $\mathbf{M}_t$. It will then be necessary to include causal variables of the causal variables, and as one forecasts further ahead, the set of variables of interest must be continually expanded. To forecast optimally an arbitrary number of steps ahead, one must find an expanded set $\mathbf{M}'_t$, including $\mathbf{M}_t$, that is self-causal. The generating mechanism for $\mathbf{M}'_t$ may be called the *complete true mechanism* for $\mathbf{M}_t$. One may well expect $\mathbf{M}'_t$ to involve many more variables than $\mathbf{M}_t$, which suggests that finding a complete true model may be very difficult. This is particularly true when it is remembered that many macroeconomic variables can be disaggregated into measurable components and that forecasts of aggregates usually are better using disaggregated data, so that components cause the total, which is another form of self-causality. Thus, by continually disaggregating and by including causal variables of all causal variables, an immense set of variables of interest can be generated from what was initially a set of modest size. If this reasoning is accepted, it becomes clear why the concept of a true generating mechanism is currently unpopular and attention is being directed toward finding models of limited size that provide adequate approximations to the true model, in some sense.

The complete true mechanism will depend on the contents of $\mathbf{M}_t$, although if a complete mechanism for Z_t is given, it will not necessarily be obvious what was the original $\mathbf{M}_t$. If the vector of variables of interest is expanded, the complete true mechanism may have to be enlarged, as is clear by adding a new self-causal variable to $\mathbf{M}_t$.

A vector of variables $\mathbf{X}_t$ may be called causal and *exogenous,* in the pure causal model case, to $\mathbf{M}_t$ if the complete information set for $\mathbf{M}_t$ includes $\mathbf{X}_t$ but also if the complete information set for $\mathbf{X}_t$ does not include $\mathbf{M}_t$. Thus, $\mathbf{X}_t$ will be causal to $\mathbf{M}_{t+1}$, but $\mathbf{M}_t$ is not causal to $\mathbf{X}_{t+1}$. When instantaneous relationships are allowed, the definition may need changing. This will be discussed later.

3 Apparent simultaneity

For this section it will be assumed that the economy, or that part of interest, is generated by a pure causal model. That is, the minimum causal lag corresponds to the sampling interval, a complete mechanism is available, and the portions of variables unexplained by the past, the ϵ_t, are independent of one another. If this is so, under which circumstances will apparent simultaneous relationships be observed? There are a number of ways that this can occur, and three will be discussed in this section.

Suppose there exists a vector $\mathbf{M}_t$ for which there exists a pure causal model, but instead one observes $\mathbf{N}_t = \mathbf{AM}_t$, where A is a square nonsingular matrix, so that each element of $\mathbf{N}_t$ is a linear combination of elements of $\mathbf{M}_t$. Then the derived generating mechanism for $\mathbf{N}_t$ will no longer be pure causal in general. As a simple example, suppose that $\mathbf{M}_t$ consists of unemployment series for each state and has a pure causal model, but we actually use data that consist of unemployment for overlapping regions; then the data used will not be pure causal, and "simultaneity" will be observed. When considering data gathered spatially, the use of overlapping regions seems unnatural. This is also true if data for, say, sales or inventories are available for separate industries but the variables used in a model use overlapping industrial groups. Similarly, it is doubtful that one should use the M1 and M2 measures of money supply in a model rather than the nonoverlapping variables M1 and M2 − M1. It is not always clear, of course, what are the natural nonoverlapping variables. Consider a set of interest rates of different term structures, for example.

In the previous section it was shown that missing causal variables can lead to instantaneous correlation between residuals, if the missing variables cause several other variables. A rather special case with similar interpretation involves control variables. A control variable is one that can be totally, or largely, controlled by some agency, which for convenience will be called the government. Let C_t be such a variable. Then, at time t the public will be able to predict C_{t+1}, using an information set $I_t(W)$, giving the mean reaction function $E[C_{t+1} \mid I_t(W)]$ and residual $\epsilon_{t+1}(C \mid W)$. This residual is the exogenous component of the control variable, and if the government hopes to partially control the variable M_t in the economy, the residual needs to be correlated to $\epsilon_{t+1}(M \mid W)$. However, appealing to the central axiom, such control occurs only if $\epsilon_{t+1}(C \mid W)$, the cause, happens at an earlier time than the variable being caused, $\epsilon_{t+1}(M \mid W)$. It can certainly be argued that this is the case. Because C_{t+1} is a controlled variable, it can be thought of as having its value selected at time t, but having a component $\epsilon_{t+1}(C \mid W)$ that although known to the government at time t is not completely observed by the public until time $t+1$. Naturally, although $\epsilon_{t+1}(C \mid W)$ is not fully known until time $t+1$, it can be thought of as being partially known between time points t and $t+1$, for the necessary reaction to occur. Thus, it is more sensible to denote C_{t+1} by C_{t+1-f}, to emphasize the fractional lead of the causal variable over the caused variables M_{t+1}. Another way of considering this situation is to note that a causal variable should be attached to the time point at which it actually occurred, rather than the point at which it was observed. Thus, if the figures for monthly employment in New York are released 6 weeks late, the variable should be associated with when it happened rather than when its value became available. To illustrate problems connected with time of occurrence rather than time of observation, consider the well-known relationship between thunder and lightning. Because lightning is observed before thunder is heard, does lightning cause thunder? Clearly not, because they occur at the same instant, but the one is detected before the other because the speed of light is greater than that of sound. Allowing for this differential in observation lags removes the spurious apparent causality and emphasizes the need to look for their common cause, which is the atmospheric electrical discharge.

It is thus seen that apparent instantaneous relationships can occur because of missing causal variables, misinterpretation of the timing of control variables, and the use of overlapping variables. A further reason for instantaneous relationships being observed, even if the true mechanism is pure causal, arises when the minimum causal lag is less than the sampling interval. This case will now be considered.

Up until this point, it has been assumed that the minimum causal lag, introduced in the first section, is identical with the sampling interval, which has been called a month. In practice, this equality is very unlikely to be true, and the miminum causal lag will not be an integer multiple of the sampling interval. The case of particular interest arises when the minimum causal lag is a fraction, f, of the sampling interval, with $0<f<1$. Consider, for example, the generating mechanism

$$\mathbf{M}_t = \alpha \mathbf{Z}_{t-1/2} + \beta \mathbf{Z}_{t-1} + \boldsymbol{\epsilon}_t$$

where the components of $\boldsymbol{\epsilon}_t$ are all independent white noises, so that if the sampling time unit is a month, say, then if the data have been gathered half-monthly, the mechanism will be purely causal. The conditional expectation of $\mathbf{M}_t$ given $\mathbf{Z}_{t-j}$ $(j \geqslant 1)$ will then be

$$E[\mathbf{M}_t \,|\, \mathbf{Z}_{t-j}, j \geqslant 1] = \alpha E[\mathbf{Z}_{t-1/2} \,|\, \mathbf{Z}_{t-j}, j \geqslant 1] + \beta \mathbf{Z}_{t-1}$$

and the unexplained residual, $\mathbf{M}_t$ minus this expectation, need not be a vector consisting of independent components, so that "instantaneous relationships" may appear to occur between these components. In the case just described, the unobserved $\mathbf{Z}_{t-1/2}$ is replaced by its optimum forecast based on the information available at time $t-1$. This will provide an "observable generating mechanism," which obviously differs from the actual mechanism. However, if one wants a model that better fits the given data, then it will generally be true that a better estimate of the missing term $\mathbf{Z}_{t-1/2}$ can be achieved from using $\mathbf{Z}_{t-j}$ $(j \geqslant 1)$ and also $\mathbf{Z}_t$. For example, if $\mathbf{Z}_t$ is generated by an AR(1) model on the half-sample interval, then the optimum interpolation or estimation of the missing $\mathbf{Z}_{t-1/2}$ will consist of a weighted sum of $\mathbf{Z}_t$ and $\mathbf{Z}_{t-1}$, using a least-squares criterion. Note that $\mathbf{Z}_t$ may contain $\mathbf{M}_t$; so some algebra and renormalizing will then be required to obtain a model explaining $\mathbf{M}_t$ in terms of current $\mathbf{Z}_t$ (other than $\mathbf{M}_t$) and past values. Consider now what happends if $\mathbf{Z}_t$ is generated by an AR(p) model with $p \geqslant 1$. It follows that the optimum interpolation will include terms $\mathbf{Z}_{t+j}$ ($j \geqslant 1$), so that now $\mathbf{M}_t$ is being "explained" by future values of $\mathbf{Z}_t$ and thus possibly future values of $\mathbf{M}_t$. The resulting equation may well fit the data well, but it can hardly be considered as a generating mechanism, because, in general, it cannot be used to generate a sequence $\mathbf{M}_t$. If, in this discussion, $\alpha \mathbf{Z}_{t-1/2}$ is replaced by $\alpha \mathbf{Z}_{t-f}$, the same considerations hold, although by estimating the model involving future values, it may be possible to estimate α and f. It does, in general, appear to be arbitrary to include $\mathbf{Z}_t$ in the model for $\mathbf{M}_t$ to help explain the missing $\mathbf{Z}_{t-f}$, but not also to recognize that this is being done as part of an interpolation and so to exclude the use of future values. The one case in which this argument loses nearly all of its impact is when f is very small compared to the sampling interval. If, for example, data are measured monthly but the economy is very efficient and quickly reacts, in a causal fashion, to new information, so that the minimum causal lag is 1 day, then $\mathbf{Z}_{t-f}$ will be effectively identical with $\mathbf{Z}_t$ if there is virtually any serially correlation or momentum in the series. Philosophically, there is a considerable difference between believing in "instantaneous causality" and believing in the time-lagged causality defined earlier. But with the minimum causal lag being very small, however, there is very little pragmatic difference between the two positions. For some parts of the economy, such as stock and commodity markets, the reaction time to new information may be short, but for other parts, such as price changes in refrigerators or the labor market, the reaction time may be very much longer. As an example of the difference between the two "philosophies" just mentioned, consider the pair of models

$$x_t = \alpha y_t + \beta Z_{t-1} + e_t$$

and

$$x_t = \alpha y_{t-f} + \beta Z_{t-1} + e_t$$

It might be tempting to write these in the alternative forms

$$y_t = a x_t - a\beta Z_{t-1} - a e_t$$

and

$$y_{t-f} = a x_t - a\beta Z_{t-1} - a e_t$$

where $a = \alpha^{-1}$. The first of these might appear to be a candidate for a generating function, but the second is not, because future values (as opposed to expected values) of variables cannot be used in a generating equation. The reversal of variables from one side of an equation to the other is also difficult to justify if the right side, apart from the residual, of the equation is taken to be a conditional expectation, because of the familiar two-regression problem of classical statistical theory.

I believe that much of the available economic theory could be better used in the specification of econometric models if the causal nature of economic relationships were specifically recognized. An appropriate specification would then be a reduced-form model in which all variables of interest were explained, or generated, by lagged causal or explanatory variables, possibly using fractional lags. The unexplained, or residual, portions of the variables of interest would be independent in the pure causal case, but not necessarily so in practice, as will be discussed in the next section. In symbols, for the linear case,

$$\mathbf{M}_t = \sum_j a_j W_{j,t-f_j} + \mathbf{a}(B)\mathbf{W}_{t-1} + \epsilon_t(M \mid W)$$

where $W_{j,t}$ are the components of the variable used in the information set, f_j are fractional lags with $0<f_j<1$, and $\mathbf{a}(B)$ is a matrix in the lag operator B. The advantages of such a specification are ease of interpretation, specific recognition of causal relationships and lags, and the removal of any need to depend on possibly unrealistic identification restrictions. This does mean that techniques to estimate the fractional lags need to be developed, and in certain simple one-way causal situations, cross-spectral techniques are already available. The model actually estimated may be a little different from those currently in use, if variables with fractional lags are approximated by weighted averages of zero and integer lagged values of the variable. If this is done, it is important to distinguish the estimated model from the generating model that it approximates, because interpretation can be quite different. The suggested use of the type of model considered here is not new; writers such as T. C. Liu and Herman Wold emphasized the use of similar models in the past, but they used a different notion of causality.

Variables that can be particularly well handled as causal, possibly with fractional lags, are those considered to be exogenous. If a variable is considered to be generated by a separate mechanism, and then the value so generated is used to help generate an endogenous variable, inevitably there seem to be some lags involved. Specifying models with exogenous variables having fractional lags may not have implications for estimation, but it does result in considerable clarification in interpretation, particularly if the models are considered in terms of generating mechanims.

It is clear that new tests for fractional lag causality need to be constructed.

4 Simultaneity

Current practice in the specification of econometric models places considerable emphasis on the simultaneous relationships between variables. It is true that apparent simultaneity is observed with actual data, but as explained in the previous sections, this could be because of missing causal variables, overlapping variables, and fractional causal lags. The interesting questions are whether or not there are any instantaneous relationships that cannot be so explained and whether or not such residual instantaneity is sufficiently important to require special attention and interpretation. To continue with the use of models specified with simultaneity, there has to be some advantages in this practice. For purposes of discussion, consider the simple model

$$\begin{aligned} \alpha x_t + \beta y_t &= m_e(Z_{t-1}) + e_t \\ \gamma x_t + \delta y_t &= m_f(Z_{t-1}) + f_t \end{aligned} \tag{3}$$

where

$$m_e(Z_{t-1}) = E[\alpha x_t + \beta y_t \,|\, Z_{t-1}]$$

and similarly for m_f, and where e_t and f_t are a pair of stationary white-noise series with zero means and variances δ_e^2 and δ_f^2, respectively, jointly normally distributed with correlation coefficient ρ. The model becomes an apparent simultaneous generating mechanism by using the normalization $\alpha=\delta=1$. It might be noted that if $\rho=0$, one has a purely causal generating mechanism for the pair of variables $x_t+\beta y_t$ and $y_t+\delta x_t$, so that solving these for x_t and y_t gives a nonpure mechanism because of the use of overlapping variables. Once the model is given, it is simple to ask what happens to y_t if x_t is changed. Although if x_t and y_t are jointly determined, the relevance of the question is unclear, particularly because if x_t becomes a control variable the relationships may well change. Answers to such questions are easily obtained, if one knows the parameters of the model, by noting that

$$E[Y|X] = a_1 + b_1 X$$

where

$$a_1 = \frac{1}{(\delta\alpha - \beta\gamma)}\,[\alpha m_f - \gamma m_e - b_1(\delta m_e - \beta m_f)]$$

and

$$b_1 = \frac{-\delta\gamma\sigma_e^2 - \beta\alpha\sigma_f^2 + (\alpha\delta + \beta\gamma)\rho\sigma_e\sigma_f}{\beta^2\sigma_f^2 + \delta^2\sigma_e^2 - 2\delta\beta\rho\sigma_e\sigma_f}$$

Similarly, if $E[X \mid Y] = a_2 + b_2 Y$, *then*

$$b_2 = \frac{-\delta\gamma\sigma_e^2 - \beta\alpha\sigma_f^2 + (\alpha\delta + \beta\sigma)\rho\sigma_e\sigma_f}{\alpha^2\sigma_f^2 + \gamma^2\sigma_e^2 - 2\alpha\delta\rho\sigma_e\sigma_f}$$

Only in rather special cases are these conditional means easily interpreted in terms of the original parameters of the model. For example, if $\alpha = \delta = 1$, $\gamma = 0$, and $\rho = 0$, one has

$$b_1 = \frac{-\beta\sigma_f^2}{\beta^2\sigma_f^2 + \sigma_e^2}$$

and $b_2 = -\beta$.

These conditions will be called case E because of their relevance to the concept of exogeneity, which will be discussed later. These conditional expectations seem to be the basis of much of the intuitive suggestions about "knowledge" of the structural simultaneous-equations parameters claimed by some economists. The complexity of these expectations, even in this simple two-equation case, indicates that such suggestions may be rather optimistic.

If a pair of random variables X, Y are found to have a joint normal distribution and to be correlated, then a variety of possible models of form (3) can equally well explain these observations. In particular, one can have the conditions of case E in which the means of e and f are constants. This is, of course, the classical identification problem. When the means of e and f are functions of predetermined variables, there obviously are potential constraints on the parameters of model (3). However, it is clear that one cannot merely have a pair of series, form their expectations with respect to an information set J, observe residuals $\epsilon_t(X \mid J)$ and $\epsilon_t(Y \mid J)$, find these to be correlated, and then hope to build and interpret a model such as (3), but with X and Y replaced by their residuals, because no unique model will result. One could specify such models in a "reduced, seemingly unrelated regression" form, with $\beta = \gamma = 0$, $\rho \neq 0$, or in "triangular" form, with $\beta \neq 0$, $\gamma = 0$, $\rho = 0$ or $\beta = 0$, $\gamma \neq 0$, $\rho = 0$, or in various forms involving more nonzero parameters, all of which might appear to be interpreted differently. As is well known, to proceed further in the modeling process, economic identification conditions must be applied by applying constraints to parameters of the whole model. If one had reasonable confidence in the manner in which these identification conditions were selected, there would be little problem with this procedure; but in practice the constraints selected are not easily defended, being selected merely for pragmatic convenience, or based on an unsophisticated and untested "theory." Such criticism is hardly new, and for a recent and very convincing account, see the work of Sims (1980), who discussed what he called "incredible identification" in dynamic models.

The questions just discussed relate to testing for what has been called instantaneous causality, as discussed by Pierce and Haugh (1977, 1979), Price (1979), and others. The concept of causality introduced in the second section of this chapter is essentially a reduced-form causality, because the time lag between cause and effect is central, and vital, for the definition. To try to define instantaneous causality, one can ask questions such as this: Can I predict X_t better using Y_{t-j} $(j \geqslant 0)$ and X_{t-j} $(j>0)$ rather than the information set Y_{t-j}, X_{t-j} $(j>0)$? Tests based on such definitions can be constructed, but the defined quantity has less satisfactory properties. Whereas, for causality as defined in Section 2, Y causing X puts no constraints on the question whether or not X causes Y; for instantaneous causality, if one finds that Y causes X instantaneously, then immediately X will cause Y instantaneously. In a sense, instantaneous causality is worth introducing only so that the difficulties with such a concept can be brought out.

The concept of exogeneity is a venerable one, and it clearly overlaps, to some extent, the definition of causality. If X does not cause Y, in the case defined in Section 2, and if X_t, Y_t obey an identified form of model (3) with conditions of type E, that is, $\beta=0$, $\rho=0$, $\alpha=\delta=1$, then X is strictly (or clearly) exogenous to Y. This definition has a different viewpoint to the classical definition of Christ (1966), based on earlier work by Koopmans and Hood, which has X_t exogenous to Y_t, in this simple model, if it is independent of the series e_t. It should be noted that Christ's definition is not very operational, because it is based on quantities, the e_t, that are not directly observed and depend on the correct specification of the model and good estimates of its parameters.

The introduction of identifiability of the model appears to have solved the question of how to decide on the direction of instantaneous causality, here embedded within the definition of exogeneity, but it should strictly be called conditional exogeneity or instantaneous causality, because its correctness depends on the correctness of the assumptions required to identify the model. As always, if these assumptions are correct, the result that X is exogenous to Y is interesting and possibly useful; but if the assumptions are incorrect, one has very little of value.

If the assumptions are testable, such difficulties are reduced, but this does not always seem to be the case.

As here defined, the concept of exogeneity is a property of variables within a generating mechanism and is useful in interpreting the mechanism. Recently, Engle, Hendry, and Richard (1979) (henceforth EHR) have approached the concept from a different viewpoint. Suppose we have a model such as (3), but with unknown coefficients that must be estimated from some available data. If, for example, β is unknown and is of interest, and thus needs estimating in model (3) with $\alpha=\delta=1$, then Y is said to be exogenous to X (with respect to β) if an efficient estimate of β can be achieved without, simultaneously, estimating the second equation of the model. Inefficiency could arise either from the usual simultaneous-equations bias or because of cross-equation parameter constraints, as, for example, if β were functionally related to parameters in the second equation, according to some theory or set of assumptions. Knowledge of exogeneity here is given practical importance, being joined with the estimation problem, but if one is given a generating mechanism, with known parameters, it has less relevance. In fact, if one is given a generating mechanism with known parameter values, it is not possible to know if a variable is exogenous according to the EHR definition. Of course, in this case the classical definition does become relevant, because the residuals e_t will then be known exactly. EHR also introduced a strong form of their definition in which to the preceding conditions is added a lack of causation (in the lagged sense) from endogenous to exogenous variables, and this suggests that their definition should be related also to an information set.

Consider, for example, the system

$$y_t = \beta x_t + e_{1t}$$

$$x_t = \gamma x_{t-1} + e_{2t}$$

$$z_t = (\gamma + \beta) z_{t-1} + e_{3t}$$

where β is the parameter of interest. The x_t is EHR exogenous to y_t with respect to the information set (x, y), but not with respect to the information set (x, y, z).

There has, unfortunately, been some confusion in the recent literature concerning the concept of exogeneity and its relationship to causality. The reports by Engle, Hendry, and Richard (1979) and Geweke (1981) should greatly reduce this confusion.

A final problem concerning simultaneous relationships between variables that has received rather little attention is the coexistence of stock and flow variables in models. The distinction between such variables has recently been discussed by Harrison (1980), and its relevance when discussing instantaneous causality has been pointed out by Hicks (1979, particularly in Chapter 5). Basically, the main point distinguishing the two types of variables is that stocks (prices, temperature, unemployment) are measured at a single point in time, whereas flows (sales, production, rainfall) are accumulations over a period of time and cannot be measured at a single instant. There is clearly no difficulty in relating X_t, a flow variable, with lagged values of Y_t, a stock variable, or vice versa, but it is difficult to explain how X_t and Y_t can be simultaneously determined. At what point in time will this occur? If sales and prices are being related, for instance, one must have a rather curiously organized market for these variables to be simultaneously selected. Markets in which, for example, a price is declared, sales result over some period, these sales suggest a new price, and so forth, would seem to be much nearer reality and fit more closely to the causality ideas being discussed in this chapter.

From these considerations, it seems that there is a lot to be said for specification of models in the form

$$x_t + \beta y_{t-d} = e_t$$

$$y_t + \gamma x_{t-d'} = f_t$$

with correlation (e_t, f_t) not constrained to be zero, and with the means of e_t, f_t possibly depending on various lagged variables. Such models take into account the causality ideas inherent in many theories and avoid many of the problems discussed here. Although the analysis of such models requires further development, their use would prevent the misunderstanding of simultaneous models that undoubtedly currently occurs.

5 Conclusions

The use of econometric models specified in a simultaneous fashion is now of long standing and is deeply rooted. The actual mechanism by which a vector of economic variables is contemporaneously and instantaneously jointly determined is, I suspect, less well understood than economic theory currently suggests. This is particularly true when exogenous variables are included in the vector, because they seem to be inherently determined before the endogenous variables. Thus, if economic models were specified totally in terms of beliefs about causality, identified by including lags, possibly fractional ones, for causal variables, and also allowing for some contemporaneous correlations between residuals, I believe that model specification would improve and fewer errors of interpretation, manipulation, and even estimation would occur. It should be noted that the resulting model would not be in a reduced form, because the fractional lagged variables would not be directly observed. The actual model estimated, using data with a given sampling interval, might not be different from those now specified, but there would be less opportunity for misunderstanding about the generating mechanism if the extra specification were taken. Methods for analyzing the model specified with fractional lags would require improvement, and further consideration of the consequences of ignoring fractional lags would be needed. Of course, the inherent difficulties of dealing with, and specifying, simultaneous models have been known for some time, as emphasized by the writings of econometricians such as T. C. Liu and Herman Wold, and I hope that the causal considerations discussed here further emphasize these questions.

REFERENCES

Christ, C. F. 1966. *Econometric Models and Methods.* New York: Wiley.

Engle, R. Hendry, D., and Richard, J. F. 1979. "Exogeneity." Unpublished CORE manuscript.

Geweke, J. 1981. "Inference and Causality in Economic Time Series Models." In *Handbook of Econometrics,* edited by Z. Griliches and M. Intriligator. Amsterdam: North-Holland.

Granger, C. W. J. 1980. "Testing For Causality—A Personal Viewpoint." *Journal of Economic Dynamics and Control* 2:329–52.

Granger, C. W. J. 1981. "Some properties of Time Series Data and Their Use in Econometric Model Specification." *Journal of Econometrics* 16:121–30.

Harrison, G. W. 1980. "The Stock-Flow Distinction: A Suggested Interpretation." *Journal of Macroeconomics* 2:111–28.

Hicks, Sir J. 1979. *Causality in Economics.* New York: Basic Books.

Pierce, D. A., and Haugh, L. D. 1977. "Causality in Temporal Systems: Characterizations and a Survey." *Journal of Econometrics* 5:265–93.

Pierce, D. A., and Haugh, L. D. 1979. "Comment on Price." *Journal of Econometrics* 10:257–60.

Price, J. M. 1979. "A Characterization of Instantaneous Causality: A Correction." *Journal of Econometrics* 10:253–6.

Sims, C. A. 1980. "Macroeconomics and Reality." *Econometrica* 68:1–48.

PART VII

ALTERNATIVE TESTS AND ESTIMATORS

CHAPTER 9

Comparing alternative asymptotically equivalent tests

Thomas J. Rothenberg

In many econometric inference problems there are a number of alternative statistical procedures available, all having the same asymptotic properties. Because the exact distributions are unknown, choice among the alternatives often is made on the basis of computational convenience. Recent work in theoretical statistics has suggested that second-order asymptotic approximations can lead to a more satisfactory basis for choice.

In this chapter I shall discuss some implications of this statistical theory for hypothesis testing in econometric models. My comments are based on current research in progress with my co-workers Chris Cavanagh, Larry Jones, Dennis Sheehan, and Darrell Turkington. This work, in turn, borrows much from earlier studies by the statisticians Chibisov, Efron, and Pfanzagl and the econometricians Durbin, Phillips, and Sargan. Although my comments will concentrate on the problem of hypothesis testing, there are, of course, parallel theories for point and interval estimation.

The basic idea underlying second-order asymptotic comparisons of tests is simple. Tests that are asymptotically equivalent often differ in finite samples. Although the exact sampling distributions may be diffi-

The research reported here was supported by the U.S. National Science Foundation under a grant administered by the Institute of Business and Economic Research at the University of California, Berkeley. The findings and conclusions do not necessarily reflect the views of the National Science Foundation. Part of the research was conducted at the International Centre for Economics and Related Disciplines, London School of Economics, whose hospitality is gratefully acknowledged.

cult to derive, the first few terms of an Edgeworth-type series expansion for the distribution functions usually are available. The tests can then be compared using the Edgeworth approximations. Of course, it is not very interesting to compare tests unless they have the same significance level. Therefore, we first approximate the distributions of the test statistics under the null hypothesis and, based on that approximation, modify the tests so that they have the same probability of a type I error. Then we use another Edgeworth series, derived under the alternative hypothesis, to approximate the power functions of the modified tests.

Although the idea is simple, the actual execution is long and tedious. Lists of regularity conditions, dozens of symbols, and pages of algebra are required. In this survey I shall ignore all of the detail and present only a general outline of the method and some typical results. Formal statements and proofs of these results can be found in the reports cited.

1 General framework

Let θ be a vector of q unknown parameters that, along with some additional "nuisance" parameters, determine the probability law for the observed data. We shall consider tests that reject the null hypothesis $\theta=\theta_0$ if some test statistic is greater than zero. We assume that each of the tests has asymptotic size α; that is, when $\theta=\theta_0$, the rejection probabilities approach α for all values of the nuisance parameters as the sample size n approaches infinity. We also assume that the tests are asymptotically equivalent when θ departs from θ_0. In particular, all the tests under consideration are assumed to have the same limiting distribution under local alternatives. That is, for each sample size n, let the true parameter value be given by $\theta_0+\delta/\sqrt{n}$, where δ is a constant q-dimensional vector. Then, for the sequence of problems as n approaches infinity, the rejection probabilities approach the function $\pi(\delta)$.

We assume further that the test statistics have distributions that can be expanded in an Edgeworth-type[1] series to order n^{-1}. Specifically, let S and T be asymptotically equivalent test statistics. Then we assume (i) that there exist modified (size-corrected) statistics

$$S^* = S + \frac{g_s}{\sqrt{n}} + \frac{h_s}{n}$$

$$T^* = T + \frac{g_t}{\sqrt{n}} + \frac{h_t}{n}$$

(where g and h are functions of the data, derived from the Edgeworth expansions of the null distributions of S and T) such that under the null hypothesis $\Pr(S^*>0) \simeq \Pr(T^*>0) \simeq \alpha$, with approximation error of order smaller than n^{-1}; (ii) that the rejection probabilities for the modified tests possess valid Edgeworth-type series approximations to order n^{-1} for local alternatives:

$$\Pr(S^* > 0) = \pi(\delta) + \frac{a_s(\delta)}{\sqrt{n}} + \frac{b_s(\delta)}{n} + o(n^{-1})$$

$$\Pr(T^* > 0) = \pi(\delta) + \frac{a_t(\delta)}{\sqrt{n}} + \frac{b_t(\delta)}{n} + o(n^{-1})$$

The first term in the series, $\pi(\delta)$, is the (first-order) asymptotic local power function. The sum of the three terms is the second-order local power function. (Some authors use the expression "second order" when referring to the $n^{-1/2}$ term and the expression "third order" when referring to the n^{-1} term; no such distinction will be made in this survey.) These power functions generally depend also on the values of the nuisance parameters; to simplify notation, we do not make this dependence explicit.

When comparing two asymptotically equivalent tests, it is useful to distinguish four possible cases:

1. S and T have identical distributions to a second order of approximation. This implies that the size corrections are the same and the second-order local power functions are the same (i.e., $g_s = g_t$, $h_s = h_t$, $a_s = a_t$, $b_s = b_t$). In this case, second-order asymptotic theory can help correct for size, but it offers no basis for choice between the two tests.
2. S and T are not identical, but S^* and T^* have the same distribution (i.e., $a_s = a_t$ and $b_s = b_t$). Again, there is no basis for choice once the size corrections are made. However, the size corrections are not the same for the two tests. One might prefer the test that involves the simplest correction.
3. S^* and T^* have different distributions, and one test dominates the other. For example, $a_s(\delta) \geqslant a_t(\delta)$ and $b_s(\delta) \geqslant b_t(\delta)$ for all relevant δ (and all values of the nuisance parameters), with strict inequality occurring for some δ.
4. S^* and T^* have different distributions, but neither test uniformly dominates the other. The second-order power curves cross.

For a given econometric testing problem and for two asymptotically equivalent tests, it would be useful to know the following: (i) Which of the preceding cases holds? (ii) How large a size correction is needed for each test? (iii) If S^* dominates T^*, how large is the difference in power? (iv) If S^* and T^* have power curves that cross, for which alternatives does each dominate?

For the case in which only one parameter is being tested ($q=1$) and a one-tailed test is performed (only positive δ are relevant), complete answers to these questions are attainable using the approach developed by Chibisov (1973) and Pfanzagl and Wefelmeyer (1978). Generally, tests based on maximum-likelihood estimates dominate tests based on minimum-distance estimates; tests that differ only in the choice between a constrained or unconstrained variance estimator are second-order equivalent after a size correction has been made. In the case of one-parameter one-tailed tests, differences in power typically occur only in the n^{-1} term, because a_s equals a_t. Thus, unless b_s and b_t differ by a large amount, power differences will be small.

2 Some econometric models

More detailed results are available for specific models. Here we shall discuss three examples in the context of regression models with non-stochastic regressors and normally distributed errors.

1. In the linear model $y=X\beta+u$, suppose the error covariance matrix depends on p unknown parameters. We test the null hypothesis that $c'\beta=1$ against the alternative that $c'\beta>1$. Breusch (1979) considered the Wald, likelihood-ratio (LR), and Lagrange-multiplier (LM) tests and showed that the Wald test statistic is always the largest and the LM statistic is always the smallest. Using second-order asymptotics, one can verify (and quantify) this inequality. Indeed, to a second order of approximation, the LR statistic is the simple average of the other two statistics. However, one can also show that, when corrected for size, all three tests have the same second-order power function. The inequality holds in the more general case in which there are q linear constraints being tested, but the result on power does not. When $q>1$, the LR statistic is still approximately the average of the Wald and LM statistics. However, the power curves for the three tests now differ, and none is uniformly most powerful.[2]

2. In the linear regression model $y=X\beta+u$, suppose the errors follow a first-order autoregression, and one tests the null hypothesis that the autocorrelation coefficient is zero against the alternative that it is positive. Again, after correction for size, the Wald, LR, and LM tests have identical second-order power functions. The Durbin–Watson test, because of its treatment of the initial values, has slightly lower power.[3]

3. Consider the nonlinear regression model $y_i=g_i(\theta)+u_i$, where the errors have a scalar covariance matrix. Suppose one tests the null hypothesis that the parameter vector θ satisfies $c'\theta=1$ against the alternative that $c'\theta>1$. The three (size-corrected) tests now generally have different second-order power functions depending on a measure of the

curvature of the g_i functions. With nonzero curvature, no one test dominates the others. The Wald test is best when power is high; the LM test is best when power is low; the LR test is best when power is near one-half. When curvature is zero, the three tests are equivalent.[4]

These results on the relative power of alternative tests are not difficult to obtain. Indeed, it should be possible to prove quite general theorems about relative power, at least when $q=1$ and the errors are normally distributed. Unfortunately, useful general results on the magnitude of the size correction do not seem to be possible. The answer depends very much on the specific model and the specific null hypothesis. Our findings so far suggest that the size corrections are large compared with differences in power. That is, $|\Pr(T>0)-\Pr(S>0)|$ often is much larger than $|\Pr(T^*>0)-\Pr(S^*>0)|$ for two asymptotically equivalent tests S and T. This implies that, once a size correction has been made, little may be lost by using a second-order inefficient test.

3 Some qualifications

Validity of the expansions. Test statistics that are smooth functions of sample moments generally have distributions that can be expanded in an Edgeworth-type series. Numerous technical conditions on the existence of moments and derivatives are required, but these appear not to be restrictive in practice. A more serious assumption, however, is that the underlying probability distribution of the data be continuous. Thus, hypothesis testing in multinomial, probit, and logit models is not covered by our methods. In principle, Edgeworth-type series can be developed for statistics from discrete distributions, but these typically are much more complex.

Accuracy of the approximations. Comparing test statistics on the basis of second-order approximations to their distribution functions makes sense only if these approximations are reasonably accurate. It is conceivable that reasonable accuracy requires a sample size so large that our n^{-1} correction terms are negligible. If so, the second-order theory is clearly useless. However, there is some evidence that for sample sizes between 25 and 50, the second-order terms are large compared with the size of the remaining error. Nevertheless, small differences in the n^{-1} term should not be taken seriously, because they may simply reflect approximation error.

Alternatives to the Edgeworth approximation. It is well documented that Edgeworth approximations often are poor when the statistic has a sharply skewed distribution (as is the case, for example, with sample correlation coefficients when the population correlation is high). In such cases, approximations based on the saddlepoint method or on normalizing transformations often are greatly superior. Unfortunately, analytic comparisons of alternative procedures are difficult when we use these approximation methods, because the power curves to be compared do not have the same functional form. More work needs to be done in this area.

Ancillarity and conditioning. We have compared the unconditional probability distributions of the test statistics. However, following the suggestion of R. A. Fisher, many statisticians would argue that the conditional distribution given any ancillary (or approximate ancillary) statistics is more appropriate. (Efron & Hinkley, 1978). The optimality results based on second-order theory seem to be sensitive to conditioning, and our results might well change if such conditioning were allowed.

Dimensionality. Most of the results presented here are for the case of $q=1$. There is no difficulty in calculating Edgeworth-type expansions (now in terms of noncentral chi-square distributions) in the more general case in which $q>1$ or in deriving size-corrected test statistics. However, uniformly most powerful tests (to second order) will be rare. The problem lies not so much in the second-order theory as in our notion of optimality. Finite-sample chi-square tests are optimal only among the class of tests that are invariant under rotations of the coordinate system. In more complex cases in which asymptotic theory is needed, none of the generally proposed tests possess this invariance, and hence our usual criterion is inapplicable.

Local power. The comparisons made here are in terms of second-order local power functions. Only parameter values "close" to the null hypothesis are considered. A different way to compare tests has been proposed by Bahadur. It uses large-deviation theory and compares the (exponentially fast) rates at which power approaches 1. It would appear to me that we are interested in comparing tests only in situations in which power is moderate (say in the range 0.2 to 0.9). If two tests both have power greater than 0.9, I would be happy with either. If both tests have power less than 0.2, I would not want to use either one. Thus the relevant range of parameter values, when comparison of tests is an issue, is the range that yields moderate power. Over this range, Edgeworth approximations based on local alternatives should be fairly accurate and should form a reasonable basis for choice among tests.

Specification search. Hypothesis testing is not always performed as an end in itself. Often one tests nuisance parameters as a first step in searching for a reasonable specification of a model containing other, more important parameters. One might test for autocorrelated errors in a linear model, for example, not because one really cares about that correlation, but because one ultimately wants to get good estimates of the regression coefficients. Sequential specification searches are not easily analyzed, partly because of the difficult distribution theory, but mostly because of the lack of a reasonable criterion for optimality. Leamer (1978) had much of interest to say about these matters. Classical power comparisons, although relevant, clearly are not the whole story when tests are part of a complex specification search.

Specification error. Second-order asymptotic theory, like all distribution theory, draws implications from basic assumptions about the probability law for the data-generating process. If these assumptions are false, then the implications are suspect. The models used by econometricians are, at best, crude approximations to reality. One would not want to rely on second-order comparisons unless the conclusions were fairly robust to small changes in the basic assumptions. Because second-order theory uses information about the first four moments of the data, whereas the usual asymptotic theory typically requires information about only the first two moments, some loss in robustness must be expected. Clearly, second-order asymptotic theory can be useful only when the econometrician is able to make detailed assumptions about the process being studied.

4 Conclusions

For moderate sample sizes, the actual significance level of a test may differ substantially from the nominal level based on (first-order) asymptotic theory. Modified test statistics, calculated from the first few terms of an Edgeworth-type series expansion of the distribution functions, typically are available and have significance levels much closer to the nominal level. Unmodified Wald, LR, and LM test statistics, although asymptotically equivalent, often assume very different numerical values. The modified (size-adjusted) statistics typically are much closer together. Because the formulas for the modified statistics are relatively simple (for LR tests it typically involves a constant degrees-of-freedom adjustment), their use should be encouraged.

Once the test statistics have been modified so that they have the same significance level (to a second order of approximation), it is possible to compare their (approximate) power functions. Here the differences often seem to be small and may possibly be swamped by the approximation error. However, when substantial differences do appear, the second-order theory provides a basis for choice among alternative tests. For example, in nonlinear problems it seems that the LR test has optimal power characteristics in the interesting central region of the power surface and may therefore be preferable to the LM and Wald tests.

NOTES

1 The usual Edgeworth series for the distribution function of a sample statistic is of the form $\Phi(x)+A(x)\phi(x)/\sqrt{n}+B(x)\phi(x)/n+\ldots$, where Φ is the normal distribution function, ϕ is the normal density function, and A and B are polynomials; the leading term is the asymptotic distribution. Test statistics that are asymptotically chi-square typically have distribution functions that can be expanded in a similar form, but Φ and ϕ are now replaced by chi-square distribution and density functions. We shall use the phrase "Edgeworth-type series" to represent any expansion of a distribution function in a power series in $n^{-1/2}$.

2 For details, see the work of Rothenberg (1977, 1981).

3 For details, see the work of Sheehan (1981).

4 For details, see the work of Cavanagh (1981).

REFERENCES

Breusch, T. S. 1979. "Conflict among Criteria for Testing Hypotheses: Extensions and Comments." *Econometrica* 47:203–8.

Cavanagh, C. 1981. "Hypothesis Testing in Nonlinear Models." Working paper, Institute of Business and Economic Research, University of California, Berkeley.

Chibisov, D. M. 1973. "Asymptotic Expansions for Some Asymptotically Optimal Tests." In *Proceedings, Prague Symposium on Asymptotic Statistics, Vol. 2,* edited by J. Hajek, pp. 37–68. Prague: Karlova.

Efron, B., and Hinkley, D. V. 1978. "Assessing the Accuracy of the Maximum Likelihood Estimator: Observed versus Expected Fisher Information." *Biometrika* 65: 457–82.

Leamer, E. 1978. *Specification Searches: Ad Hoc Inference with Nonexperimental Data.* New York: Wiley.

Pfanzagl, J., and Wefelmeyer, W. 1978. "An Asymptotically Complete Class of Tests." *Zeitschrift für Wahrscheinlichkeitstheorie* 45:49–72.

Rothenberg, T. J. 1977. "Edgeworth Expansions for Multivariate Test Statistics." Working paper IP-255, Center for Research in Management, University of California, Berkeley.

Rothenberg, T. J. 1981. "Hypothesis Testing in Linear Models when the Error Covariance Matrix Is Nonscalar." Working paper, Institute of Business and Economic Research, University of California, Berkeley.

Sheehan, D. 1981. "Approximating the Distribution of Some Time-Series Estimators and Test Statistics." Ph.D. Thesis, University of California, Berkeley.

CHAPTER 10

Conflict among testing procedures in a linear regression model with lagged dependent variables

G. B. A. Evans and N. E. Savin

1 Introduction

Three general principles employed for hypothesis testing in econometrics are the likelihood-ration (LR), Wald (W), and Lagrange-multiplier (LM) criteria. The W test was introduced by Wald (1943) and the LM test by Aitchison and Silvey (1958) and Silvey (1959). The LM test, which is also the same as the score test of Rao (1947), has been the subject of recent reports by Breusch (1979), Godfrey (1978a, 1978b, 1978c), and Breusch and Pagan (1979, 1980).

Savin (1976) and Berndt and Savin (1977) showed that a systematic numerical inequality exists for the test statistics for testing linear restrictions on the coefficients of certain linear models. The inequality relationship for the values of the test statistics is $W \geqslant LR \geqslant LM$. Breusch (1979) established that the inequality relationship holds for a general linear model with normal disturbances, provided that the unknown elements of the covariance matrix can be estimated by maximum likelihood (ML) and that the ML estimates of the coefficient parameters are asymptotically uncorrelated with those of the covariance matrix parameters.

The exact sampling distributions of the three test statistics can be complicated, so that in practice the critical regions of the tests commonly are based on asymptotic approximations. In regular problems the

This research was supported in part by Social Science Research Council Grant HR 7048/1. The authors wish to thank G. A. Hughes, G. E. Mizon, K. F. Wallis, and T. J. Rothenberg for helpful comments.

test statistics have the same asymptotic chi-square distribution under the null hypothesis. When the tests use the asymptotic chi-square value, they have the same critical region, and they are asymptotically equivalent. The inequality relationship among the test statistics implies that there are samples for which the large-sample tests will produce conflicting inferences. Among the questions that arise with respect to the large-sample tests are these: How large are the differences between the truc and nominal significance levels? How do the true powers of the three tests differ? How large is the probability of conflict?

Evans and Savin (1981) investigated the probability of conflict in the classical linear regression model. They found that the probability of conflict can be substantial when the number of restrictons tested is large compared with the degrees of freedom. In this chapter we shall examine the probability of conflict in a linear regression model with lagged dependent variables. For this model there are at least two variants of the W and LM statistics, because there are at least two methods for estimating the information matrix for a stable first-order stochastic difference equation. We calculate the true powers of a particular version of the large-sample W and LM tests and the probabilities of conflict. The case considered has two special features. The first is that there is no conflict between the two tests when they are based on exact distributions, and the second is that they can be calculated with relative ease. The results show that even in the case of one restriction the probability of conflict can be substantial when the absolute value of the root of the stochastic difference equation is near unity.

The organization of this chapter is as follows: The three test procedures will be reviewed in Section 2, and the linear regression model with lagged dependent variables and the F statistic will be presented in Section 3. In Section 4 we shall develop the three test statistics in the context of a simple first-order stochastic difference equation. The powers and the probabilities of conflict for a particular version of the large-sample W and LM tests will be presented in Section 5. Concluding comments will be given in Section 6.

2 Testing procedures

Consider the density function $f(y;\theta)$, where y is a $T\times 1$ random vector. It is assumed that the functional form of the density is known but that the $(p\times 1)$-parameter vector θ is not known, except that it is an element of the set Ω in R^p. A typical hypothesis of interest asserts that θ is a member of some subset Ω_0 of Ω; that is, $H_0:\theta\in\Omega_0$, with the alternative hypothesis being $\theta\in\Omega_1=\Omega-\Omega_0$. The subset Ω_0 frequently is defined by a set of constraint equations, say the r equations $\phi(\theta)=0$ that hold among the components of θ in Ω_0.

Writing the logarithm of the likelihood as $l(\theta;y)=\ln f(y;\theta)$, the $p\times 1$ score vector is

$$s(\theta;y) = \partial l(\theta;y)/\partial\theta$$

and the $p\times p$ information matrix is

$$R(\theta) = E(ss')$$

where $s=s(\theta;y)$. In regular problems, the information matrix is minus the expectation of the matrix of second partial derivatives of $l(\theta;y)$ with respect to θ. We shall assume that $R(\theta)$ is a nonsingular matrix.

Suppose the null hypothesis is $H_0:\phi(\theta)=0$, where the $p\times r$ matrix

$$\partial\phi(\theta)/\partial\theta = H(\theta)$$

has full column rank. Denote by $\hat{\theta}$ the vector of estimates given by maximizing $l(\theta)$ when the hypothesized restrictions are ignored, and by $\tilde{\theta}$ the vector of estimates that maximizes $l(\theta)$ subject to the hypothesis $\phi(\theta)=0$. Then the three test statistics for testing H_0 are the following:

1. The likelihood-ration statistic is

$$\text{(2.1)}\qquad \text{LR} = 2[l(\hat{\theta};y) - l(\tilde{\theta};y)]$$

which involves both the constrained and unconstrained ML estimates.

2. The Wald statistic is

$$\text{(2.2)}\qquad \text{W} = \phi(\hat{\theta})'(\hat{H}'\hat{R}^{-1}\hat{H})^{-1}\phi(\hat{\theta})$$

where $\hat{H}=H(\hat{\theta})$ and $\hat{R}=R(\hat{\theta})$, which requires only unconstrained ML estimation.

3. The Lagrange-multiplier or score-test statistic is

$$\text{(2.3)}\qquad \text{LM} = \tilde{s}'\tilde{R}^{-1}\tilde{s}$$

where $\tilde{s}=s(\tilde{\theta};y)$ and $\tilde{R}=R(\tilde{\theta})$, which uses only the constrained estimates. The Lagrangian function is $l(\theta;y)-\lambda'\phi(\theta)$, where λ is an $r\times 1$ vector of Lagrange multipliers. The first-order conditions for a constrained maximum yield $\tilde{s}=\tilde{H}\tilde{\lambda}$, where $\tilde{H}=H(\tilde{\theta})$, so that an alternative expression for (2.3) is $\text{LM}=\tilde{\lambda}'\tilde{H}'\tilde{R}^{-1}\tilde{H}\tilde{\lambda}$.

In regular problems, the three test statistics are asymptotically equivalent. When H_0 is true, they have the same limiting chi-square distribution, and under a sequence of local alternatives they have the same limiting noncentral chi-square distribution. Each gives a consistent test, and they are asymptotically most powerful against local alternatives.

3 The lagged dependent variable model and the F statistic

Consider the linear model

(3.1) $$y = X\beta + \epsilon$$

where y is a $T\times 1$ vector of observations on the dependent variable, X is a $T\times k$ matrix of observations on the explanatory variables, β is a $k\times 1$ parameter vector, and ϵ is a $T\times 1$ vector of random disturbances. The explanatory variables of this model include one or more lagged dependent variables. The assumption is that the systematic part of the stochastic difference equation is stable. It is also assumed that the presample values of the lagged dependent variables are fixed numbers, that $X'X/T$ converges in probability to a positive definite matrix, and that X has full column rank. Finally, it is assumed that ϵ is distributed as $N(0, \sigma^2 I)$.

Suppose the null hypothesis is

(3.2) $$H_0: C\beta = c$$

where C is a known $r\times k$ matrix of full row rank and c is a known $r\times 1$ vector. Letting $\theta' = (\beta', \sigma^2)$, we can write the null hypothesis as $\phi(\theta) = C\beta - c = 0$. The p $(=k+1) \times r$ matrix

$$\partial\phi/\partial\theta = H(\theta) = \begin{bmatrix} C' \\ 0 \end{bmatrix}$$

has full column rank by assumption.

The log likelihood function is

$$l(\theta) = \text{constant} - (T/2)\ln\sigma^2 - (y - X\beta)'(y - X\beta)/2\sigma^2$$

The score vector is

(3.3) $$s(\theta) = \begin{bmatrix} X'(y - X\beta)/2\sigma^2 \\ -T/2\sigma^2 + (y - X\beta)'(y - X\beta)/\sigma^4 \end{bmatrix}$$

and the information matrix is

(3.4) $$R(\theta) = \begin{bmatrix} E(X'X)/\sigma^2 & 0 \\ 0 & T/2\sigma^4 \end{bmatrix}$$

The unrestricted ML estimators are the least-square estimator $\hat\beta = (X'X)^{-1}X'y$ and $\hat\sigma^2 = (y - X\hat\beta)'(y - X\hat\beta)/T$. The restricted ML estimators are the restricted least-squares estimator

$$\tilde\beta = \hat\beta - (X'X)^{-1}C'[C(X'X)^{-1}C']^{-1}(C\hat\beta - c)$$

and $\tilde{\sigma}^2 = (y - X\tilde{\beta})'(y - X\tilde{\beta})/T$. Finally, the Lagrange multiplier is

$$\tilde{\lambda} = -[C(X'X)^{-1}C']^{-1}(C\hat{\beta} - c)/\tilde{\sigma}^2$$

The three test statistics for testing H_0 are

$$\text{LR} = T[\ln \tilde{\sigma}^2 - \ln \hat{\sigma}^2] \tag{3.5}$$

$$\text{W} = (C\hat{\beta} - c)'[\hat{\sigma}^2 C\hat{Q}^{-1}C']^{-1}(C\hat{\beta} - c) \tag{3.6}$$

$$\text{LM} = (C\hat{\beta} - c)'[\tilde{\sigma}^2 C\tilde{Q}^{-1}C']^{-1}(C\hat{\beta} - c) \tag{3.7}$$

where the W and LM statistics differ by different estimates of the relevant submatrix of the information matrix [i.e., $Q/\sigma^2 = E(X'X)/\sigma^2$].

One method of estimation replaces $E(X'X)$ by its sample analogue $X'X$. Applying this method, the W and LM statistics in the lagged dependent variable model are the same as in the classical linear model. Define the unrestricted residual sum of squares as URSS= $(y - X\hat{\beta})'(y - X\tilde{\beta})$ and the restricted residual sum of squares as RRSS$= (y - X\tilde{\beta})(y - X\tilde{\beta})$. Then the W statistic can be written as

$$\text{W} = T(\text{RRSS} - \text{URSS})/\text{URSS} \tag{3.8}$$

(Maddala, 1977, p. 458). The LM statistic can be written as

$$\begin{aligned} \text{LM} &= T(\text{RRSS} - \text{URSS})/\text{RRSS} \\ &= [\text{W}/(1 + \text{W}/T)] \end{aligned} \tag{3.9}$$

and the LR statistic as

$$\text{LR} = T\ln(\text{RRSS}/\text{URSS}) = T\ln(1 + \text{W}/T) \tag{3.10}$$

Hence the LM and LR statistics are functions of the W statistic.

The three test statistics obey the inequality relationship W$\geqslant$LR$\geqslant$LM. This inequality relationship can be written as

$$\text{W} \geqslant T\ln(1 + \text{W}/T) \geqslant \text{W}/(1 + \text{W}/T)$$

where the LR and LM statistics are expressed as functions of W. The left-hand inequality

$$\text{W}/T \geqslant \ln(1 + \text{W}/T)$$

follows from the inequality $x \geqslant \ln(1+x)$ $(x \geqslant 0)$, and the right-hand inequality

$$\ln(1 + \text{W}/T) \geqslant (\text{W}/T)/(1 + \text{W}/T)$$

from the inequality $\ln(1+x) \geqslant x/(1+x)$ $(x \geqslant 0)$. The relevant inequalities on logarithms are found in the work of Hardy, Littlewood, and Polya (1967, pp. 103, 106). See the work of Breusch (1979) for a proof that does not use these inequalities.

A further result on the relationship of the three statistics can be established in the case of large samples. From the expansions $\ln(1+x) = x - x^2/2 + \ldots$ and $x/(1+x) = x - x^2 + \ldots$ $(-1 < x \leqslant 1)$ it follows that to a second order of approximation

$$x - \ln(1+x) \simeq \ln(1+x) - x/(1+x) \simeq x^2/2$$

Replacing x by W/T and multiplying through by T gives

$$\mathrm{W} - \mathrm{LR} \simeq \mathrm{LR} - \mathrm{LM} \simeq \mathrm{W}^2/2T^2$$

In words, for W much less than T, the W statistic is greater than the LR statistic by approximately the same amount that the LM statistic is smaller than the LR statistic. A similar result has been obtained by Rothenberg (1977) in the context of the classical multivariate linear regression model.

When $E(X'X)$ is replaced by $X'X$, the three test statistics are functions of the familiar F statistic:

$$F = \frac{\mathrm{RRSS} - \mathrm{URSS}}{\mathrm{URSS}} \frac{n}{r}$$

where $n = T - k$. This follows from the fact that $\mathrm{W} = TrF/n$. Each test statistic is a different function of the F statistic, and hence they have different exact sampling distributions. As a result, the critical values for the three test statistics are different. When the tests employ the critical values based on the exact sampling distributions, they are referred to as exact tests; the exact tests have the correct significance level.

The fact that each test statistic is a function of the F statistic implies that the three exact tests are equivalent; in the original T-dimensional sample space the three exact tests have the same critical region. In other words, when the exact W test accepts H_0 at significance level α, the exact LM and LR tests also accept H_0 at level α, and similarly if the exact W test rejects H_0. As a consequence, the exact tests have the same power function. Hence, there can be no conflict between the exact tests. In the case of test statistics (3.8), (3.9), and (3.10), conflict is due entirely to the fact that the tests use different critical regions in the original T-dimensional sample space.

In the classical linear regression model (X fixed in repeated samples) the F statistic has a noncentral F distribution. However, this is no longer true in the presence of lagged dependent variables. In fact, the exact sampling distributions of the three test statistics (3.8), (3.9), and (3.10) cannot be readily computed. For this reason we do not compute the critical regions and powers of these exact tests.

Under the null hypothesis H_0, the three test statistics (3.8), (3.9), and (3.10) have the same asymptotic chi-square distribution. For asymptotic theory in the lagged dependent variable model, see Theorems 5.5.13 and 5.5.14 in the work of Anderson (1971, Section 5.5). When the exact distribution is approximated by the asymptotic chi-square distribution, the critical value for an α-level test of H_0 is approximated by the chi-square critical value. The tests based on this approximate critical value are referred to as large-sample tests. Because the exact distribution of each test statistic may differ substantially from the asymptotic distribution, the exact critical values may differ substantially from the chi-square critical value. As a result, the large-sample tests may not have the correct significance level. The inequality relation $\mathrm{W} \geqslant \mathrm{LR} \geqslant \mathrm{LM}$ implies that the true significance levels of these large-sample tests are not equal. Hence, the true powers of the large-sample tests cannot be equal. The inequality relationship also implies that there are samples for which the large-sample tests will produce conflicting inferences. It will be remembered that the conflict is due solely to the difference between the true significance levels.

4 A simple lagged dependent model

The expectations $E(X'X)$ can be expressed as functions of the parameters β and σ^2, the values of the nonstochastic variables, and the presample values of the lagged dependent variables. Another method of estimation replaces the unknown parameters in $E(X'X)$ by their unrestricted ML estimates in the W statistic and by their restricted ML estimates in the LM statistic. This method produces W and LM statistics that are not functions of the F statistic and that do not satisfy the inequality relationship.

We now illustrate the different versions of the W and LM statistics using the stable first-order stochastic difference equation

$$(4.1) \qquad y_t = \mu + \beta y_{t-1} + \epsilon_t, \quad |\beta| < 1, \quad t = 1, 2, \ldots, T$$

where y_0 is a known constant and the ϵ_t are independently and identically distributed $N(0, \sigma^2)$ variates. We investigate tests of the hypothesis

$$H_0 : \beta = \beta_0$$

against alternatives $\beta \neq \beta_0$ where $|\beta_0| < 1$.

It will prove convenient to write model (4.1) as

(4.2) $$z_t = \gamma + \beta z_{t-1} + w_t, \quad t = 1, 2, \ldots, T$$

where $z_t = (y_t - y_0)/\sigma$, $\gamma = [\mu + y_0(\beta - 1)]/\sigma$, and $w_t = \epsilon_t/\sigma$. The presample value of $z_0 = 0$, and the variance of the disturbance w_t is unity. A useful interpretation of γ follows from noting that large values of γ correspond to small values of σ relative to the units of measurement (i.e., for models with relatively little noise).

The unrestricted maximum likelihood estimators of μ and β, conditional on y_0, are the least-squares estimators

$$\hat{\mu}_T = \bar{y} - \hat{\beta}_T \bar{y}_{-1}$$

$$\hat{\beta}_T = \sum_{t=1}^{T} (y_{t-1} - \bar{y}_{-1}) y_t \Big/ S$$

where

$$\bar{y} = \sum_{t=1}^{T} y_t / T, \qquad \bar{y}_{-1} = \sum_{t=1}^{T} y_{t-1} / T$$

$$S = \sum_{t=1}^{T} (y_{t-1} - \bar{y}_{-1})^2$$

The restricted maximum likelihood estimators that satisfy the null hypothesis $H_0 : \beta = \beta_0$ are

$$\tilde{\mu}_T = \bar{y} - \beta_0 \bar{y}_{-1}, \qquad \tilde{\beta}_T = \beta_0$$

For the unrestricted and restricted estimators of σ^2 we use

$$\hat{\sigma}_T^2 = \sum_{t=1}^{T} (y_t - \hat{\mu}_T - \hat{\beta}_T y_{t-1})^2 / (T-2)$$

and

$$\tilde{\sigma}_T^2 = \sum_{t=1}^{T} (y_t - \tilde{\mu} - \tilde{\beta}_T y_{t-1})^2 / (T-2)$$

respectively.

The information matrix is

$$R = \frac{1}{\sigma^2} \begin{bmatrix} T & E\sum_{t=1}^{T} y_{t-1} & 0 \\ E\sum_{t=1}^{T} y_{t-1} & E\sum_{t=1}^{T} y_{t-1}^2 & 0 \\ 0 & 0 & T/2\sigma^2 \end{bmatrix}$$

The second diagonal element of the inverse of R is used in the subsequent development. This element is $R^{22} = \sigma^2/\text{SE}$ where

$$\text{(4.3)} \quad \mathrm{SE} = E\sum_{t=1}^{T} y_{t-1}^2 - \left(E\sum_{t=1}^{T} y_{t-1}\right)^2 \Big/ T$$

Taking expectations

$$\text{(4.4)} \quad \mathrm{SE}/\sigma^2 = \mathrm{SE}(\gamma, \beta)$$
$$= \frac{\gamma^2}{(1-\beta)^2}\left[\frac{1-\beta^{2T}}{1-\beta^2} - \frac{(1-\beta^T)^2}{T(1-\beta)^2}\right]$$
$$+ \frac{1}{1-\beta^2}\left[T - \frac{1-\beta^{2T}}{1-\beta^2}\right], \quad |\beta| < 1$$

with $\gamma = [\mu + y_0(\beta - 1)]/\sigma$.

The three tests statistics for testing $H: \beta = \beta_0$ are

$$\text{(4.5)} \quad \mathrm{LR} = T[\ln \tilde{\sigma}_T^2 - \ln \hat{\sigma}_T^2]$$

$$\text{(4.6)} \quad \mathrm{W} = (\hat{\beta}_T - \beta_0)^2[\hat{R}^{22}]^{-1}$$

$$\text{(4.7)} \quad \mathrm{LM} = (\hat{\beta}_T - \beta_0)^2 \tilde{R}^{22}[S/\tilde{\sigma}_T^2]^2$$

where $\hat{R}^{22}$ and $\tilde{R}^{22}$ are estimates of R^{22} based on the unrestricted and restricted estimates, respectively.

In the W and LM statistics an estimator is required for R^{22}. Variants of the W and LM statistics are obtained by using different estimators for the unknown R^{22}. The first method replaces the expectations $E\Sigma y_{t-1}$ and $E\Sigma y_{t-1}^2$ in SE by their sample analogues Σy_{t-1} and Σy_{t-1}^2, that is, replaces SE by $S = \Sigma(t_{t-1} - \bar{y}_{t-1})^2$. The unknown σ^2 is replaced by $\hat{\sigma}_T^2$ in the W statistic and by $\tilde{\sigma}_T^2$ in the LM statistic. Applying this method, the W and LM statistics are

$$\text{(4.8)} \quad \mathrm{W} = (\hat{\beta}_T - \beta_0)^2/\hat{V}$$

$$\text{(4.9)} \quad \mathrm{LM} = (\hat{\beta}_T - \beta_0)^2/\tilde{V}$$

where $\hat{V} = \hat{\sigma}_T^2/S$ and $\tilde{V} = \tilde{\sigma}_T^2/S$. The W and LM statistics (4.8) and (4.9) are squared t ratios that are distinguished by different estimators of the standard error of $\hat{\beta}_T$.

The second method of estimating R^{22} replaces the unknown parameters in SE by unrestricted estimates in the case of the W statistic and by restricted estimates in the case of the LM statistic. Again σ^2 is replaced by $\hat{\sigma}_T^2$ in the W statistic and by $\tilde{\sigma}_T^2$ in the LM statistic. This method yields the test statistics

$$\text{(4.10)} \quad \mathrm{W} = (\hat{\beta}_T - \beta_0)^2 \mathrm{SE}(\hat{\gamma}_T, \hat{\beta}_T)$$

$$\text{(4.11)} \quad \mathrm{LM} = (\hat{\beta}_T - \beta_0)^2 \mathrm{SE}(\tilde{\gamma}_T, \tilde{\beta}_T)$$

where $\hat{\gamma}_T = [\hat{\mu}_T + y_0(\hat{\beta}_T - 1)]/\sigma^2$ and $\tilde{\gamma}_T = [\tilde{\mu}_T + y_0(\beta_0 - 1)]/\tilde{\sigma}^2$. Further, in the LM statistic (4.11), S has been replaced by $\mathrm{SE}(\tilde{\gamma}_T, \beta_0)$. These W and LM statistics are also squared t ratios that are distinguished by different estimators of the standard error of $\hat{\beta}_T$. When H is true, $\mathrm{SE}(\hat{\gamma}_T, \hat{\beta}_T)$ and $\mathrm{SE}(\tilde{\gamma}_T, \beta_0)$ converge in probability to $\mathrm{SE}(\gamma, \beta_0)$, and similarly $\hat{\sigma}_T^2$ and $\tilde{\sigma}_T^2$ converge in probability to σ^2, so that (4.10) and (4.11) have the same limiting distribution if a limiting distribution exists. These W and LM statistics are no longer functions of a single statistic. Hence, when the exact sample distributions of these statistics are used in testing the hypothesis H_0, the resulting tests are not equivalent; that is, even for exact tests there can be conflict between the criteria. Further, these two statistics do not satisfy the inequality $\mathrm{W} \geqslant \mathrm{LM}$.

A large-sample version of the statistics (4.10) and (4.11) is used in practice. When $|\beta| < 1$, we have

$$\operatorname*{plim}_{T\to\infty} (S/T\sigma^2) = \lim_{T\to\infty} (\mathrm{SE}/T\sigma^2) = 1/(1-\beta^2)$$

Hence, when the hypothesis specifies that $|\beta| < 1$, it is common to estimate $[R^{22}]^{-1}$ by $T(1-\beta^2)^{-1}$, with β replaced by $\hat{\beta}_T$ in the W statistic and by the hypothesized value β_0 in the LM statistic. This approach produces the statistics

$$\mathrm{W} = T(\hat{\beta}_T - \beta_0)^2/(1 - \hat{\beta}_T^2) \tag{4.12}$$

$$\mathrm{LM} = T(\hat{\beta}_T - \beta_0)^2/(1 - \beta_0^2) \tag{4.13}$$

The denominator $(1-\beta_0^2)$ is always positive if H specifies $|\beta_0| < 1$, whereas $(1-\hat{\beta}_T^2)$ can be negative, because even if $|\beta| < 1$ there is a positive probability that $|\hat{\beta}_T| > 1$. Thus the W statistic, as calculated in (4.12), can take on negative values. On the other hand, the W statistic (4.10) is always nonnegative.

There is the question how to define the acceptance region of the large-sample W test based on (4.12). In practice, if $|\hat{\beta}_T| \geqslant 1$, the investigator will revert to another version of the W statistic, namely (4.10). This is analogous to the situation encountered when testing for autocorrelation using Durbin's h statistic. When the h statistic is not calculable, the investigator switches to another version of the LM statistic for testing autocorrelation (Breusch & Pagan, 1980, pp. 243–4). For the purpose of looking at the performance of an α-level W test of the hypothesis $H_0: \beta = \beta_0$ $(|\beta_0| < 1)$, we define the acceptance region to be $0 < \mathrm{W} < \chi_\alpha^2(1)$, so that in consequence H_0 is rejected for negative values of W. In other words, we take the acceptance region to be values of $\hat{\beta}_T$ for which $(\hat{\beta}_T - \beta_0)^2 \leqslant (1 - \hat{\beta}_T^2)\chi_\alpha^2(1)$, that is, values of $\hat{\beta}_T$ between

$$[\beta_0 \pm gu(1 + g^2u^2/T^2)^{1/2}]/(1 + u/T)$$

where $g = T/(1-\beta_0^2)^{1/2}$ and $u = (\chi_\alpha^2(1))^{1/2}$. The corresponding critical region will include all values of $|\hat{\beta}_T| \geqslant 1$.

When $E(X'X)$ is replaced by its sample analogue $X'X$, the LR statistic can be written as

$$\text{LR} = -T\ln(1 - \text{LM}/T) \tag{4.14}$$

because for this estimate of the information matrix $(1+\text{W}/T)\times(1-\text{LM}/T)=1$. Engle (1978) has suggested using the relationship between the W and LM statistics to construct new statistics based wholly on the restricted estimates in situations in which it is difficult to compute the unrestricted estimates. Such statistics may have the advantage of a more rapid approach to the limiting chi-square distribution than the conventional LM statistics. There are several versions of the LM statistic that can be used in the expression (4.14) to construct new statistics. Although these statistics are not LR statistics, it is convenient to continue to refer to them as LR statistics provided this causes no confusion. We shall investigate the performance of the statistic (4.14) where the LM statistic is (4.13). As a consequence, the LR statistic (4.14) is necessarily greater than or equal to the LM statistic (4.13). However, there is no systematic ordering of the W and LR or W and LM statistics; that is, the inequalities W $\geqslant$ LR and W $\geqslant$ LM no longer hold.

The three statistics (4.12), (4.13), and (4.14) are functions of the single statistic $\hat{\beta}_T$. Hence, when the exact sampling distributions of the three statistics are used in testing the hypothesis $H_0: \beta = \beta_0$, the three tests are equivalent; that is, in the case of exact tests, there is no conflict among the criteria. If $H_0: \beta = \beta_0$ is true and $|\beta_0| < 1$, the W statistic (4.12) has a limiting $\chi^2(1)$ distribution, and similarly for (4.13) and (4.14). When this limiting distribution is used in testing the hypothesis H_0 at nominal level α, the three tests employ the same critical region. Even though these statistics do not satisfy the inequality W $\geqslant$ LR $\geqslant$ LM, there are samples such that these large-sample tests will produce conflicting inferences. It is worth remarking that when using large-sample tests the inequality is a sufficient condition but not a necessary condition for conflict among the criteria. When all three tests use the same critical region, what is necessary is that the statistics have different exact sampling distributions.

5 Power functions and conflict

We investigated the null hypothesis $H_0: \beta = \beta_0$ for $\beta_0 = 0.0$, 0.5, and 0.95. The large-sample tests are based on the statistics (4.12), (4.13), and

(4.14). The powers of the large-sample tests and the probabilities of conflict are calculated by using the fact that these three statistics are functions of $\hat{\beta}_T$. The true size of the exact tests and the nominal size of the large-sample tests is $\alpha=0.05$. The powers and the probabilities of conflict are strongly influenced by the value of γ as well as β when $\beta=0.95$. The powers of the exact and large-sample tests and the probabilities of conflict are computed for values of $\gamma=0.0$, 0.25, 0.5, and 1.0, for values of β from -0.5 to 1.05, and for sample sizes $T=25$, 50, and 100. The calculation of the finite sample distribution of $\hat{\beta}_T$ has been described by Evans and Savin (1980). Selected results are reported in Tables 10.1, 10.2, and 10.3 and Figures 10.1 and 10.2.

The exact test of $H:\beta=\beta_0$ is based on the distribution of $\hat{\beta}_T$ for $\gamma=0$. The critical region of this test is of the form

$$P[\hat{\beta}_T < a \mid \gamma = 0, \beta = \beta_0] = P[\hat{\beta}_T > b \mid \gamma=0, \beta = \beta_0] \tag{5.1}$$

(i.e., it is equal-tailed). Because the probability of rejecting $H:\beta=\beta_0$ depends on γ, the fact that γ is unknown complicates the construction of a test of specified size. The size of the significance level of a test of $H:\beta=\beta_0$ based on the critical region C is α if

$$\sup_{\gamma} P[\hat{\beta}_T \in C \mid \gamma, \beta_0] = \alpha$$

Roughly speaking, the size is the maximum probability of rejecting H when H is true. We construct a test of size $\alpha=0.05$ by adjusting the critical values a and b such that the test remains equal-tailed for $\gamma=0$ and at the same time achieves the desired size.

To test $H_0:\beta=0$ with sample size T, we calculated a critical region (5.1) with probability of rejection equal to 0.05. Using this critical region, the probability of rejection was then calculated for $\beta=0$ and $\gamma=0.25$, 0.5, 1.0, 2.0, and 4.0. Because these probabilities were declining as γ increased, we concluded that the size of this critical region was $\alpha=0.05$. To test $H_0:\beta=0.5$, critical regions of size $\alpha=0.05$ were similarly determined. For $H_0:\beta=0.95$, a more complicated procedure of numerical evaluation was required to achieve critical regions of size $\alpha=0.05$. In this case, for $T=25$, the probability of rejection was 0.0322 at $\gamma=0$ and 0.05 at $\gamma=0.62$. The corresponding figures for $T=50$ were 0.0443 at $\gamma=0$ and 0.05 at $\gamma=0.53$.

For the large-sample tests based on (4.12), (4.13), and (4.14), the probability of rejecting H_0 when it is true has been calculated for $\gamma=0.0$, 0.25, 0.5, and 1.0. The true size of a large-sample test is greater than or equal to the maximum of these probabilities. Because these probabilities decline as γ increases from $\gamma=0$, it would seem reasonable

Table 10.1 *Power functions and probabilities of conflict when testing $\beta = 0.0$ at significance level $\alpha = 0.05$*

		$T = 25$					$T = 50$				
β	γ	E	W	LR	LM	Conflict	E	W	LR	LM	Conflict
−0.50	0.0	0.674	0.768	0.749	0.725	0.044	0.935	0.954	0.951	0.948	0.007
−0.50	0.25	0.674	0.769	0.749	0.725	0.044	0.935	0.954	0.951	0.948	0.007
−0.50	0.50	0.674	0.769	0.749	0.725	0.044	0.936	0.955	0.951	0.948	0.007
−0.50	1.00	0.675	0.770	0.751	0.726	0.044	0.936	0.955	0.952	0.948	0.007
−0.25	0.0	0.213	0.312	0.288	0.261	0.051	0.406	0.481	0.467	0.452	0.029
−0.25	0.25	0.212	0.312	0.288	0.261	0.051	0.406	0.481	0.467	0.452	0.029
−0.25	0.50	0.212	0.311	0.287	0.260	0.051	0.406	0.481	0.467	0.451	0.030
−0.25	1.00	0.208	0.309	0.285	0.257	0.051	0.405	0.481	0.466	0.451	0.030
0.0	0.0	0.050	0.068	0.058	0.049	0.019	0.050	0.058	0.054	0.049	0.009
0.0	0.25	0.050	0.067	0.058	0.048	0.019	0.050	0.058	0.054	0.049	0.009
0.0	0.50	0.049	0.066	0.057	0.047	0.019	0.049	0.058	0.053	0.049	0.009
0.0	1.00	0.045	0.062	0.053	0.044	0.018	0.048	0.056	0.051	0.047	0.009
0.25	0.0	0.210	0.179	0.162	0.142	0.037	0.401	0.364	0.351	0.336	0.028
0.25	0.25	0.210	0.179	0.161	0.142	0.037	0.401	0.364	0.351	0.337	0.028
0.25	0.50	0.210	0.179	0.161	0.141	0.038	0.402	0.364	0.351	0.337	0.028
0.25	1.00	0.209	0.176	0.158	0.138	0.038	0.403	0.365	0.351	0.337	0.028
0.50	0.0	0.638	0.596	0.572	0.542	0.054	0.925	0.912	0.907	0.901	0.011
0.50	0.25	0.641	0.599	0.574	0.544	0.054	0.926	0.913	0.908	0.902	0.011
0.50	0.50	0.648	0.605	0.580	0.550	0.055	0.928	0.915	0.910	0.904	0.011
0.50	1.00	0.673	0.630	0.604	0.573	0.057	0.936	0.924	0.919	0.913	0.010
0.95	0.0	0.982	0.978	0.976	0.972	0.006					
0.95	0.25	0.989	0.987	0.985	0.983	0.004					
0.95	0.50	0.998	0.997	0.997	0.996	0.001					
0.95	1.00	1.000	1.000	1.000	1.000	0.000					

Table 10.2 *Power functions and probabilities of conflict when testing $\beta = 0.5$ at significance level $\alpha = 0.05$*

		$T = 25$					$T = 50$				
β	γ	E	W	LR	LM	Conflict	E	W	LR	LM	Conflict
0.0	0.0	0.557	0.777	0.859	0.844	0.083	0.914	0.963	0.979	0.978	0.016
0.0	0.25	0.557	0.777	0.859	0.845	0.083	0.914	0.963	0.979	0.978	0.016
0.0	0.50	0.557	0.777	0.860	0.845	0.083	0.915	0.963	0.980	0.978	0.016
0.0	1.00	0.555	0.778	0.862	0.847	0.084	0.916	0.964	0.980	0.979	0.016
0.25	0.0	0.167	0.355	0.475	0.450	0.120	0.371	0.532	0.629	0.617	0.097
0.25	0.25	0.167	0.354	0.474	0.449	0.120	0.370	0.532	0.629	0.616	0.097
0.25	0.50	0.164	0.352	0.472	0.447	0.120	0.369	0.532	0.629	0.616	0.097
0.25	1.00	0.153	0.342	0.464	0.439	0.123	0.365	0.530	0.628	0.615	0.099
0.50	0.0	0.050	0.088	0.127	0.116	0.058	0.050	0.068	0.089	0.084	0.039
0.50	0.25	0.049	0.086	0.125	0.113	0.058	0.049	0.068	0.088	0.083	0.039
0.50	0.50	0.046	0.081	0.119	0.108	0.056	0.048	0.065	0.086	0.081	0.039
0.50	1.00	0.036	0.064	0.098	0.088	0.050	0.042	0.057	0.077	0.072	0.036
0.75	0.0	0.294	0.212	0.093	0.075	0.152	0.573	0.487	0.348	0.330	0.158
0.75	0.25	0.300	0.215	0.092	0.074	0.155	0.577	0.491	0.350	0.332	0.160
0.75	0.50	0.317	0.224	0.090	0.071	0.163	0.590	0.502	0.357	0.339	0.164
0.75	1.00	0.373	0.254	0.085	0.065	0.192	0.636	0.541	0.381	0.361	0.180
0.95	0.0	0.671	0.584	0.389	0.350	0.237	0.954	0.936	0.896	0.889	0.047
0.95	0.25	0.757	0.680	0.494	0.454	0.228	0.975	0.964	0.936	0.932	0.032
0.95	0.50	0.899	0.851	0.702	0.664	0.188	0.996	0.993	0.985	0.984	0.009
0.95	1.00	0.996	0.991	0.952	0.934	0.057	1.000	1.000	1.000	1.000	0.000

to take the size of these tests to be the probability of rejection when $\gamma=0$.

The main finding is that when testing $H_0:\beta=0.95$ the probability of conflict may be high. For example, when the null is $H_0:\beta=0$, the probability of conflict reported in Table 10.1 is less than 0.06 for $T=25$ and less than 0.03 for $T=50$. On the other hand, when the null is $H_0:\beta=0.95$, the probability of conflict at some alternatives is greater than 0.90 for $T=25$, and similarly for $T=50$. Hence, in the lagged dependent variable model, the probability of conflict can be high even when testing only one restriction.

The results for the case $H_0:\beta=0$ reveal some interesting features. The true size of the large-sample tests are not very different from the nominal size, even for samples as small as $T=25$. In addition, the powers of the large-sample tests are not very different from the powers of the exact test when $\beta=0.25$, 0.5, and 0.95, but they do differ when $\beta=-0.25$ and -0.5 (Figure 10.1). Note that the inequality relation $\mathrm{W}\geqslant\mathrm{LR}\geqslant\mathrm{LM}$ is satisfied for the tabled values of γ and β and that the nuisance parameter γ has only a slight effect on the powers of the exact and large-sample tests. It is evident from Table 10.1 and Figure 10.1 that when testing $H_0:\beta=0$, the large-sample tests are good approximations to the exact test.

Turning to the case $H_0:\beta=0.5$, the true sizes of the large-sample tests can be very different from the nominal size for samples $T=25$ and $T=50$. This is particularly the case for the LR and LM tests. For example, the true size of the LM test is at least 11.6% when $T=25$ and 8.4% when $T=50$. The powers of the large-sample tests can also be very different from the powers of the exact test. For instance, the power of the LM test at $\beta=0.25$ and $\gamma=0.0$ is 45% when $T=25$ and 61.7% when $T=50$. The power of the exact test at this alternative is 16.7% when $T=25$ and 37.1% when $T=50$. The powers of the LR and LM tests are very similar. The results show that the power of the W test is closest to the power of the exact test. The powers of the large-sample tests are less than the power of the exact test when $\beta=0.75$ and 0.95 and vice versa when $\beta=0.0$ and 0.25. The inequality relation $\mathrm{W}\geqslant\mathrm{LR}\geqslant\mathrm{LM}$ no longer holds for the tabled results, and the nuisance parameter γ has a substantial impact on the powers of the exact and large-sample tests when the alternative β is near unity. It appears when testing $H_0:\beta=0.5$ that the large-sample properties of the W, LR, and LM statistics are substantially achieved for $T\geqslant100$.

A review of the case $H_0:\beta=0.95$ shows that the true sizes of the large-sample tests can differ dramatically from the nominal size. For example, when $T=50$ the true size is at least 18.5% for the W test,

Table 10.3 *Power functions and probabilities of conflict when testing $\beta = 0.95$ at significance level $\alpha = 0.05$*

		$T = 25$					$T = 50$				
β	γ	E	W	LR	LM	Conflict	E	W	LR	LM	Conflict
0.50	0.0	0.341	0.928	0.999	0.998	0.070	0.924	0.999	1.000	1.000	0.001
0.50	0.25	0.339	0.929	0.999	0.998	0.070	0.924	0.999	1.000	1.000	0.001
0.50	0.50	0.332	0.929	0.999	0.999	0.069	0.925	0.999	1.000	1.000	0.001
0.50	1.00	0.306	0.932	0.999	0.999	0.067	0.928	1.000	1.000	1.000	0.000
0.90	0.0	0.032	0.296	0.730	0.717	0.452	0.050	0.294	0.664	0.656	0.374
0.90	0.25	0.027	0.254	0.687	0.673	0.457	0.039	0.263	0.639	0.631	0.381
0.90	0.50	0.019	0.164	0.582	0.566	0.452	0.020	0.189	0.576	0.567	0.391
0.90	1.00	0.007	0.035	0.351	0.331	0.341	0.002	0.057	0.420	0.408	0.364
0.95	0.0	0.032	0.237	0.633	0.618	0.436	0.044	0.185	0.475	0.467	0.315
0.95	0.25	0.038	0.190	0.528	0.513	0.409	0.046	0.134	0.379	0.372	0.286
0.95	0.50	0.048	0.118	0.319	0.305	0.323	0.050	0.090	0.203	0.196	0.166
0.95	1.00	0.038	0.067	0.056	0.050	0.119	0.032	0.012	0.023	0.021	0.034
0.99	0.0	0.046	0.206	0.527	0.513	0.406	0.088	0.150	0.321	0.315	0.269
0.99	0.25	0.083	0.194	0.358	0.345	0.353	0.221	0.185	0.141	0.136	0.245
0.99	0.50	0.152	0.224	0.121	0.113	0.285	0.426	0.288	0.017	0.015	0.291
0.99	1.00	0.196	0.314	0.005	0.004	0.312	0.669	0.399	0.000	0.000	0.398
1.00	0.0	0.053	0.203	0.493	0.479	0.396	0.123	0.160	0.276	0.270	0.265
1.00	0.25	0.107	0.214	0.316	0.304	0.349	0.356	0.283	0.102	0.098	0.315
1.00	0.50	0.208	0.293	0.094	0.087	0.326	0.682	0.519	0.015	0.013	0.511
1.00	1.00	0.304	0.460	0.006	0.004	0.456	0.949	0.793	0.000	0.000	0.792
1.01	0.0	0.065	0.206	0.455	0.442	0.386	0.189	0.196	0.229	0.223	0.280
1.01	0.25	0.141	0.247	0.277	0.266	0.357	0.553	0.460	0.084	0.080	0.464
1.01	0.50	0.289	0.390	0.079	0.071	0.399	0.911	0.816	0.027	0.023	0.795

1.01	1.00	0.463	0.645	0.009	0.006	0.639	1.000	0.992	0.001	0.001	0.991
1.025	0.0	0.095	0.225	0.395	0.382	0.378	0.394	0.363	0.170	0.164	0.403
1.025	0.25	0.222	0.333	0.231	0.220	0.403	0.816	0.778	0.120	0.107	0.720
1.025	0.50	0.467	0.586	0.077	0.067	0.564	0.995	0.992	0.112	0.090	0.903
1.025	1.00	0.772	0.902	0.019	0.013	0.888		1.000	0.032	0.019	0.981
1.05	0.0	0.213	0.336	0.300	0.288	0.427	0.785	0.776	0.440	0.404	0.451
1.05	0.25	0.465	0.568	0.206	0.190	0.568					
1.05	0.50	0.834	0.890	0.148	0.121	0.793					
1.05	1.00	0.998	1.000	0.100	0.065	0.934					

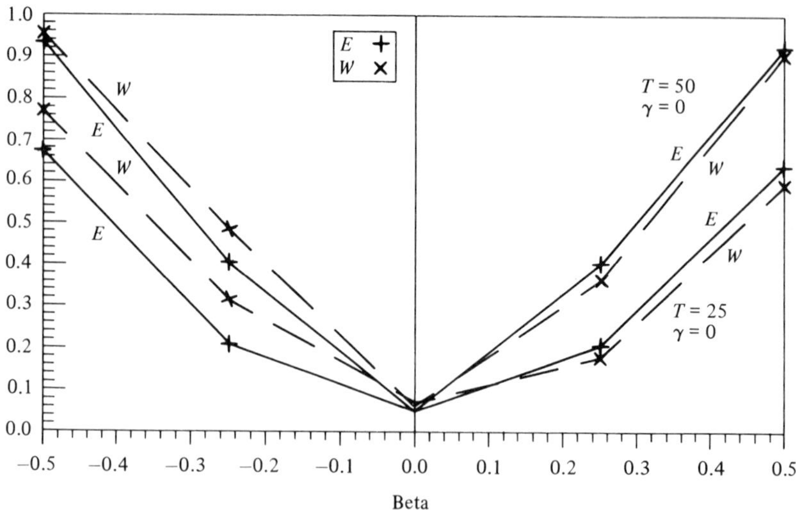

Figure 10.1. Power curves for the exact test (E) and for the asymptotic Wald test (W) when testing $H_0:\beta=0$ with (nominal) size 0.05.

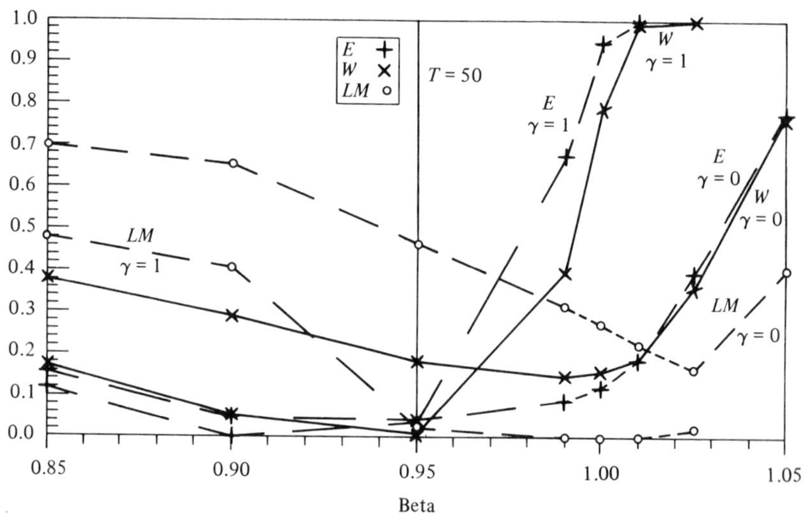

Figure 10.2. Power curves for the exact test (E) and for the asymptotic Wald (W) and Lagrange-multiplier (LM) tests when testing $H_0:\beta=0.95$ with (nominal) size 0.05.

47.5% for the LR test, and 46.7% for the LM test. Further, the powers of the large-sample tests can be strikingly different from the power of the exact test. For instance, at $\beta=\gamma=1.0$, with $T=50$, the power is 94.9% for the exact test, 79.3% for the W test, and 0.0 for both the LR and LM tests. Again, the powers of the LR and LM tests are very similar. Aside from a few exceptions, the results indicate that the power of the W test is closest to the power of the exact test. This is illustrated in Figure 10.2. The powers are strongly influenced by the nuisance parameter γ. For $\beta>0.95$, as γ increases from 0 to 1.0, the powers of the exact and W tests are increased, and the powers of the LR and LM tests are decreased.

6 Concluding comments

In the lagged dependent variable there are at least two methods of estimating the relevant submatrix of the information matrix. One method replaces $E(X'X)$ by its sample analogue $X'X$. When this method is employed, the W, LR, and LM statistics are functions of the usual F statistic. In this case there is no conflict between the three tests when they are based on exact sampling distributions. When the three tests are based on the chi-square critical values, the true significance level of each test may differ substantially from the nominal level. It is this that accounts for the difference between the power functions of each large-sample test and hence accounts for the probability of conflict.

Another method of estimation replaces the unknown parameters in $E(X'X)$ by their unrestricted estimates in the W statistic and their restricted estimates in the LM statistic. This method produces W and LM statistics that are not functions of the F statistic and that do not satisfy the inequality relationship. Further, when the exact sampling distributions of these W and LM statistics are used, the resulting exact tests are not equivalent; that is, there can be conflict even in the case of exact tests.

For the case of a first-order stochastic difference equation, our calculations show that the probability of conflict depends on the stability of the model. The W and LM tests used in these calculations are functions of a single statistic; hence, when the tests are based on exact sampling distributions, there is no conflict. When the tests are based on the chi-square critical values, the true significance level of each test can differ substantially from the nominal level. In particular, our results show that the probability of conflict can be substantial when the root of the equation is near unity. This is because the true sizes of the tests are very different from the nominal size. Roughly speaking, the less stable the model the higher the probability of conflict.

When the root is near unity, but below unity, the chi-square critical values need to be modified in order to produce a test of the correct size. One approach is to use the Edgeworth approximation to the true critical value. For a first-order stochastic difference equation without a constant term, Phillips (1977) has shown that the Edgeworth approximation is poor when the root is near but below unity. Hence, there is a need for further research on correction factors for the chi-square critical values. Our results suggest that in the context of lagged dependent variable models, tests should be interpreted with caution, particularly when the model is on the border of instability.

REFERENCES

Aitchison, J., and Silvey, D. 1958. "Maximum Likelihood Estimation of Parameters Subject to Restraints." *Annals of Mathematical Statistics* 29:813–28.

Anderson, T. W. 1971. *The Statistical Analysis of Time Series.* New York: Wiley.

Berndt, E., and Savin, N. E. 1977. "Conflict Among Criteria for Testing Hypotheses in the Multivariate Linear Regression Model." *Econometrica* 45:1263–78.

Breusch, T. S. 1979. "Conflict Among Criteria for Testing Hypotheses: Extension and Comment." *Econometrica* 47:203–8.

Breusch, T. S., and Pagan, A. R. 1979. "A Simple Test for Heteroscedasticity and Random Coefficient Variation." *Econometrica* 47:1287–94.

Breusch, T. S., and Pagan, A. R. 1980. "The Language Multiplier Test and Its Application to Model Specification in Econometrics." *Review of Economic Studies* 47:239–54.

Engle, R. F. 1978. "The Lagrange Multiplier Test as a Regression Diagnostic." Discussion paper 78-6, Department of Economics, University of California, San Diego.

Evans, G. B. A., and Savin, N. E. 1980. "Testing Unit Roots—II." Unpublished manuscript, Faculty of Economics and Politics, Cambridge University.

Evans, G. B. A., and Savin, N. E. 1981. "Conflict among Criteria Revisited; The W, LR and LM Tests." *Econometrica (in press).*

Godfrey, L. S. 1978a. "Testing for Multiplicative Heteroscedasticity." *Journal of Econometrics* 8:227–36.

Godfrey, L. S. 1978b. "Testing against General Autoregressive and Moving Average Error Models when the Regressors Include Lagged Dependent Variables." *Econometrica* 46:1293–1302.

Godfrey, L. S. 1978c. "Testing for Higher Order Serial Correlation in Regression Equations when the Regressors Include Lagged Dependent Variables." *Econometrica* 46:1303–10.

Hardy, G. H., Littlewood, J. E., and Polya, G. 1967. *Inequalities.* Cambridge University Press.

Maddala, G. S. 1977. *Econometrics.* New York: McGraw-Hill.

Phillips, P. C. B. 1977. "Approximations to Some Finite Sample Distributions Associated with a First-Order Stochastic Difference Equation." *Econometrica* 45:463–85.

Rao, C. R. 1947. "Large Sample Tests of Statistical Hypotheses Concerning Several Parameters with Applications to Problems of Estimation." *Proceedings of the Cambridge Philosophical Society* 44:50–7.

Rothenberg, T. J. 1977. "Edgeworth Expansions for Multivariate Test Statistics." Working paper in economic theory and econometrics IP–225, Center for Research in Management Science, Institute for Business and Economic Research, University of California, Berkeley.

Savin, N. E. 1976. "Conflict Among Testing Procedures in a Linear Regression Model with Autoregressive Disturbances." *Econometrica* 44:1303–15.

Silvey, S. D. 1959. "The Lagrange Multiplier Test." *Annals of Mathematical Statistics* 30:389–407.

Wald, A. 1943. "Tests of Hypotheses Concerning Several Parameters When the Number of Observations Is Large." *Transactions of the American Mathematical Society* 54:426–82.

PART VIII

MODELING CENTRALLY PLANNED ECONOMIES

CHAPTER 11

Macroeconomic modeling based on econometric and simulation models for the Polish economy

Zbigniew Czerwiński and Władysław Welfe

1 Introduction

In this chapter we shall review two approaches to building macroeconomic models and their potential use in medium-term planning for a socialist economy. The first approach concerns a system of models built by Czerwiński and associates at the Academy of Economics, Poznań, based on a Leontief-type dynamic multisectoral model extended by the use of demographic and econometric models of consumers' expenditures. It is aimed at simulating the planning procedures for building a 5-year plan. The second approach deals with macroeconometric W models built by Welfe and associates exemplified by the medium-size W-3 model of the Polish economy, which optionally includes a static input–output equation system. It is aimed not only at explaining the real flows in the medium term but also at simulating the alternative economic policies and revealing the imbalances of different sectors of the national economy.

2 A system of simulation for planning models

At the Institute of Economic Cybernetics of the Academy of Economics on Poznań, an attempt has been made to simulate the medium-term planning procedure at the central level of the economy by means of a series of interrelated models. The basic idea of the procedure is as follows.

A plan is understood to be a set of consistent paths of growth of selected variables describing the state of the economy, compatible with some accepted targets. Variables are divided into three groups: target, autonomous, and outcome variables.[1] Autonomous paths of growth of the population and of its social and professional components are assumed. Increases of incomes in distinguished groups of the population (wages, salaries, pensions) within the planning horizon are postulated, and hence the path of growth of total income of the population, being one of the target variables, is derived. This path is split up into the path of growth of expenditures on selected groups of commodities and the path of savings. These paths are converted into the paths of growth of individual (consumption) demand for output of productive sectors. The planned government investment and consumption activities in non-material-services sector (housing, public transportation, education, health, etc.) create collective demand. Achieving some goals in these fields is considered as important as increasing population incomes. Collective demand is, therefore, another target variable. The third target variable is employment in non-material-services sector, which is also assumed as given.

Individual demand and collective demand add up to total final demand (excluding productive investment and exports). Once the path of growth of the final demand distributed by productive sectors and by type of demand (consumption or investment in nonproductive sector) is fixed, the paths of growth of outcome variables are to be determined. The outcome variables are the following: gross output of productive sectors, current and capital intersectoral flows, import and export flows. Imports are divided into three components: final consumption imports, final investment imports, and intermediate imports, these components being related respectively to final (individual and collective) consumption, to (productive and nonproductive) investment, and to gross output of material-product sectors. Some constraints are imposed on the level and structure of exports.

The paths of growth of investment and of employment in material-product sectors are another outcome of computations. The resulting path of growth of employment in these sectors is compared with the path of growth of the professionally active population assumed as the starting point, reduced by employment in non-material-services sector. If these two paths either coincide or differ insignificantly, the procedure ends. Otherwise, targets are changed, a new path of growth of final demand is obtained, and computations are repeated. A simplified block diagram of the procedure is shown in Figure 11.1.

At every step of the procedure, different models were tried: demo-

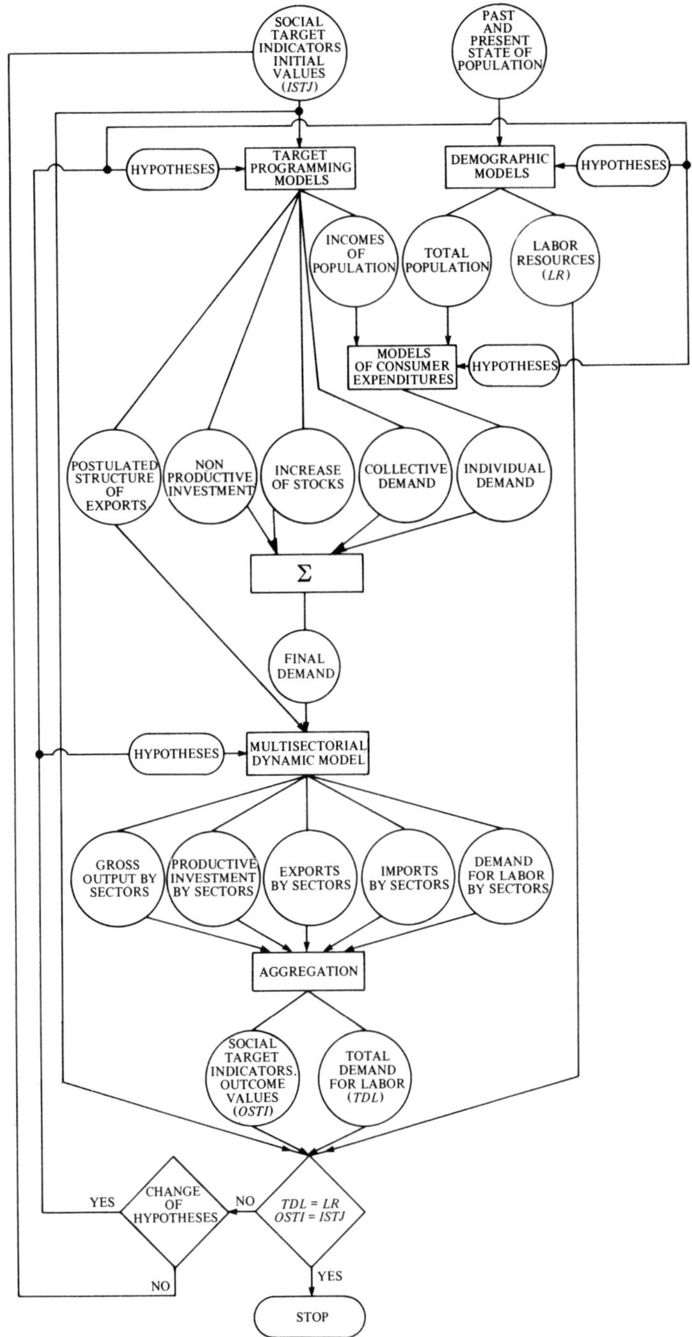
SOCIAL TARGET INDICATORS INITIAL VALUES (ISTJ)
PAST AND PRESENT STATE OF POPULATION
HYPOTHESES
TARGET PROGRAMMING MODELS
DEMOGRAPHIC MODELS
HYPOTHESES
INCOMES OF POPULATION
TOTAL POPULATION
LABOR RESOURCES (LR)
MODELS OF CONSUMER EXPENDITURES
HYPOTHESES
POSTULATED STRUCTURE OF EXPORTS
NON PRODUCTIVE INVESTMENT
INCREASE OF STOCKS
COLLECTIVE DEMAND
INDIVIDUAL DEMAND
Σ
FINAL DEMAND
HYPOTHESES
MULTISECTORIAL DYNAMIC MODEL
GROSS OUTPUT BY SECTORS
PRODUCTIVE INVESTMENT BY SECTORS
EXPORTS BY SECTORS
IMPORTS BY SECTORS
DEMAND FOR LABOR BY SECTORS
AGGREGATION
SOCIAL TARGET INDICATORS, OUTCOME VALUES (OSTI)
TOTAL DEMAND FOR LABOR (TDL)
YES
CHANGE OF HYPOTHESES
NO
TDL = LR
OSTI = ISTJ
NO
YES
STOP

Figure 11.1.

graphic models (to project the growth of population), models of consumer expenditures and savings (to derive paths of growth of individual demand for groups of commodities), etc. As the core of the procedure, a variant of the Leontief dynamic multisectoral model was used. This model relates the path of growth of final demand to those of gross output, of productive-sectors intersectoral flows, imports, exports, and productive investment. Capital flows are assumed to be proportional to the increase of gross output and distributed in time.

The systems of equations and inequalities constituting the core model are the following. The core model of the planning procedure:
Final demand inequality:

$$(1) \qquad Q_t - \bar{A}Q_t - J_t^P - E_t + M_t = \bar{J}_t^N + \bar{C}_t^N + \bar{C}_t^I$$

Productive investments:

$$(2) \qquad J_t^P = \sum_{\tau=1}^{4} \bar{B}^\tau \Delta Q_{t+\tau-1}$$

Exports:

$$(3) \qquad E_t = z_t^1 \bar{S}^1 + z_t^2 \bar{S}^2$$

Imports:

$$(4) \qquad M_t = \bar{A}^Q Q_t + \bar{H}^K (K_t^P + \bar{K}_t^N) + \bar{H}^C (\bar{C}_t^N + \bar{C}_t^I)$$

Explanation of symbols:

t: time index (year)
Q: gross output
J^P: productive investment inputs by sectors of origin
E: exports
M: imports
$\Delta Q_t = Q_{t+1} - Q_t$
$\bar{J}^N$: collective demand created by investment activity in the non-material-services sector
$\bar{C}^N$: collective demand created by consumption activity in the non-material-services sector
$\bar{C}^I$: individual consumers' demands

All variables are 15-dimensional vectors.

$\bar{A}$: current input coefficients (15×15 matrix). The vector $\bar{A}Q$ denotes current productive inputs by sectors of origin.
$\bar{B}$: capital input coefficients (15×15 matrix) with nonzero elements in only 7 rows. The coefficient b_{ij} denotes input of the ith sector per unit of the increase of output of the jth sector between years t and $t+1$, which

takes place in the year $t-\tau$; b_{ij} are positive only if the index i represents a capital-producing sector. Note: Productive investment in the jth sector (sector of destination) in the year t is equal to $J_{tj}=\sum_{\tau=1}^{4}\sum_{i=\tau}^{15} b_{ij}\times Q_{t+\tau-1,j}$

$\bar{S}^l$: desired structures of exports (15-dimensional vectors)

z_t^l: scalars determining the levels and structures of exports that are to be positive linear combinations of the desired structures ($l=1,2$)

$\bar{A}^Q$: intermediate import input coefficients (15×15 matrix)

$\bar{H}^K, \bar{H}^C$: coefficients relating investment and consumption imports to the level of (productive and nonproductive) investment and to that of (individual and collective) consumption (15×15 matrices)

Note: Symbols with bars are parameters of the core model. The remaining symbols represent variables.

The preceding system of equations was supplemented by a series of initial conditions and by the condition of nonnegativity of variables. Because the system has many feasible solutions, some "reasonable" optimality criteria were imposed to obtain a unique solution. It turned out that the choice of optimality criteria was practically immaterial. The differences between solutions obtained with different criteria were practically insignificant.

The entire simulation procedure was tested experimentally using the data for the 5-year plan for the period 1970–75. The assumed targets were those explicitly or implicitly contained in the government plan. All parameters necessary to derive the paths of growth of target variables, and then those of outcome variables, were estimated on the basis of the data available in 1970. Obviously, many auxiliary assumptions had to be made to obtain reasonable estimates. The greatest difficulty met by the authors was that of estimating capital-input coefficients and their time distribution.

Fifteen productive sectors were distinguished, and among them there were seven capital-producing sectors (i.e., sectors whose outputs were used as inputs in the investment process). Capital inputs were assumed to be distributed over a period of at most 4 years. The paths of growth of gross output, productive investment and employment, imports and exports (divided by sectors) were derived and compared with those actually planned for the period in question and with the real paths. The general conclusion is that the procedure outlined is a useful and relatively simple tool to elaborate the framework of a 5-year plan (i.e., a consistent set of paths of growth of basic variables describing the state of the economy, compatible with the targets assumed in advance). The paths of growth derived by means of our procedure did not differ significantly from those implicitly or explicitly contained in the official plan, and some of them turned out to be more realistic (i.e., better fitted to the observed paths of growth).[2]

At the moment, an attempt is being made to apply the procedure to elaborate the plan for the next 5-year planning period (1981–85), taking into account the changes in the economic milieu and policy.

3 Econometric macromodels: economic analysis, forecasting, and simulation

The model W-3 built at the Institute of Econometrics and Statistics, University of Łódź, can be regarded as a representative of the econometric-type macromodels used both in economic analysis and forecasting and more recently in historical and ex-ante policy simulations.[3] It is an annual econometric macromodel of the Polish economy operating since 1977 and covering the sample period starting from 1960. It is updated each year when a new observation is added. Its 1980 version has been enlarged and takes into account the changes in the structure and economic policies in Poland in the late 1970s and the expected changes in the early 1980s.

It contains over 400 equations, approximately 200 of which are stochastic. It covers the entire national economy, including the static input–output relationships (optional) and the major financial processes. The disaggregation goes into 15 industries (including 2 non-material-services sectors); more disaggregation is to be found in the W-2 model, which is under construction.

The model has been built in several versions accentuating different economic situations of the Polish economy. Originally, to reflect the mechanisms prevailing in the early 1970s, it was mainly demand-determined. It thus represented the same demand orientation as the planning model described earlier. The final demands on the consumer side and on investments were determined endogenously. They, together with export demands, were converted into the demand for industrial and agricultural output (in terms of net output) by industries using either generalized static input–output relationships or their stochastic approximations. The net output requirements, on the other hand, determined the demands for labor, imports, and real assets by industries (it has been assumed that the capacities were not fully utilized or that they can be easily extended). The net outputs or their increments also influenced directly the requirements for investment outlays, taking into account the replacement needs. The inventory changes and foreign trade were regarded as control variables, which help to balance the commodity markets, prices being nonelastic. Prices, changes in wage rates, and investment allocation were treated as instruments (policy variables) introduced in the form of changes in structural parameters (i.e., by means of using dummies). These relationships are illustrated in Figure 11.2.

The disequilibria that spread over the Polish economy in the late 1970s induced the development of further versions: a supply-determined version analogous to the early models of the socialist economies and a mixed model that explicitly takes account of temporary disequilibria and simulates both the demands and supplies of commodity groups and primary factors of production.

The supply version of the model W-3 explicitly introduces the production functions that mirror not only constraints in fixed assets and labor force but also the bottlenecks in different industries resulting in constraints in material supplies that cannot be easily overcome because of severe limitations imposed on imports. Then an allocation procedure for outputs of particular industries, their sales and supplies, is introduced that allows us to determine the supplies of consumer and investment goods. Alternatively, a system of static input–output equations can be used to determine the final supplies of goods (Tomaszewicz & Welfe, 1979). The supplies of investment goods are further distributed among industries, and afterward they are related to the fixed-assets increments, taking into account particular lag distributions in the investment process. These are estimated assuming either Almon or geometric distributions. Thus the supplies of investment goods influence the capacities. A maximizing behavior is assumed for exports, whereas financial constraints

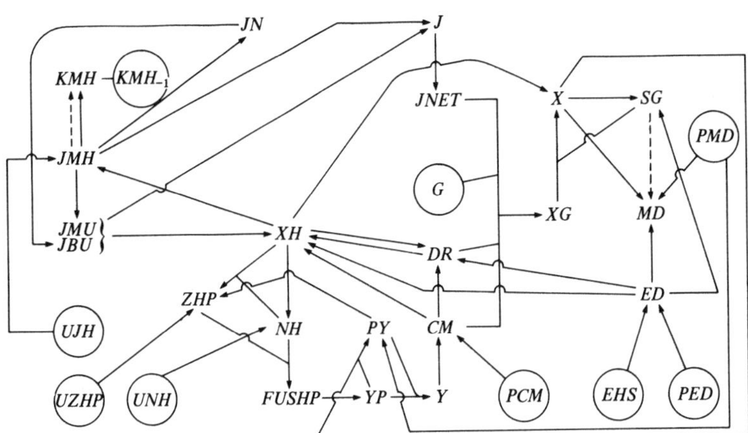

Figure 11.2. Simplified flow chart of W-3 model, demand-oriented version. $H = R, L, Q, B, T, H$ (national economy sector); dash line indicates lagged relationships.

are assumed for imports. The preceding system of relationships is represented in simplified form in Figure 11.3.

The systems of equations for both the demand and supply versions of the W-3 model containing more than 400 equations cannot be fully described in this chapter. However, the typical forms of equations for each of the 10 main blocks of the model are shown in Table 11.1 in compact fashion. This will permit short-cut comparisons between the two versions, which by no means are purely demand- or supply-oriented, and also will give rough insight into the structure of the equations. The linear forms of the equations are shown, although nonlinear forms were also tried, especially with regard to personal consumption and production equations. The alternative input–output equations for linking final demand with net output are also given in Table 11.1.

The equations (10) in the demand-oriented version defining the requirements for gross output by industries given the final demand by users' categories can be substituted by respective input–output equation systems. The same can be easily done with regard to the link between gross and net output, equation (11).

We have

$$(17) \qquad QH = H(XK)$$

where QH is a $1 \times H$ vector of gross output by industries, $XK^T =$

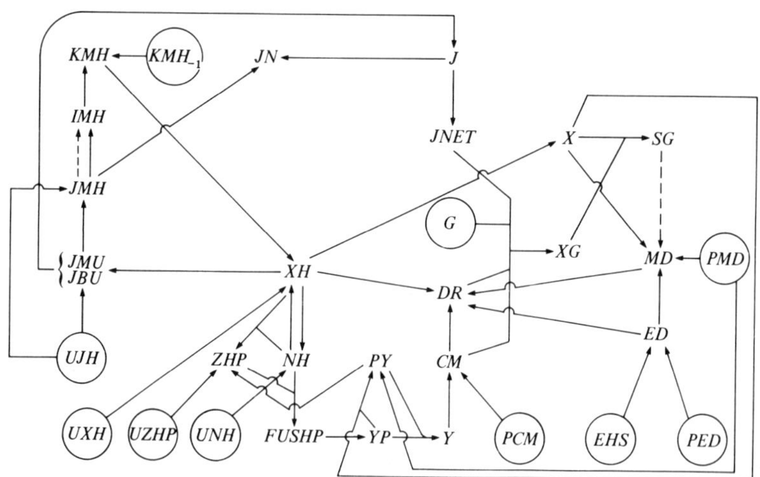

Figure 11.3. Simplified flow chart of W-3 model, supply-oriented version. $H = R, L, Q, B, T, H$ (national economy sector); dash line indicates lagged relationships.

$[CK^T GK^T DRK^T JK^T EH^T - MH^T]$ is a raw vector $K \times 1$ of final demand by categories of users (and commodity groups within these categories), and H is an $H \times K$ transformation matrix.

In the supply version the equations showing the distribution (allocation) of domestic gross output, equations (6), equations (14) can be substituted for the following input–output equations (imports must also be added):

(18) $$XK = K(QH)$$

where K is a $K \times H$ transformation matrix that can be decomposed with regard to separate final users:

$$K^T = [KC^T KG^T KDR^T KJ^T KEM^T]$$

hence

$$CK = (KC)(QH), \quad \text{etc.}$$

In both cases, either the coefficients of transformation matrices must be allowed to change or suitable adjustments of simulated values of outcomes must be introduced (the simulated values of residuals are added using the equations explaining the residuals in the sample period) (Tomaszewicz & Welfe, 1979).

The meanings of some symbols used have been explained earlier. The full list of variables used is as follows:

A	scrappings
C	personal consumption
CM	personal consumption of material goods
DR	inventory changes
e_b	disturbance term in equation explaining variable B
ED	exports
EMD	proxy for foreign debt
EHS^*	world trade (world exports)
$FUSHP$	wage bill nominal, socialized sector
G^*	consumption of material goods, nonmaterial sector
I	investments put into operation
IM	investments put into operation in material production sector
J	investment outlays, total
JBU	investment outlays, constructions
JM	investment outlays in material production sector
JMU	investment outlays, machinery equipment
JN	investment outlays, non-material-services sector
$JNET$	net investment outlays
K	fixed assets, end of year
KM	fixed assets in material production sector, end of year

Table 11.1 *Typical specification of equations in the W-3 model*

	Demand version	Supply version
	Net material product X and national income distributed XG:	
(5)	$X = XG + SG, \quad SG = a_0 + a_1(ED - MD) + a_2X$ $XG = CM + G + JNET + DR$	The same equations that determine *DR*
	Personal consumption CM:	
(6)	$CK = a_0 + a_1CK_{-1} + a_2Y + PCKR + e_c$ $CM = \Sigma_K CK$	$CK = b_0 + b_1QH + b_2MH - b_3EH + e_c$ $CM = \Sigma_K CK$
	Inventories R:	
(7)	$DRH = a_0 + a_1RH_{-1} + a_2QH + a_3MH - a_4XGK + e_r$ $DR = \Sigma_H DRH$	Determined from (5)
	Exports ED:	
(8)	$EH = a_0 + a_1EH_{-1} + a_2EHS + a_3PEH + e_e$ $ED = \Sigma_H EH$	The same as in demand version
	Imports MD:	
(9)	$MH = b_0 + b_1CK + b_2QH + b_3JK + b_4EMD_{-1} + e_m$ $MD = \Sigma_H MH, \quad EMD = \Sigma_{i=0}^{T}(ED_{-i} - MD_{-i})$	The same as in demand version
	Gross output Q:	
(10)	$QH = a_0 + a_1CK + a_2JK + a_3QD + a_4EH + e_q$	$QH = b_0 + b_1XH + b_2MH + b_3QS + e_q$
	Net output X:	
(11)	$XH = a_0 + a_1QH - a_2MH - a_3QS + e_x$	$XH = b_0 + b_1KMH \cdot WZH + b_2NMH + b_3UDMH + b_4t + e_x$

	Employment N:	
(12)	$NMH = a_0 + a_1 XH + a_2 (KMH/NMH)_{-1} + a_3 UNH + e_n$ $NN = N - \Sigma_H NMH, \quad N = LA \cdot LPR$ $LA = c_0 + c_1 t + c_2 (YP/FUSHP) + e_l$	$NMH = b_0 + b_1 N + b_2 (XH/NMH)_{-1} + b_3 UNH + e_n$ $NN = N - \Sigma_H NMH, \quad N = LA \cdot LPR$ $LA = c_0 + c_1 t + c_2 (YP/FUSHP) + e_l$
	Fixed assets K:	
(13)	The same as in supply version	$KH = KH_{-1} + IH - AH, \quad AH = a_0 + a_1 KH_{-1} + e_a$ $IH = b_0 + b_1 \Sigma_{i=0}^{T} j_i JH_{-i} + b_2 UIH + e_i$
	Investment outlays J:	
(14)	$JMH = a_0 + a_1 JMH_{-1} + a_2 DXH + a_3 UJH + e_j$ $JM = \Sigma_H JMH, \quad JN = c_0 + c_1 JM + c_2 G + e_{jm}$ $J = JM + JN, \quad JNET = d_0 + d_1 J + e_{jt}$	$JMH = b_0 + b_1 JM + b_2 DXH + b_3 MH + b_4 UJH + e_j$ $JM = e_0 + e_1 J + e_2 UJM + e_{jm}, \quad JN = J - JM$ $J = f_0 + f_1 QH + f_2 MH + f_3 UJ + e_f$ $JNET = d_0 + d_1 J + e_{jt}$
	Average wages Z, wage bills F, and incomes Y (the same for both versions):	
(15)	$ZMHP = a_0 + a_1 (XH/NMH) + a_2 PY + a_3 UZMHP + e_{zm}$ $ZNP = b_0 + b_1 ZMHP_{-1} + e_{zn}, \quad FUSHP = ZHP \cdot NH, \quad FUSP = \Sigma_H FUSHP$ $YP = FUSP + YOP, \quad YOP = c_0 + c_1 FUSP + c_2 UYOP + e_y, \quad Y = YP/PY$	
	Prices P (the same for both versions):	
(16)	$PY = a_0 + a_1 PY_{-1} + a_2 (YP/X) + a_3 PM + e_{py}$ $PX = b_0 + b_1 PY + b_2 PJ + b_3 PM + e_{px}$ $PE = c_0 + c_1 PEHS + c_2 DPX + e_{pe}$	

LA	participation ratio of the labor force
LPR	population at productive age (labor force)
MD	imports
N	employment
NM	employment in material production sector
NN	employment in nonmaterial services
PC	prices of consumer goods, index
PCM	total personal consumption deflator
PE	domestic export prices, deflator
*PEHS**	world export prices, index
*PJ**	investment outlays, deflator
*PM**	import prices, deflator
PX	net material product deflator
PY	deflator of personal incomes
Q	gross output
QD	gross output of buying industries
QS	gross output of supplying industries
R	inventories, end of year
t	time
WZ	number of shifts, proxy for potential utilization measure
X	net material product
XG	national income distributed
$SG = X - XG$	surplus of exports over imports plus losses and statistical discrepancies
Y	real personal income
YO	other income (except for wage bills)
Z	average wages
ZM	average wages in material product sector
ZN	average wages in non-material-services sector

Note: Small letters are used to indicate structural parameters.

* denotes an exogenous variable
D added before a symbol denotes first differences
H added after a symbol indicates the branch of industry
K added after a symbol indicates the particular commodity group
P added after a symbol indicates that the variable has been expressed in current prices, otherwise in constant prices
U added before a symbol denotes a dummy variable that plays the role of the instrument of the economic policy occurring in the equation explaining the endogenous variable that this instrument must affect. For example, if the dummy variable *UJH* (indicating decision) assumes a value equal to unity, then the investment outlays in the branch *H* should be changed by the value equal to the value of the parameter standing with this variable *UJH*. Of course, all dummies are exogenous.

Variables shown in figures in circles are predetermined variables (exogenous or lagged exogenous). All variables indicating values are expressed in billions of zlotys, except for foreign trade, where U.S. dollars are used. Constant prices of January 1, 1977, are applied over the sample period.

Both the demand- and supply-oriented versions of the model represent interdependent systems containing the basic feedbacks linking in the long term the production and investment activities, but in a reverse form. The demand-oriented version assumes an accelerator-type simultaneous relationship such that the investment outlays depend on expected increments of output.[4]

The increased demands for investment outlays influence the demands for the outputs of industries producing investment goods. This, in turn, involves their capacity increase and thus new investments in these industries.

Analogous (on reverse) mechanisms can be observed in the supply-oriented version. The supplies of investment goods increase the capacities of industries producing the investment goods, which makes it possible to accelerate the future supplies of these goods.

Both of these feedbacks are dynamic, and the time span extends for several years, being dependent on the length of the investment completion period.

Both versions of the model described earlier also contain equations explaining the financial processes with regard to personal income generation and prices of consumer goods. The wage bills depend on employment and average monthly wages, which change because of changes in labor productivity and government wage regulations. The wage bills and the incomes of individual farmers and other private units add up to total personal income. The consumer price deflator is endogenously determined, being related to labor costs and financial accumulation pressures.

The demand-oriented version contains a feedback of a multiplier type: An increase in output causes an increase in wage bills (strengthened by a parallel increase in labor productivity). This, in turn, determines the rise of nominal and real personal income, which influences consumer demand and afterward the requirements for output by industries, and this again causes the wage bill to increase. The supply-oriented version lacks this feedback, because there is no direct link between the demands for products by industries and their outputs.

Detailed descriptions of particular equations, with regard to earlier versions of the W-3 model, are contained in several publications (Welfe, 1975, 1978, 1979).[5] The paramters of the system have been estimated using, for several versions, several different estimation procedures. OLS procedures have been extensively used for the initial evaluation and for testing single equations. TSLS procedures were applied to estimate the parameters of simultaneous blocks of equations. Iterative methods (e.g., fix-point and IIV) have also been tried in cooperation with the Institute of Statistics, University of Uppsala (Bergström, 1980).

The system as a whole has been solved and tested for two main versions and several special versions using Gauss–Seidel procedures.

The two versions of the W-3 model just described are not pure demand- or supply-oriented versions; several equations have the same structure (e.g., the export functions explain in both cases foreign demand but not domestic supplies), and others contain disequilibria indicators used as proxies either to represent the excess demand (e.g., to explain the forced substitution due to the excess demand for durables in the 1970s) or to measure the constraints imposed on the utilization of available capacities and resources (e.g., to explain in production functions the results of electricity and fuel constraints in 1978–79). Nevertheless, the description of existing and expected disequilibria is by no means complete, and an attempt has been made to construct the unbalanced version of the model.[6] Its simplified structure is characterized in Figure 11.4.

This version, called also a mixed model, explicitly defines the demands for and supplies of commodities at both the main final user and producer levels, as well as the primary production factors. The equations typically contain disequilibria indicators mentioned earlier. This permits proper identification of demand and supply functions, thus making feasible simulation exercises aimed at studying the possible strains and evaluating the likely magnitude of imbalance. It must be admitted that no consistent estimation procedures are available at the moment, and only constrained OLS procedures should be applied to estimate the structural parameters of the whole system. Nevertheless, it is hoped that the biases are not of sufficiently high order to make the estimates and simulation results meaningless. This hope is based on theoretical considerations showing that the existence of disequilibria indicators in an equation diminishes the bias (Charemza, 1980), as well as on quasi experimentations and comparisons of the empirical results with those obtained earlier using consistent estimation techniques and with the available a priori evidence.

The preceding characteristics do not apply to the estimates of excess demand and excess supply. Their estimates show a low degree of accuracy, because they typically are derived as differences between (estimated) demand and supply or simply in the form of residuals. This is the reason they often do not intervene in the subsequent equations. The notable exceptions are the coefficients of capacity utilization (which depend on the number of shifts worked) that influence the investment outlays and the inventory changes intervening in many equations.

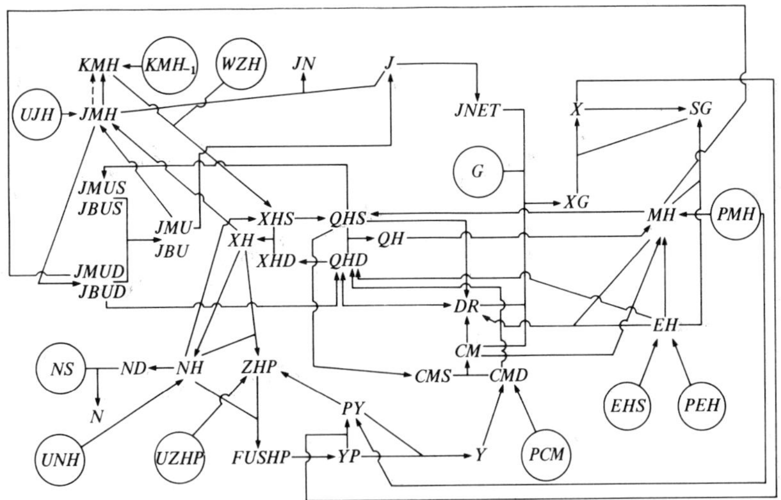

Figure 11.4. Simplified flow chart of W-3 model, unbalanced version. S at the end of a symbol stands for supply, D for demand.

For this reason, in simulation exercises, where the shocks might be sufficiently large to produce significant discrepancies between supply and demand, additional "regulating" subsystems of equations are used (mostly based on iterative procedures), aiming either at eliminating (balanced systems) or at diminishing these discrepancies (quasi-balanced systems). For example, simulating the economic policy alternatives, one typically assumes full employment, that is, the existence of a mechanism (procedure) diminishing the excess demand for labor force, either by means of increasing the rate of participation or reducing the demand using administrative measures (i.e., introducing constant adjustments in equations explaining demand for employees) or by means of productivity of labor increase (i.e., introducing changes in structural parameters standing with variables being proxies for technical progress, etc., in the previously mentioned equations).

The economic policy simulations can also be easily extended to cover the problems of balanced growth. We have in mind, first of all, the studies of the results of likely changes (decreases) in the rate of investment and its allocation among different sectors and industries. Because the investments are endogenous, the shocks are initiated by means of suitable changes of structural parameters standing with variables explaining investment outlays (i.e., net output levels or their increments).

Thus, at the stage of model utilization, the simulation analysis problems and procedures evolve toward the problems and techniques used in systems analysis. This helps to bring together the two seemingly different types of macromodels (the econometric type and systems-analysis-oriented models) and construct large systems of models apt to perform economic policy analysis of the past and possibly future worlds.

NOTES

1 This distinction corresponds roughly to the division of variables into policy, strictly exogenous, and endogenous variables.

2 Typewritten materials are available from the Institute of Economic Cybernetics, Academy of Economics, Poznań. An extensive report of the results of the research will be published (Czerwiński et al., 1981). Another example of the simulation planning models recently built independently by Pawilno-Pacewicz (1980) is available.

3 Similar targets and structure are revealed by another family of econometric macromodels constructed by Maciejewski and Zajchowski (1974). See also the work of Maciejewski (1976).

4 In the W-3 model (opposite to the previously described planning model) the future increments of production (unknown in the sample period) are substituted by past increases (or levels) of net output.

5 The full description of the 1980 version of the model will be available in the forthcoming publications of the Institute of Econometrics and Statistics (Prace IEiS) being provided by a team including, besides W. Welfe, A. Czyżewski, J. Gajda, N. Lapinska-Sobczak, L. Tomaszewicz, and P. Tomczyk.

6 It should be noted that the first version, the W-1 model of the Polish economy, being the predecessor of the W-3 model, was built principally as a disequilibrium-type model (Welfe, 1973). However, the numerical constraints have prevented its further use in the enlarged versions of the model.

REFERENCES

Bergström, R. 1980. "Estimation of Large Econometric Models by Consistent Methods. The Case of the Polish W-3 Model." Mimeograph, Uppsala University.

Charemza, W. *Ekonometryczne modele nierównowagi. Problemy specyfikacji i estymacji* (Disequilibrium Econometric Models. Problems of Specification and Estimation). Gdańsk: Uniwersytet Gdański, Wydawnictwo Uczelniane.

Czerwiński, Z., Guzik, B., Jurek, W., Panek, E., Runka, H., and Sledziński, W. 1981. *System symulacyjnych modeli planowania* (A System of Simulation Planning Models). Warszawa: PWN.

Maciejewski, W. 1976. *Zastosowania ekonometrycznych modeli rozwoju gospodarki narodowej* (The Applications of Econometric Models of National Economy Development). Warszawa: PWE.

Maciejewski, W., and Zajchowski, J. 1974. "Ogólna idea modelu ekonometrycznego gospodarki narodowej KP-II." (A General Concept of the